PUBLISHER
DAMIAN A. WASSEL
EDITOR-IN-CHIEF
ADRIAN F. WASSEL
ART DIRECTOR
NATHAN C. GOODEN
BRANDING & DESIGN
TIM DANIEL
MANAGING EDITOR
REBECCA TAYLOR
DIRECTOR OF MARKETING
DAVID DISSANAYAKE
PRODUCTION MANAGER
IAN BALDESSARI
PRINCIPAL
DAMIAN A. WASSEL SR.

WINTER'S TEETH

WRITTEN BY
TIM SEELEY

DRAWN BY
DEVMALYA PRAMANIK

THE ANARCH TALES

WRITTEN BY
TINI HOWARD & BLAKE HOWARD

DRAWN BY
NATHAN GOODEN

ALL TALES

COLORED BY
ADDISON DUKE

LETTERED BY
ANDWORLD

COVERS BY

AARON CAMPBELL   DAVID MACK

MANAGING PRODUCER: **JOE LEFAVI** | GENUINE ENTERTAINMENT

VAULT COMICS PRESENTS

WINTER'S TEETH BOOK ONE

VAMPIRE

THE MASQUERADE

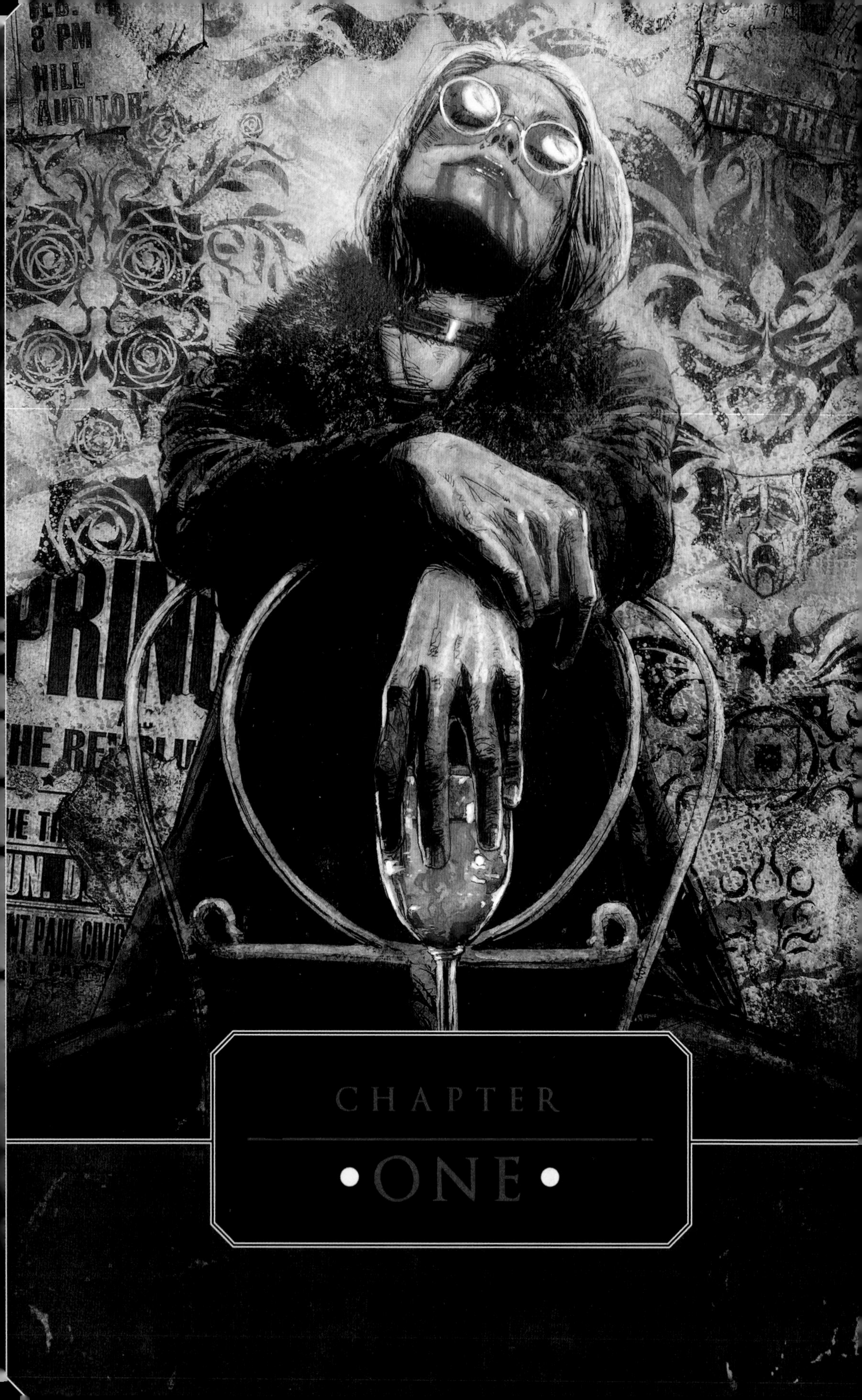
8 PM
HILL

CHAPTER ONE

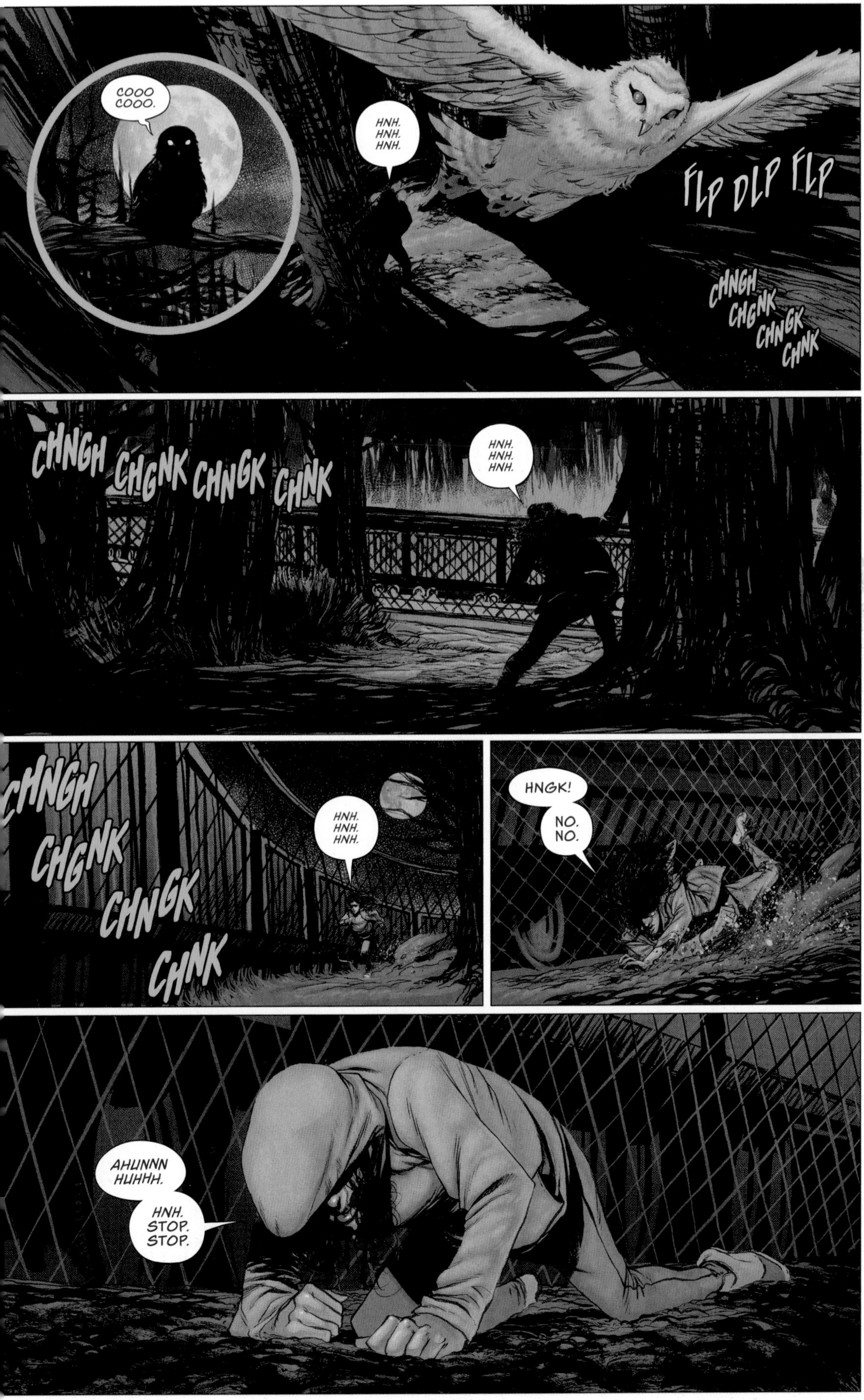
COOO COOO.
HNH. HNH. HNH.
FLP DLP FLP
CHNGH CHGNK CHNGK CHNK
CHNGH CHGNK CHNGK CHNK
HNH. HNH. HNH.
CHNGH CHGNK CHNGK CHNK
HNH. HNH. HNH.
HNGK!
NO. NO.
AHUNNN HUHHH.
HNH. STOP. STOP.

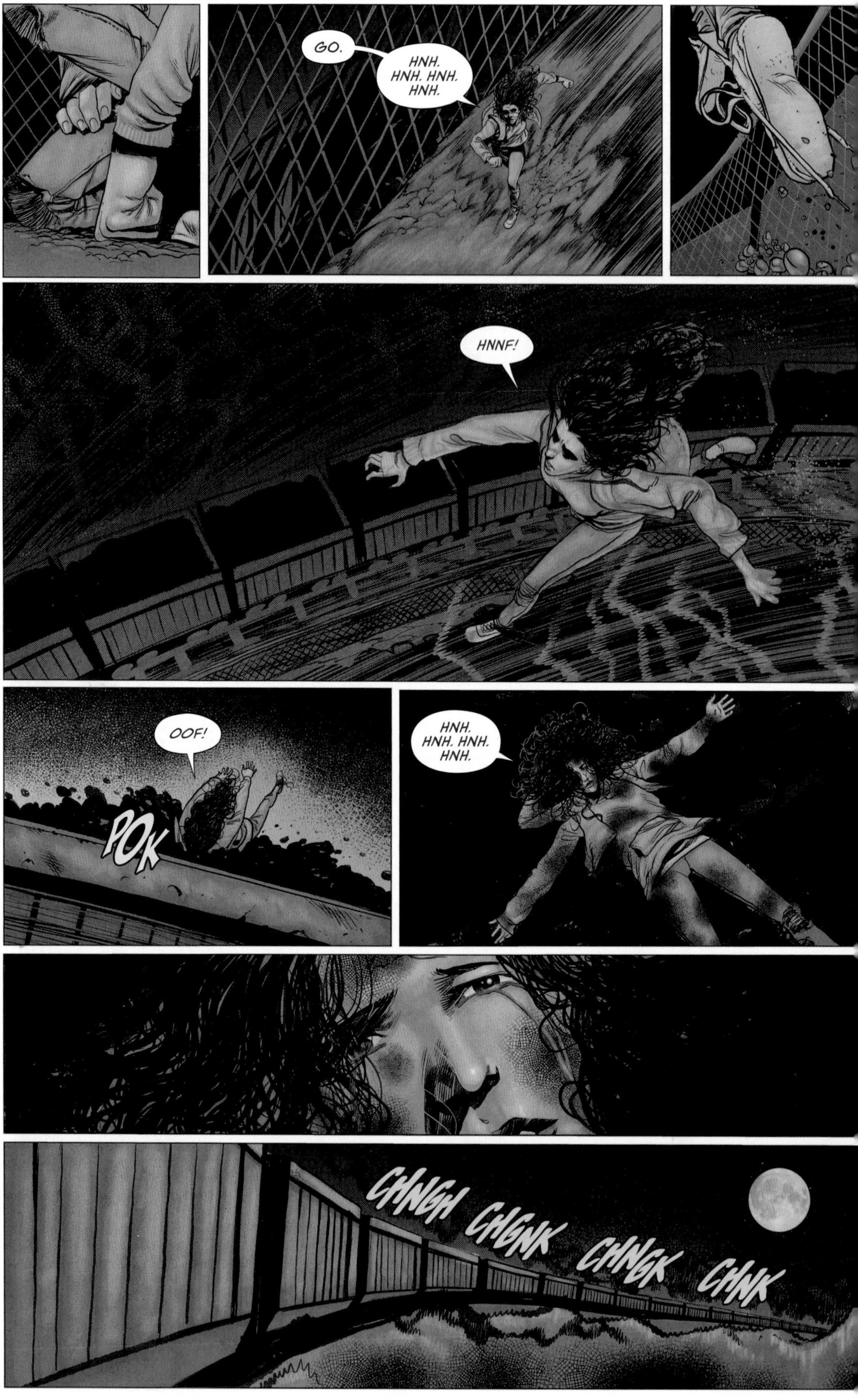
GO.
HNH. HNH. HNH. HNH.
HNNF!
OOF!
POK
HNH. HNH. HNH. HNH.
CHNGH
CHGNK
CHNGK
CHNK

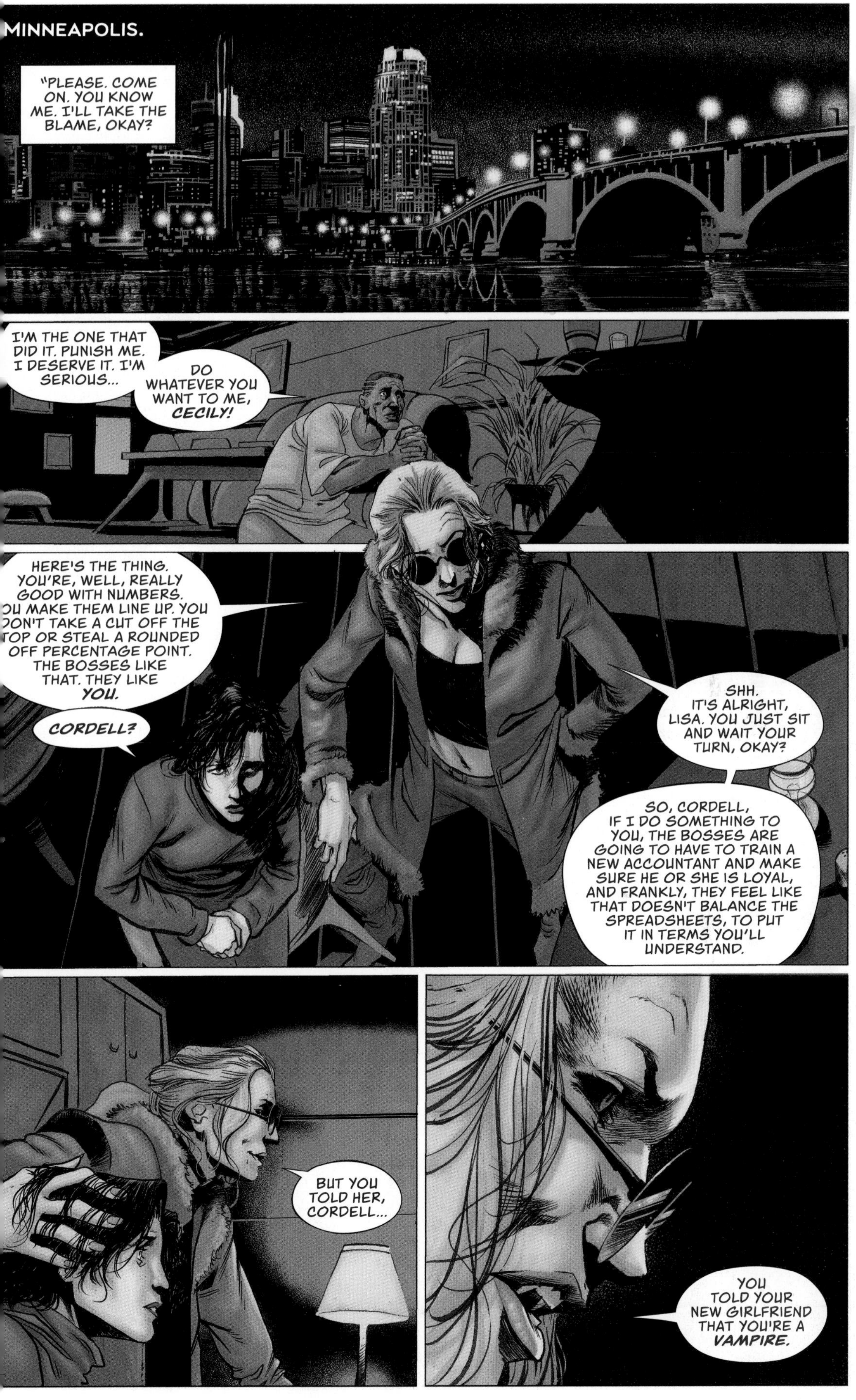
MINNEAPOLIS.
"PLEASE. COME ON. YOU KNOW ME. I'LL TAKE THE BLAME, OKAY?
I'M THE ONE THAT DID IT. PUNISH ME. I DESERVE IT. I'M SERIOUS...
DO WHATEVER YOU WANT TO ME, CECILY!
HERE'S THE THING. YOU'RE, WELL, REALLY GOOD WITH NUMBERS. OU MAKE THEM LINE UP. YOU ON'T TAKE A CUT OFF THE TOP OR STEAL A ROUNDED OFF PERCENTAGE POINT. THE BOSSES LIKE THAT. THEY LIKE YOU.
CORDELL?
SHH. IT'S ALRIGHT, LISA. YOU JUST SIT AND WAIT YOUR TURN, OKAY?
SO, CORDELL, IF I DO SOMETHING TO YOU, THE BOSSES ARE GOING TO HAVE TO TRAIN A NEW ACCOUNTANT AND MAKE SURE HE OR SHE IS LOYAL, AND FRANKLY, THEY FEEL LIKE THAT DOESN'T BALANCE THE SPREADSHEETS, TO PUT IT IN TERMS YOU'LL UNDERSTAND.
BUT YOU TOLD HER, CORDELL...
YOU TOLD YOUR NEW GIRLFRIEND THAT YOU'RE A VAMPIRE.

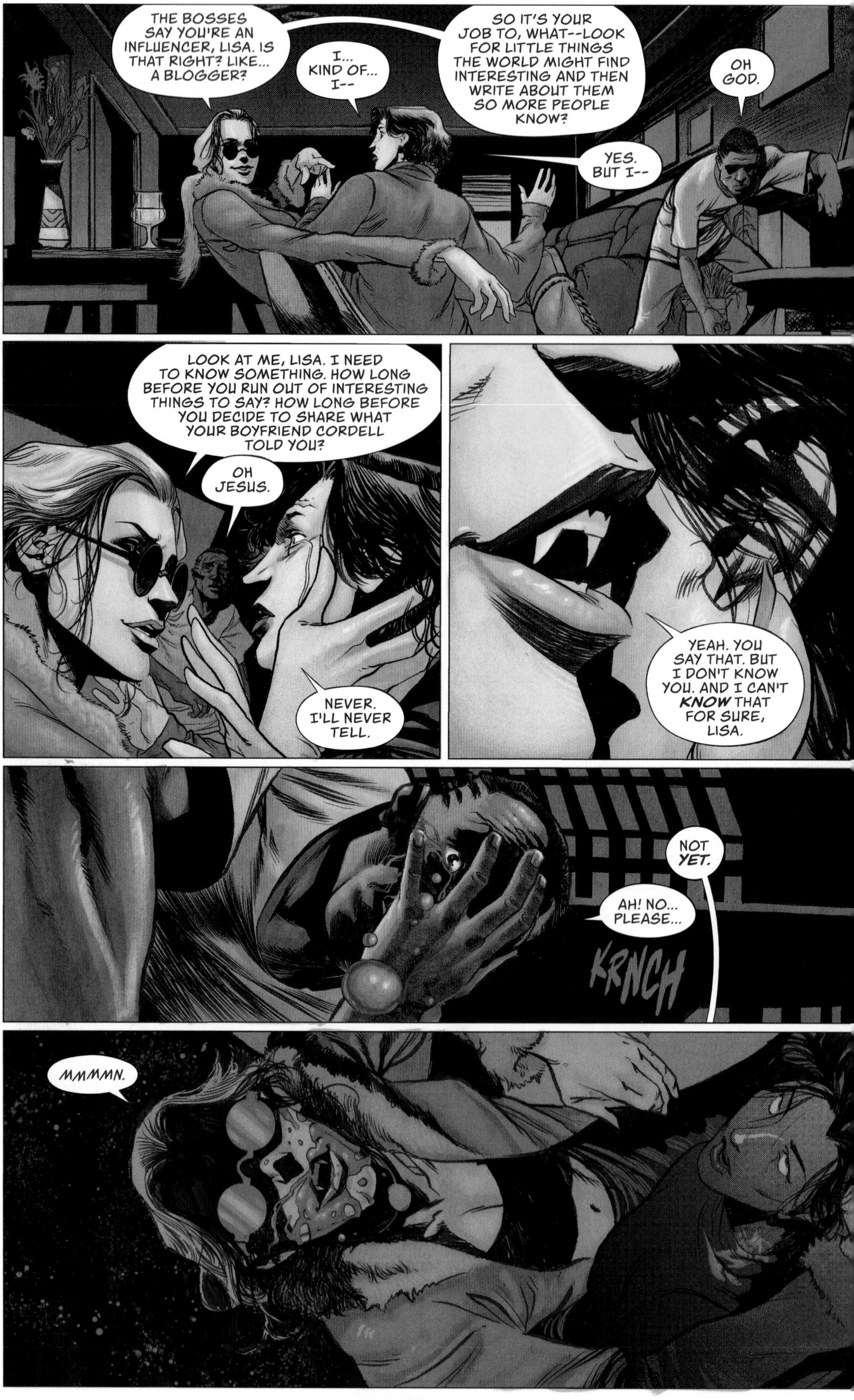
THE BOSSES SAY YOU'RE AN INFLUENCER, LISA. IS THAT RIGHT? LIKE... A BLOGGER?
I... KIND OF... I--
SO IT'S YOUR JOB TO, WHAT--LOOK FOR LITTLE THINGS THE WORLD MIGHT FIND INTERESTING AND THEN WRITE ABOUT THEM SO MORE PEOPLE KNOW?
YES. BUT I--
OH GOD.
LOOK AT ME, LISA. I NEED TO KNOW SOMETHING. HOW LONG BEFORE YOU RUN OUT OF INTERESTING THINGS TO SAY? HOW LONG BEFORE YOU DECIDE TO SHARE WHAT YOUR BOYFRIEND CORDELL TOLD YOU?
OH JESUS.
NEVER. I'LL NEVER TELL.
YEAH. YOU SAY THAT. BUT I DON'T KNOW YOU. AND I CAN'T KNOW THAT FOR SURE, LISA.
NOT YET.
AH! NO... PLEASE...
KRNCH
MMMMN.

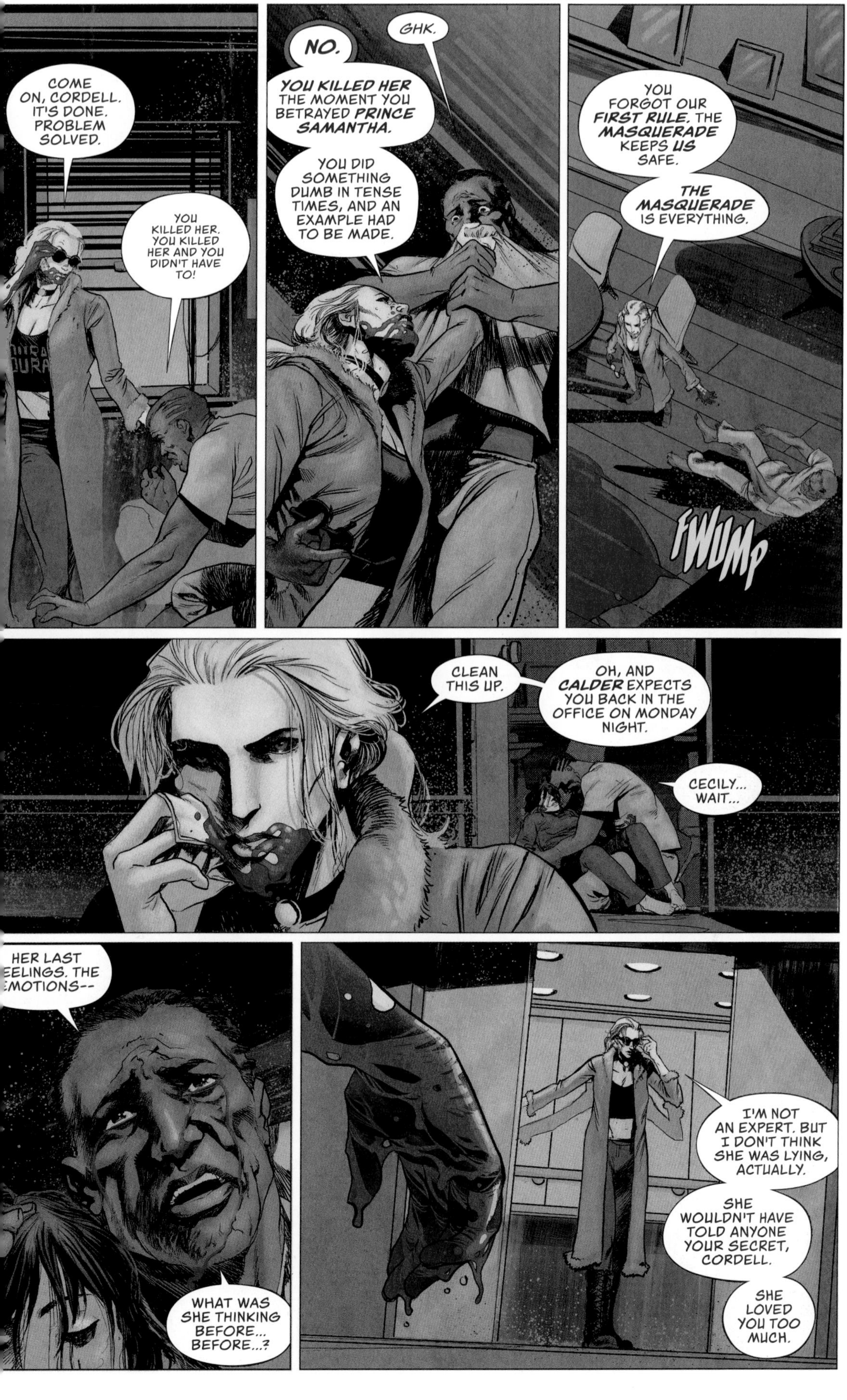
COME ON, CORDELL. IT'S DONE. PROBLEM SOLVED.
YOU KILLED HER. YOU KILLED HER AND YOU DIDN'T HAVE TO!
NO.
GHK.
YOU KILLED HER THE MOMENT YOU BETRAYED PRINCE SAMANTHA.
YOU DID SOMETHING DUMB IN TENSE TIMES, AND AN EXAMPLE HAD TO BE MADE.
YOU FORGOT OUR FIRST RULE. THE MASQUERADE KEEPS US SAFE.
THE MASQUERADE IS EVERYTHING.
FWUMP
CLEAN THIS UP.
OH, AND CALDER EXPECTS YOU BACK IN THE OFFICE ON MONDAY NIGHT.
CECILY... WAIT...
HER LAST EELINGS. THE EMOTIONS--
WHAT WAS SHE THINKING BEFORE... BEFORE...?
I'M NOT AN EXPERT. BUT I DON'T THINK SHE WAS LYING, ACTUALLY.
SHE WOULDN'T HAVE TOLD ANYONE YOUR SECRET, CORDELL.
SHE LOVED YOU TOO MUCH.

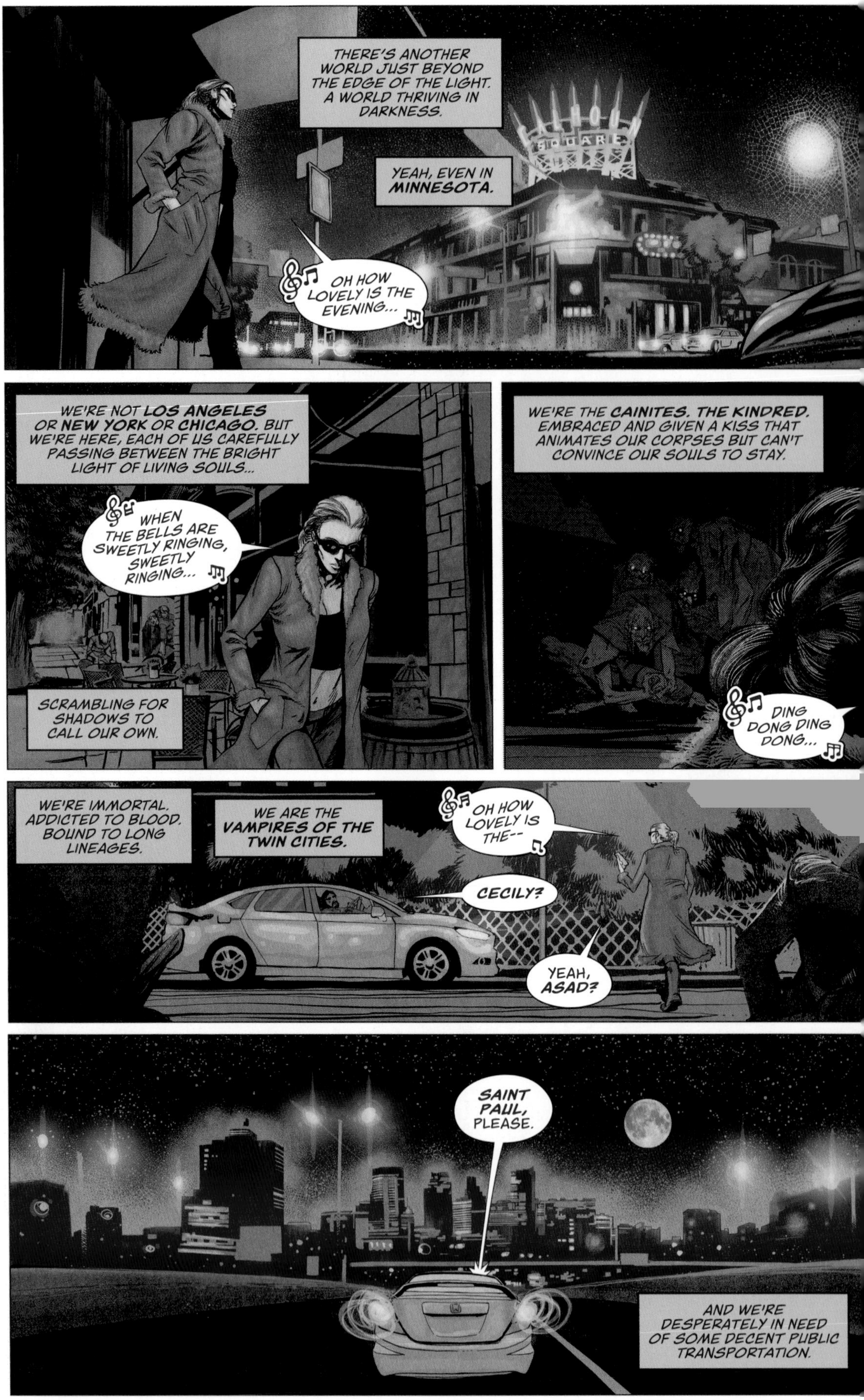
THERE'S ANOTHER WORLD JUST BEYOND THE EDGE OF THE LIGHT. A WORLD THRIVING IN DARKNESS.
YEAH, EVEN IN **MINNESOTA.**
OH HOW LOVELY IS THE EVENING...
CALHOUN SQUARE
WE'RE NOT **LOS ANGELES** OR **NEW YORK** OR **CHICAGO.** BUT WE'RE HERE, EACH OF US CAREFULLY PASSING BETWEEN THE BRIGHT LIGHT OF LIVING SOULS...
WHEN THE BELLS ARE SWEETLY RINGING, SWEETLY RINGING...
SCRAMBLING FOR SHADOWS TO CALL OUR OWN.
WE'RE THE **CAINITES. THE KINDRED.** EMBRACED AND GIVEN A KISS THAT ANIMATES OUR CORPSES BUT CAN'T CONVINCE OUR SOULS TO STAY.
DING DONG DING DONG...
WE'RE IMMORTAL. ADDICTED TO BLOOD. BOUND TO LONG LINEAGES.
WE ARE THE **VAMPIRES OF THE TWIN CITIES.**
OH HOW LOVELY IS THE--
CECILY?
YEAH, **ASAD?**
SAINT PAUL, PLEASE.
AND WE'RE DESPERATELY IN NEED OF SOME DECENT PUBLIC TRANSPORTATION.

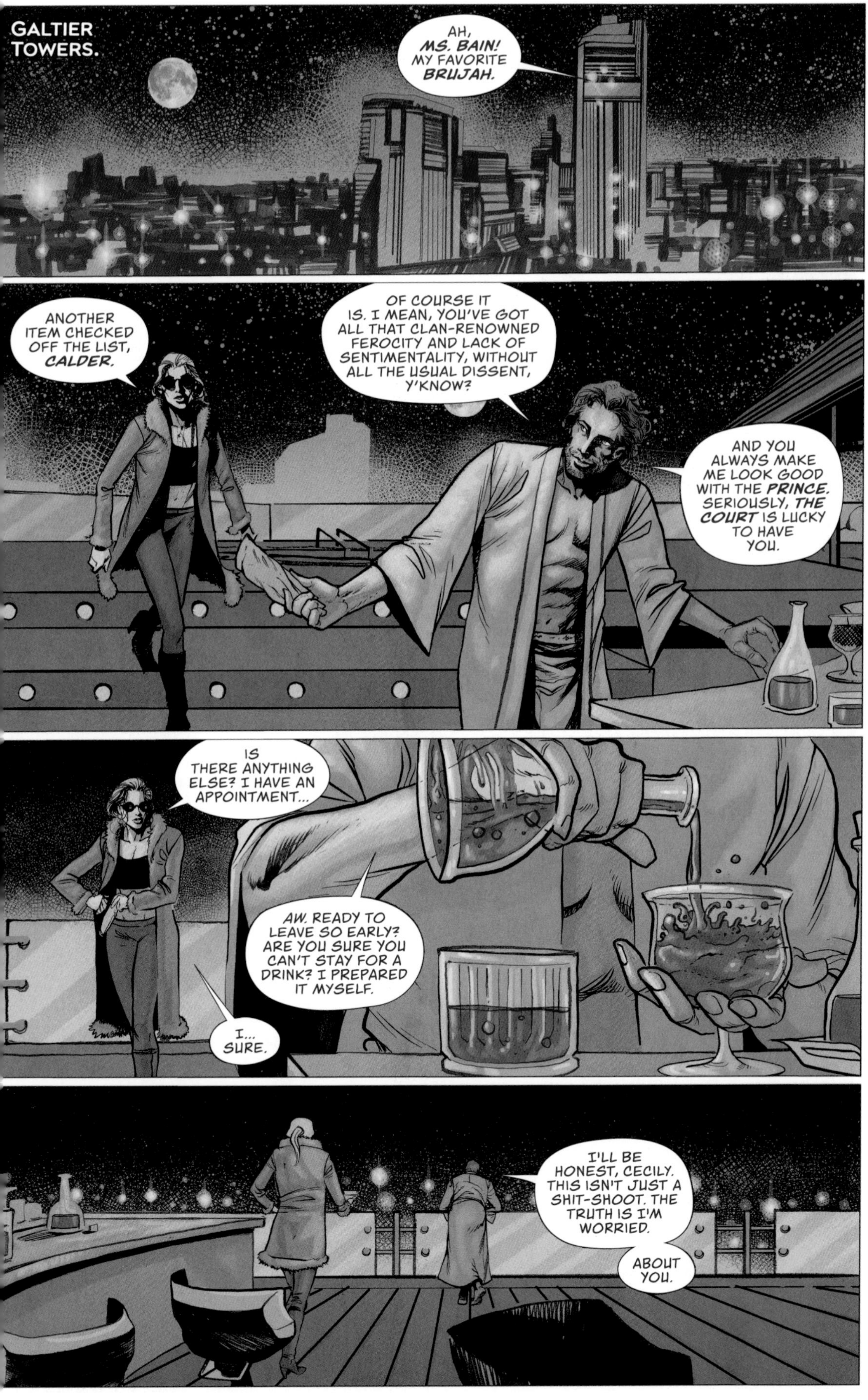
GALTIER TOWERS.
AH, MS. BAIN! MY FAVORITE BRUJAH.
ANOTHER ITEM CHECKED OFF THE LIST, CALDER.
OF COURSE IT IS. I MEAN, YOU'VE GOT ALL THAT CLAN-RENOWNED FEROCITY AND LACK OF SENTIMENTALITY, WITHOUT ALL THE USUAL DISSENT, Y'KNOW?
AND YOU ALWAYS MAKE ME LOOK GOOD WITH THE PRINCE. SERIOUSLY, THE COURT IS LUCKY TO HAVE YOU.
IS THERE ANYTHING ELSE? I HAVE AN APPOINTMENT...
AW. READY TO LEAVE SO EARLY? ARE YOU SURE YOU CAN'T STAY FOR A DRINK? I PREPARED IT MYSELF.
I... SURE.
I'LL BE HONEST, CECILY. THIS ISN'T JUST A SHIT-SHOOT. THE TRUTH IS I'M WORRIED.
ABOUT YOU.

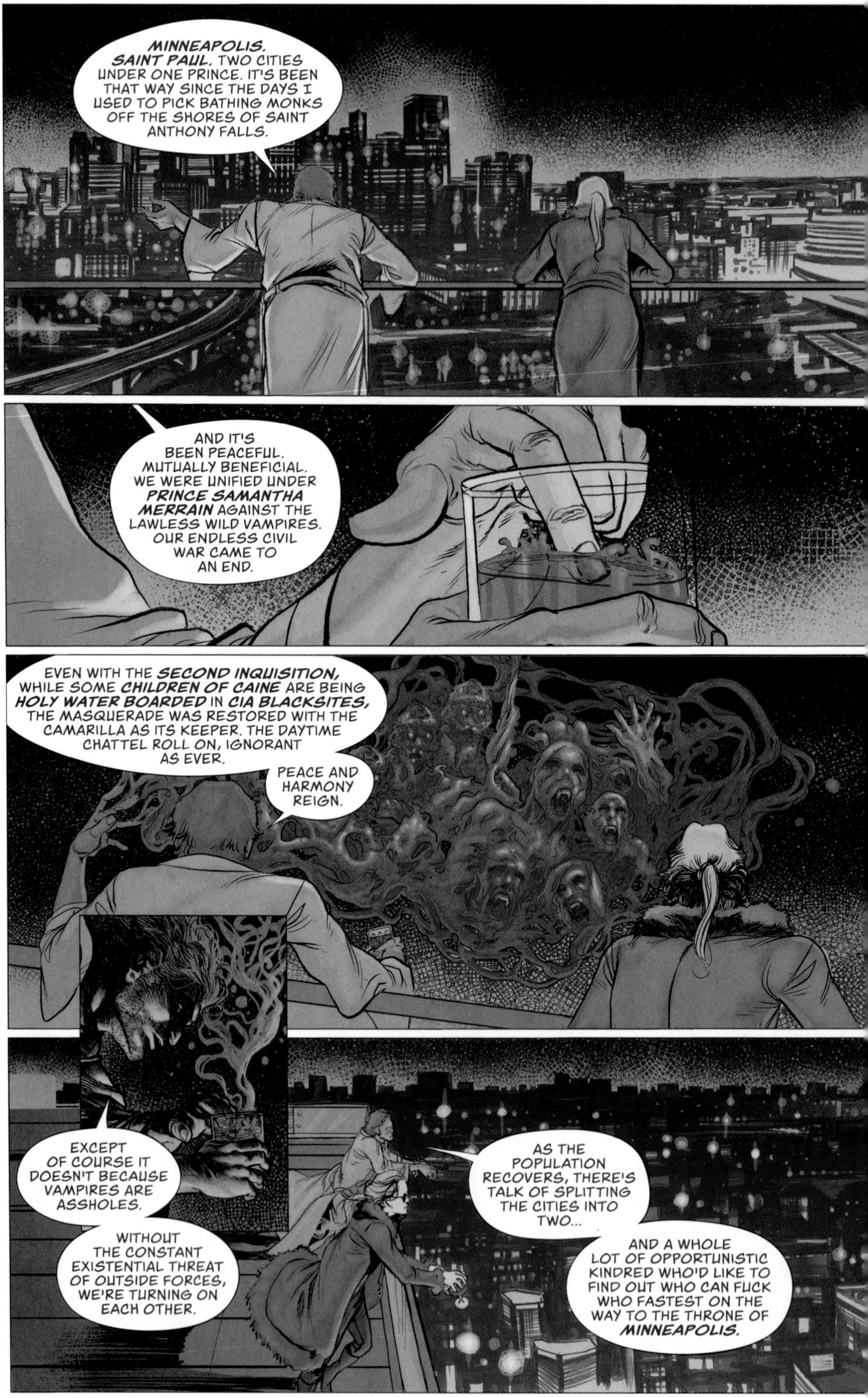

MINNEAPOLIS. SAINT PAUL. TWO CITIES UNDER ONE PRINCE. IT'S BEEN THAT WAY SINCE THE DAYS I USED TO PICK BATHING MONKS OFF THE SHORES OF SAINT ANTHONY FALLS.
AND IT'S BEEN PEACEFUL. MUTUALLY BENEFICIAL. WE WERE UNIFIED UNDER PRINCE SAMANTHA MERRAIN AGAINST THE LAWLESS WILD VAMPIRES. OUR ENDLESS CIVIL WAR CAME TO AN END.
EVEN WITH THE SECOND INQUISITION, WHILE SOME CHILDREN OF CAINE ARE BEING HOLY WATER BOARDED IN CIA BLACKSITES, THE MASQUERADE WAS RESTORED WITH THE CAMARILLA AS ITS KEEPER. THE DAYTIME CHATTEL ROLL ON, IGNORANT AS EVER.
PEACE AND HARMONY REIGN.
EXCEPT OF COURSE IT DOESN'T BECAUSE VAMPIRES ARE ASSHOLES.
WITHOUT THE CONSTANT EXISTENTIAL THREAT OF OUTSIDE FORCES, WE'RE TURNING ON EACH OTHER.
AS THE POPULATION RECOVERS, THERE'S TALK OF SPLITTING THE CITIES INTO TWO...
AND A WHOLE LOT OF OPPORTUNISTIC KINDRED WHO'D LIKE TO FIND OUT WHO CAN FUCK WHO FASTEST ON THE WAY TO THE THRONE OF MINNEAPOLIS.

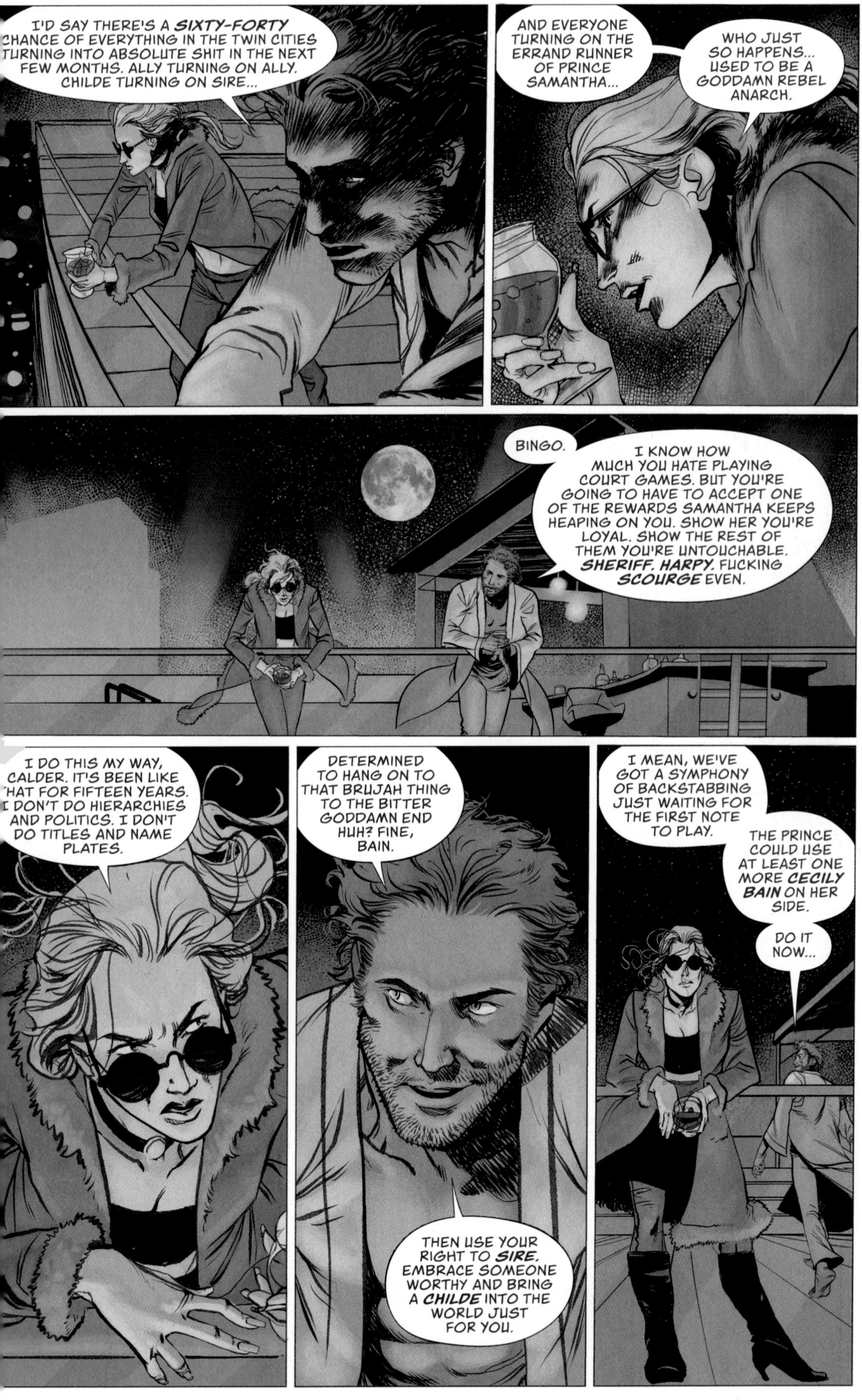
I'D SAY THERE'S A SIXTY-FORTY CHANCE OF EVERYTHING IN THE TWIN CITIES TURNING INTO ABSOLUTE SHIT IN THE NEXT FEW MONTHS. ALLY TURNING ON ALLY. CHILDE TURNING ON SIRE...
AND EVERYONE TURNING ON THE ERRAND RUNNER OF PRINCE SAMANTHA...
WHO JUST SO HAPPENS... USED TO BE A GODDAMN REBEL ANARCH.
BINGO.
I KNOW HOW MUCH YOU HATE PLAYING COURT GAMES. BUT YOU'RE GOING TO HAVE TO ACCEPT ONE OF THE REWARDS SAMANTHA KEEPS HEAPING ON YOU. SHOW HER YOU'RE LOYAL. SHOW THE REST OF THEM YOU'RE UNTOUCHABLE. SHERIFF. HARPY. FUCKING SCOURGE EVEN.
I DO THIS MY WAY, CALDER. IT'S BEEN LIKE THAT FOR FIFTEEN YEARS. I DON'T DO HIERARCHIES AND POLITICS. I DON'T DO TITLES AND NAME PLATES.
DETERMINED TO HANG ON TO THAT BRUJAH THING TO THE BITTER GODDAMN END HUH? FINE, BAIN.
THEN USE YOUR RIGHT TO SIRE. EMBRACE SOMEONE WORTHY AND BRING A CHILDE INTO THE WORLD JUST FOR YOU.
I MEAN, WE'VE GOT A SYMPHONY OF BACKSTABBING JUST WAITING FOR THE FIRST NOTE TO PLAY.
THE PRINCE COULD USE AT LEAST ONE MORE CECILY BAIN ON HER SIDE.
DO IT NOW...

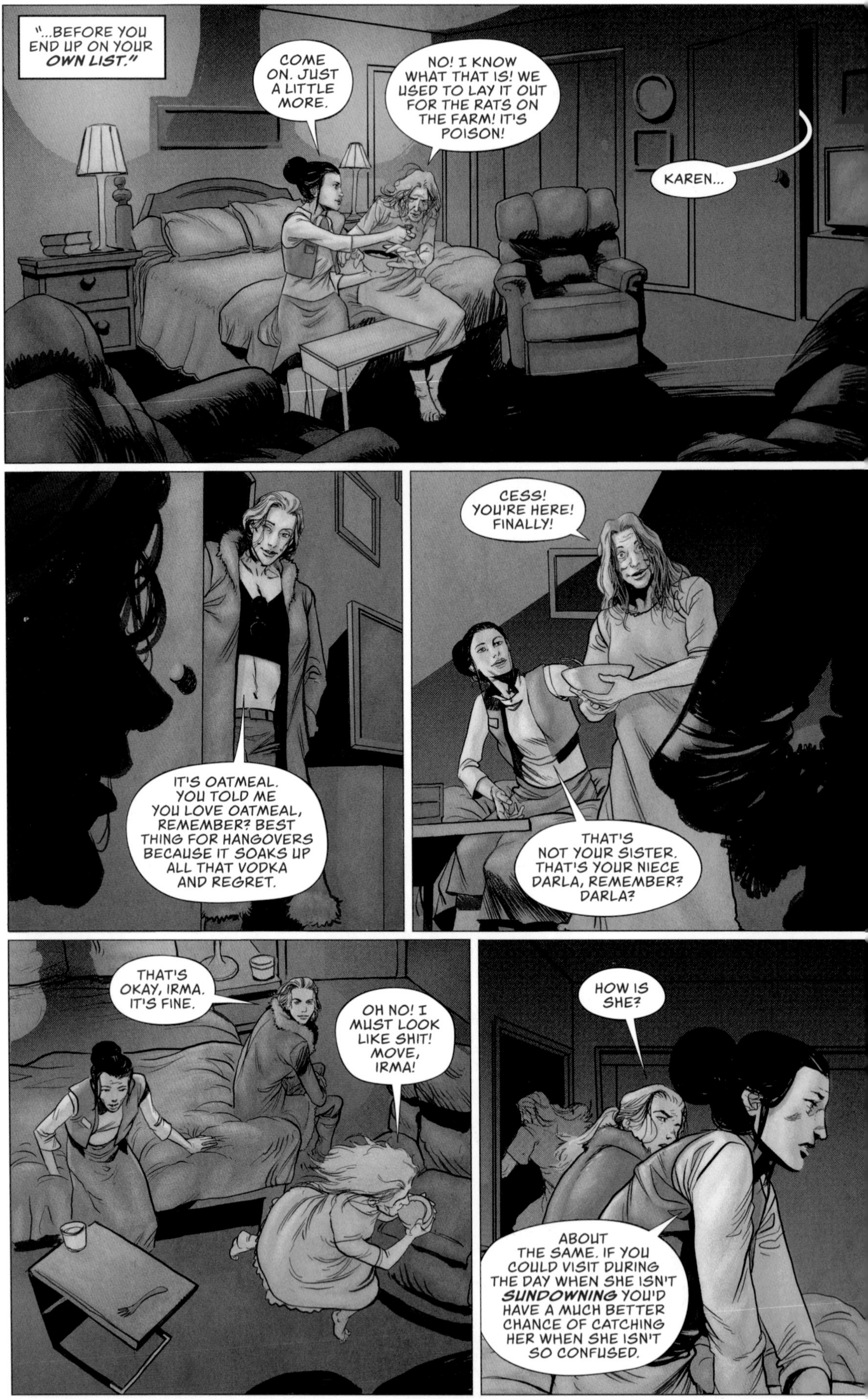
"...BEFORE YOU END UP ON YOUR *OWN LIST.*"
COME ON. JUST A LITTLE MORE.
NO! I KNOW WHAT THAT IS! WE USED TO LAY IT OUT FOR THE RATS ON THE FARM! IT'S POISON!
KAREN...
IT'S OATMEAL. YOU TOLD ME YOU LOVE OATMEAL, REMEMBER? BEST THING FOR HANGOVERS BECAUSE IT SOAKS UP ALL THAT VODKA AND REGRET.
CESS! YOU'RE HERE! FINALLY!
THAT'S NOT YOUR SISTER. THAT'S YOUR NIECE DARLA, REMEMBER? DARLA?
THAT'S OKAY, IRMA. IT'S FINE.
OH NO! I MUST LOOK LIKE SHIT! MOVE, IRMA!
HOW IS SHE?
ABOUT THE SAME. IF YOU COULD VISIT DURING THE DAY WHEN SHE ISN'T *SUNDOWNING* YOU'D HAVE A MUCH BETTER CHANCE OF CATCHING HER WHEN SHE ISN'T SO CONFUSED.

I WISH I COULD. BUT WITH WORK BEING SO BUSY AND... Y'KNOW.

SURE. OF COURSE. THAT'S GOOD.

SO, I MEAN, YOU KNOW, IF YOU CAN--YOU KNOW I WOULDN'T IF I DIDN'T HAVE TO BUT IT'S EXPENSIVE AND...

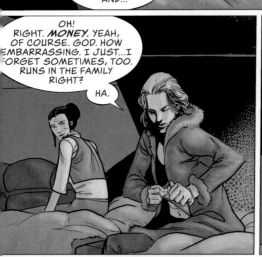

OH! RIGHT. *MONEY.* YEAH, OF COURSE. GOD. HOW EMBARRASSING. I JUST...I FORGET SOMETIMES, TOO. RUNS IN THE FAMILY RIGHT?

HA.

UM. ANYWAY. THANK YOU, IRMA. THANKS FOR EVERYTHING YOU DO FOR...FOR MY *AUNT.*

SURE, DARLA. I'LL LEAVE YOU TWO TO IT.

ALRIGHT, YOU BITCH!

GET ME THE FUCK OUT OF HERE! CUZ I'M READY TO PARTY!

HOLY SHIT, GIRL! YOU LOOK HOTTER 'N GODDAMN DEBBIE HARRY!

BUT, KAREN, HUN...IT'S EARLY. NOBODY WHO'S ANYBODY WILL BE AT *LONGHORN* YET, AND *SUICIDE COMMANDOS* NEVER START PLAYING UNTIL AFTER MIDNIGHT ANYWAY.

BUT--!

SERIOUSLY, YOU DON'T WANNA BE LAME. LET'S JUST CHILL FOR A LITTLE BIT SO WE DON'T BURN OUT EARLY. TRUST ME, I KNOW THESE THINGS. I'M THE OLDER, WISER SISTER.

YEAH. THAT'S WHAT YOU ALWAYS SAY.

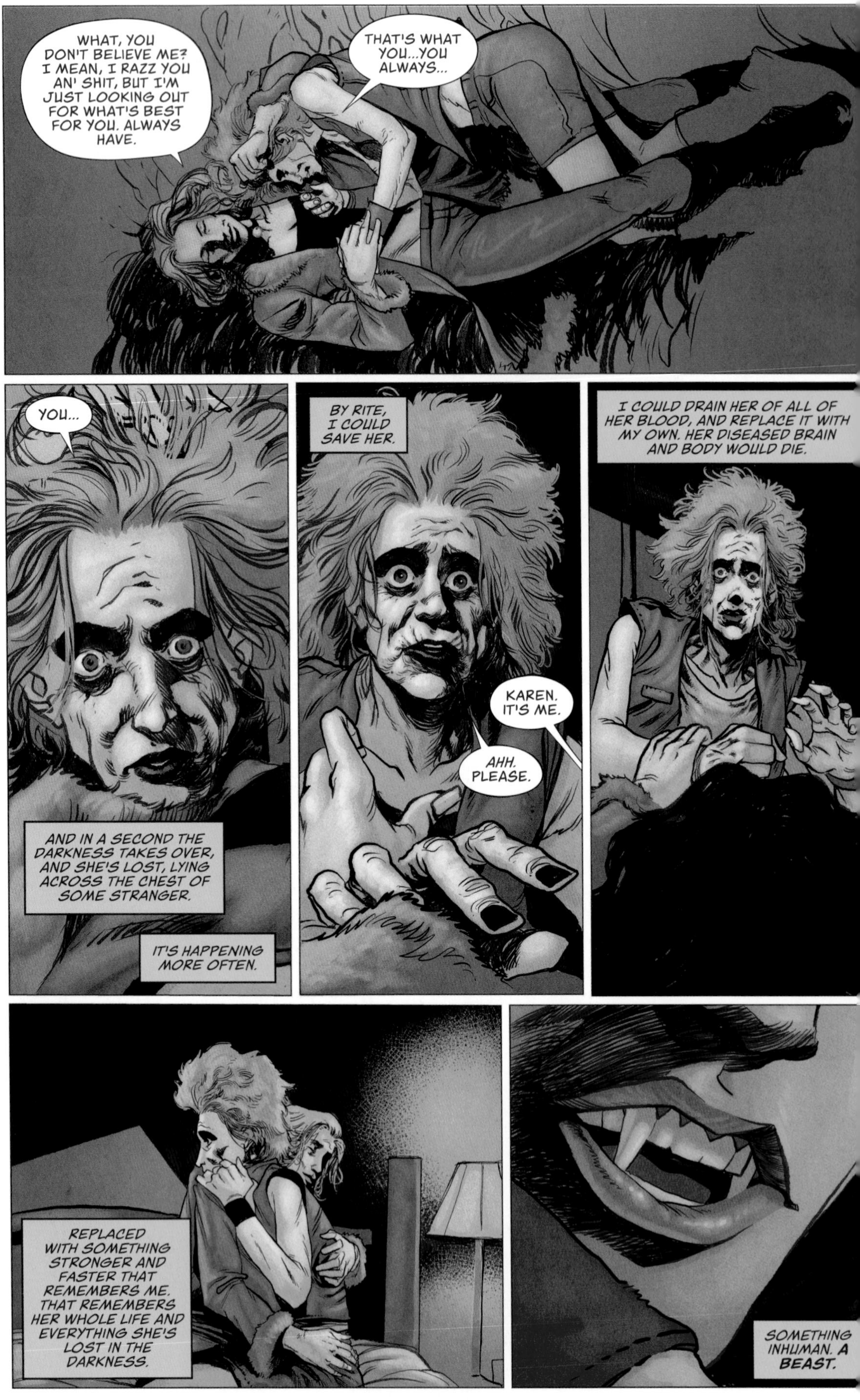

WHAT, YOU DON'T BELIEVE ME? I MEAN, I RAZZ YOU AN' SHIT, BUT I'M JUST LOOKING OUT FOR WHAT'S BEST FOR YOU. ALWAYS HAVE.
THAT'S WHAT YOU...YOU ALWAYS...
YOU...
AND IN A SECOND THE DARKNESS TAKES OVER, AND SHE'S LOST, LYING ACROSS THE CHEST OF SOME STRANGER.
IT'S HAPPENING MORE OFTEN.
BY RITE, I COULD SAVE HER.
KAREN. IT'S ME.
AHH. PLEASE.
I COULD DRAIN HER OF ALL OF HER BLOOD, AND REPLACE IT WITH MY OWN. HER DISEASED BRAIN AND BODY WOULD DIE.
REPLACED WITH SOMETHING STRONGER AND FASTER THAT REMEMBERS ME. THAT REMEMBERS HER WHOLE LIFE AND EVERYTHING SHE'S LOST IN THE DARKNESS.
SOMETHING INHUMAN. A BEAST.

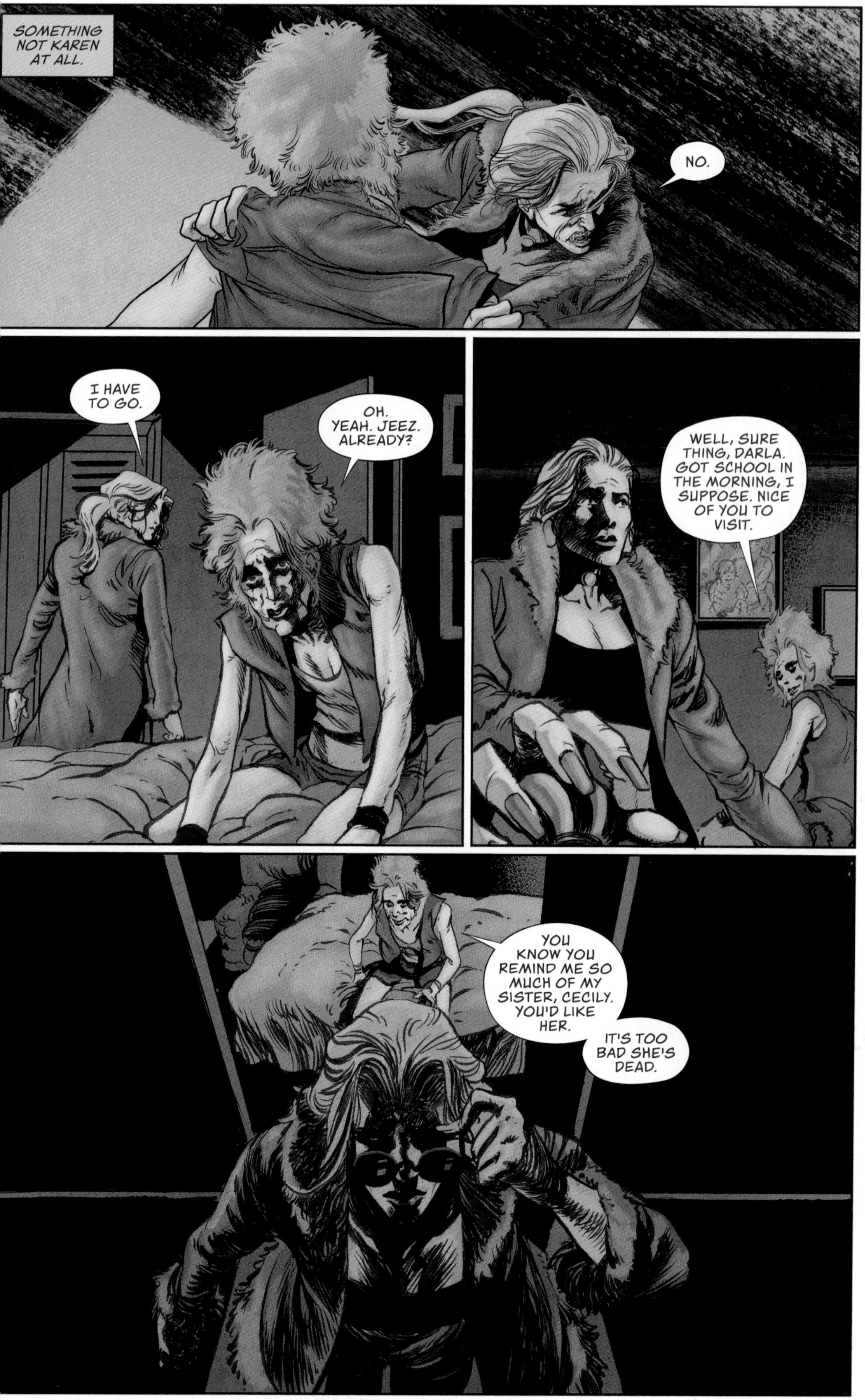
SOMETHING NOT KAREN AT ALL.
NO.
I HAVE TO GO.
OH. YEAH. JEEZ. ALREADY?
WELL, SURE THING, DARLA. GOT SCHOOL IN THE MORNING, I SUPPOSE. NICE OF YOU TO VISIT.
YOU KNOW YOU REMIND ME SO MUCH OF MY SISTER, CECILY. YOU'D LIKE HER.
IT'S TOO BAD SHE'S DEAD.

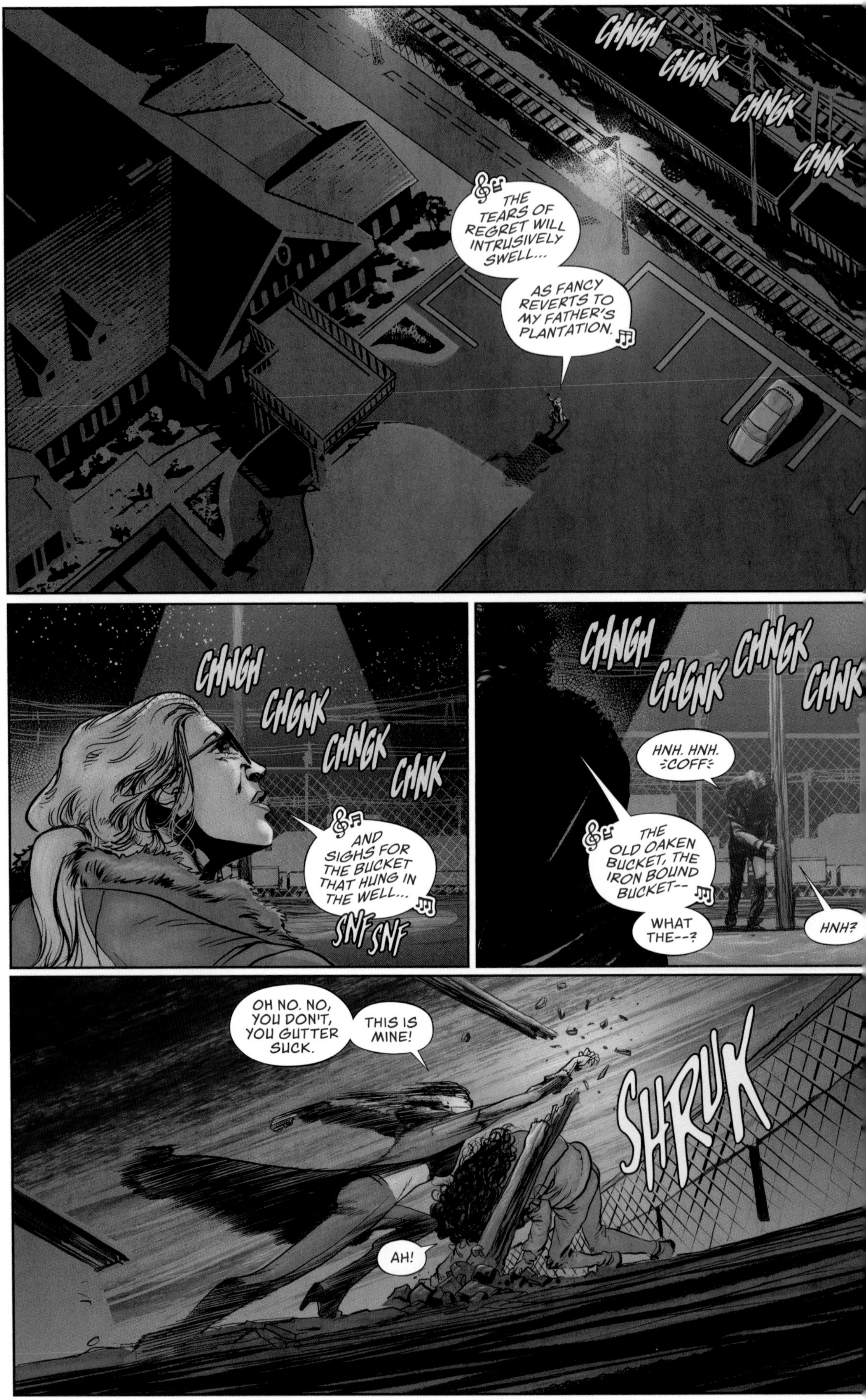
CHNGH
CHGNK
CHNGK
CHNK
THE TEARS OF REGRET WILL INTRUSIVELY SWELL...
AS FANCY REVERTS TO MY FATHER'S PLANTATION.
CHNGH
CHGNK
CHNGK
CHNK
AND SIGHS FOR THE BUCKET THAT HUNG IN THE WELL...
SNF SNF
CHNGH
CHGNK
CHNGK
CHNK
HNH. HNH. COFF
THE OLD OAKEN BUCKET, THE IRON BOUND BUCKET--
WHAT THE--?
HNH?
OH NO. NO, YOU DON'T, YOU GUTTER SUCK.
THIS IS MINE!
SHRUK
AH!

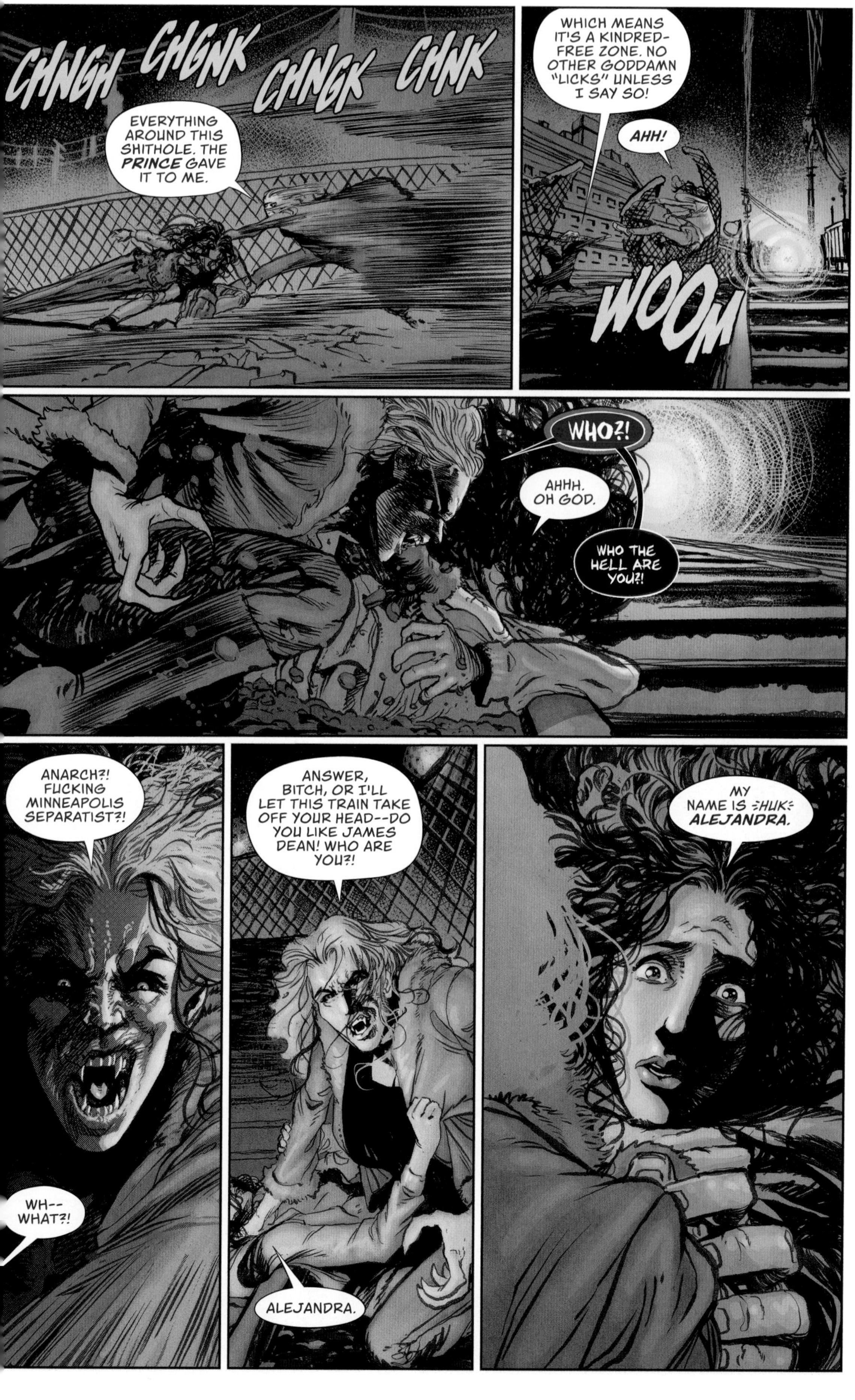
CHNGH CHGNK CHNGK CHNK
EVERYTHING AROUND THIS SHITHOLE. THE PRINCE GAVE IT TO ME.
WHICH MEANS IT'S A KINDRED-FREE ZONE. NO OTHER GODDAMN "LICKS" UNLESS I SAY SO!
AHH!
WOOM
WHO?!
AHHH. OH GOD.
WHO THE HELL ARE YOU?!
ANARCH?! FUCKING MINNEAPOLIS SEPARATIST?!
WH-- WHAT?!
ANSWER, BITCH, OR I'LL LET THIS TRAIN TAKE OFF YOUR HEAD--DO YOU LIKE JAMES DEAN! WHO ARE YOU?!
ALEJANDRA.
MY NAME IS -HUK- ALEJANDRA.

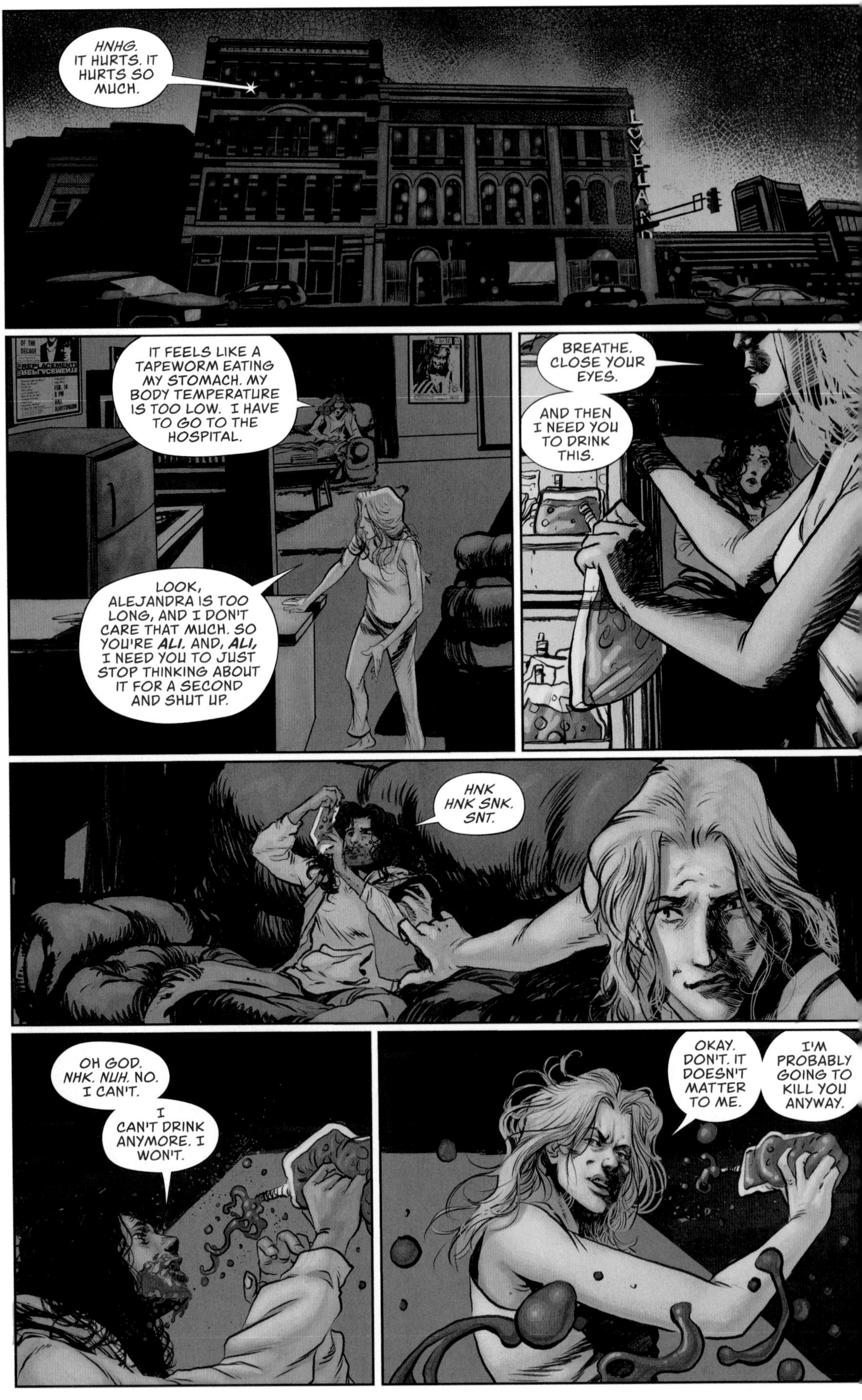
HNHG. IT HURTS. IT HURTS SO MUCH.
LOVELAND
IT FEELS LIKE A TAPEWORM EATING MY STOMACH. MY BODY TEMPERATURE IS TOO LOW. I HAVE TO GO TO THE HOSPITAL.
LOOK, ALEJANDRA IS TOO LONG, AND I DON'T CARE THAT MUCH. SO YOU'RE ALI. AND, ALI, I NEED YOU TO JUST STOP THINKING ABOUT IT FOR A SECOND AND SHUT UP.
BREATHE. CLOSE YOUR EYES.
AND THEN I NEED YOU TO DRINK THIS.
HNK HNK SNK. SNT.
OH GOD. NHK. NUH. NO. I CAN'T.
I CAN'T DRINK ANYMORE. I WON'T.
OKAY. DON'T. IT DOESN'T MATTER TO ME.
I'M PROBABLY GOING TO KILL YOU ANYWAY.

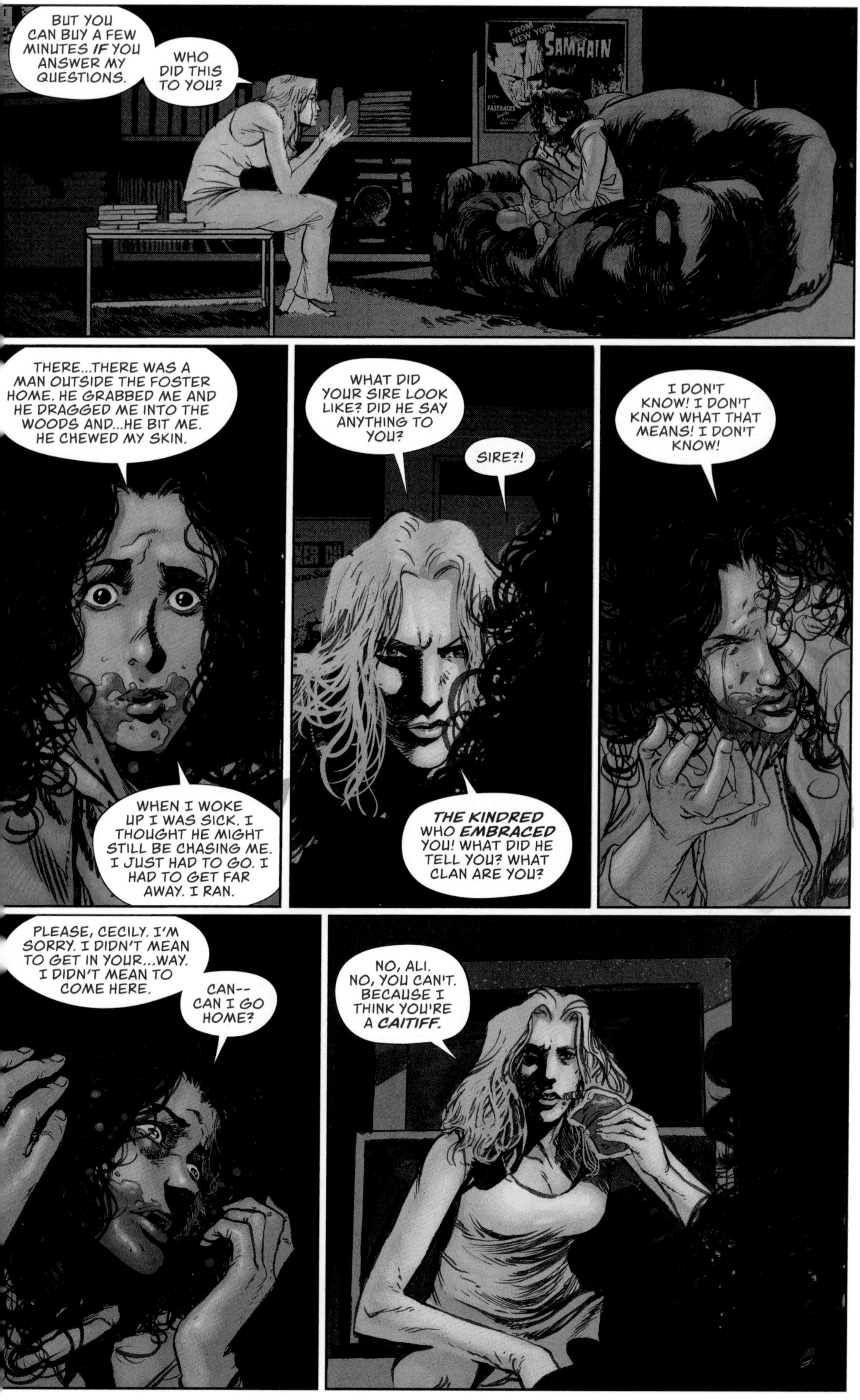
BUT YOU CAN BUY A FEW MINUTES IF YOU ANSWER MY QUESTIONS.
WHO DID THIS TO YOU?
FROM NEW YORK SAMHAIN
FASTBACKS
THERE...THERE WAS A MAN OUTSIDE THE FOSTER HOME. HE GRABBED ME AND HE DRAGGED ME INTO THE WOODS AND...HE BIT ME. HE CHEWED MY SKIN.
WHEN I WOKE UP I WAS SICK. I THOUGHT HE MIGHT STILL BE CHASING ME. I JUST HAD TO GO. I HAD TO GET FAR AWAY. I RAN.
WHAT DID YOUR SIRE LOOK LIKE? DID HE SAY ANYTHING TO YOU?
SIRE?!
THE KINDRED WHO EMBRACED YOU! WHAT DID HE TELL YOU? WHAT CLAN ARE YOU?
I DON'T KNOW! I DON'T KNOW WHAT THAT MEANS! I DON'T KNOW!
PLEASE, CECILY. I'M SORRY. I DIDN'T MEAN TO GET IN YOUR...WAY. I DIDN'T MEAN TO COME HERE.
CAN-- CAN I GO HOME?
NO, ALI. NO, YOU CAN'T. BECAUSE I THINK YOU'RE A CAITIFF.

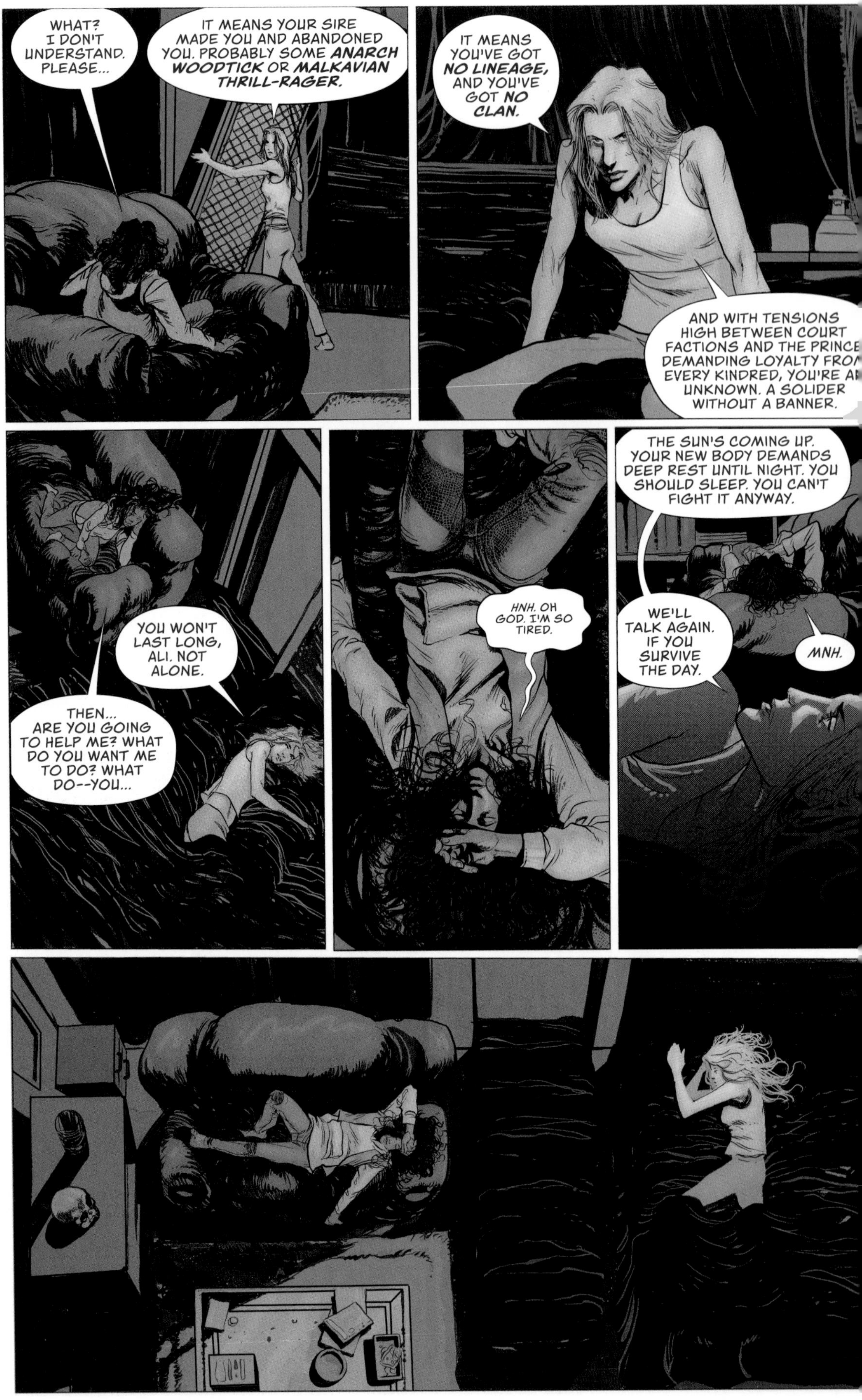
WHAT? I DON'T UNDERSTAND. PLEASE...
IT MEANS YOUR SIRE MADE YOU AND ABANDONED YOU. PROBABLY SOME ANARCH WOODTICK OR MALKAVIAN THRILL-RAGER.
IT MEANS YOU'VE GOT NO LINEAGE, AND YOU'VE GOT NO CLAN.
AND WITH TENSIONS HIGH BETWEEN COURT FACTIONS AND THE PRINCE DEMANDING LOYALTY FROM EVERY KINDRED, YOU'RE AN UNKNOWN. A SOLIDER WITHOUT A BANNER.
YOU WON'T LAST LONG, ALI. NOT ALONE.
THEN... ARE YOU GOING TO HELP ME? WHAT DO YOU WANT ME TO DO? WHAT DO--YOU...
HNH. OH GOD. I'M SO TIRED.
THE SUN'S COMING UP. YOUR NEW BODY DEMANDS DEEP REST UNTIL NIGHT. YOU SHOULD SLEEP. YOU CAN'T FIGHT IT ANYWAY.
WE'LL TALK AGAIN. IF YOU SURVIVE THE DAY.
MNH.

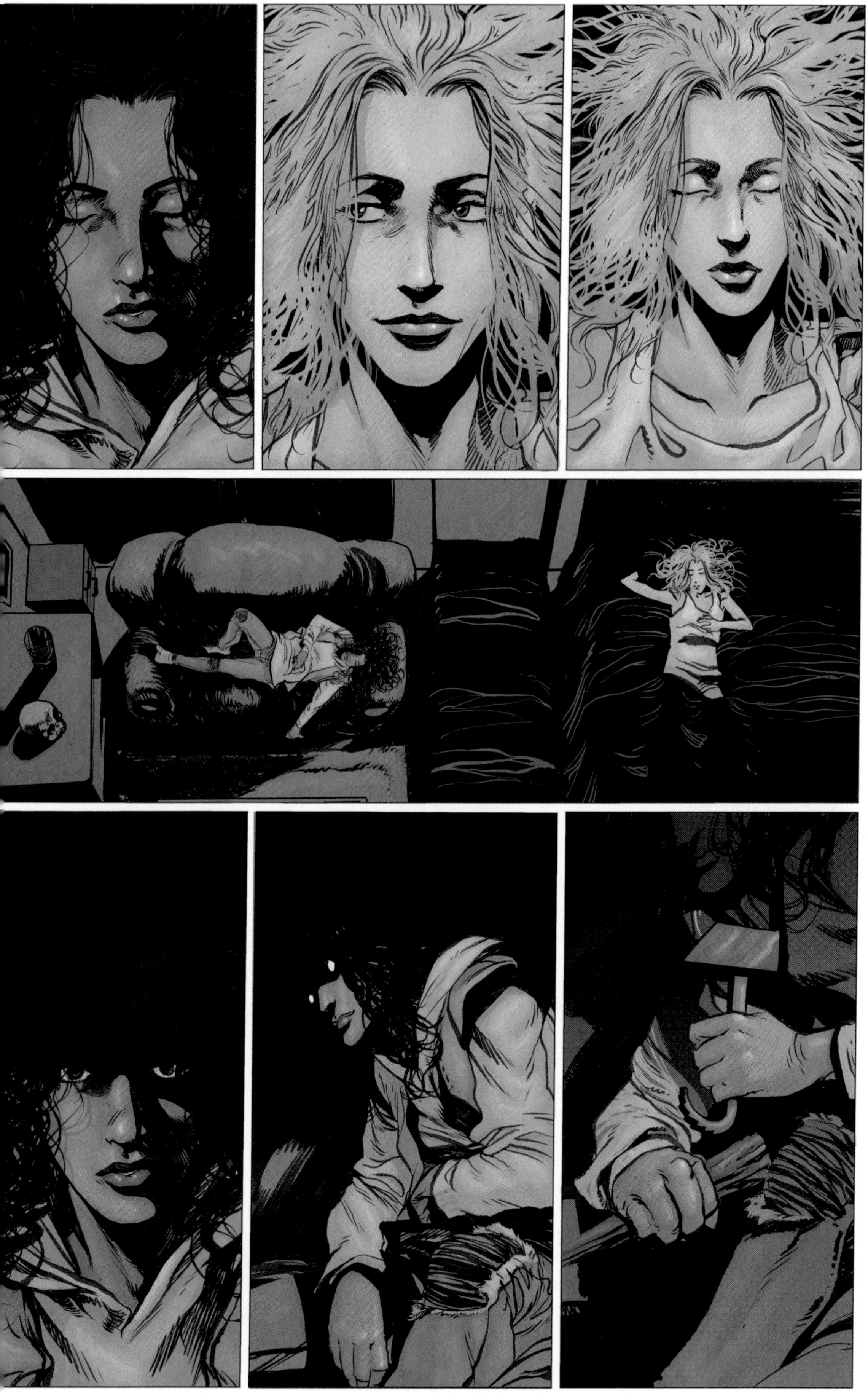

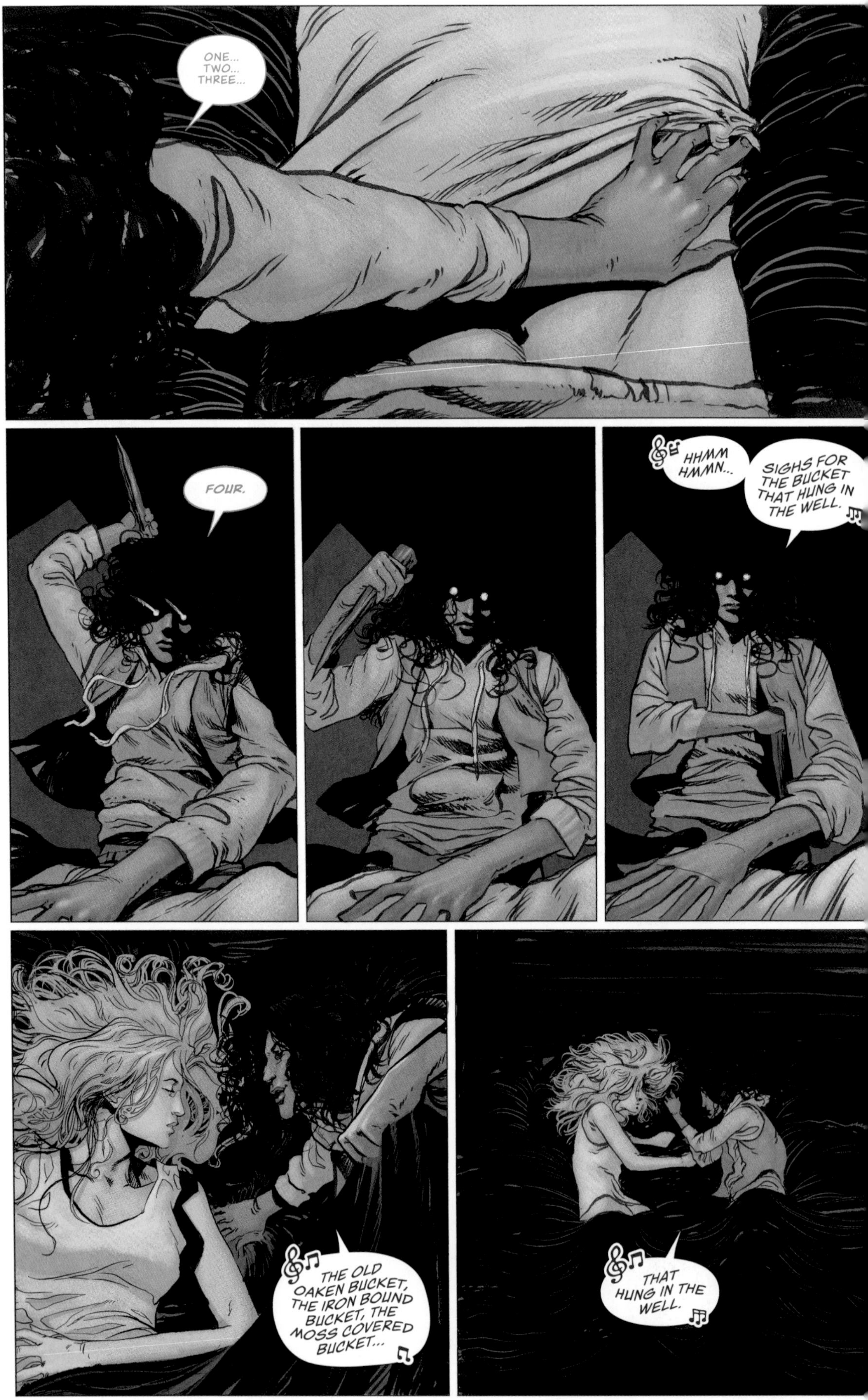

ONE... TWO... THREE...
FOUR.
HHMM HMMN...
SIGHS FOR THE BUCKET THAT HUNG IN THE WELL.
THE OLD OAKEN BUCKET, THE IRON BOUND BUCKET, THE MOSS COVERED BUCKET...
THAT HUNG IN THE WELL.

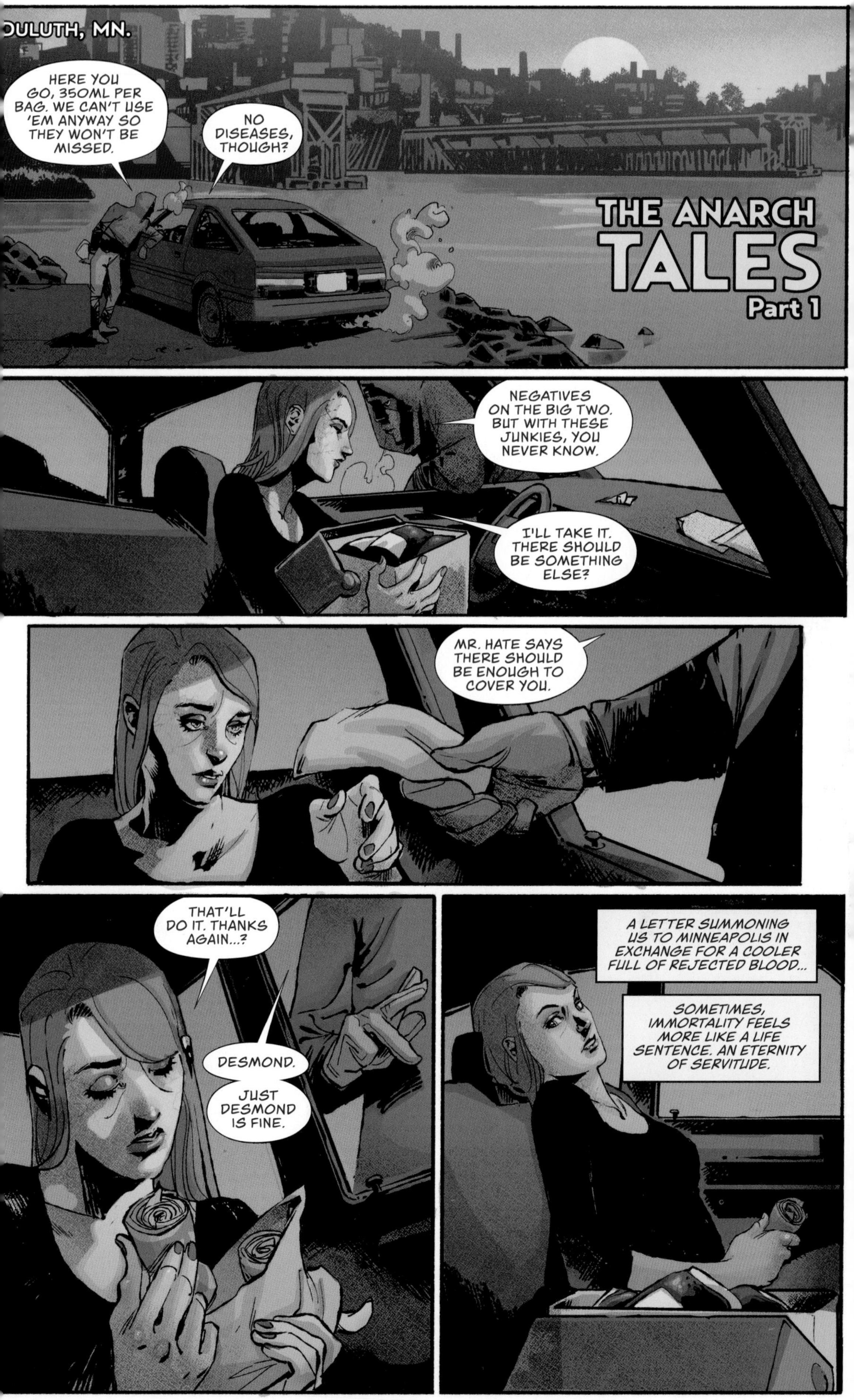
DULUTH, MN.
HERE YOU GO, 350ML PER BAG. WE CAN'T USE 'EM ANYWAY SO THEY WON'T BE MISSED.
NO DISEASES, THOUGH?
THE ANARCH TALES
Part 1
NEGATIVES ON THE BIG TWO. BUT WITH THESE JUNKIES, YOU NEVER KNOW.
I'LL TAKE IT. THERE SHOULD BE SOMETHING ELSE?
MR. HATE SAYS THERE SHOULD BE ENOUGH TO COVER YOU.
THAT'LL DO IT. THANKS AGAIN...?
DESMOND.
JUST DESMOND IS FINE.
A LETTER SUMMONING US TO MINNEAPOLIS IN EXCHANGE FOR A COOLER FULL OF REJECTED BLOOD...
SOMETIMES, IMMORTALITY FEELS MORE LIKE A LIFE SENTENCE. AN ETERNITY OF SERVITUDE.

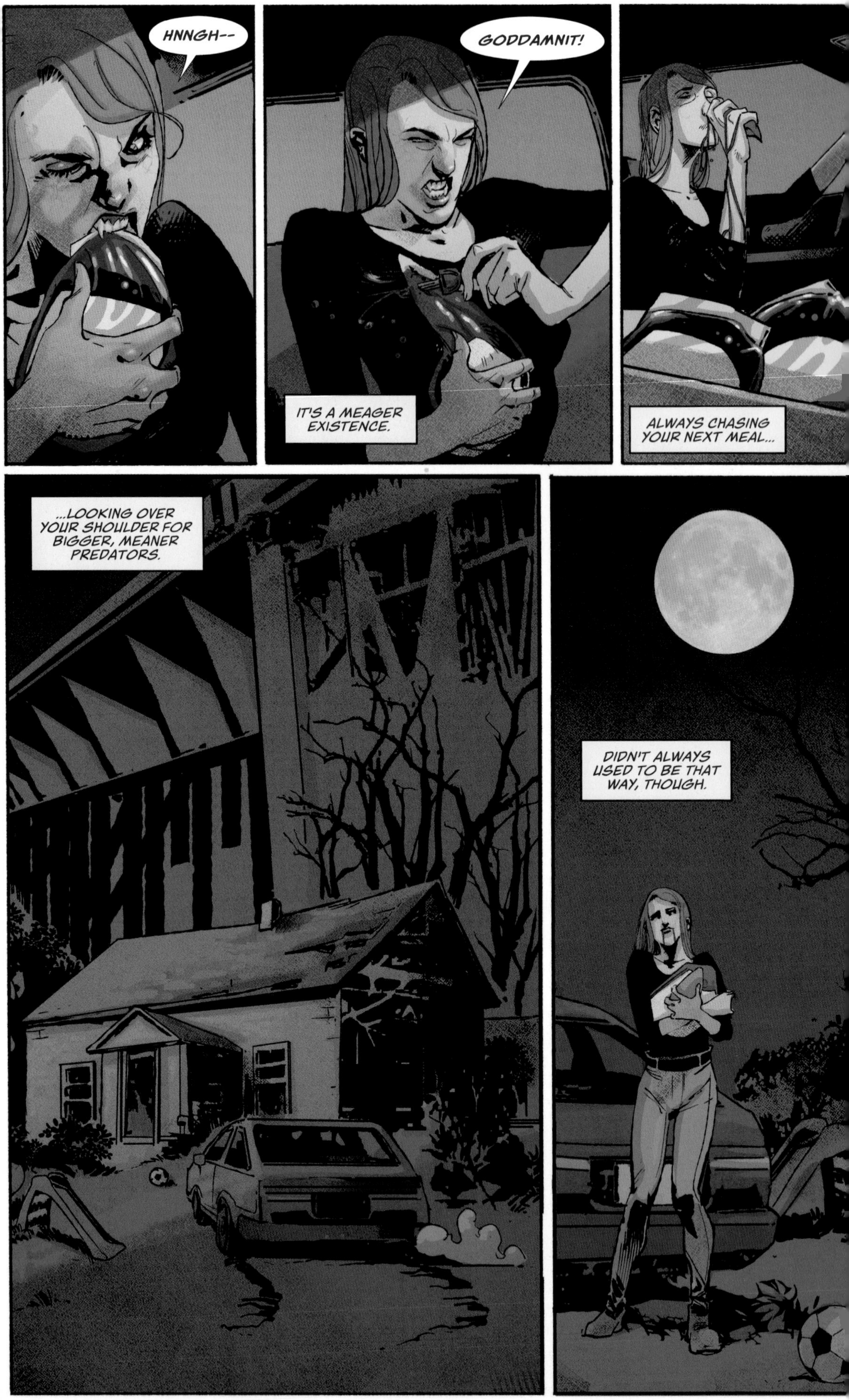
HNNGH--
GODDAMNIT!
IT'S A MEAGER EXISTENCE.
ALWAYS CHASING YOUR NEXT MEAL...
...LOOKING OVER YOUR SHOULDER FOR BIGGER, MEANER PREDATORS.
DIDN'T ALWAYS USED TO BE THAT WAY, THOUGH.

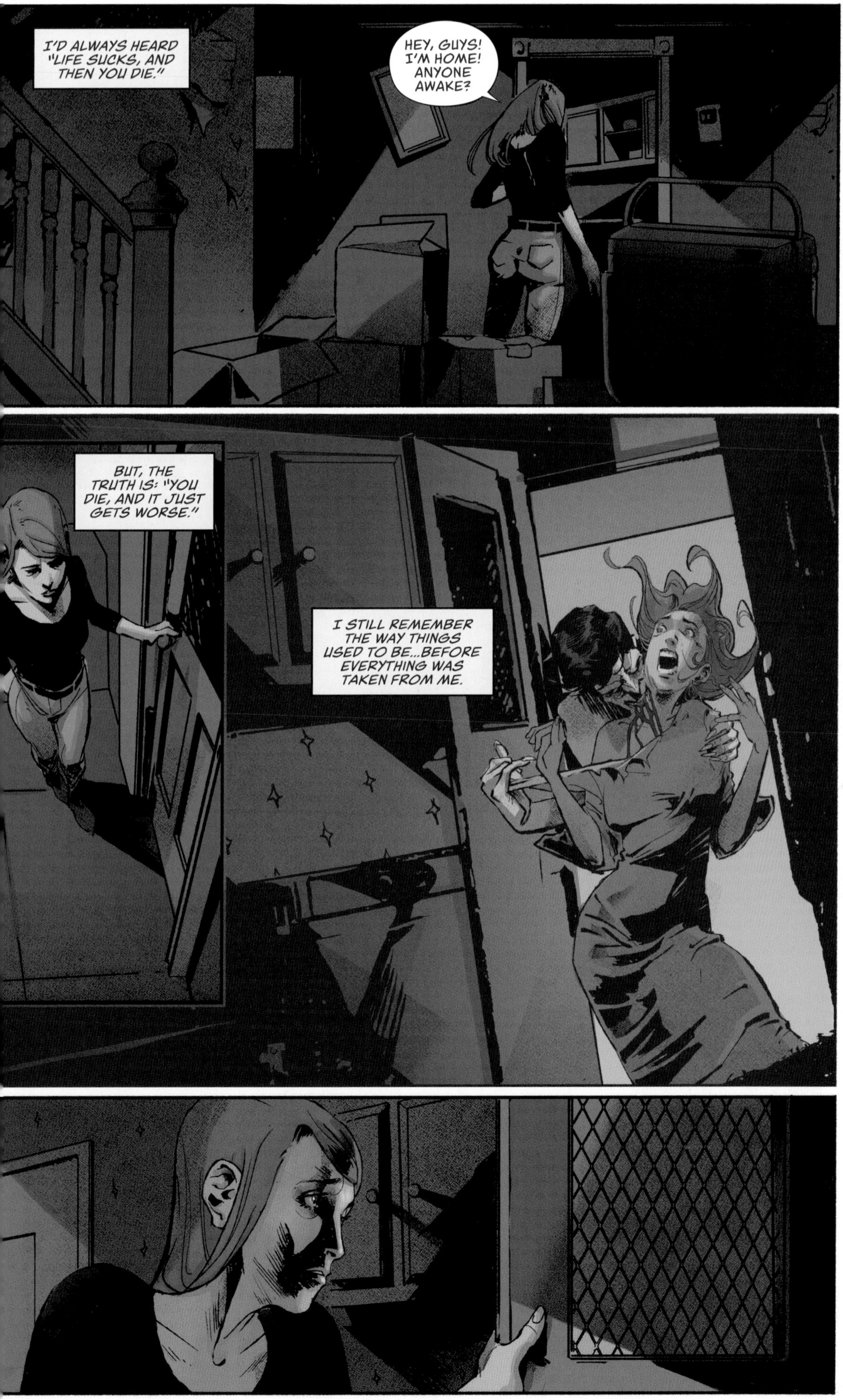
I'D ALWAYS HEARD "LIFE SUCKS, AND THEN YOU DIE."
HEY, GUYS! I'M HOME! ANYONE AWAKE?
BUT, THE TRUTH IS: "YOU DIE, AND IT JUST GETS WORSE."
I STILL REMEMBER THE WAY THINGS USED TO BE...BEFORE EVERYTHING WAS TAKEN FROM ME.

KING, HONEY? YOU UP?

HEY, COLLEEN... S'THERE FOOD?

ON THE TABLE.

BAGS AGAIN?

"YOU GET WHAT YOU GET, AND YOU DON'T THROW A FIT."

UNLIKE ME, THEY HAVE TO SLEEP ALL DAY.

BUT I DON'T SLEEP AT NIGHT. I CAN'T SLEEP AT ALL-- MORE EXHAUSTED THAN EVER.

WHEN THE SU... STINGS MY EYE... I JUST GET... HEADACHE.

MAYBE THE BLOOD SWEATS. UNLIKE OTHER VAMPIRES...

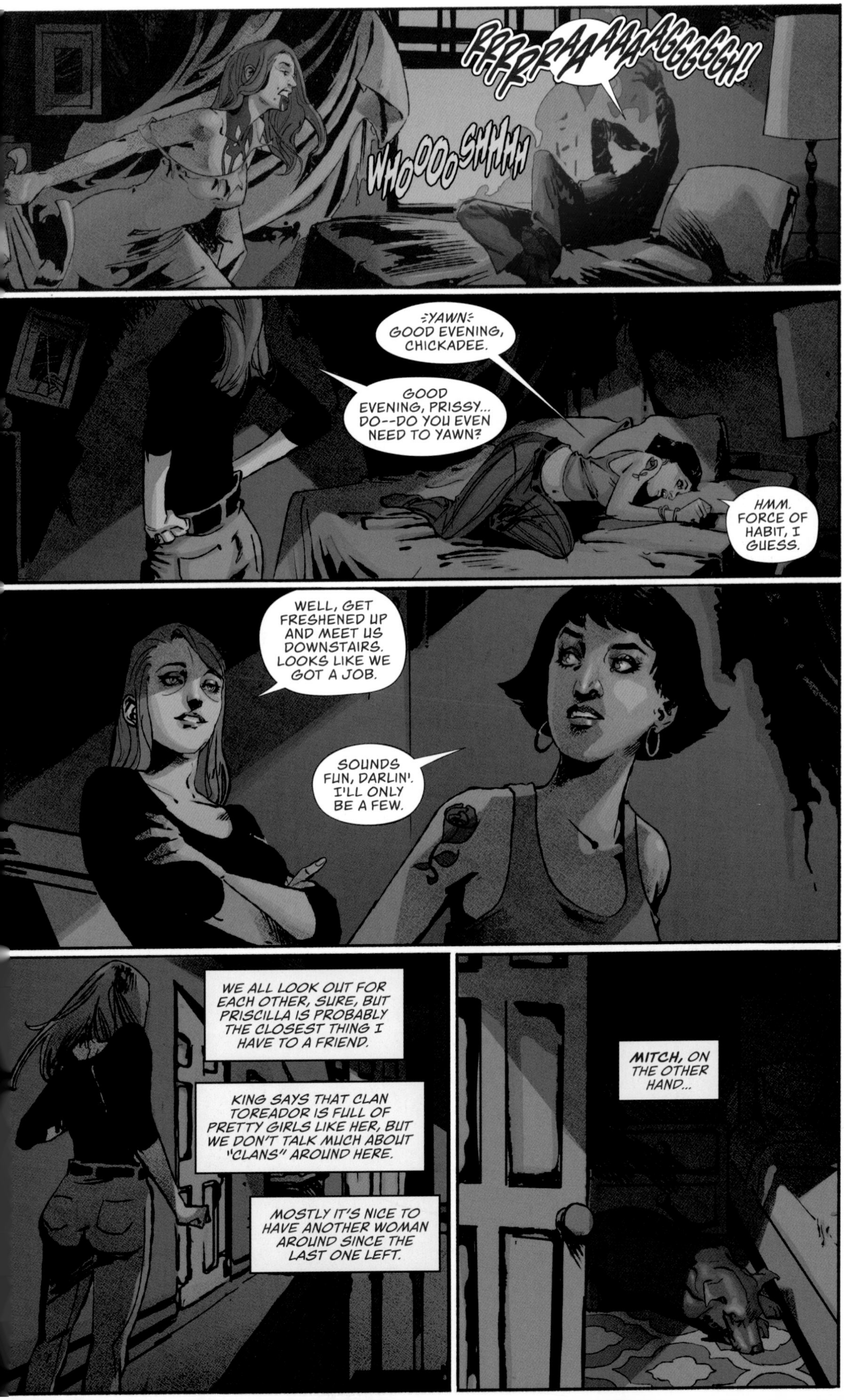
RRRRRAAAAAAGGGGGH!
WHOOOOSHHHH
=YAWN= GOOD EVENING, CHICKADEE.
GOOD EVENING, PRISSY... DO--DO YOU EVEN NEED TO YAWN?
HMM. FORCE OF HABIT, I GUESS.
WELL, GET FRESHENED UP AND MEET US DOWNSTAIRS. LOOKS LIKE WE GOT A JOB.
SOUNDS FUN, DARLIN'. I'LL ONLY BE A FEW.
WE ALL LOOK OUT FOR EACH OTHER, SURE, BUT PRISCILLA IS PROBABLY THE CLOSEST THING I HAVE TO A FRIEND.
KING SAYS THAT CLAN TOREADOR IS FULL OF PRETTY GIRLS LIKE HER, BUT WE DON'T TALK MUCH ABOUT "CLANS" AROUND HERE.
MOSTLY IT'S NICE TO HAVE ANOTHER WOMAN AROUND SINCE THE LAST ONE LEFT.
MITCH, ON THE OTHER HAND...

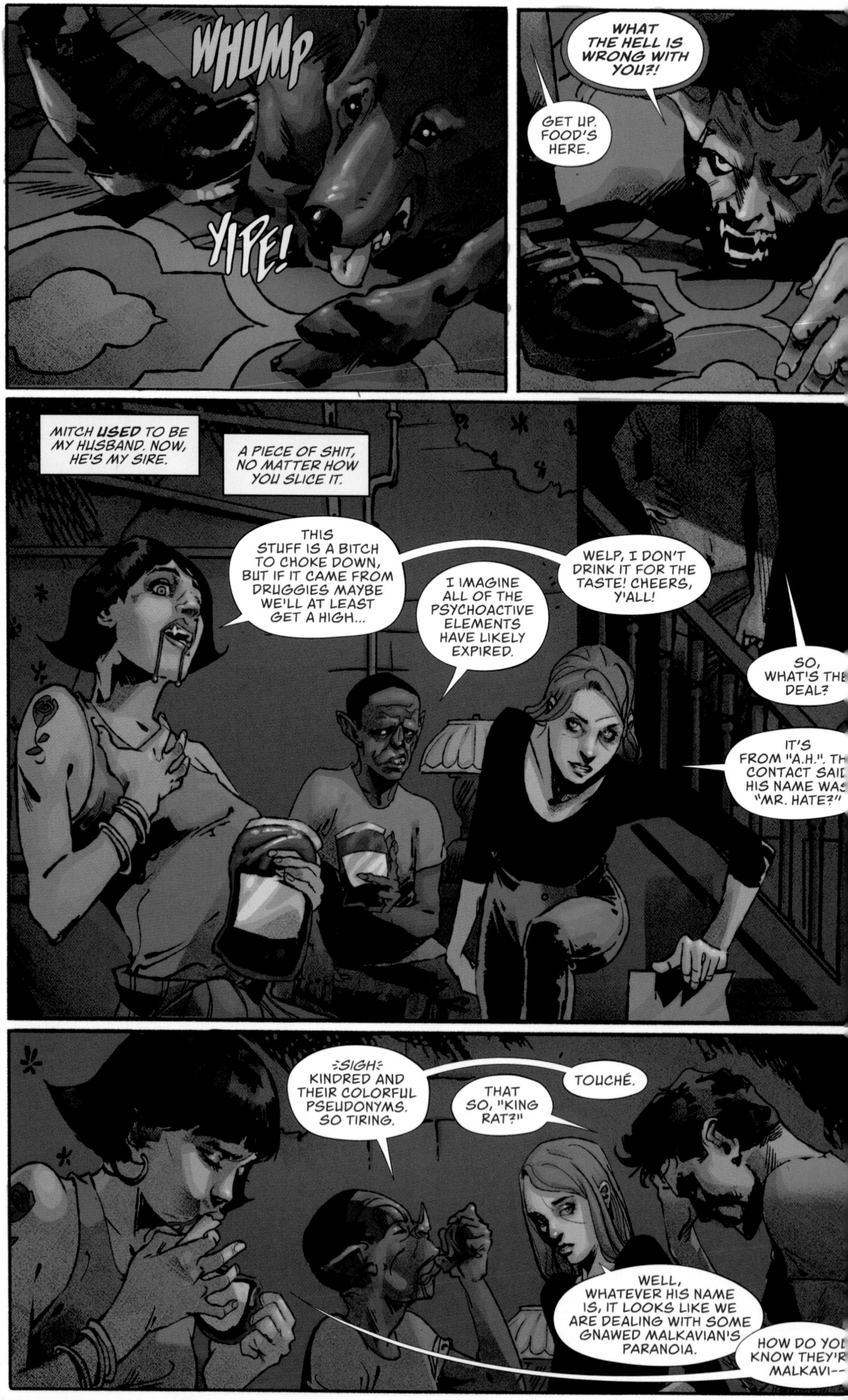
WHUMP
YIPE!
WHAT THE HELL IS WRONG WITH YOU?!
GET UP. FOOD'S HERE.
MITCH **USED** TO BE MY HUSBAND. NOW, HE'S MY SIRE.
A PIECE OF SHIT, NO MATTER HOW YOU SLICE IT.
THIS STUFF IS A BITCH TO CHOKE DOWN, BUT IF IT CAME FROM DRUGGIES MAYBE WE'LL AT LEAST GET A HIGH...
WELP, I DON'T DRINK IT FOR THE TASTE! CHEERS, Y'ALL!
I IMAGINE ALL OF THE PSYCHOACTIVE ELEMENTS HAVE LIKELY EXPIRED.
SO, WHAT'S THE DEAL?
IT'S FROM "A.H.". THE CONTACT SAID HIS NAME WAS "MR. HATE?"
=SIGH= KINDRED AND THEIR COLORFUL PSEUDONYMS. SO TIRING.
TOUCHÉ.
THAT SO, "KING RAT?"
WELL, WHATEVER HIS NAME IS, IT LOOKS LIKE WE ARE DEALING WITH SOME GNAWED MALKAVIAN'S PARANOIA.
HOW DO YOU KNOW THEY'RE MALKAVI--

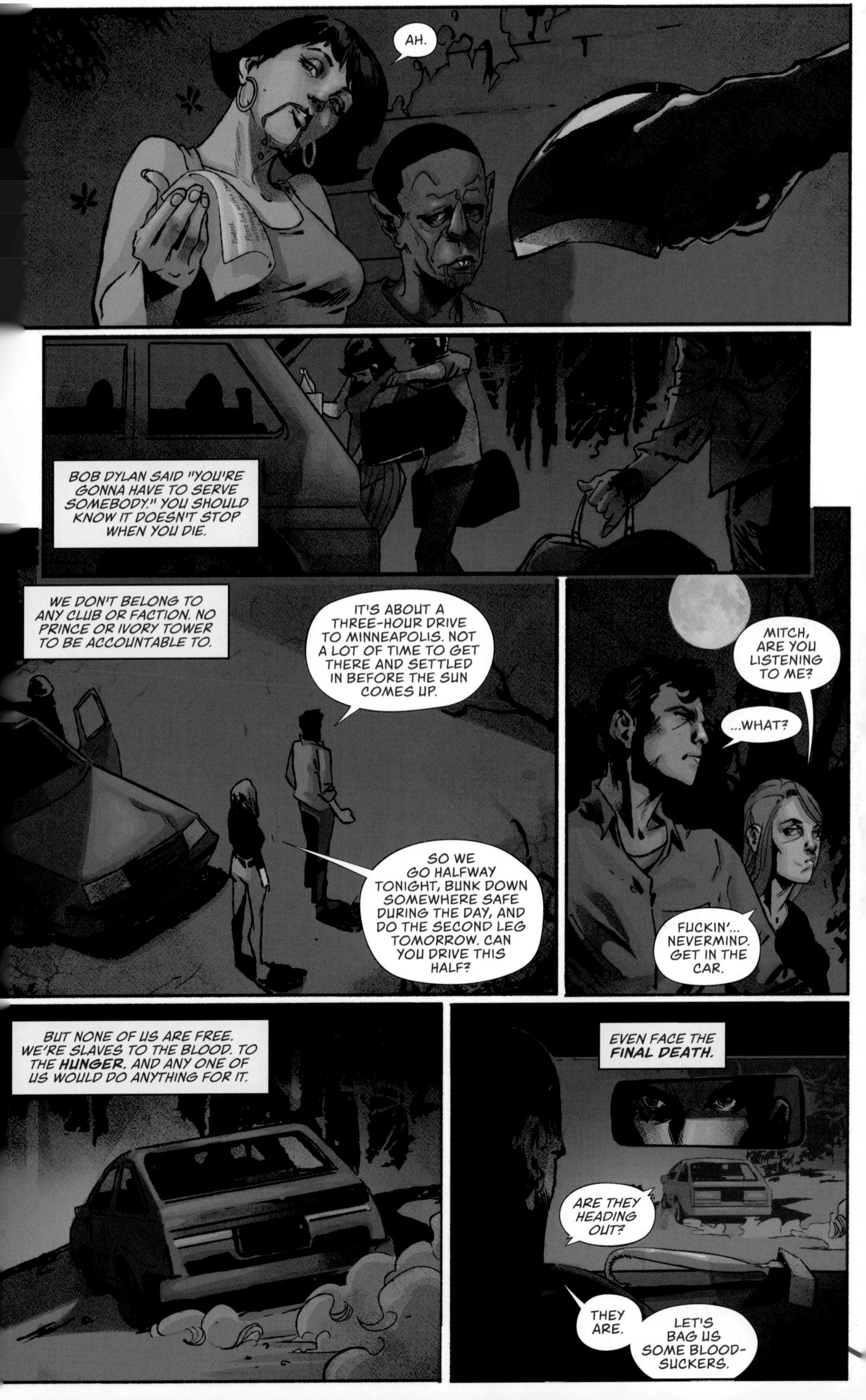
AH.
BOB DYLAN SAID "YOU'RE GONNA HAVE TO SERVE SOMEBODY." YOU SHOULD KNOW IT DOESN'T STOP WHEN YOU DIE.
WE DON'T BELONG TO ANY CLUB OR FACTION. NO PRINCE OR IVORY TOWER TO BE ACCOUNTABLE TO.
IT'S ABOUT A THREE-HOUR DRIVE TO MINNEAPOLIS. NOT A LOT OF TIME TO GET THERE AND SETTLED IN BEFORE THE SUN COMES UP.
SO WE GO HALFWAY TONIGHT, BUNK DOWN SOMEWHERE SAFE DURING THE DAY, AND DO THE SECOND LEG TOMORROW. CAN YOU DRIVE THIS HALF?
MITCH, ARE YOU LISTENING TO ME?
...WHAT?
FUCKIN'... NEVERMIND. GET IN THE CAR.
BUT NONE OF US ARE FREE. WE'RE SLAVES TO THE BLOOD. TO THE HUNGER. AND ANY ONE OF US WOULD DO ANYTHING FOR IT.
EVEN FACE THE FINAL DEATH.
ARE THEY HEADING OUT?
THEY ARE.
LET'S BAG US SOME BLOOD-SUCKERS.

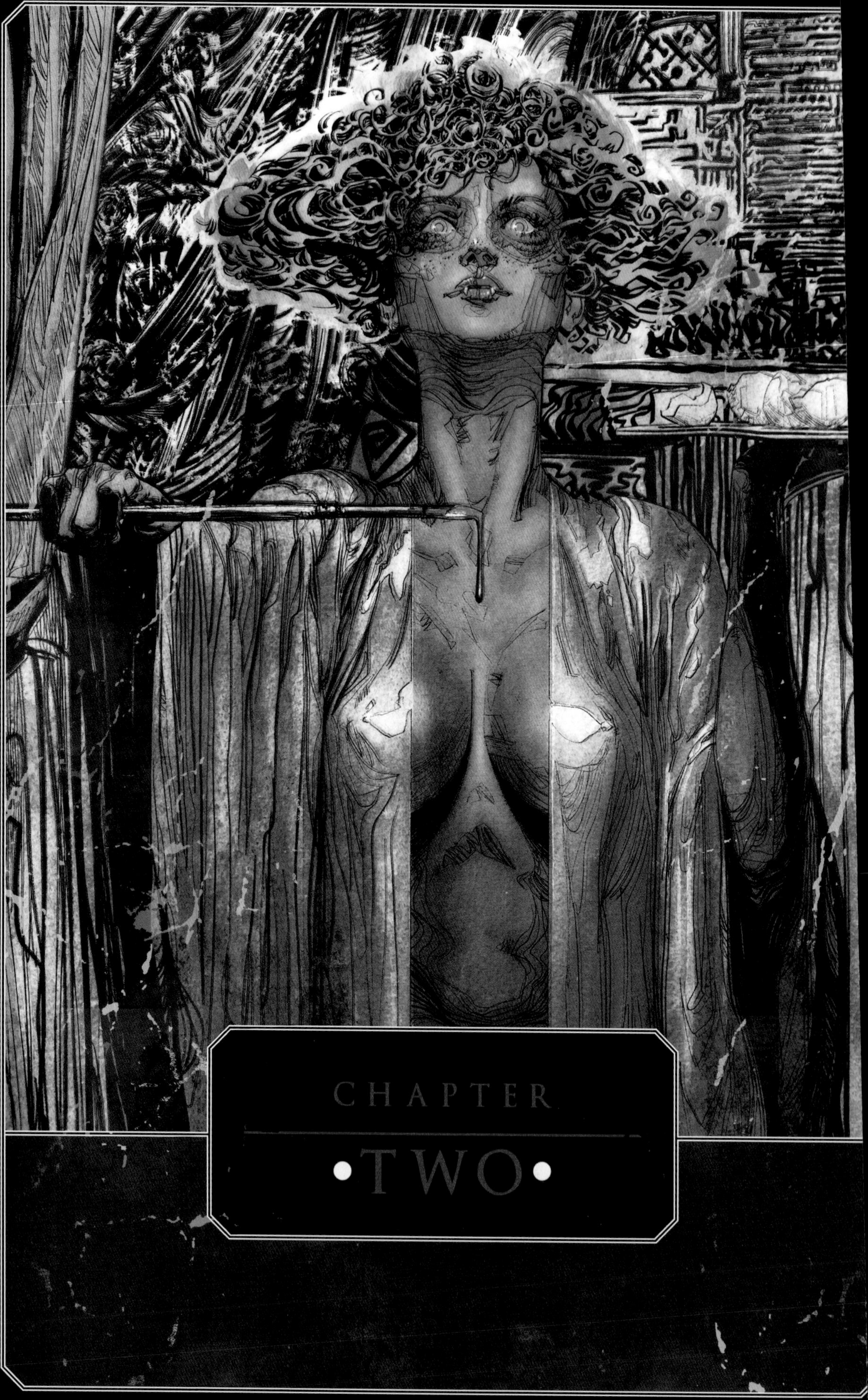

CHAPTER
•TWO•

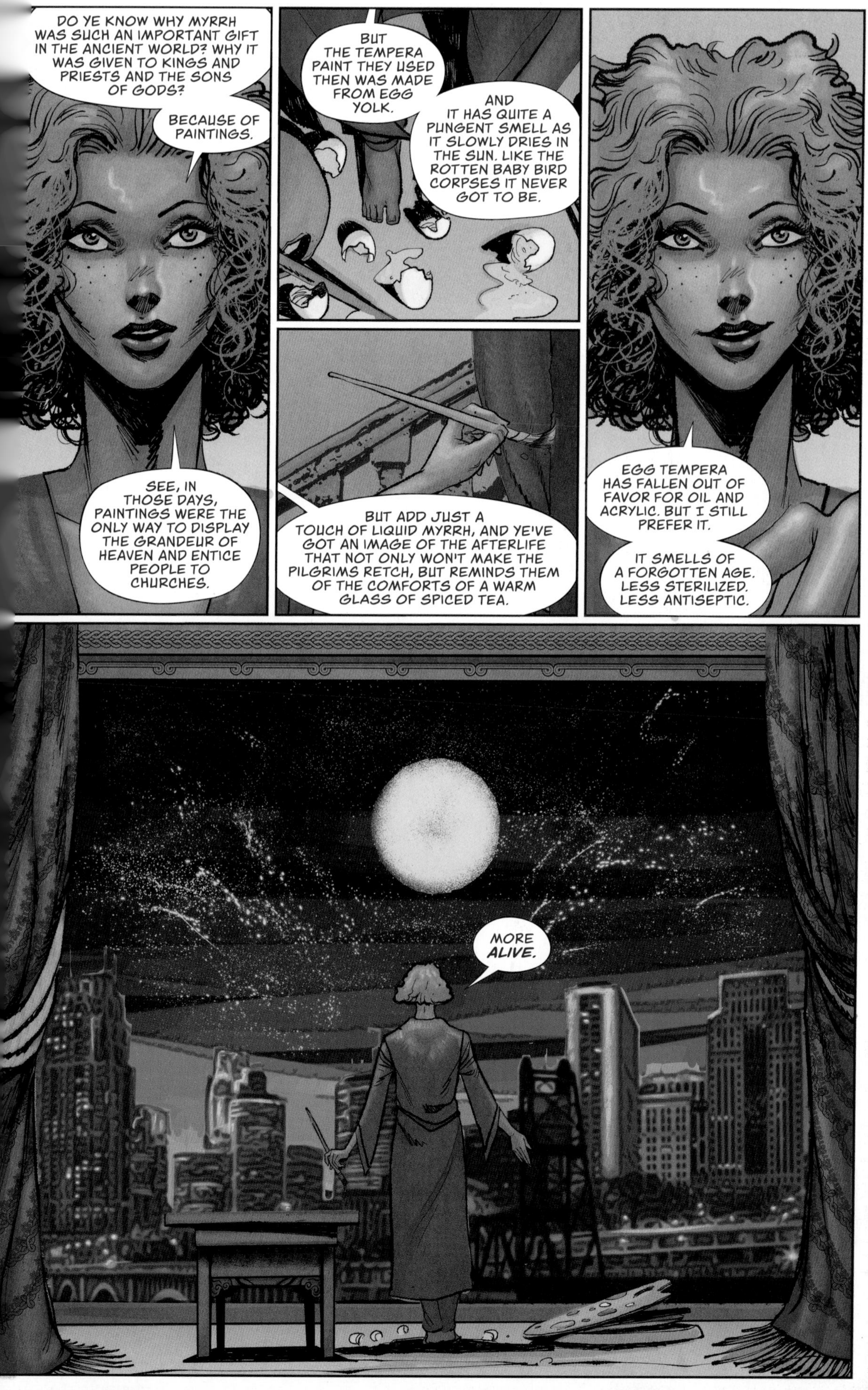
DO YE KNOW WHY MYRRH WAS SUCH AN IMPORTANT GIFT IN THE ANCIENT WORLD? WHY IT WAS GIVEN TO KINGS AND PRIESTS AND THE SONS OF GODS?
BECAUSE OF PAINTINGS.
SEE, IN THOSE DAYS, PAINTINGS WERE THE ONLY WAY TO DISPLAY THE GRANDEUR OF HEAVEN AND ENTICE PEOPLE TO CHURCHES.
BUT THE TEMPERA PAINT THEY USED THEN WAS MADE FROM EGG YOLK.
AND IT HAS QUITE A PUNGENT SMELL AS IT SLOWLY DRIES IN THE SUN. LIKE THE ROTTEN BABY BIRD CORPSES IT NEVER GOT TO BE.
BUT ADD JUST A TOUCH OF LIQUID MYRRH, AND YE'VE GOT AN IMAGE OF THE AFTERLIFE THAT NOT ONLY WON'T MAKE THE PILGRIMS RETCH, BUT REMINDS THEM OF THE COMFORTS OF A WARM GLASS OF SPICED TEA.
EGG TEMPERA HAS FALLEN OUT OF FAVOR FOR OIL AND ACRYLIC. BUT I STILL PREFER IT.
IT SMELLS OF A FORGOTTEN AGE. LESS STERILIZED. LESS ANTISEPTIC.
MORE ALIVE.

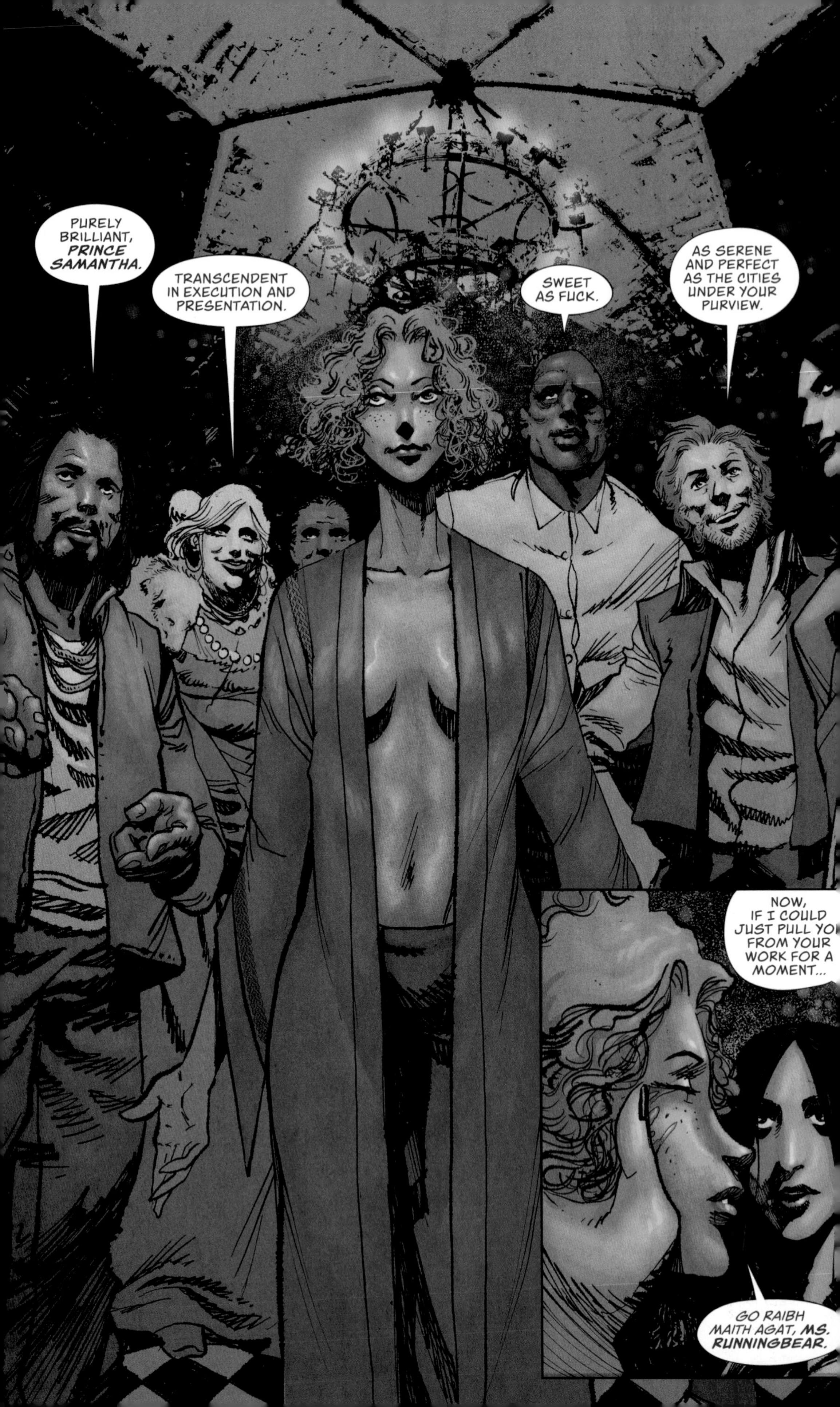
PURELY BRILLIANT, **PRINCE SAMANTHA.**
TRANSCENDENT IN EXECUTION AND PRESENTATION.
SWEET AS FUCK.
AS SERENE AND PERFECT AS THE CITIES UNDER YOUR PURVIEW.
NOW, IF I COULD JUST PULL YO FROM YOUR WORK FOR A MOMENT...
GO RAIBH MAITH AGAT, **MS. RUNNINGBEAR.**

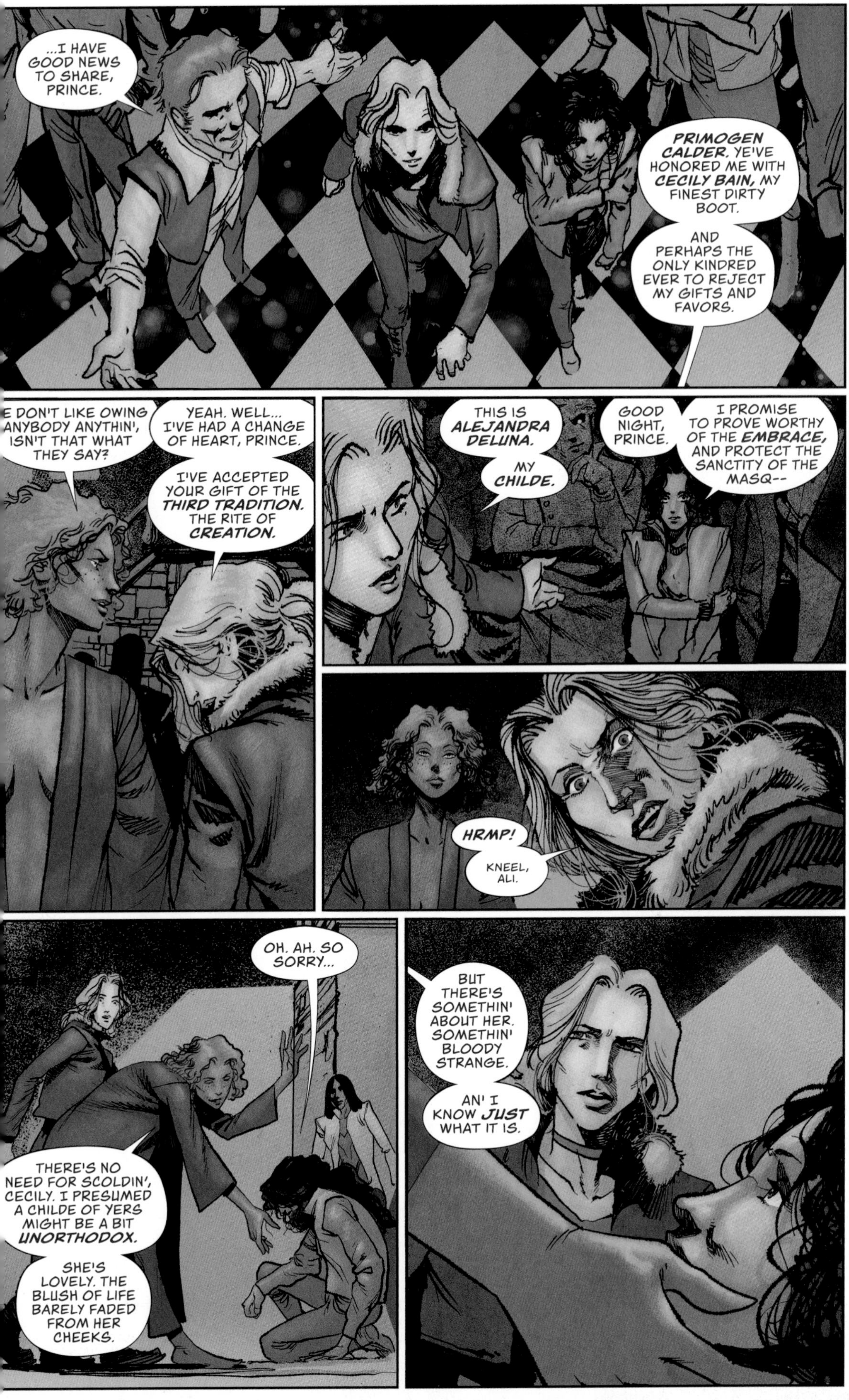
...I HAVE GOOD NEWS TO SHARE, PRINCE.
PRIMOGEN CALDER. YE'VE HONORED ME WITH CECILY BAIN, MY FINEST DIRTY BOOT.
AND PERHAPS THE ONLY KINDRED EVER TO REJECT MY GIFTS AND FAVORS.
E DON'T LIKE OWING ANYBODY ANYTHIN', ISN'T THAT WHAT THEY SAY?
YEAH. WELL... I'VE HAD A CHANGE OF HEART, PRINCE.
I'VE ACCEPTED YOUR GIFT OF THE THIRD TRADITION. THE RITE OF CREATION.
THIS IS ALEJANDRA DELUNA.
MY CHILDE.
GOOD NIGHT, PRINCE.
I PROMISE TO PROVE WORTHY OF THE EMBRACE, AND PROTECT THE SANCTITY OF THE MASQ--
HRMP!
KNEEL, ALI.
OH. AH. SO SORRY...
THERE'S NO NEED FOR SCOLDIN', CECILY. I PRESUMED A CHILDE OF YERS MIGHT BE A BIT UNORTHODOX.
SHE'S LOVELY. THE BLUSH OF LIFE BARELY FADED FROM HER CHEEKS.
BUT THERE'S SOMETHIN' ABOUT HER. SOMETHIN' BLOODY STRANGE.
AN' I KNOW JUST WHAT IT IS.

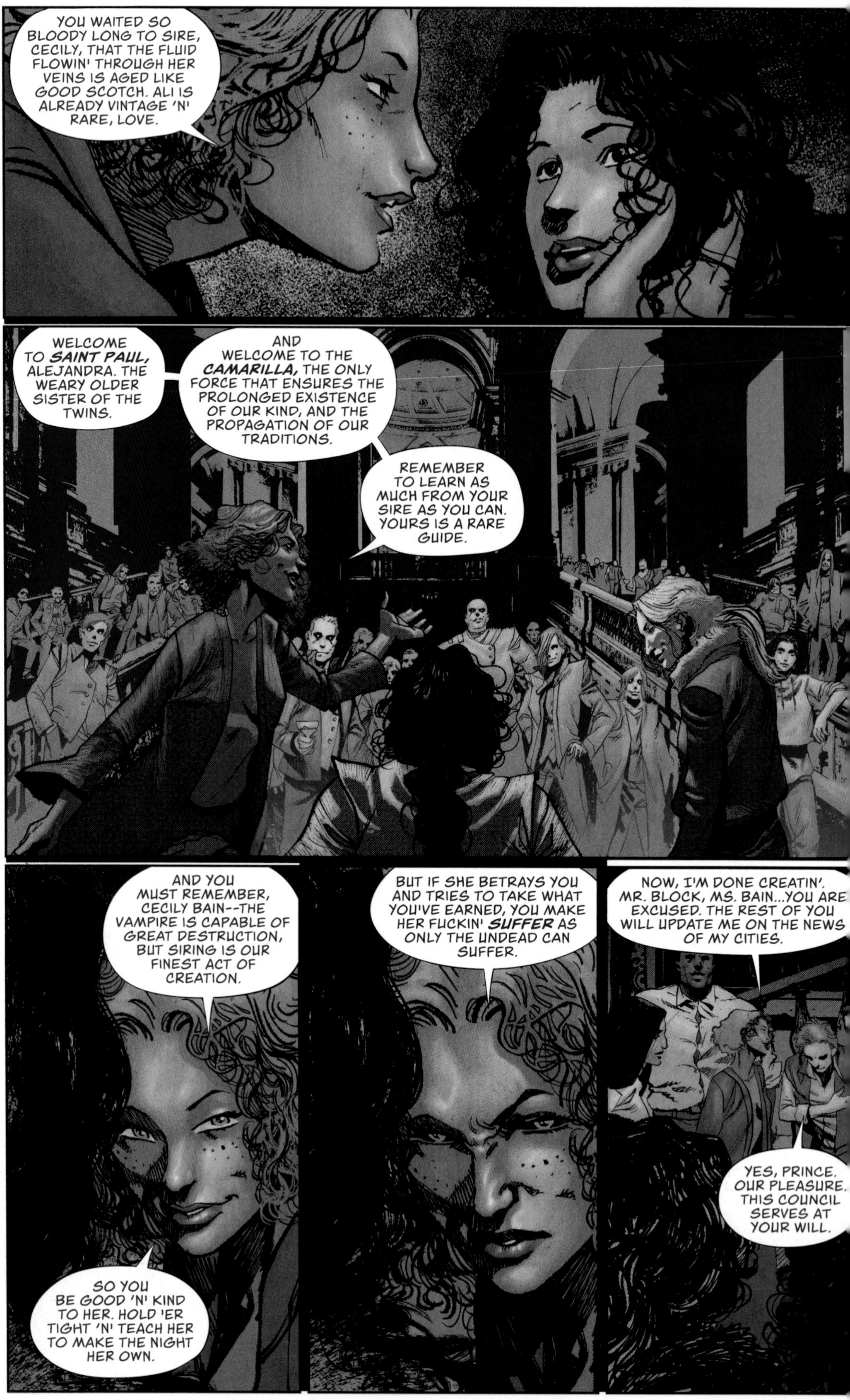
YOU WAITED SO BLOODY LONG TO SIRE, CECILY, THAT THE FLUID FLOWIN' THROUGH HER VEINS IS AGED LIKE GOOD SCOTCH. ALI IS ALREADY VINTAGE 'N' RARE, LOVE.
WELCOME TO SAINT PAUL, ALEJANDRA. THE WEARY OLDER SISTER OF THE TWINS.
AND WELCOME TO THE CAMARILLA, THE ONLY FORCE THAT ENSURES THE PROLONGED EXISTENCE OF OUR KIND, AND THE PROPAGATION OF OUR TRADITIONS.
REMEMBER TO LEARN AS MUCH FROM YOUR SIRE AS YOU CAN. YOURS IS A RARE GUIDE.
AND YOU MUST REMEMBER, CECILY BAIN--THE VAMPIRE IS CAPABLE OF GREAT DESTRUCTION, BUT SIRING IS OUR FINEST ACT OF CREATION.
SO YOU BE GOOD 'N' KIND TO HER. HOLD 'ER TIGHT 'N' TEACH HER TO MAKE THE NIGHT HER OWN.
BUT IF SHE BETRAYS YOU AND TRIES TO TAKE WHAT YOU'VE EARNED, YOU MAKE HER FUCKIN' SUFFER AS ONLY THE UNDEAD CAN SUFFER.
NOW, I'M DONE CREATIN'. MR. BLOCK, MS. BAIN...YOU ARE EXCUSED. THE REST OF YOU WILL UPDATE ME ON THE NEWS OF MY CITIES.
YES, PRINCE. OUR PLEASURE. THIS COUNCIL SERVES AT YOUR WILL.

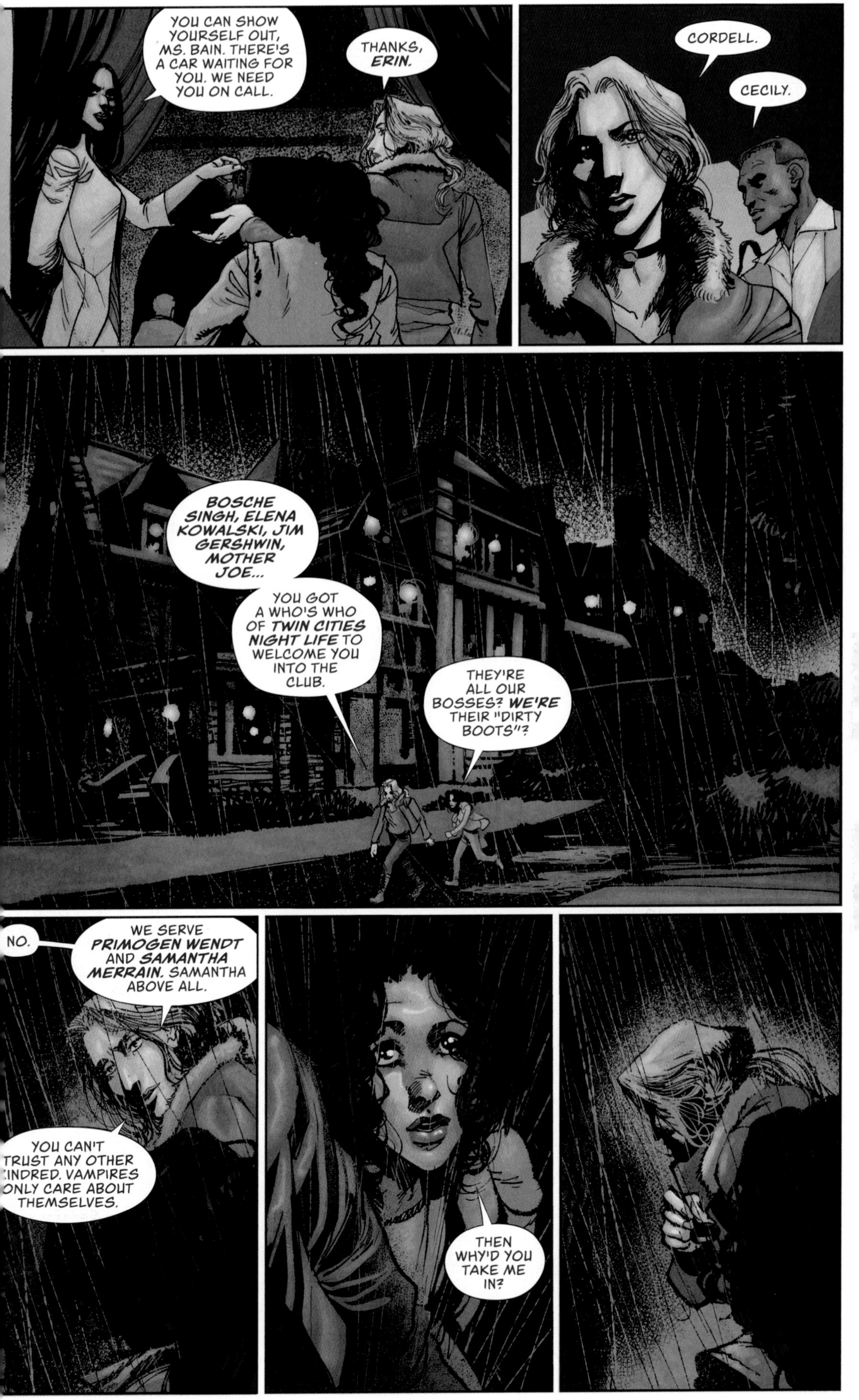

YOU CAN SHOW YOURSELF OUT, MS. BAIN. THERE'S A CAR WAITING FOR YOU. WE NEED YOU ON CALL.
THANKS, *ERIN.*
CORDELL.
CECILY.
BOSCHE SINGH, ELENA KOWALSKI, JIM GERSHWIN, MOTHER JOE...
YOU GOT A WHO'S WHO OF *TWIN CITIES NIGHT LIFE* TO WELCOME YOU INTO THE CLUB.
THEY'RE ALL OUR BOSSES? *WE'RE* THEIR "DIRTY BOOTS"?
NO.
WE SERVE *PRIMOGEN WENDT* AND *SAMANTHA MERRAIN.* SAMANTHA ABOVE ALL.
YOU CAN'T TRUST ANY OTHER KINDRED. VAMPIRES ONLY CARE ABOUT THEMSELVES.
THEN WHY'D YOU TAKE ME IN?

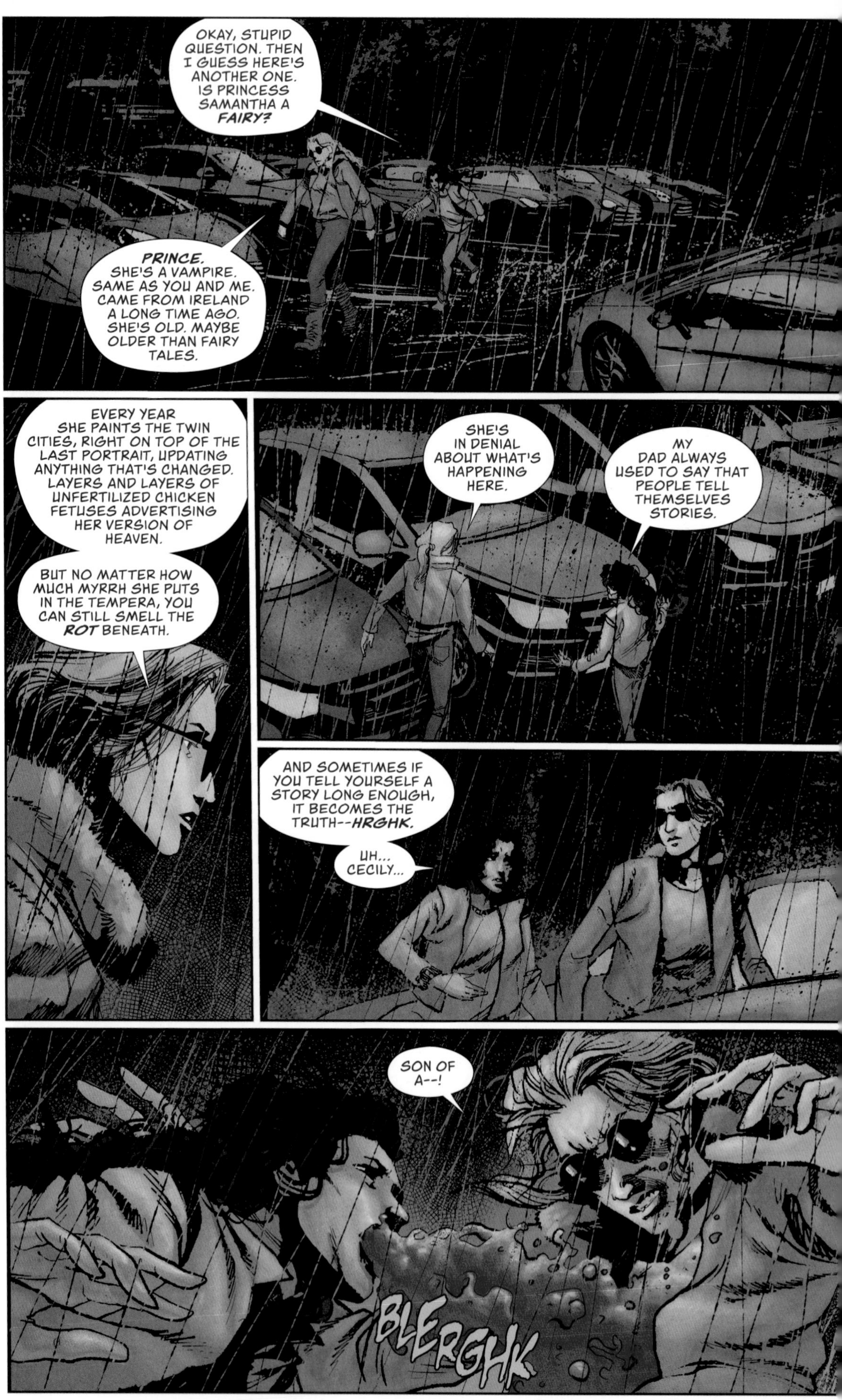

OKAY, STUPID QUESTION. THEN I GUESS HERE'S ANOTHER ONE. IS PRINCESS SAMANTHA A *FAIRY?*
PRINCE. SHE'S A VAMPIRE. SAME AS YOU AND ME. CAME FROM IRELAND A LONG TIME AGO. SHE'S OLD. MAYBE OLDER THAN FAIRY TALES.
EVERY YEAR SHE PAINTS THE TWIN CITIES, RIGHT ON TOP OF THE LAST PORTRAIT, UPDATING ANYTHING THAT'S CHANGED. LAYERS AND LAYERS OF UNFERTILIZED CHICKEN FETUSES ADVERTISING HER VERSION OF HEAVEN.
BUT NO MATTER HOW MUCH MYRRH SHE PUTS IN THE TEMPERA, YOU CAN STILL SMELL THE *ROT* BENEATH.
SHE'S IN DENIAL ABOUT WHAT'S HAPPENING HERE.
MY DAD ALWAYS USED TO SAY THAT PEOPLE TELL THEMSELVES STORIES.
AND SOMETIMES IF YOU TELL YOURSELF A STORY LONG ENOUGH, IT BECOMES THE TRUTH--*HRGHK.*
UH... CECILY...
SON OF A--!
BLERGHK

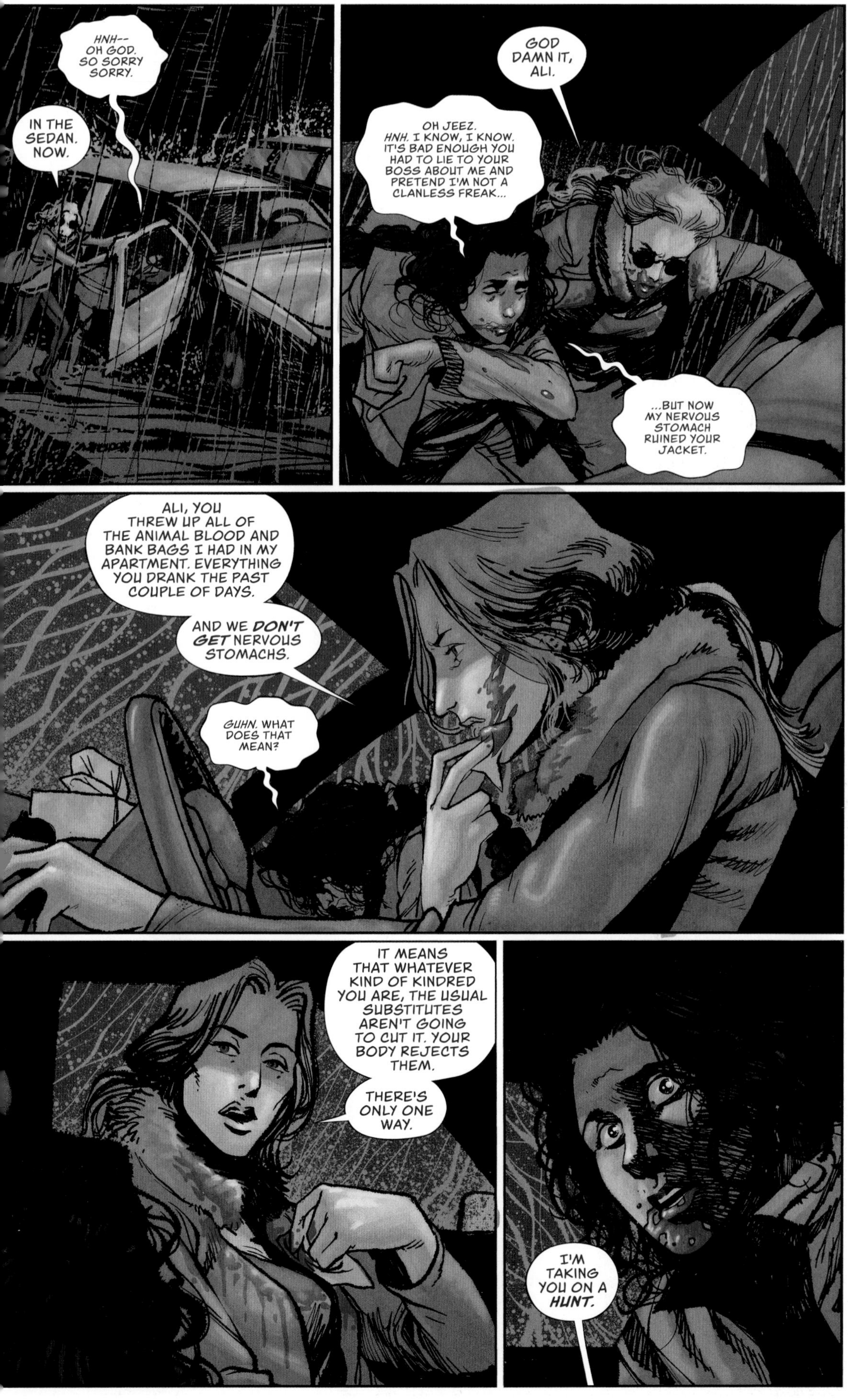

HNH-- OH GOD. SO SORRY SORRY.
IN THE SEDAN. NOW.
GOD DAMN IT, ALI.
OH JEEZ. *HNH.* I KNOW, I KNOW. IT'S BAD ENOUGH YOU HAD TO LIE TO YOUR BOSS ABOUT ME AND PRETEND I'M NOT A CLANLESS FREAK...
...BUT NOW MY NERVOUS STOMACH RUINED YOUR JACKET.
ALI, YOU THREW UP ALL OF THE ANIMAL BLOOD AND BANK BAGS I HAD IN MY APARTMENT. EVERYTHING YOU DRANK THE PAST COUPLE OF DAYS.
AND WE ***DON'T GET*** NERVOUS STOMACHS.
GUHN. WHAT DOES THAT MEAN?
IT MEANS THAT WHATEVER KIND OF KINDRED YOU ARE, THE USUAL SUBSTITUTES AREN'T GOING TO CUT IT. YOUR BODY REJECTS THEM.
THERE'S ONLY ONE WAY.
I'M TAKING YOU ON A ***HUNT.***

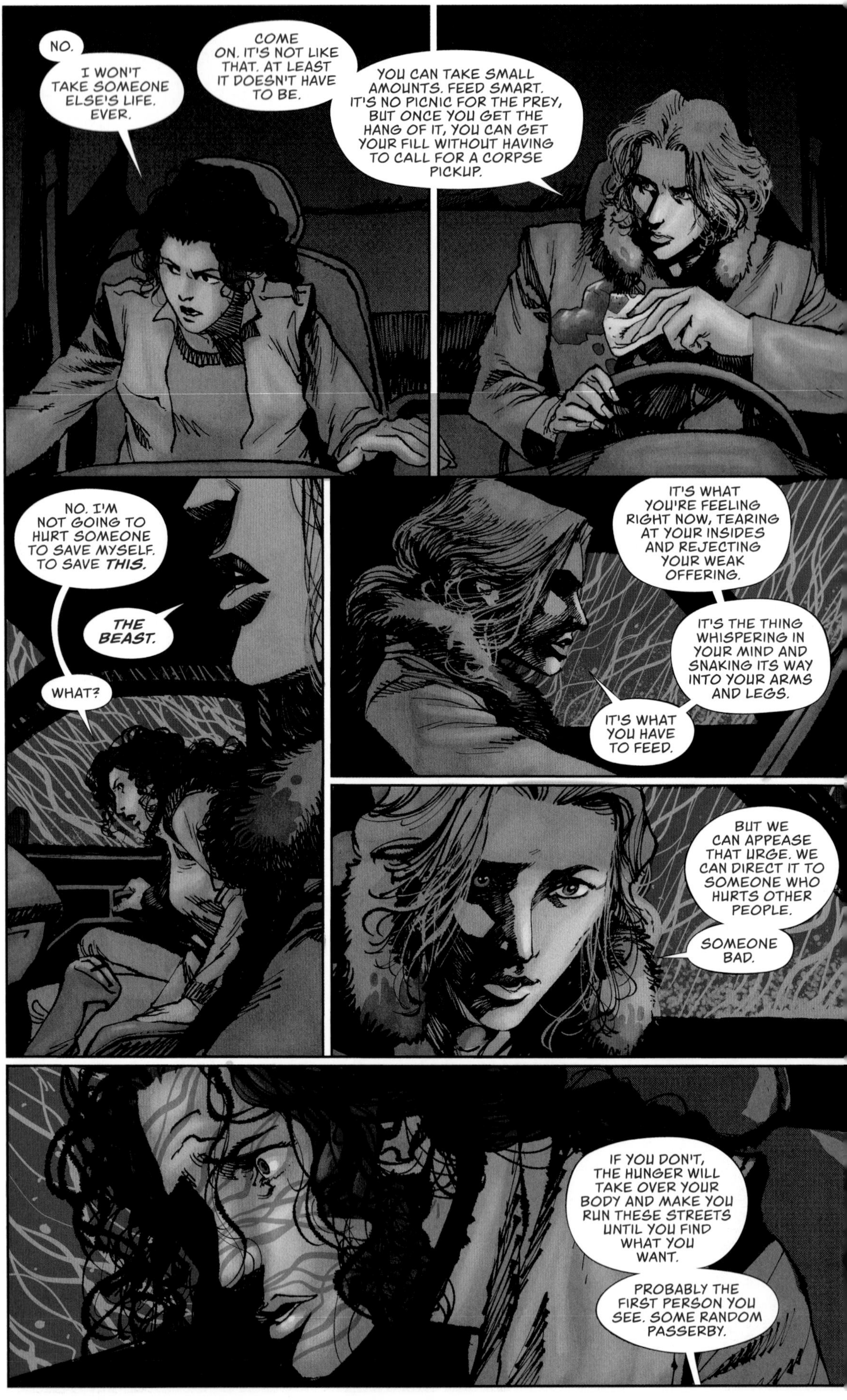

NO.
I WON'T TAKE SOMEONE ELSE'S LIFE. EVER.
COME ON. IT'S NOT LIKE THAT. AT LEAST IT DOESN'T HAVE TO BE.
YOU CAN TAKE SMALL AMOUNTS. FEED SMART. IT'S NO PICNIC FOR THE PREY, BUT ONCE YOU GET THE HANG OF IT, YOU CAN GET YOUR FILL WITHOUT HAVING TO CALL FOR A CORPSE PICKUP.
NO. I'M NOT GOING TO HURT SOMEONE TO SAVE MYSELF. TO SAVE *THIS.*
THE BEAST.
WHAT?
IT'S WHAT YOU'RE FEELING RIGHT NOW, TEARING AT YOUR INSIDES AND REJECTING YOUR WEAK OFFERING.
IT'S THE THING WHISPERING IN YOUR MIND AND SNAKING ITS WAY INTO YOUR ARMS AND LEGS.
IT'S WHAT YOU HAVE TO FEED.
BUT WE CAN APPEASE THAT URGE. WE CAN DIRECT IT TO SOMEONE WHO HURTS OTHER PEOPLE.
SOMEONE BAD.
IF YOU DON'T, THE HUNGER WILL TAKE OVER YOUR BODY AND MAKE YOU RUN THESE STREETS UNTIL YOU FIND WHAT YOU WANT.
PROBABLY THE FIRST PERSON YOU SEE. SOME RANDOM PASSERBY.

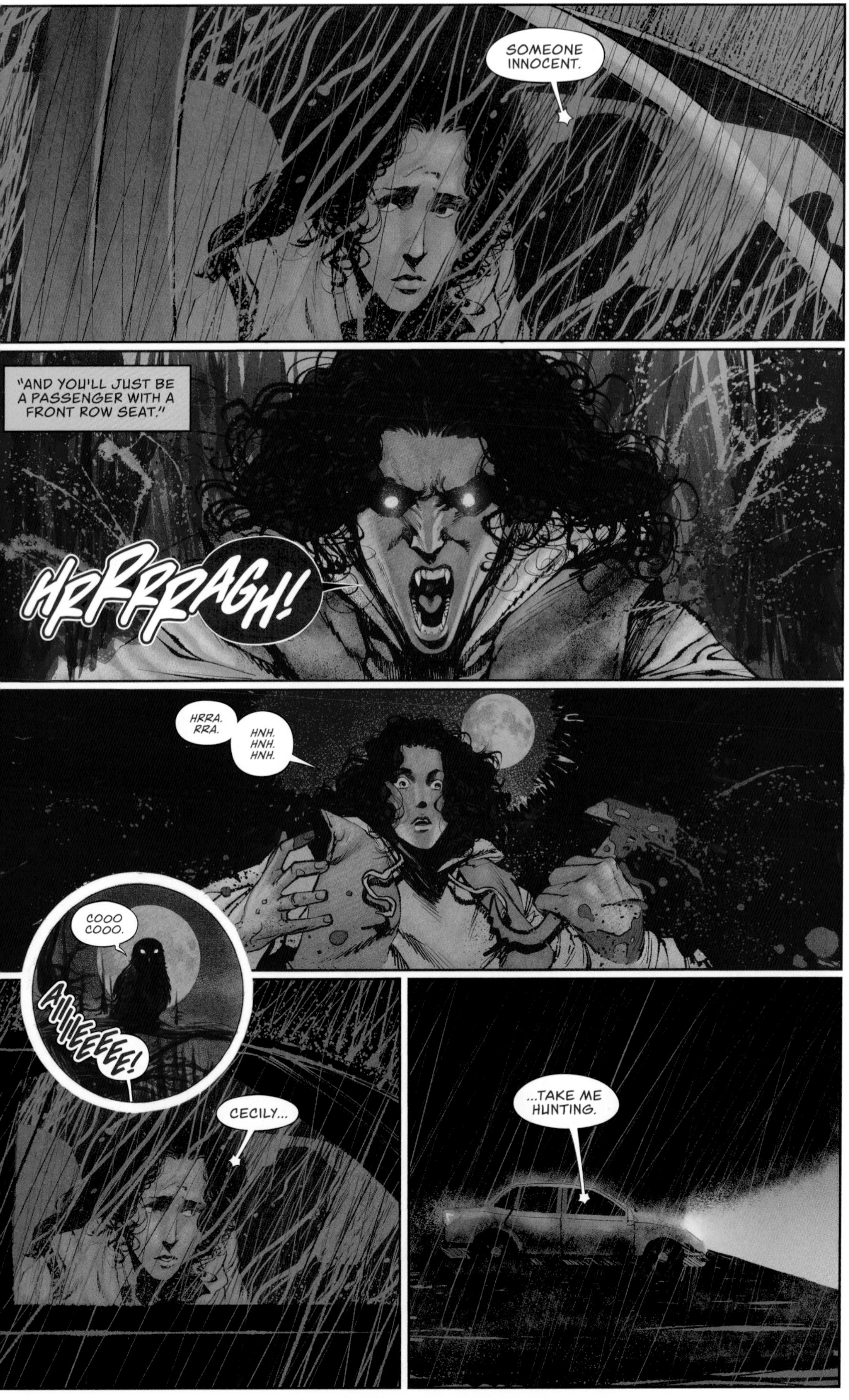
SOMEONE INNOCENT.
"AND YOU'LL JUST BE A PASSENGER WITH A FRONT ROW SEAT."
HRRRRAGH!
HRRA. RRA.
HNH. HNH. HNH.
COOO COOO.
AIIIEEEEE!
CECILY...
...TAKE ME HUNTING.

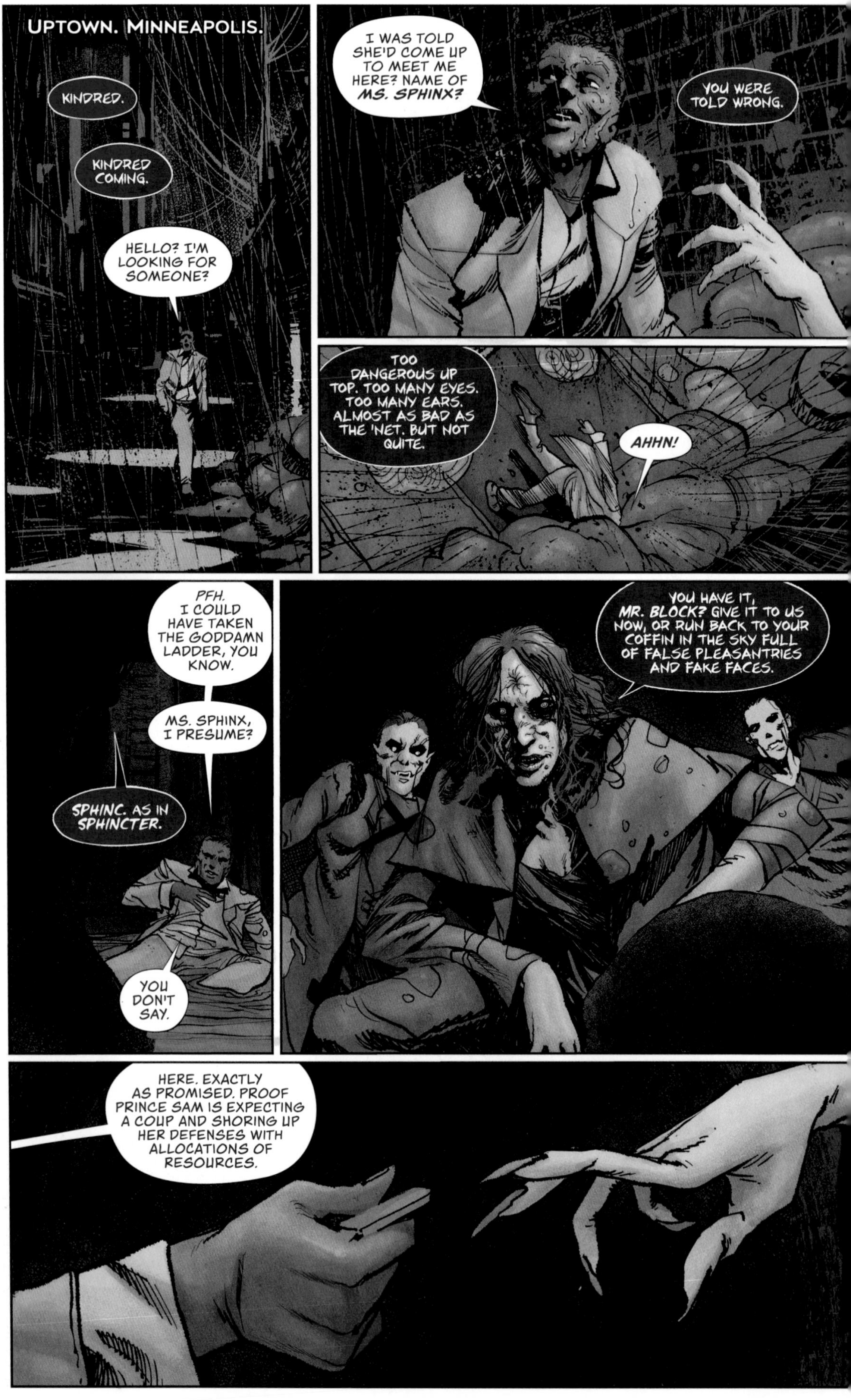
UPTOWN. MINNEAPOLIS.
KINDRED.
KINDRED COMING.
HELLO? I'M LOOKING FOR SOMEONE?
I WAS TOLD SHE'D COME UP TO MEET ME HERE? NAME OF MS. SPHINX?
YOU WERE TOLD WRONG.
TOO DANGEROUS UP TOP. TOO MANY EYES. TOO MANY EARS. ALMOST AS BAD AS THE 'NET. BUT NOT QUITE.
AHHN!
PFH. I COULD HAVE TAKEN THE GODDAMN LADDER, YOU KNOW.
MS. SPHINX, I PRESUME?
SPHINC. AS IN SPHINCTER.
YOU DON'T SAY.
YOU HAVE IT, MR. BLOCK? GIVE IT TO US NOW, OR RUN BACK TO YOUR COFFIN IN THE SKY FULL OF FALSE PLEASANTRIES AND FAKE FACES.
HERE. EXACTLY AS PROMISED. PROOF PRINCE SAM IS EXPECTING A COUP AND SHORING UP HER DEFENSES WITH ALLOCATIONS OF RESOURCES.

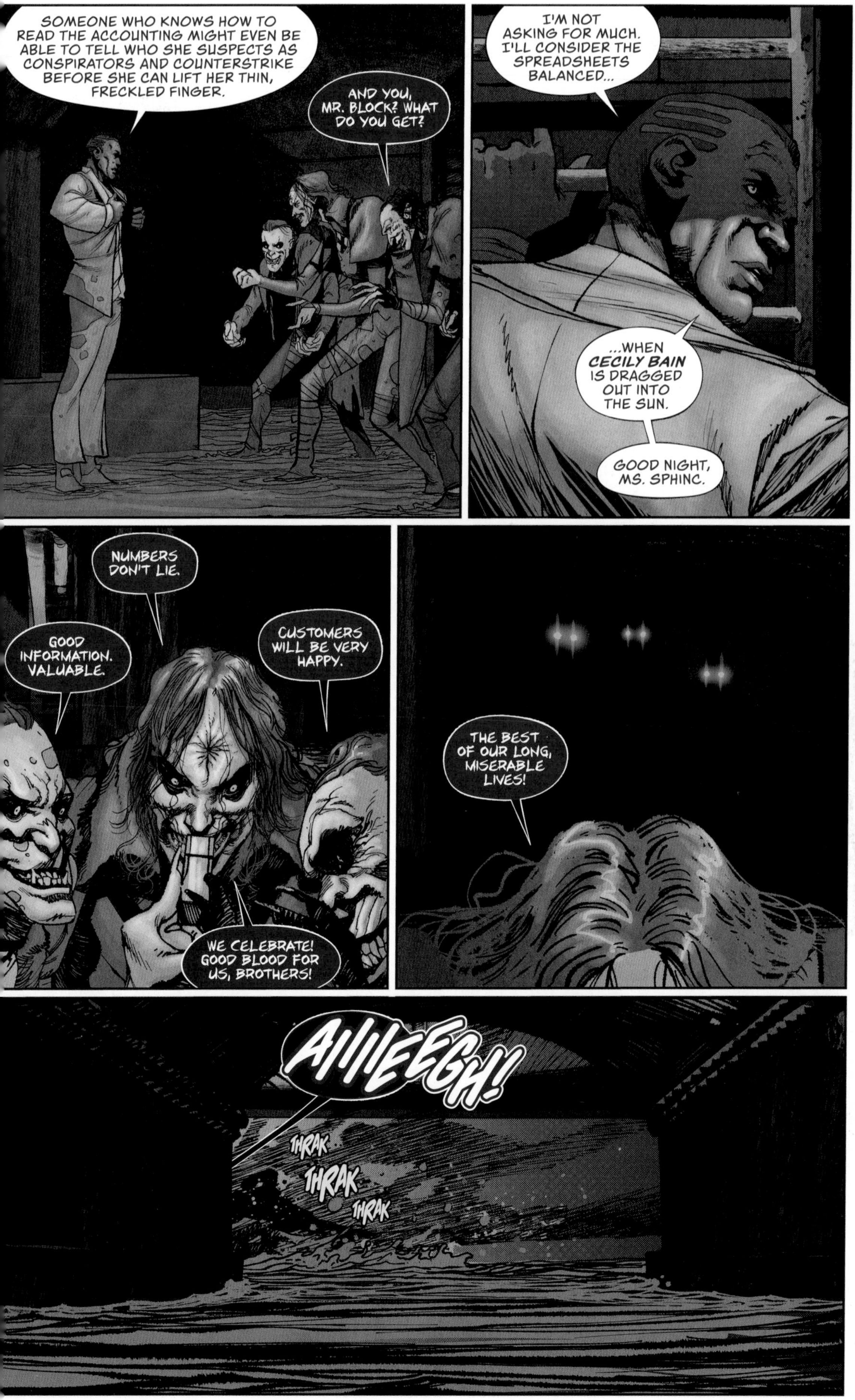
SOMEONE WHO KNOWS HOW TO READ THE ACCOUNTING MIGHT EVEN BE ABLE TO TELL WHO SHE SUSPECTS AS CONSPIRATORS AND COUNTERSTRIKE BEFORE SHE CAN LIFT HER THIN, FRECKLED FINGER.
AND YOU, MR. BLOCK? WHAT DO YOU GET?
I'M NOT ASKING FOR MUCH. I'LL CONSIDER THE SPREADSHEETS BALANCED...
...WHEN CECILY BAIN IS DRAGGED OUT INTO THE SUN.
GOOD NIGHT, MS. SPHINC.
NUMBERS DON'T LIE.
GOOD INFORMATION. VALUABLE.
CUSTOMERS WILL BE VERY HAPPY.
WE CELEBRATE! GOOD BLOOD FOR US, BROTHERS!
THE BEST OF OUR LONG, MISERABLE LIVES!
AIIIEEGH!
THRAK
THRAK
THRAK

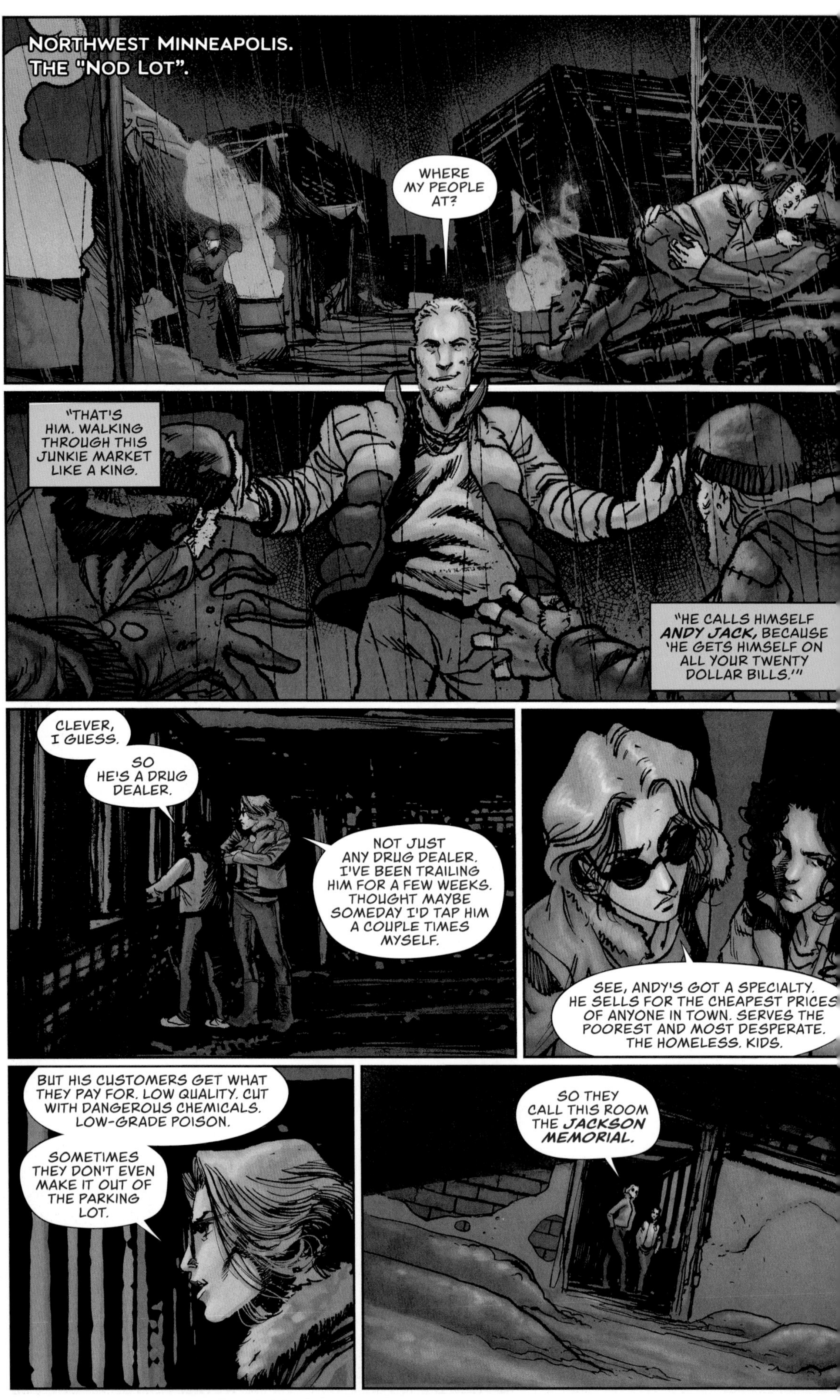

NORTHWEST MINNEAPOLIS.
THE "NOD LOT".
WHERE MY PEOPLE AT?
"THAT'S HIM. WALKING THROUGH THIS JUNKIE MARKET LIKE A KING.
"HE CALLS HIMSELF ANDY JACK, BECAUSE 'HE GETS HIMSELF ON ALL YOUR TWENTY DOLLAR BILLS.'"
CLEVER, I GUESS.
SO HE'S A DRUG DEALER.
NOT JUST ANY DRUG DEALER. I'VE BEEN TRAILING HIM FOR A FEW WEEKS. THOUGHT MAYBE SOMEDAY I'D TAP HIM A COUPLE TIMES MYSELF.
SEE, ANDY'S GOT A SPECIALTY. HE SELLS FOR THE CHEAPEST PRICES OF ANYONE IN TOWN. SERVES THE POOREST AND MOST DESPERATE. THE HOMELESS. KIDS.
BUT HIS CUSTOMERS GET WHAT THEY PAY FOR. LOW QUALITY. CUT WITH DANGEROUS CHEMICALS. LOW-GRADE POISON.
SOMETIMES THEY DON'T EVEN MAKE IT OUT OF THE PARKING LOT.
SO THEY CALL THIS ROOM THE JACKSON MEMORIAL.

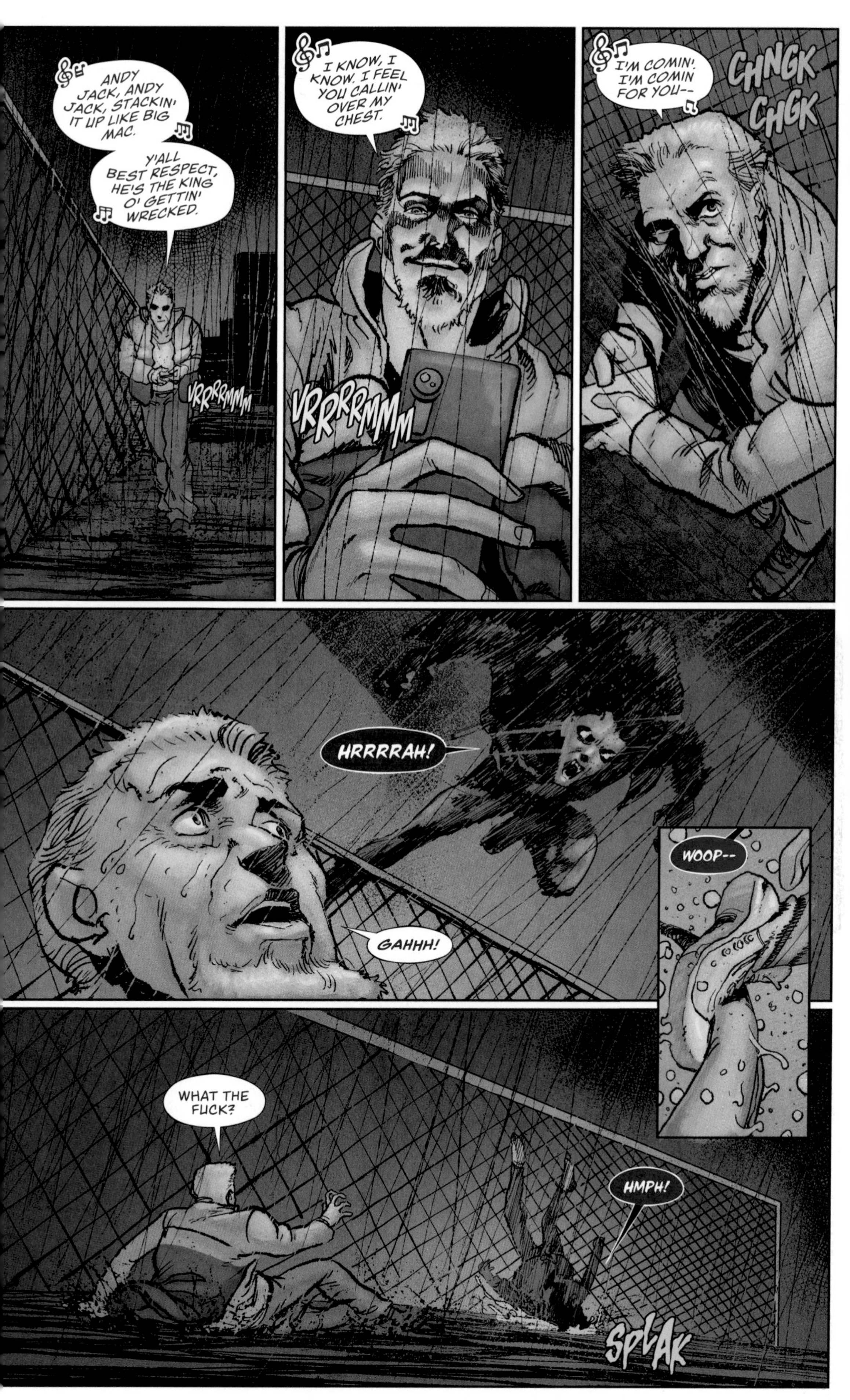
ANDY JACK, ANDY JACK, STACKIN' IT UP LIKE BIG MAC.
Y'ALL BEST RESPECT, HE'S THE KING O' GETTIN' WRECKED.
VRRRRMMM
I KNOW, I KNOW. I FEEL YOU CALLIN' OVER MY CHEST.
VRRRRMMM
I'M COMIN'. I'M COMIN FOR YOU--
CHNGK CHGK
HRRRRAH!
GAHHH!
WOOP--
WHAT THE FUCK?
HMPH!
SPLAK

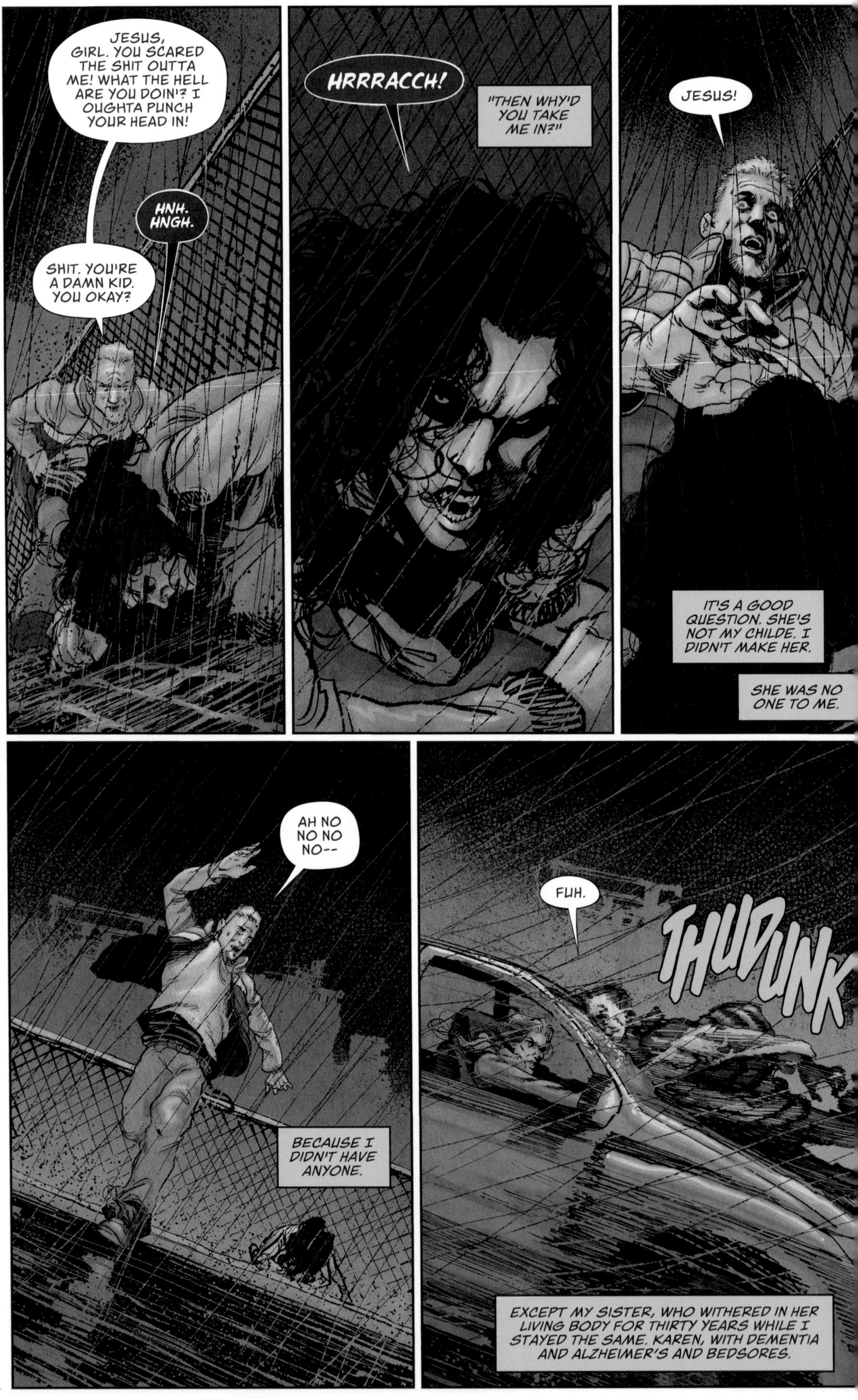

JESUS, GIRL. YOU SCARED THE SHIT OUTTA ME! WHAT THE HELL ARE YOU DOIN'? I OUGHTA PUNCH YOUR HEAD IN!
HNH. HNGH.
SHIT. YOU'RE A DAMN KID. YOU OKAY?
HRRRACCH!
"THEN WHY'D YOU TAKE ME IN?"
JESUS!
IT'S A GOOD QUESTION. SHE'S NOT MY CHILDE. I DIDN'T MAKE HER.
SHE WAS NO ONE TO ME.
AH NO NO NO NO--
BECAUSE I DIDN'T HAVE ANYONE.
FUH.
THUDUNK
EXCEPT MY SISTER, WHO WITHERED IN HER LIVING BODY FOR THIRTY YEARS WHILE I STAYED THE SAME. KAREN, WITH DEMENTIA AND ALZHEIMER'S AND BEDSORES.

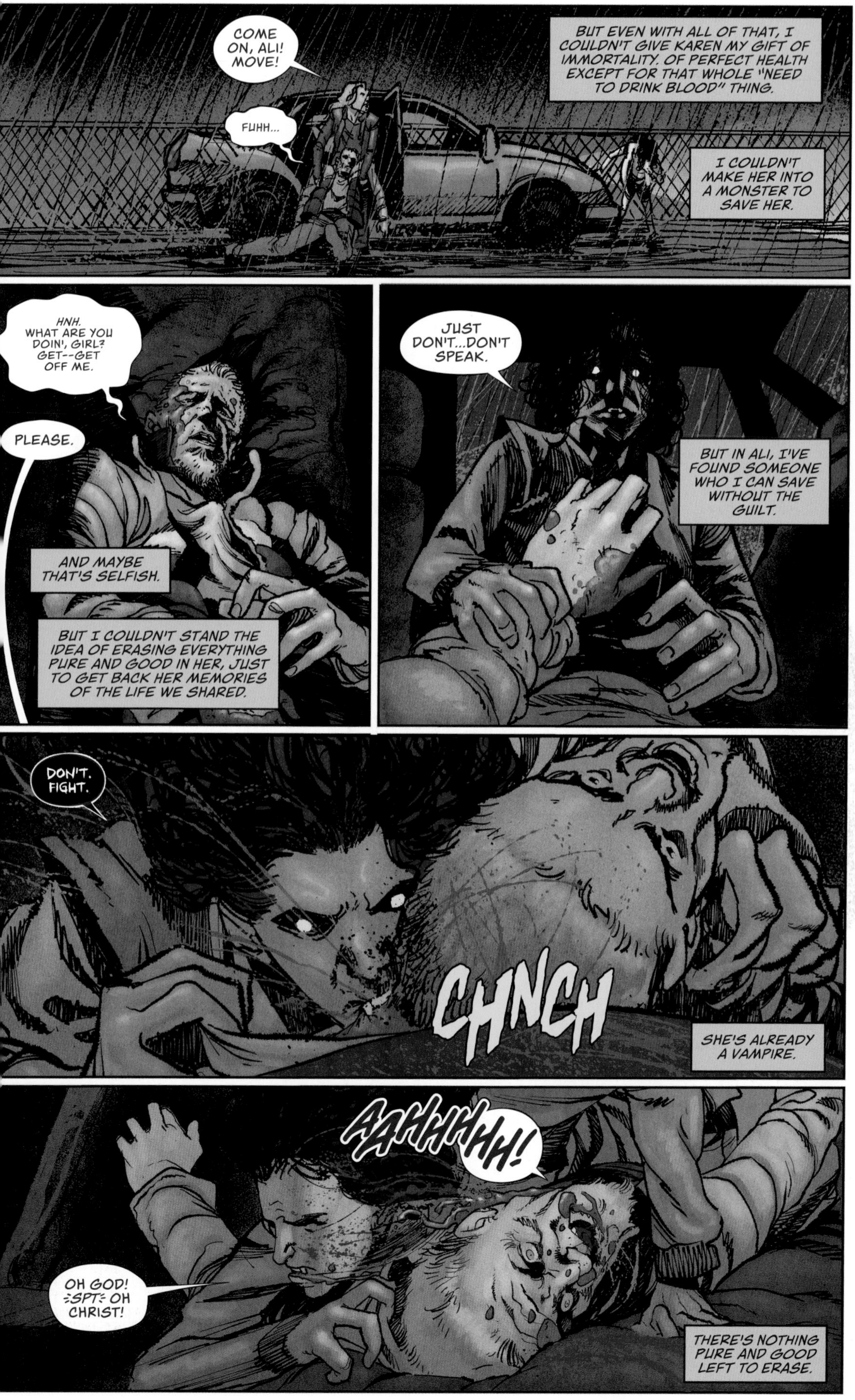
COME ON, ALI! MOVE!
BUT EVEN WITH ALL OF THAT, I COULDN'T GIVE KAREN MY GIFT OF IMMORTALITY. OF PERFECT HEALTH EXCEPT FOR THAT WHOLE "NEED TO DRINK BLOOD" THING.
FUHH...
I COULDN'T MAKE HER INTO A MONSTER TO SAVE HER.
HNH. WHAT ARE YOU DOIN', GIRL? GET--GET OFF ME.
PLEASE.
AND MAYBE THAT'S SELFISH.
BUT I COULDN'T STAND THE IDEA OF ERASING EVERYTHING PURE AND GOOD IN HER, JUST TO GET BACK HER MEMORIES OF THE LIFE WE SHARED.
JUST DON'T...DON'T SPEAK.
BUT IN ALI, I'VE FOUND SOMEONE WHO I CAN SAVE WITHOUT THE GUILT.
DON'T. FIGHT.
CHNCH
SHE'S ALREADY A VAMPIRE.
AAHHHHH!
OH GOD! SPT OH CHRIST!
THERE'S NOTHING PURE AND GOOD LEFT TO ERASE.

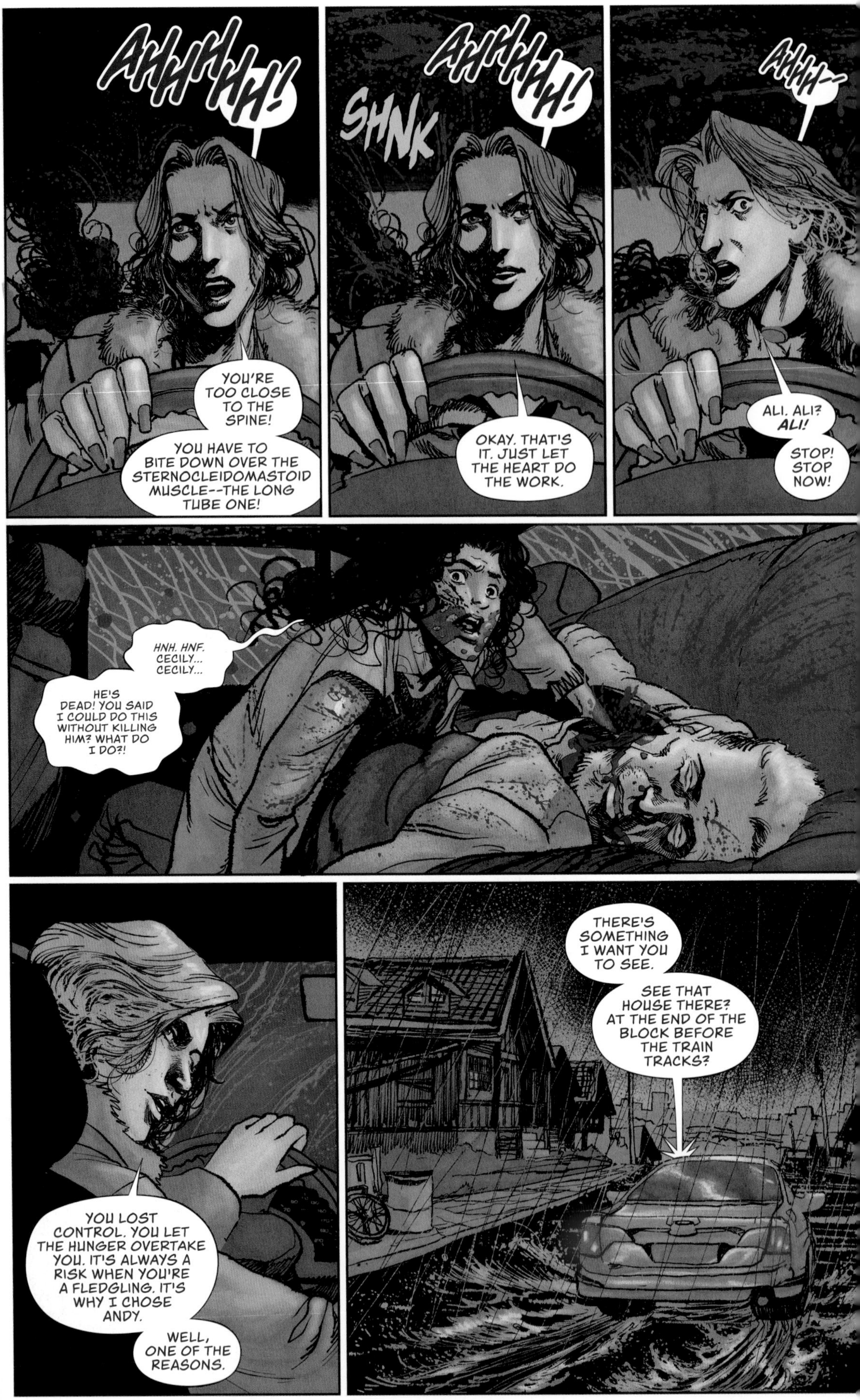
AHHHHHH!
YOU'RE TOO CLOSE TO THE SPINE!
YOU HAVE TO BITE DOWN OVER THE STERNOCLEIDOMASTOID MUSCLE--THE LONG TUBE ONE!
SHNK
AHHHHHH!
OKAY. THAT'S IT. JUST LET THE HEART DO THE WORK.
AHHH-
ALI. ALI? ALI!
STOP! STOP NOW!
HNH. HNF. CECILY... CECILY...
HE'S DEAD! YOU SAID I COULD DO THIS WITHOUT KILLING HIM? WHAT DO I DO?!
YOU LOST CONTROL. YOU LET THE HUNGER OVERTAKE YOU. IT'S ALWAYS A RISK WHEN YOU'RE A FLEDGLING. IT'S WHY I CHOSE ANDY.
WELL, ONE OF THE REASONS.
THERE'S SOMETHING I WANT YOU TO SEE.
SEE THAT HOUSE THERE? AT THE END OF THE BLOCK BEFORE THE TRAIN TRACKS?

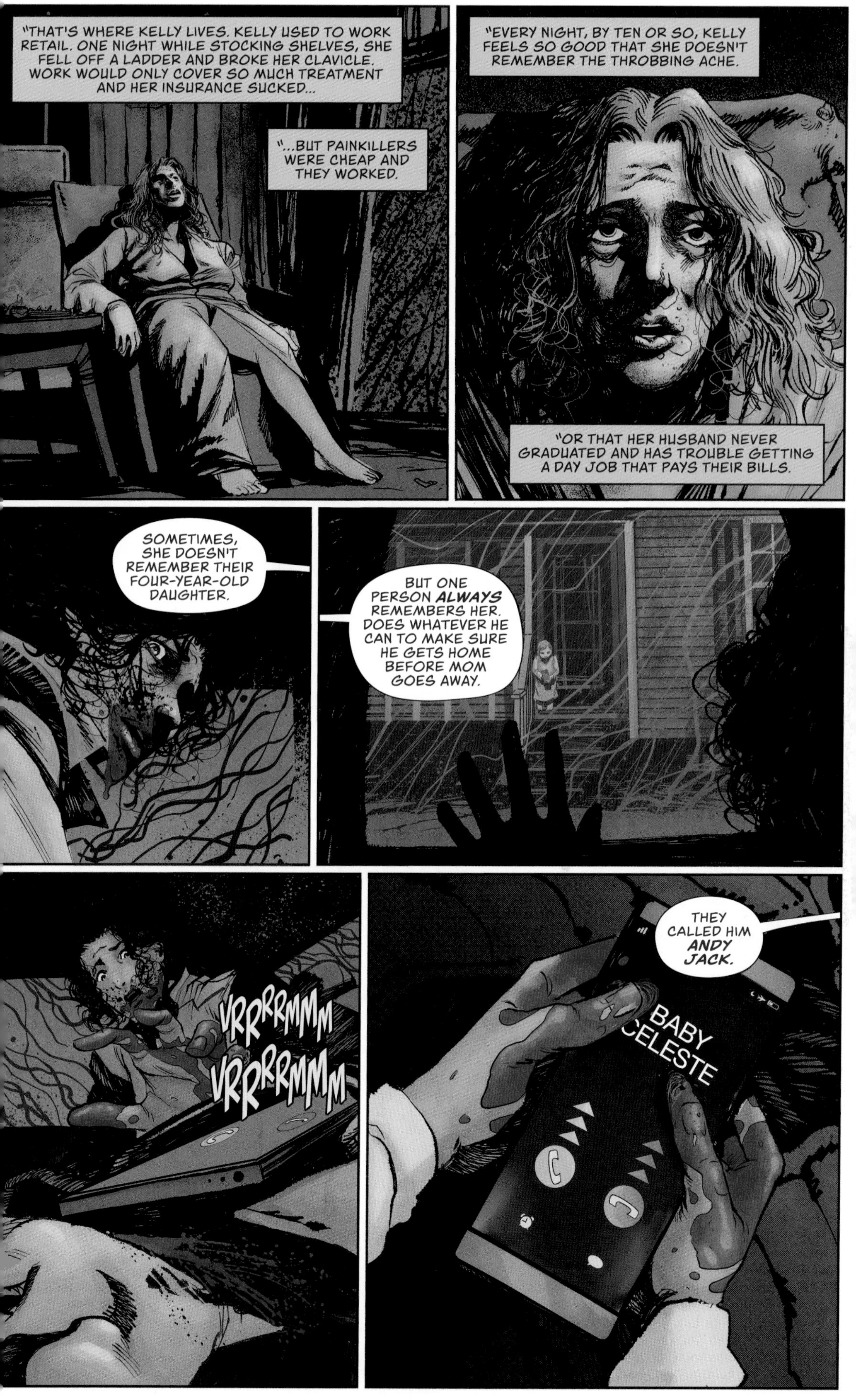
"THAT'S WHERE KELLY LIVES. KELLY USED TO WORK RETAIL. ONE NIGHT WHILE STOCKING SHELVES, SHE FELL OFF A LADDER AND BROKE HER CLAVICLE. WORK WOULD ONLY COVER SO MUCH TREATMENT AND HER INSURANCE SUCKED...
"...BUT PAINKILLERS WERE CHEAP AND THEY WORKED.
"EVERY NIGHT, BY TEN OR SO, KELLY FEELS SO GOOD THAT SHE DOESN'T REMEMBER THE THROBBING ACHE.
"OR THAT HER HUSBAND NEVER GRADUATED AND HAS TROUBLE GETTING A DAY JOB THAT PAYS THEIR BILLS.
SOMETIMES, SHE DOESN'T REMEMBER THEIR FOUR-YEAR-OLD DAUGHTER.
BUT ONE PERSON ***ALWAYS*** REMEMBERS HER. DOES WHATEVER HE CAN TO MAKE SURE HE GETS HOME BEFORE MOM GOES AWAY.
VRRRRMMM
VRRRRMMM
THEY CALLED HIM ***ANDY JACK.***
BABY CELESTE

OH GOD.

WHY...WHY WOULD YOU DO THAT TO ME? MAKE ME DO THIS?

WHY WOULD YOU LIE TO ME?!

I DIDN'T LIE, ALI. I SHOWED YOU THE TRUTH ABOUT FEEDING. ON WHO WE CHOOSE.

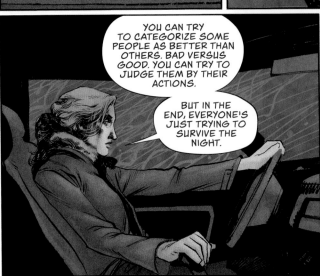

YOU CAN TRY TO CATEGORIZE SOME PEOPLE AS BETTER THAN OTHERS. BAD VERSUS GOOD. YOU CAN TRY TO JUDGE THEM BY THEIR ACTIONS.

BUT IN THE END, EVERYONE'S JUST TRYING TO SURVIVE THE NIGHT.

BECAUSE EVERYONE HAS SOMETHING THEY HAVE TO FEED.

OH GOD. I'M HORRIBLE. I HATE MYSELF. I WISH I HAD DIED.

NO. GET THAT OUT OF YOUR HEAD RIGHT NOW.

THIS IS A *CURSE*. YOU DON'T HAVE A CHOICE. SOMEONE FORCED THIS ON YOU, ALI.

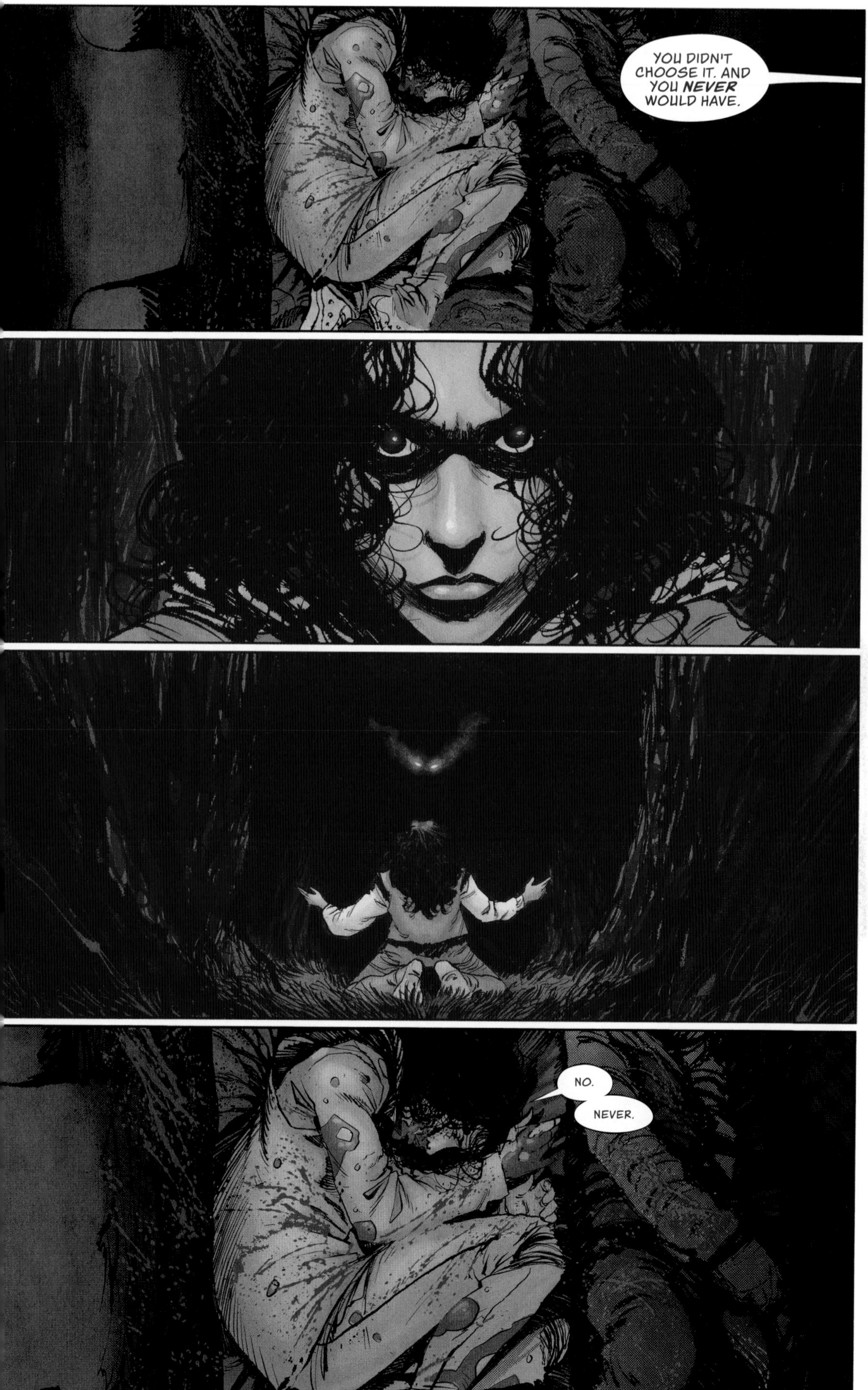
YOU DIDN'T CHOOSE IT. AND YOU NEVER WOULD HAVE.
NO.
NEVER.

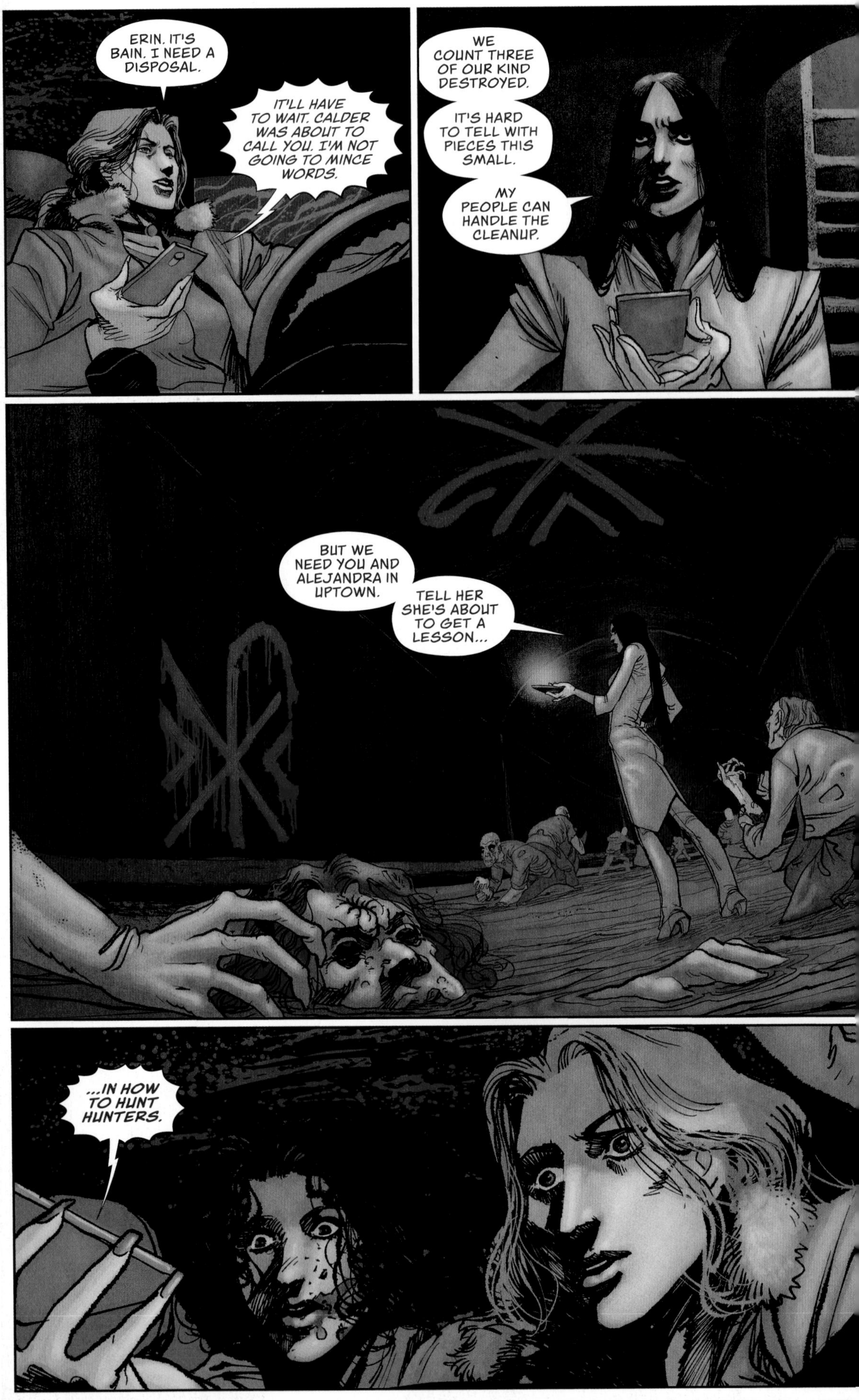
ERIN. IT'S BAIN. I NEED A DISPOSAL.
IT'LL HAVE TO WAIT. CALDER WAS ABOUT TO CALL YOU. I'M NOT GOING TO MINCE WORDS.
WE COUNT THREE OF OUR KIND DESTROYED.
IT'S HARD TO TELL WITH PIECES THIS SMALL.
MY PEOPLE CAN HANDLE THE CLEANUP.
BUT WE NEED YOU AND ALEJANDRA IN UPTOWN.
TELL HER SHE'S ABOUT TO GET A LESSON...
...IN HOW TO HUNT HUNTERS.

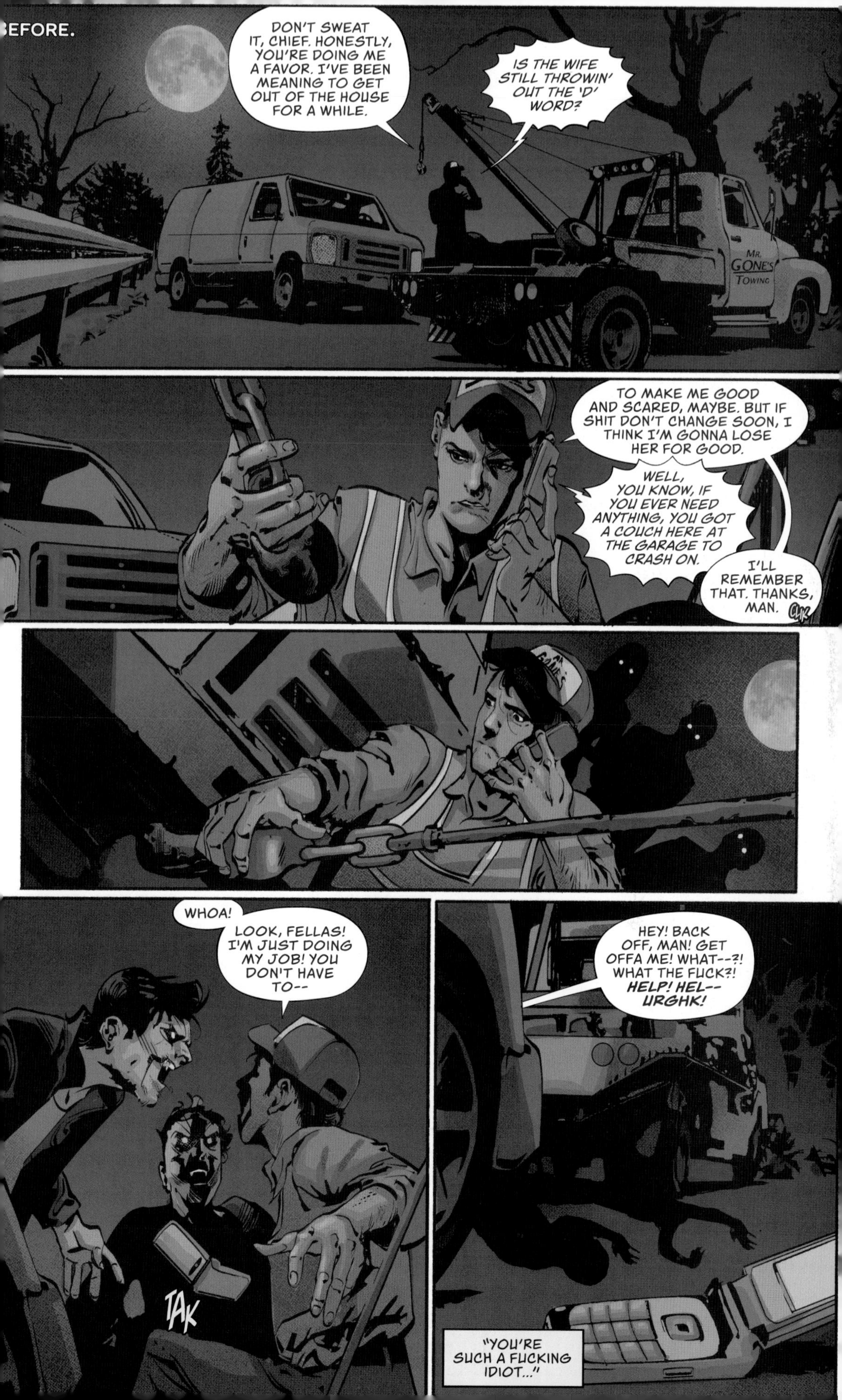
BEFORE.
DON'T SWEAT IT, CHIEF. HONESTLY, YOU'RE DOING ME A FAVOR. I'VE BEEN MEANING TO GET OUT OF THE HOUSE FOR A WHILE.
IS THE WIFE STILL THROWIN' OUT THE 'D' WORD?
MR. GONE'S TOWING
TO MAKE ME GOOD AND SCARED, MAYBE. BUT IF SHIT DON'T CHANGE SOON, I THINK I'M GONNA LOSE HER FOR GOOD.
WELL, YOU KNOW, IF YOU EVER NEED ANYTHING, YOU GOT A COUCH HERE AT THE GARAGE TO CRASH ON.
I'LL REMEMBER THAT. THANKS, MAN.
CLIK
WHOA!
LOOK, FELLAS! I'M JUST DOING MY JOB! YOU DON'T HAVE TO--
TAK
HEY! BACK OFF, MAN! GET OFFA ME! WHAT--?! WHAT THE FUCK?! HELP! HEL-- URGHK!
"YOU'RE SUCH A FUCKING IDIOT..."

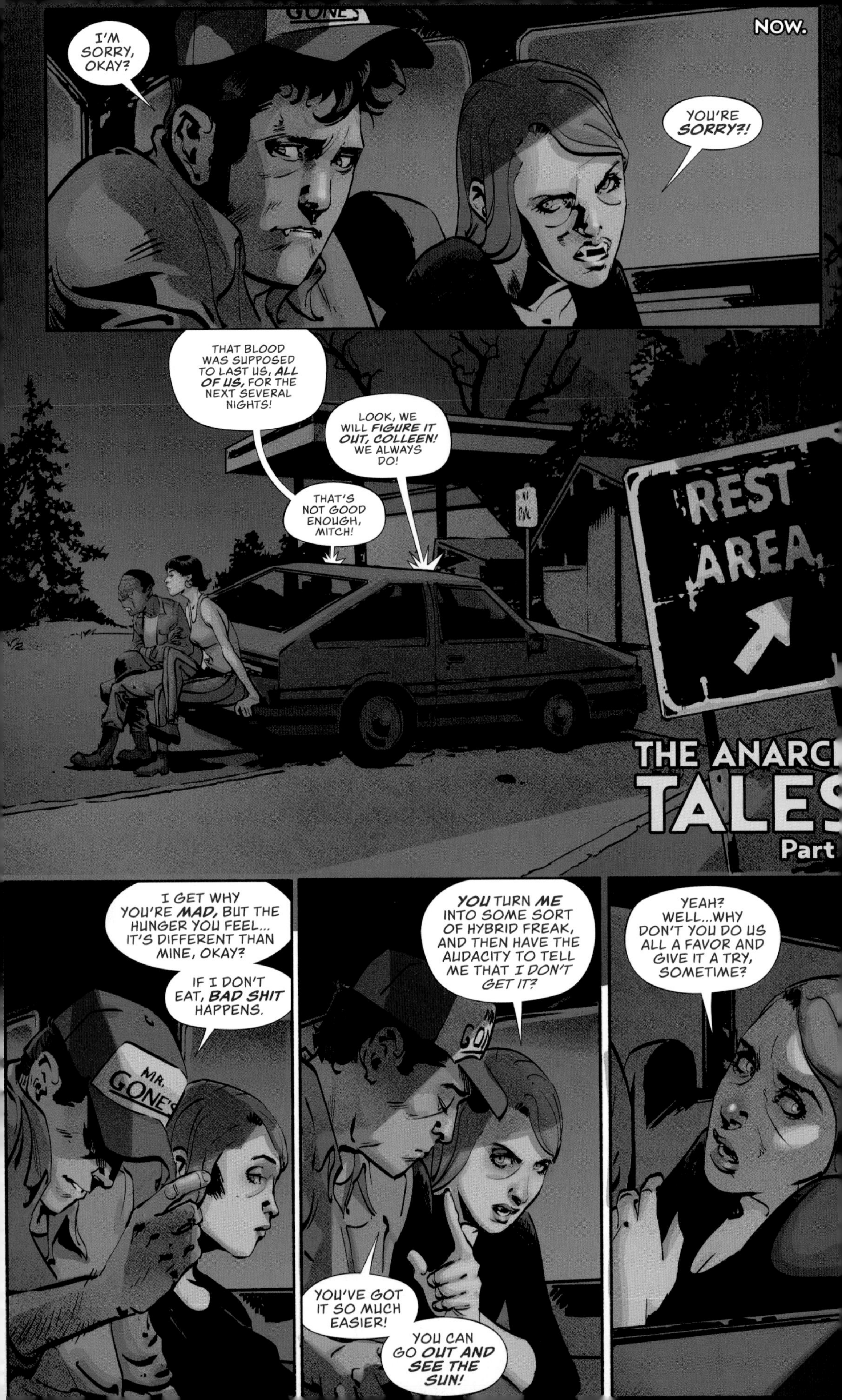

NOW.
I'M SORRY, OKAY?
YOU'RE SORRY?!
THAT BLOOD WAS SUPPOSED TO LAST US, ALL OF US, FOR THE NEXT SEVERAL NIGHTS!
LOOK, WE WILL FIGURE IT OUT, COLLEEN! WE ALWAYS DO!
THAT'S NOT GOOD ENOUGH, MITCH!
REST AREA
THE ANARC
TALES
Part
I GET WHY YOU'RE MAD, BUT THE HUNGER YOU FEEL... IT'S DIFFERENT THAN MINE, OKAY?
IF I DON'T EAT, BAD SHIT HAPPENS.
MR. GONE'S
YOU TURN ME INTO SOME SORT OF HYBRID FREAK, AND THEN HAVE THE AUDACITY TO TELL ME THAT I DON'T GET IT?
YOU'VE GOT IT SO MUCH EASIER!
YOU CAN GO OUT AND SEE THE SUN!
YEAH? WELL...WHY DON'T YOU DO US ALL A FAVOR AND GIVE IT A TRY, SOMETIME?

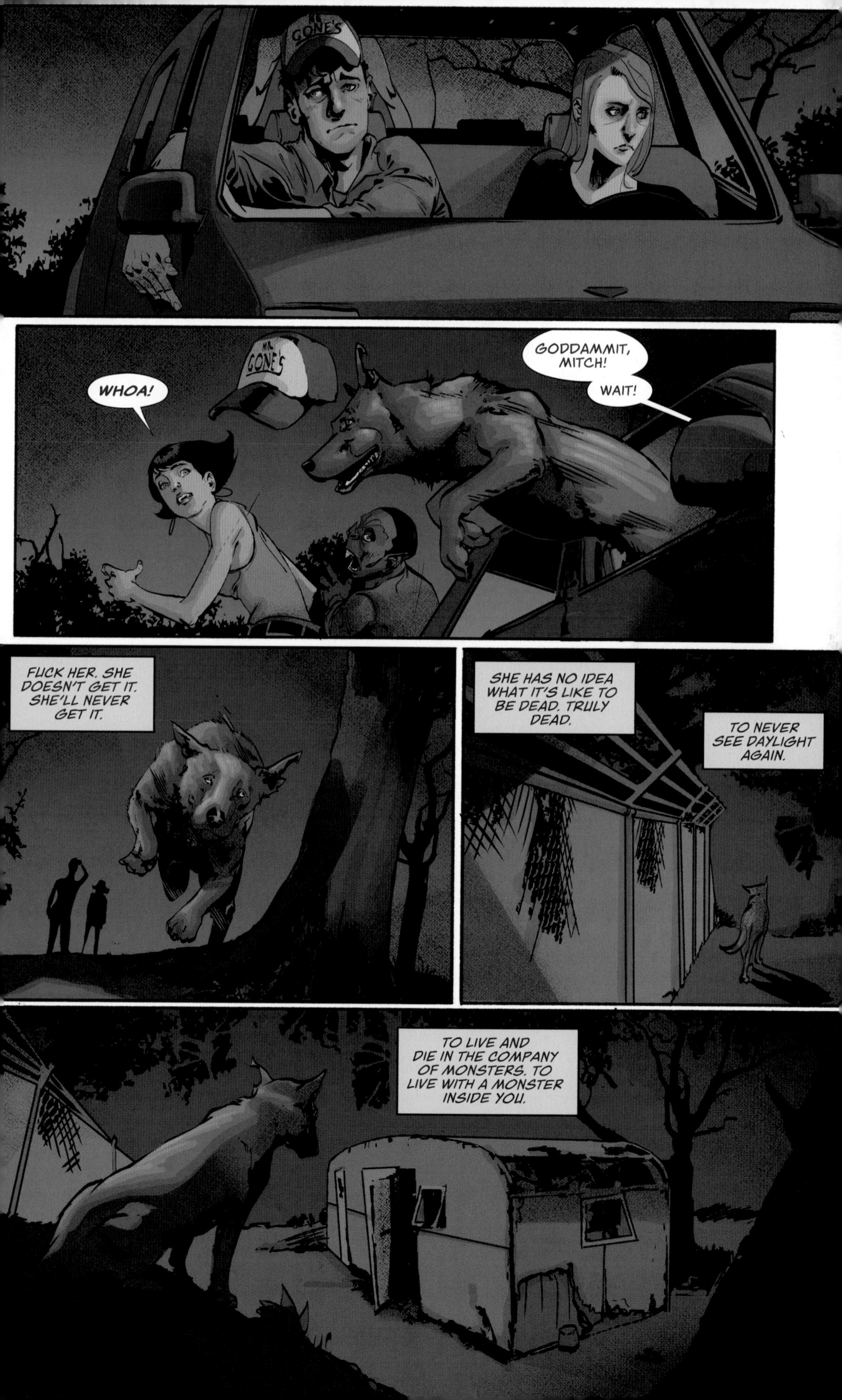

MR. GONE'S
WHOA!
GODDAMMIT, MITCH!
WAIT!
FUCK HER. SHE DOESN'T GET IT. SHE'LL NEVER GET IT.
SHE HAS NO IDEA WHAT IT'S LIKE TO BE DEAD. TRULY DEAD.
TO NEVER SEE DAYLIGHT AGAIN.
TO LIVE AND DIE IN THE COMPANY OF MONSTERS. TO LIVE WITH A MONSTER INSIDE YOU.

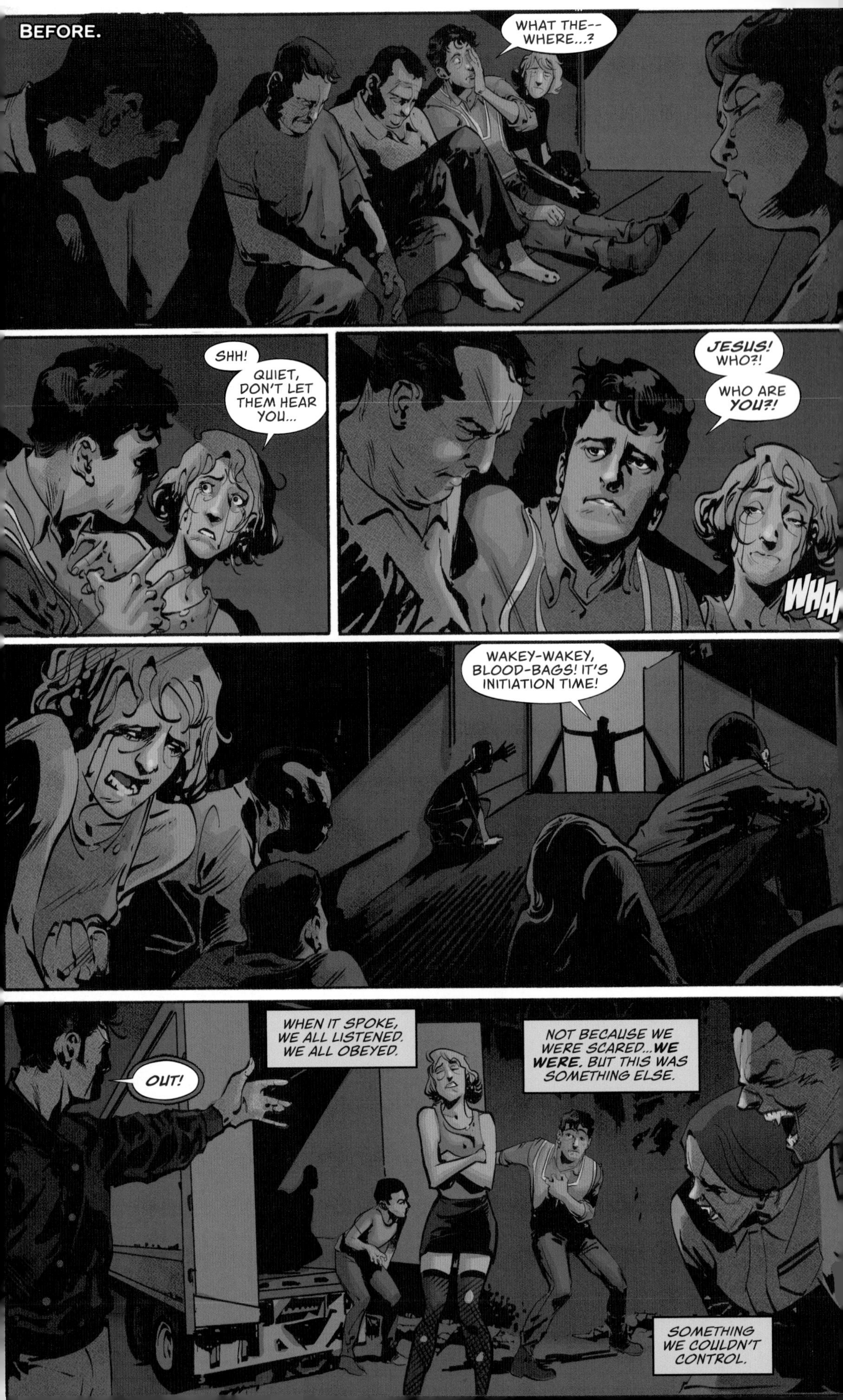
BEFORE.
WHAT THE--
WHERE...?
SHH!
QUIET, DON'T LET THEM HEAR YOU...
JESUS! WHO?!
WHO ARE YOU?!
WHA
WAKEY-WAKEY, BLOOD-BAGS! IT'S INITIATION TIME!
OUT!
WHEN IT SPOKE, WE ALL LISTENED. WE ALL OBEYED.
NOT BECAUSE WE WERE SCARED...WE WERE. BUT THIS WAS SOMETHING ELSE.
SOMETHING WE COULDN'T CONTROL.

WE ONLY STOPPED TO DIG.

WE DUG UNTIL OUR HANDS WERE BLISTERED AND BLEEDING AND THE PIT WAS DEEP AND WIDE.

WE KNEW [W]E'D DUG OUR [O]WN GRAVE.

THEY SEEMED TO BE SAYING SOMETHING. CHANTING SOMETHING. BUT I COULDN'T RECKON WHAT IT WAS. IT WASN'T LIKE A LANGUAGE.

MORE LIKE THE SCRAPPING AND HOLLERING OF BEASTS.

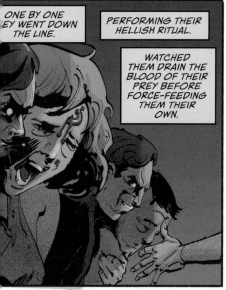

ONE BY ONE [TH]EY WENT DOWN THE LINE.

PERFORMING THEIR HELLISH RITUAL.

WATCHED THEM DRAIN THE BLOOD OF THEIR PREY BEFORE FORCE-FEEDING THEM THEIR OWN.

WHEN MY TIME CAME...I WAS TOO SCARED TO MOVE.

TOO SCARED TO DO ANYTHING BUT PRAY.

LORD JESUS, FORGIVE ME...

TK

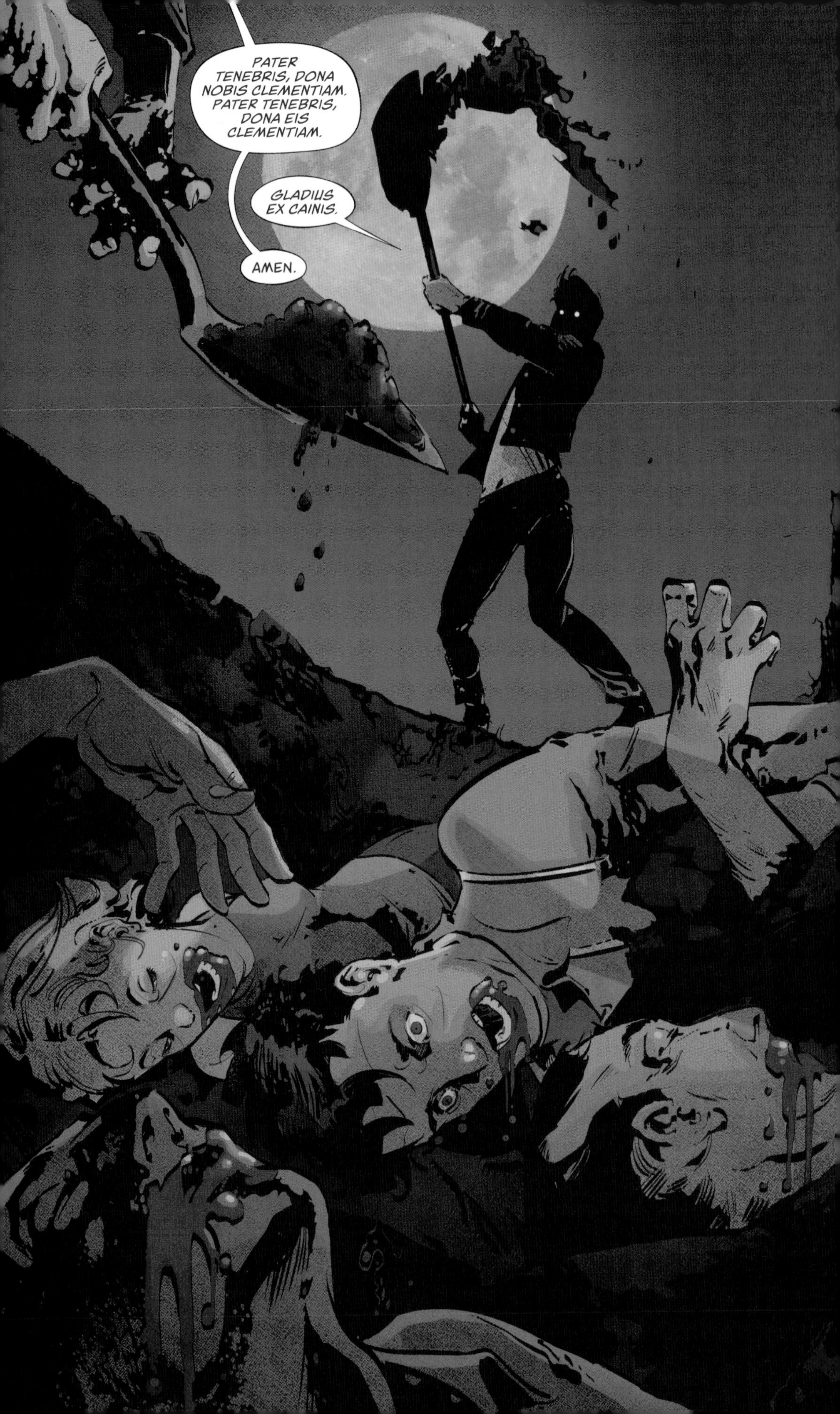
PATER TENEBRIS, DONA NOBIS CLEMENTIAM. PATER TENEBRIS, DONA EIS CLEMENTIAM.
GLADIUS EX CAINIS.
AMEN.

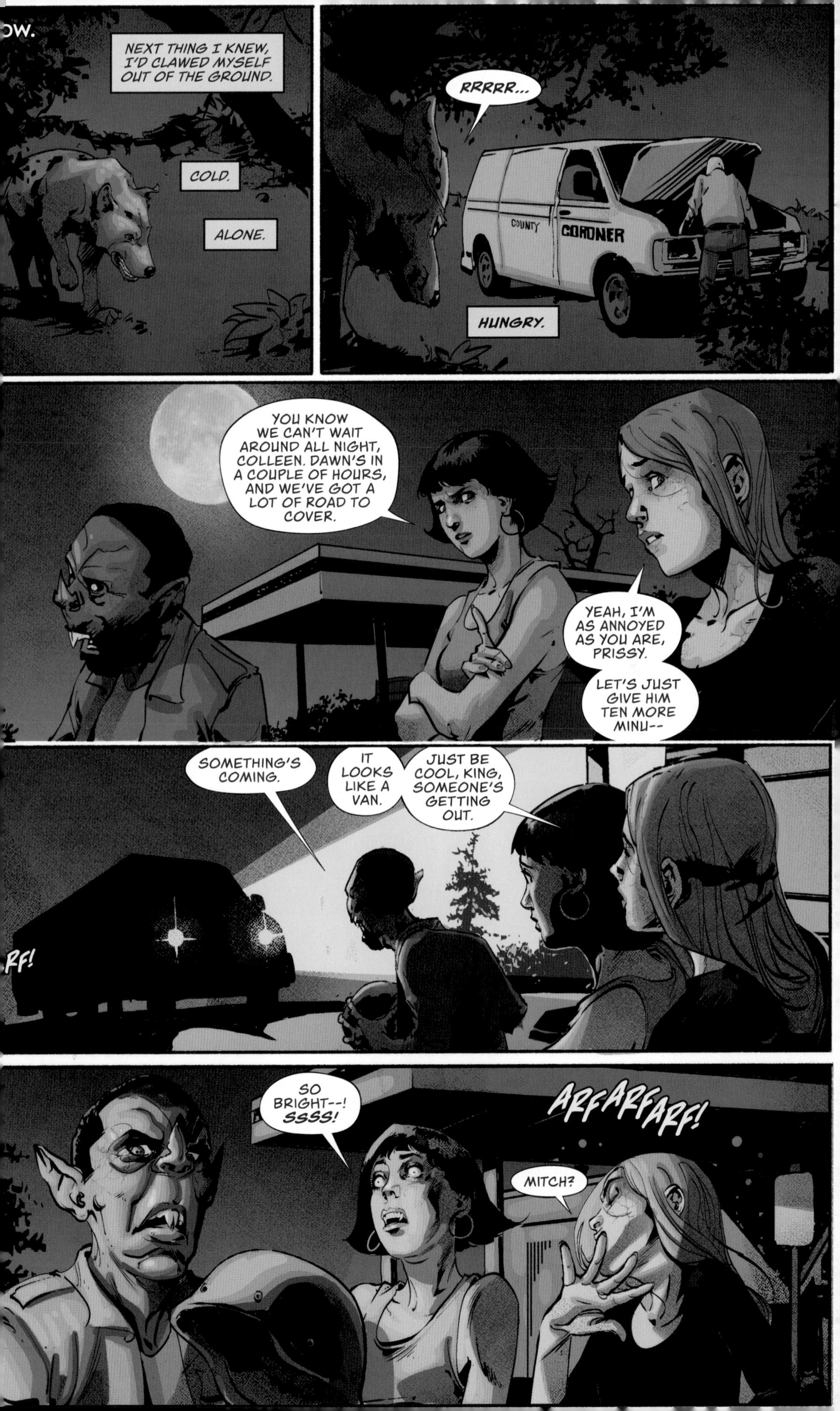
OW.
NEXT THING I KNEW, I'D CLAWED MYSELF OUT OF THE GROUND.
COLD.
ALONE.
RRRRR...
COUNTY CORONER
HUNGRY.
YOU KNOW WE CAN'T WAIT AROUND ALL NIGHT, COLLEEN. DAWN'S IN A COUPLE OF HOURS, AND WE'VE GOT A LOT OF ROAD TO COVER.
YEAH, I'M AS ANNOYED AS YOU ARE, PRISSY.
LET'S JUST GIVE HIM TEN MORE MINU--
SOMETHING'S COMING.
IT LOOKS LIKE A VAN.
JUST BE COOL, KING, SOMEONE'S GETTING OUT.
RF!
SO BRIGHT--! SSSS!
ARFARFARF!
MITCH?

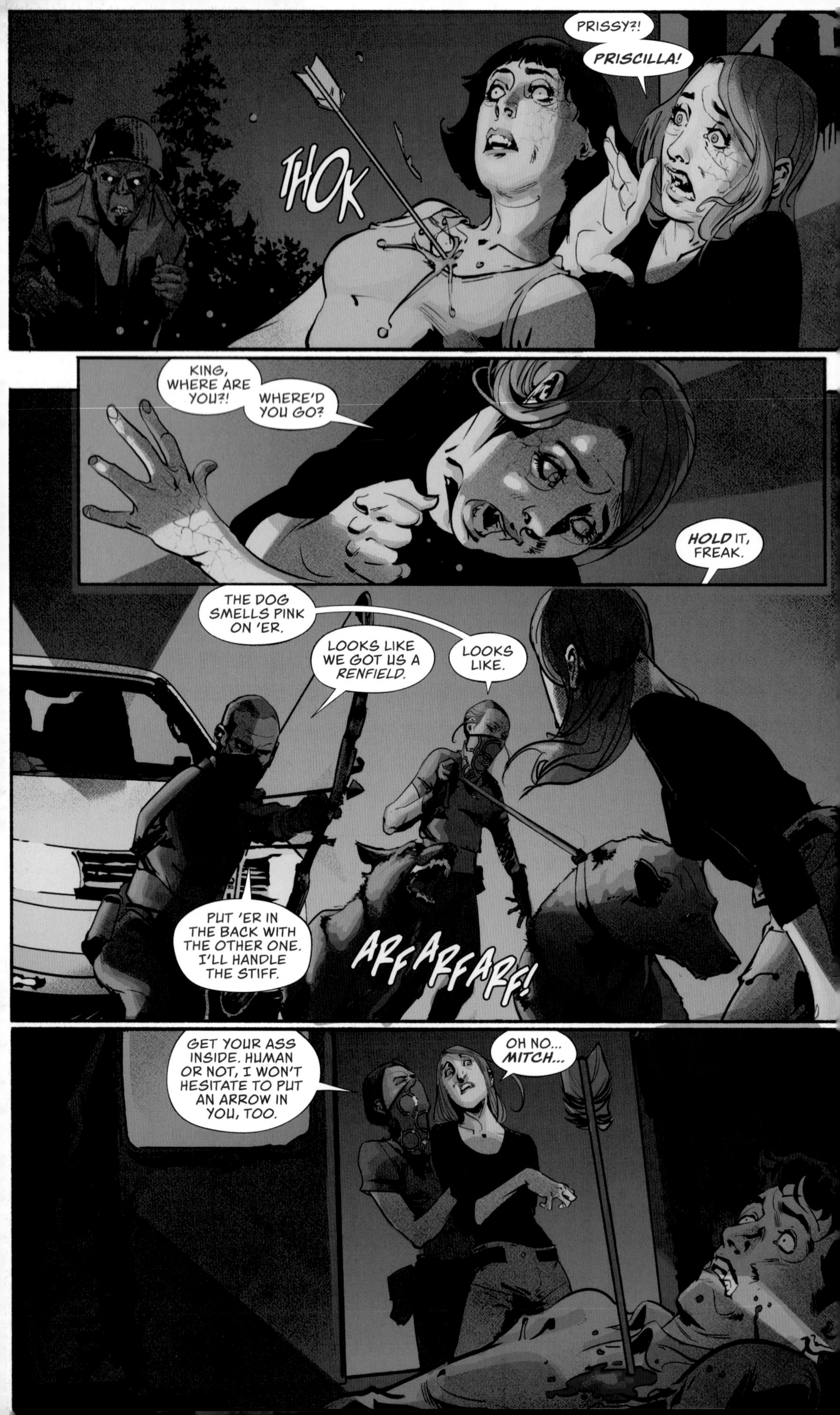
PRISSY?!
PRISCILLA!
THOK
KING, WHERE ARE YOU?!
WHERE'D YOU GO?
HOLD IT, FREAK.
THE DOG SMELLS PINK ON 'ER.
LOOKS LIKE WE GOT US A RENFIELD.
LOOKS LIKE.
PUT 'ER IN THE BACK WITH THE OTHER ONE. I'LL HANDLE THE STIFF.
ARF ARF ARF!
GET YOUR ASS INSIDE. HUMAN OR NOT, I WON'T HESITATE TO PUT AN ARROW IN YOU, TOO.
OH NO... MITCH...

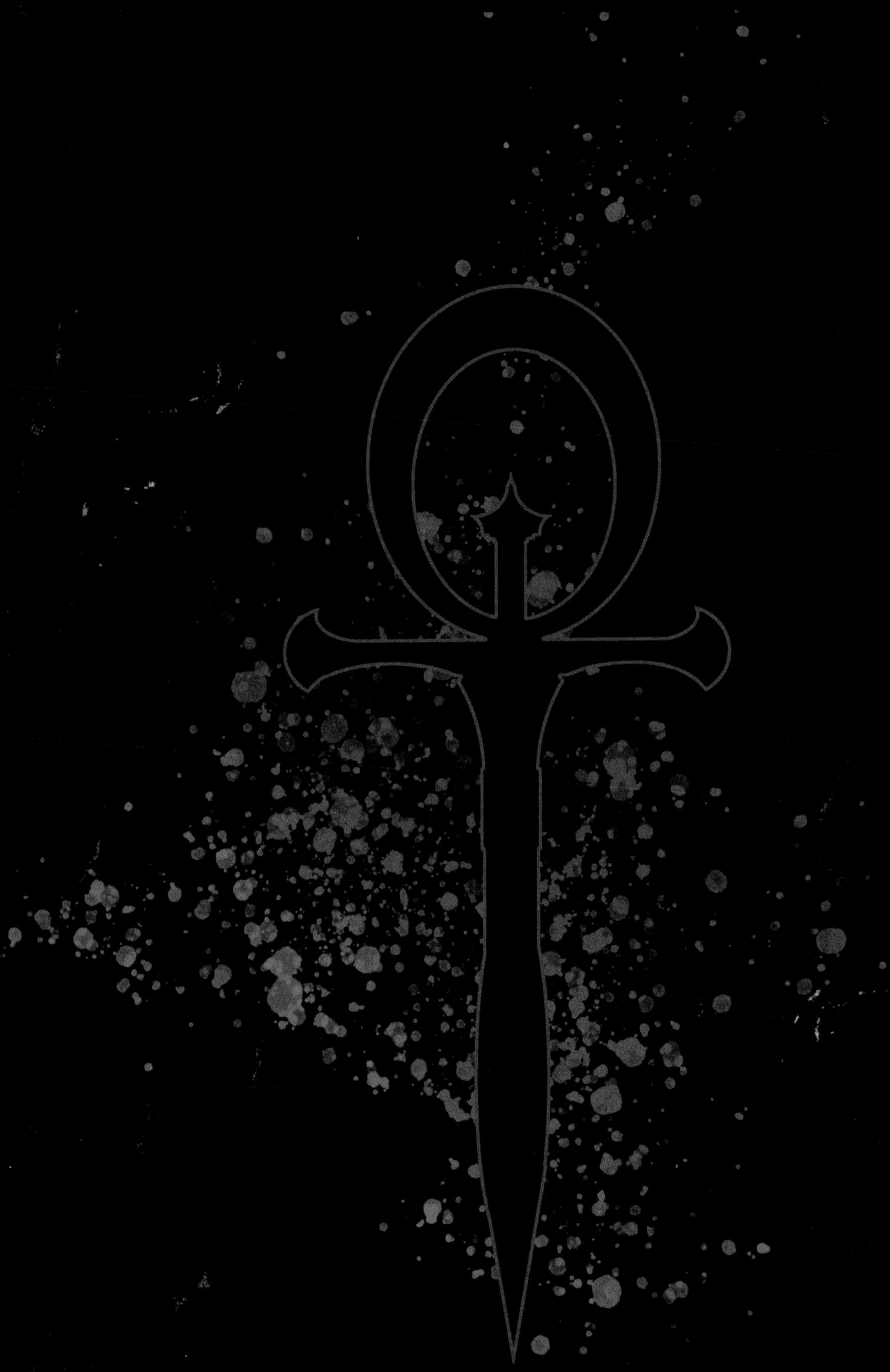

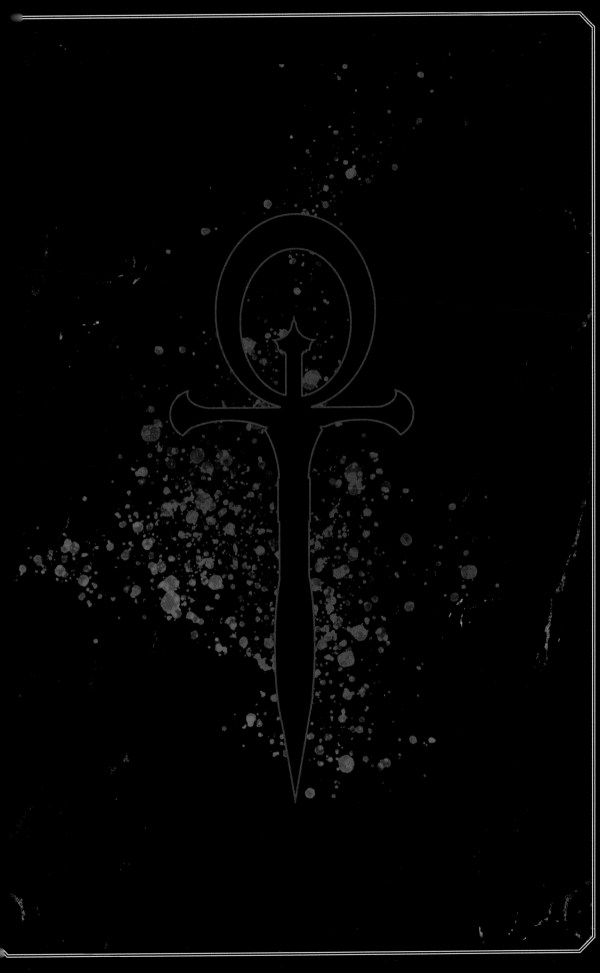

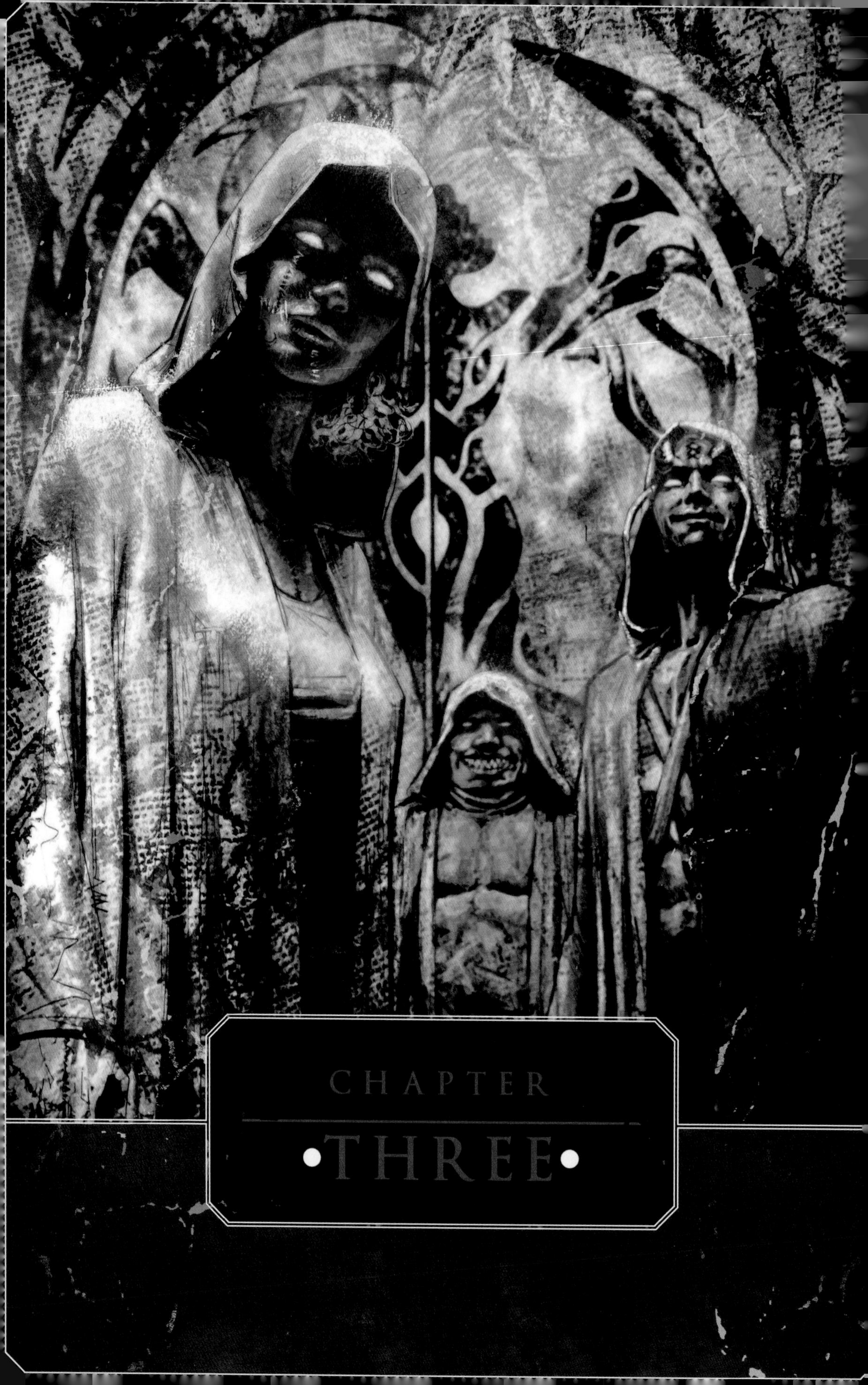

CHAPTER THREE

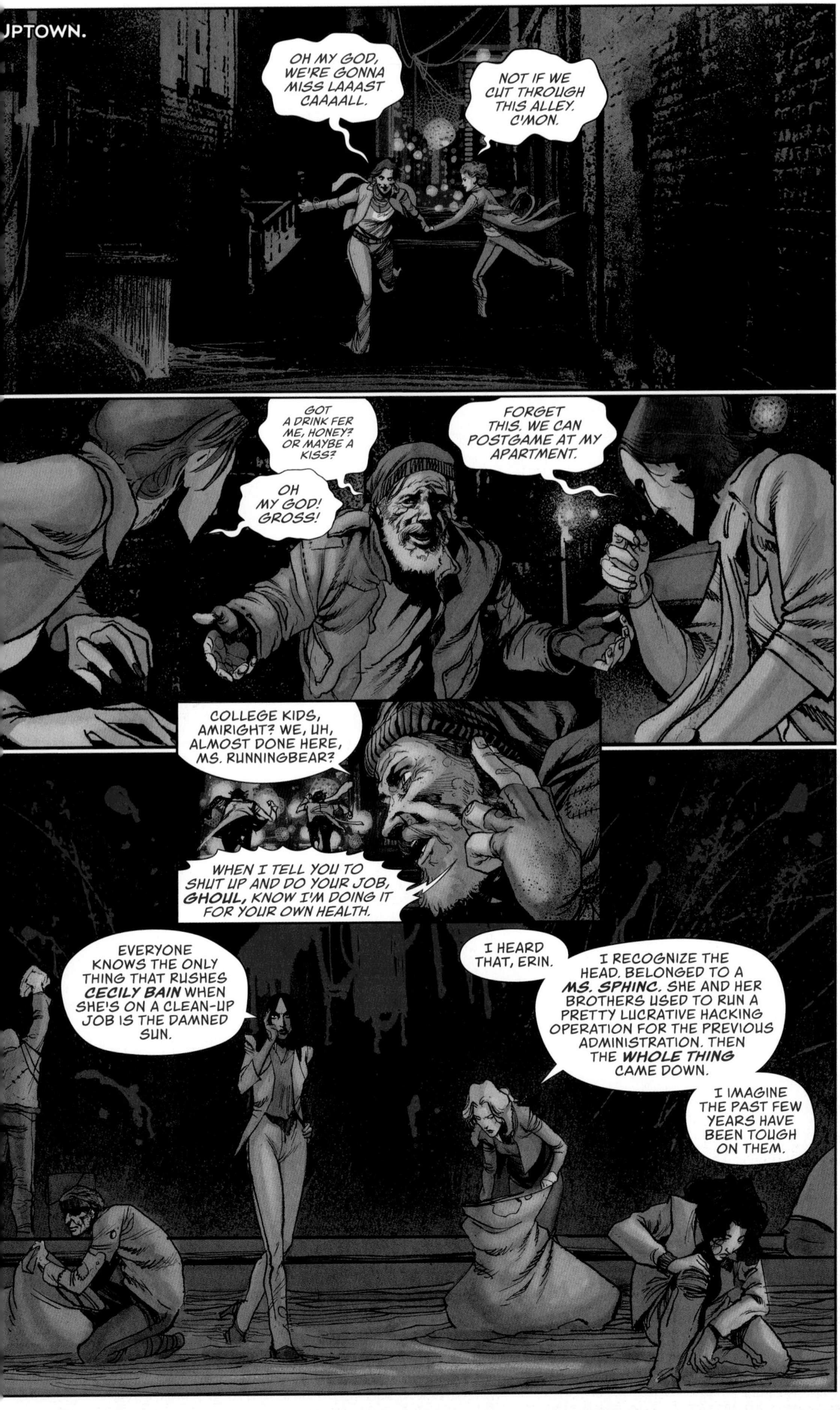

UPTOWN.
OH MY GOD, WE'RE GONNA MISS LAAAST CAAAALL.
NOT IF WE CUT THROUGH THIS ALLEY. C'MON.
GOT A DRINK FER ME, HONEY? OR MAYBE A KISS?
OH MY GOD! GROSS!
FORGET THIS. WE CAN POSTGAME AT MY APARTMENT.
COLLEGE KIDS, AMIRIGHT? WE, UH, ALMOST DONE HERE, MS. RUNNINGBEAR?
WHEN I TELL YOU TO SHUT UP AND DO YOUR JOB, GHOUL, KNOW I'M DOING IT FOR YOUR OWN HEALTH.
EVERYONE KNOWS THE ONLY THING THAT RUSHES CECILY BAIN WHEN SHE'S ON A CLEAN-UP JOB IS THE DAMNED SUN.
I HEARD THAT, ERIN.
I RECOGNIZE THE HEAD. BELONGED TO A MS. SPHINC. SHE AND HER BROTHERS USED TO RUN A PRETTY LUCRATIVE HACKING OPERATION FOR THE PREVIOUS ADMINISTRATION. THEN THE WHOLE THING CAME DOWN.
I IMAGINE THE PAST FEW YEARS HAVE BEEN TOUGH ON THEM.

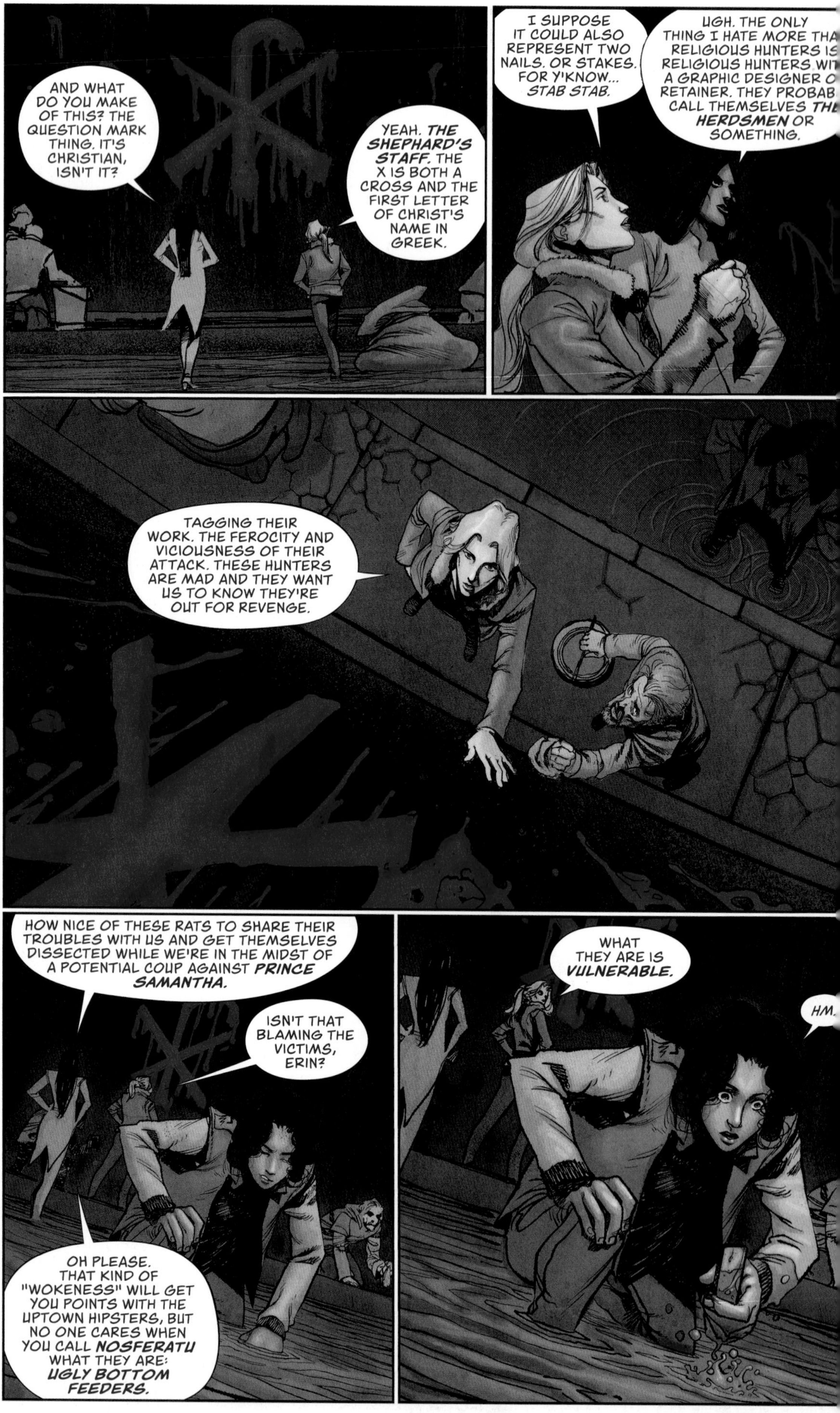
AND WHAT DO YOU MAKE OF THIS? THE QUESTION MARK THING. IT'S CHRISTIAN, ISN'T IT?
YEAH. THE SHEPHARD'S STAFF. THE X IS BOTH A CROSS AND THE FIRST LETTER OF CHRIST'S NAME IN GREEK.
I SUPPOSE IT COULD ALSO REPRESENT TWO NAILS. OR STAKES. FOR Y'KNOW... STAB STAB.
UGH. THE ONLY THING I HATE MORE THA RELIGIOUS HUNTERS IS RELIGIOUS HUNTERS WIT A GRAPHIC DESIGNER O RETAINER. THEY PROBAB CALL THEMSELVES THE HERDSMEN OR SOMETHING.
TAGGING THEIR WORK. THE FEROCITY AND VICIOUSNESS OF THEIR ATTACK. THESE HUNTERS ARE MAD AND THEY WANT US TO KNOW THEY'RE OUT FOR REVENGE.
HOW NICE OF THESE RATS TO SHARE THEIR TROUBLES WITH US AND GET THEMSELVES DISSECTED WHILE WE'RE IN THE MIDST OF A POTENTIAL COUP AGAINST PRINCE SAMANTHA.
ISN'T THAT BLAMING THE VICTIMS, ERIN?
OH PLEASE. THAT KIND OF "WOKENESS" WILL GET YOU POINTS WITH THE UPTOWN HIPSTERS, BUT NO ONE CARES WHEN YOU CALL NOSFERATU WHAT THEY ARE: UGLY BOTTOM FEEDERS.
WHAT THEY ARE IS VULNERABLE.
HM.

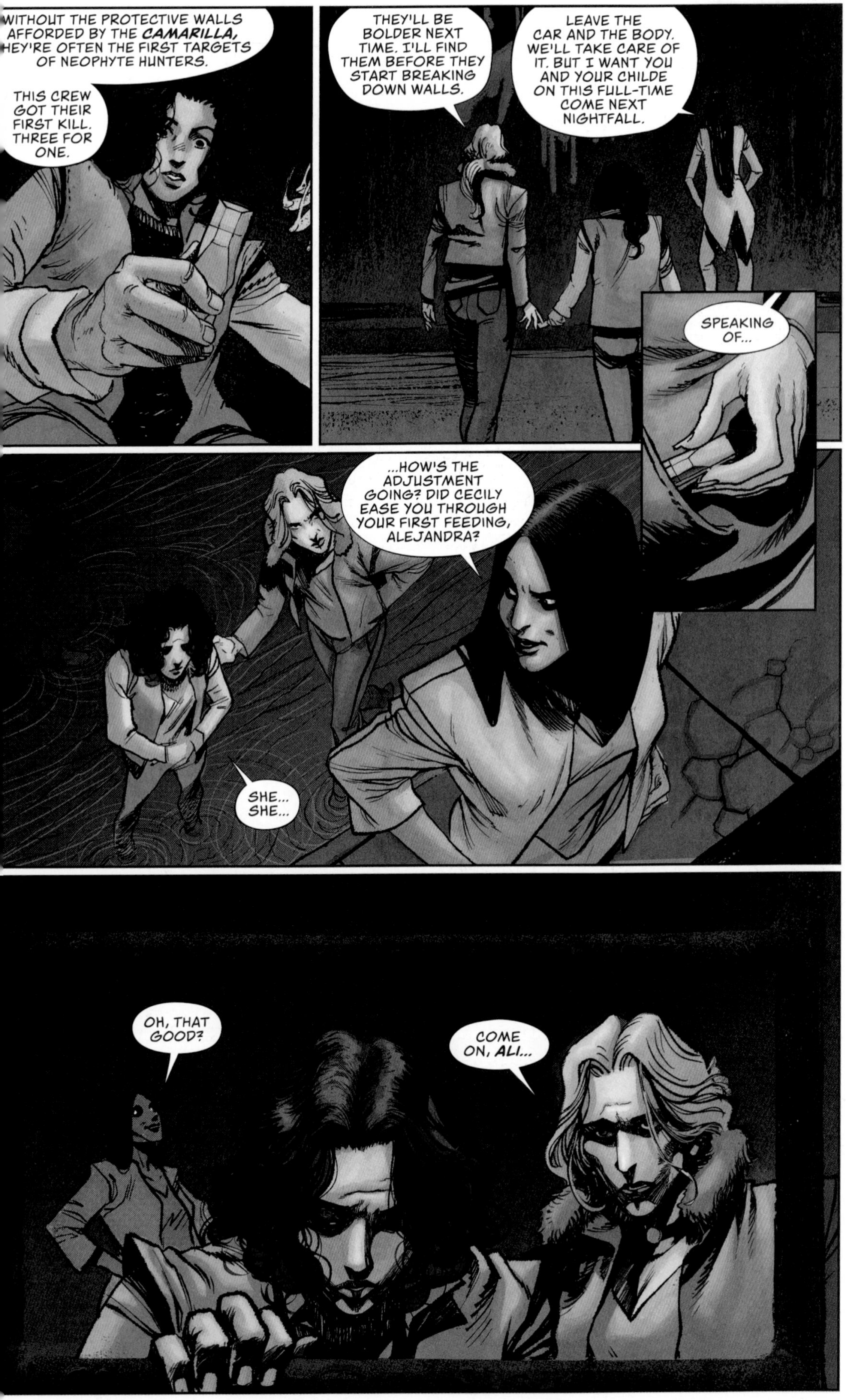
WITHOUT THE PROTECTIVE WALLS AFFORDED BY THE CAMARILLA, HEY'RE OFTEN THE FIRST TARGETS OF NEOPHYTE HUNTERS.
THIS CREW GOT THEIR FIRST KILL. THREE FOR ONE.
THEY'LL BE BOLDER NEXT TIME. I'LL FIND THEM BEFORE THEY START BREAKING DOWN WALLS.
LEAVE THE CAR AND THE BODY. WE'LL TAKE CARE OF IT. BUT I WANT YOU AND YOUR CHILDE ON THIS FULL-TIME COME NEXT NIGHTFALL.
SPEAKING OF...
...HOW'S THE ADJUSTMENT GOING? DID CECILY EASE YOU THROUGH YOUR FIRST FEEDING, ALEJANDRA?
SHE... SHE...
OH, THAT GOOD?
COME ON, ALI...

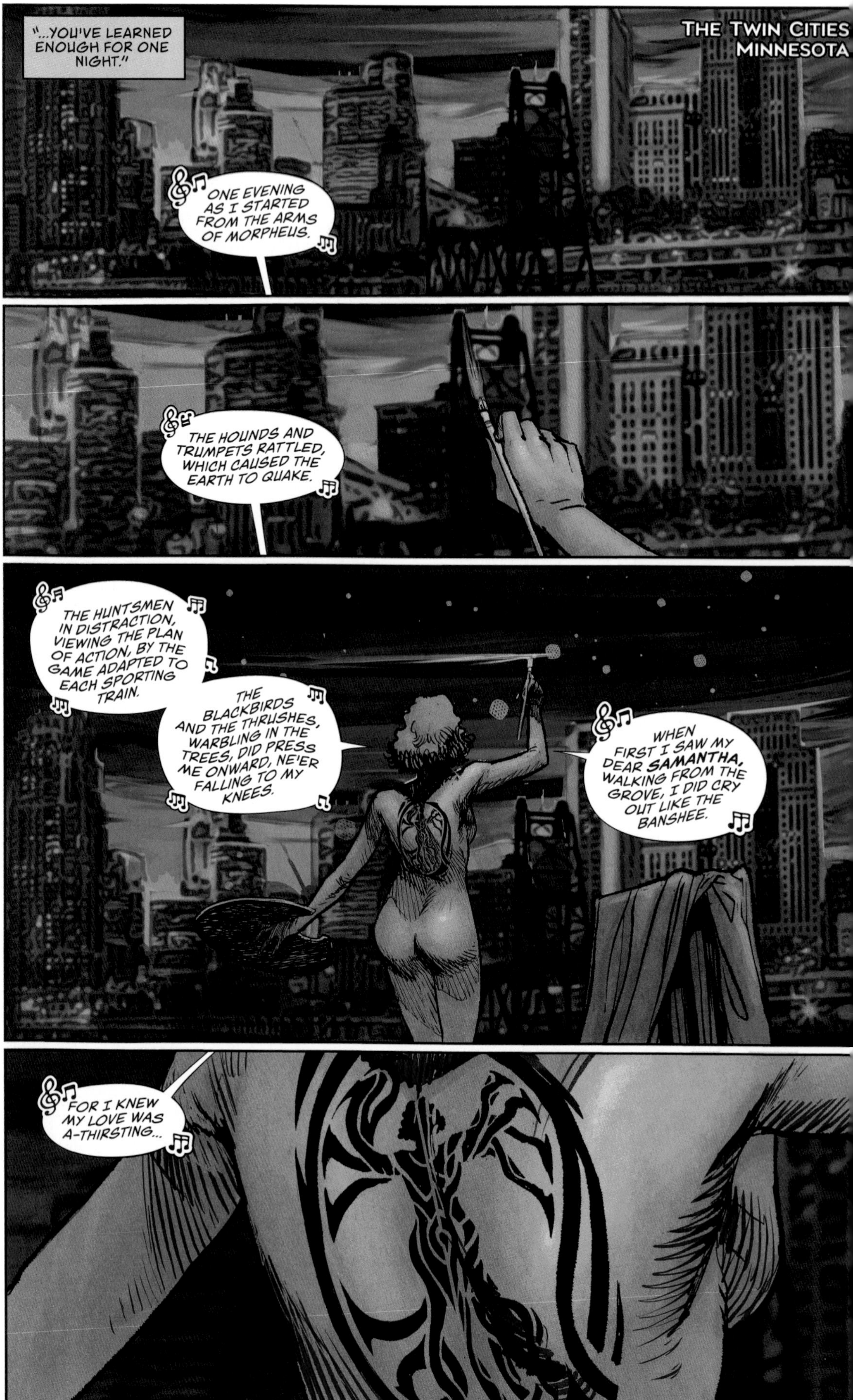
"...YOU'VE LEARNED ENOUGH FOR ONE NIGHT."
THE TWIN CITIES MINNESOTA
ONE EVENING AS I STARTED FROM THE ARMS OF MORPHEUS.
THE HOUNDS AND TRUMPETS RATTLED, WHICH CAUSED THE EARTH TO QUAKE.
THE HUNTSMEN IN DISTRACTION, VIEWING THE PLAN OF ACTION, BY THE GAME ADAPTED TO EACH SPORTING TRAIN.
THE BLACKBIRDS AND THE THRUSHES, WARBLING IN THE TREES, DID PRESS ME ONWARD, NE'ER FALLING TO MY KNEES.
WHEN FIRST I SAW MY DEAR SAMANTHA, WALKING FROM THE GROVE, I DID CRY OUT LIKE THE BANSHEE.
FOR I KNEW MY LOVE WAS A-THIRSTING...

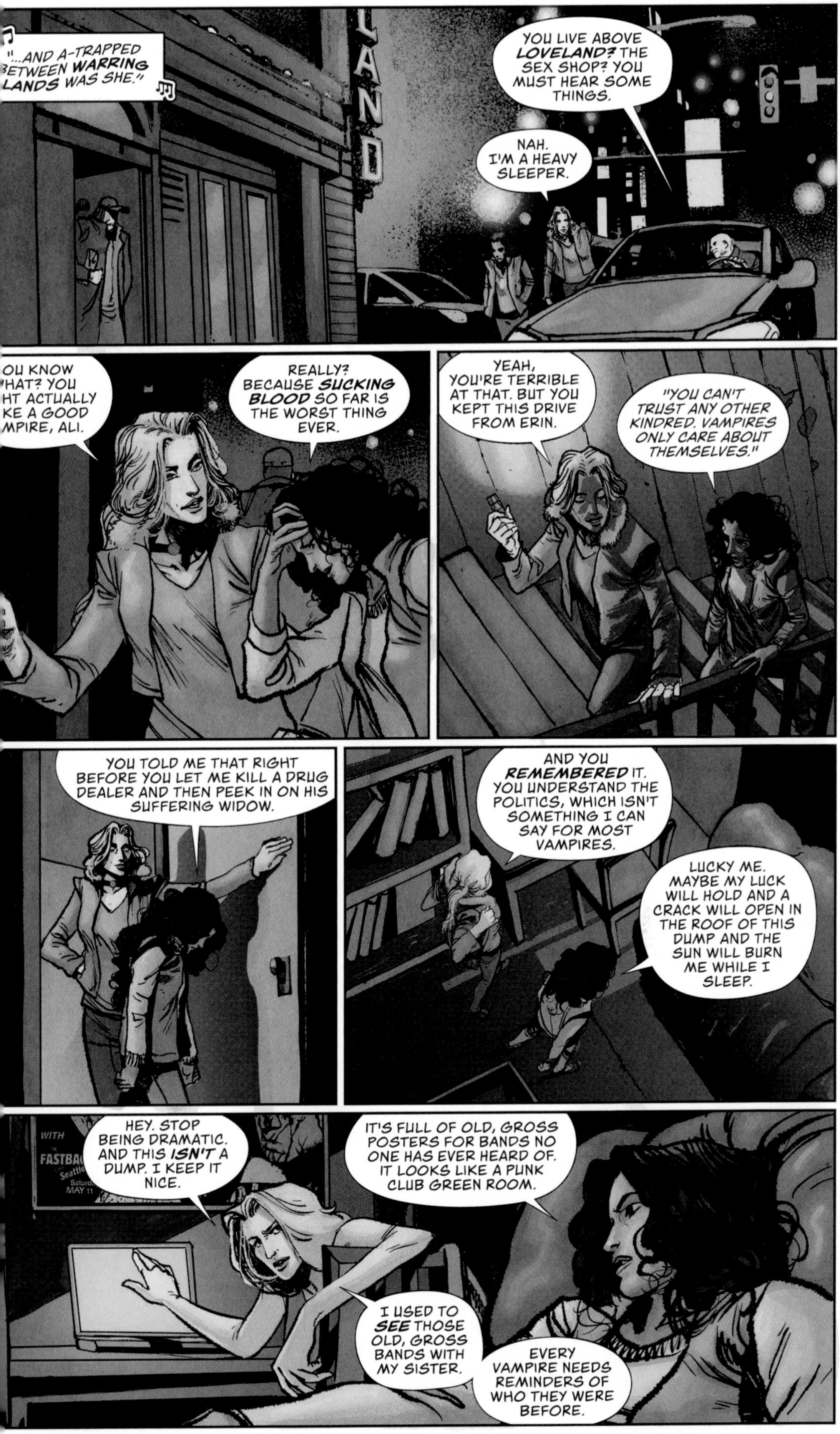
"...AND A-TRAPPED
BETWEEN WARRING
LANDS WAS SHE."
YOU LIVE ABOVE LOVELAND? THE SEX SHOP? YOU MUST HEAR SOME THINGS.
NAH. I'M A HEAVY SLEEPER.
OU KNOW HAT? YOU HT ACTUALLY KE A GOOD MPIRE, ALI.
REALLY? BECAUSE SUCKING BLOOD SO FAR IS THE WORST THING EVER.
YEAH, YOU'RE TERRIBLE AT THAT. BUT YOU KEPT THIS DRIVE FROM ERIN.
"YOU CAN'T TRUST ANY OTHER KINDRED. VAMPIRES ONLY CARE ABOUT THEMSELVES."
YOU TOLD ME THAT RIGHT BEFORE YOU LET ME KILL A DRUG DEALER AND THEN PEEK IN ON HIS SUFFERING WIDOW.
AND YOU REMEMBERED IT. YOU UNDERSTAND THE POLITICS, WHICH ISN'T SOMETHING I CAN SAY FOR MOST VAMPIRES.
LUCKY ME. MAYBE MY LUCK WILL HOLD AND A CRACK WILL OPEN IN THE ROOF OF THIS DUMP AND THE SUN WILL BURN ME WHILE I SLEEP.
HEY. STOP BEING DRAMATIC. AND THIS ISN'T A DUMP. I KEEP IT NICE.
IT'S FULL OF OLD, GROSS POSTERS FOR BANDS NO ONE HAS EVER HEARD OF. IT LOOKS LIKE A PUNK CLUB GREEN ROOM.
I USED TO SEE THOSE OLD, GROSS BANDS WITH MY SISTER.
EVERY VAMPIRE NEEDS REMINDERS OF WHO THEY WERE BEFORE.

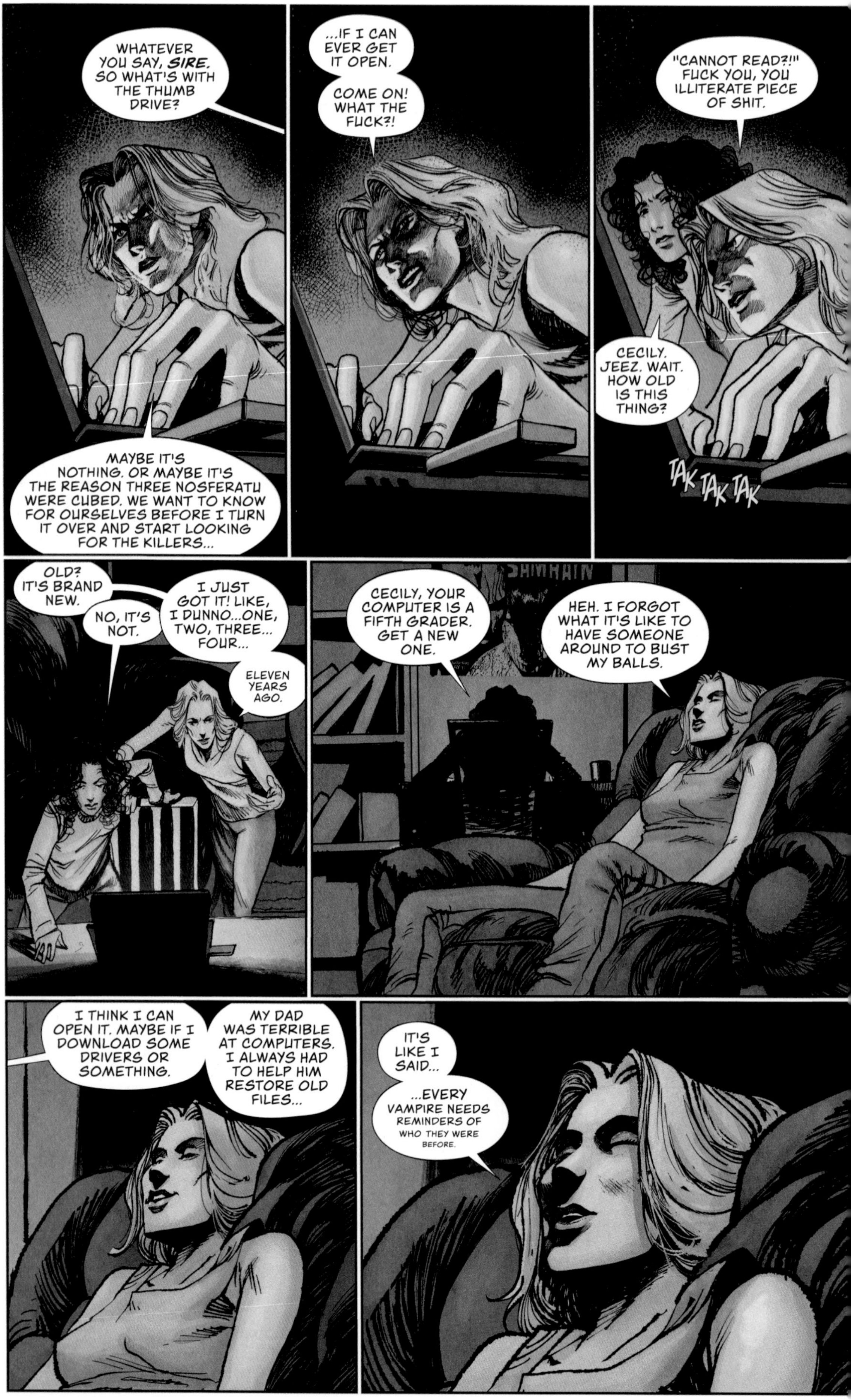
WHATEVER YOU SAY, SIRE. SO WHAT'S WITH THE THUMB DRIVE?
MAYBE IT'S NOTHING. OR MAYBE IT'S THE REASON THREE NOSFERATU WERE CUBED. WE WANT TO KNOW FOR OURSELVES BEFORE I TURN IT OVER AND START LOOKING FOR THE KILLERS...
...IF I CAN EVER GET IT OPEN.
COME ON! WHAT THE FUCK?!
"CANNOT READ?!" FUCK YOU, YOU ILLITERATE PIECE OF SHIT.
CECILY. JEEZ. WAIT. HOW OLD IS THIS THING?
TAK TAK TAK
OLD? IT'S BRAND NEW.
NO, IT'S NOT.
I JUST GOT IT! LIKE, I DUNNO...ONE, TWO, THREE... FOUR...
ELEVEN YEARS AGO.
SAMHAIN
CECILY, YOUR COMPUTER IS A FIFTH GRADER. GET A NEW ONE.
HEH. I FORGOT WHAT IT'S LIKE TO HAVE SOMEONE AROUND TO BUST MY BALLS.
I THINK I CAN OPEN IT. MAYBE IF I DOWNLOAD SOME DRIVERS OR SOMETHING.
MY DAD WAS TERRIBLE AT COMPUTERS. I ALWAYS HAD TO HELP HIM RESTORE OLD FILES...
IT'S LIKE I SAID...
...EVERY VAMPIRE NEEDS REMINDERS OF WHO THEY WERE BEFORE.

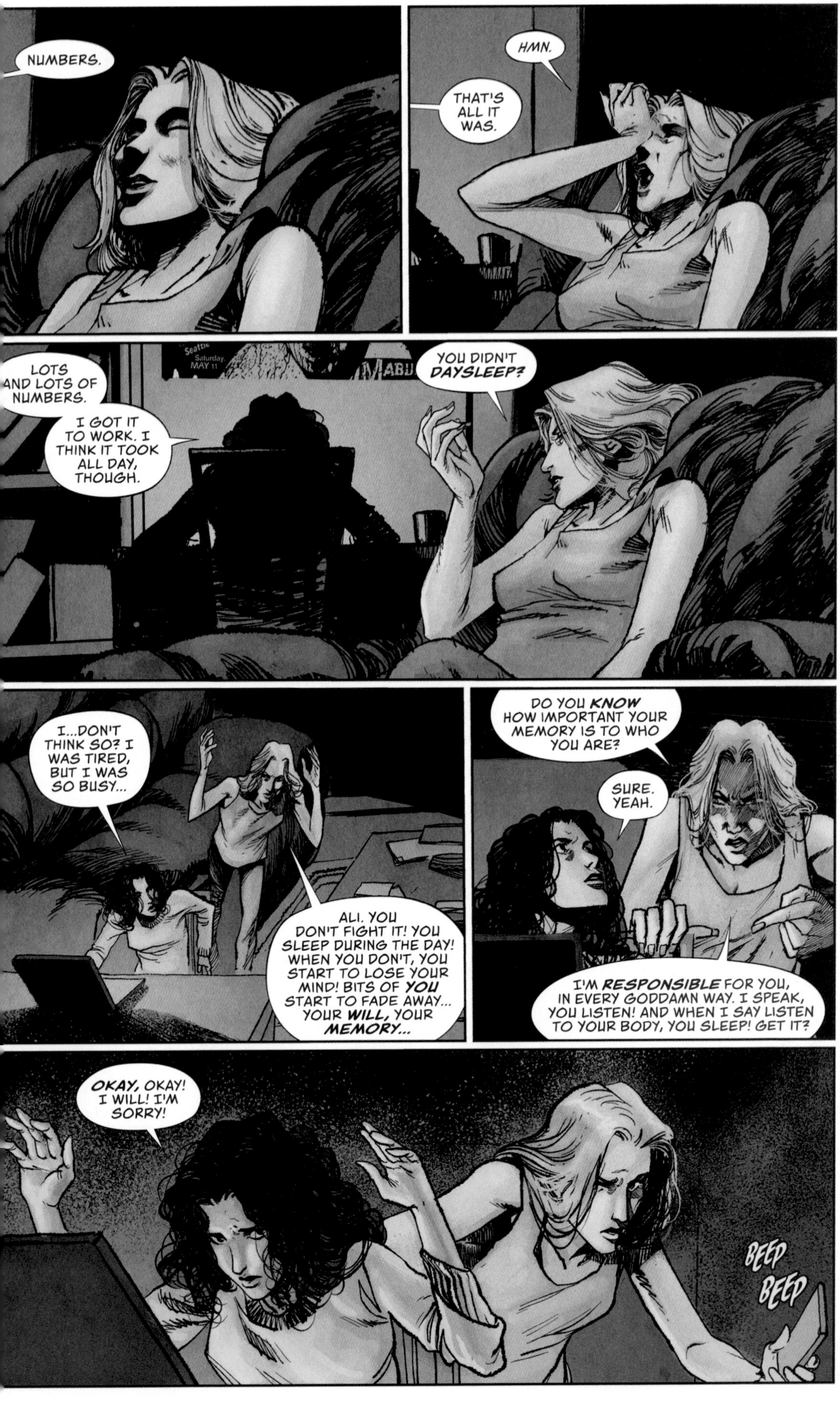
NUMBERS.
HMN.
THAT'S ALL IT WAS.
Seattle Saturday, MAY 11
LOTS AND LOTS OF NUMBERS.
YOU DIDN'T DAYSLEEP?
I GOT IT TO WORK. I THINK IT TOOK ALL DAY, THOUGH.
I...DON'T THINK SO? I WAS TIRED, BUT I WAS SO BUSY...
ALI. YOU DON'T FIGHT IT! YOU SLEEP DURING THE DAY! WHEN YOU DON'T, YOU START TO LOSE YOUR MIND! BITS OF YOU START TO FADE AWAY... YOUR WILL, YOUR MEMORY...
DO YOU KNOW HOW IMPORTANT YOUR MEMORY IS TO WHO YOU ARE?
SURE. YEAH.
I'M RESPONSIBLE FOR YOU, IN EVERY GODDAMN WAY. I SPEAK, YOU LISTEN! AND WHEN I SAY LISTEN TO YOUR BODY, YOU SLEEP! GET IT?
OKAY, OKAY! I WILL! I'M SORRY!
BEEP BEEP

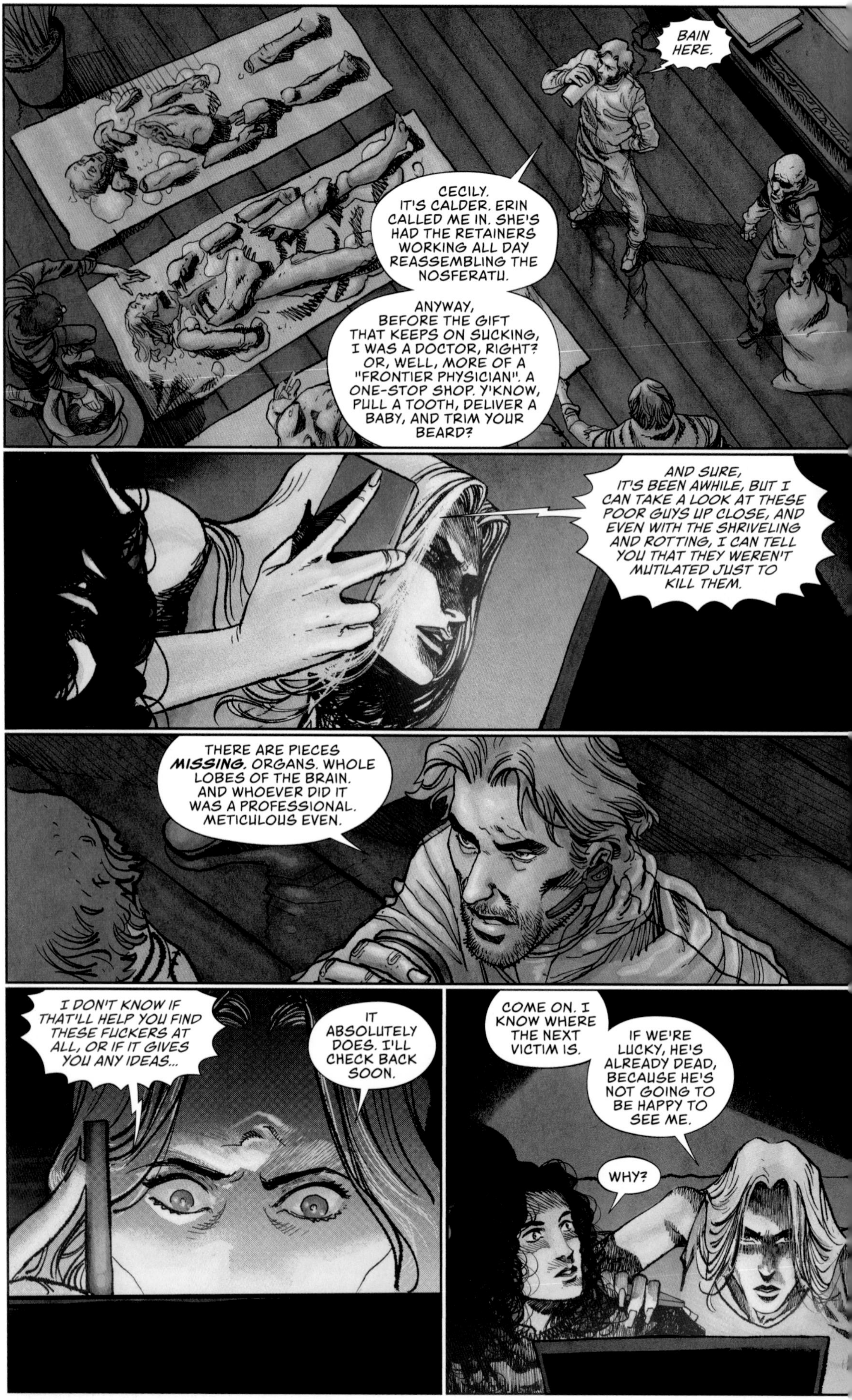
BAIN HERE.
CECILY. IT'S CALDER. ERIN CALLED ME IN. SHE'S HAD THE RETAINERS WORKING ALL DAY REASSEMBLING THE NOSFERATU.
ANYWAY, BEFORE THE GIFT THAT KEEPS ON SUCKING, I WAS A DOCTOR, RIGHT? OR, WELL, MORE OF A "FRONTIER PHYSICIAN". A ONE-STOP SHOP. Y'KNOW, PULL A TOOTH, DELIVER A BABY, AND TRIM YOUR BEARD?
AND SURE, IT'S BEEN AWHILE, BUT I CAN TAKE A LOOK AT THESE POOR GUYS UP CLOSE, AND EVEN WITH THE SHRIVELING AND ROTTING, I CAN TELL YOU THAT THEY WEREN'T MUTILATED JUST TO KILL THEM.
THERE ARE PIECES MISSING. ORGANS. WHOLE LOBES OF THE BRAIN. AND WHOEVER DID IT WAS A PROFESSIONAL. METICULOUS EVEN.
I DON'T KNOW IF THAT'LL HELP YOU FIND THESE FUCKERS AT ALL, OR IF IT GIVES YOU ANY IDEAS...
IT ABSOLUTELY DOES. I'LL CHECK BACK SOON.
COME ON. I KNOW WHERE THE NEXT VICTIM IS.
IF WE'RE LUCKY, HE'S ALREADY DEAD, BECAUSE HE'S NOT GOING TO BE HAPPY TO SEE ME.
WHY?

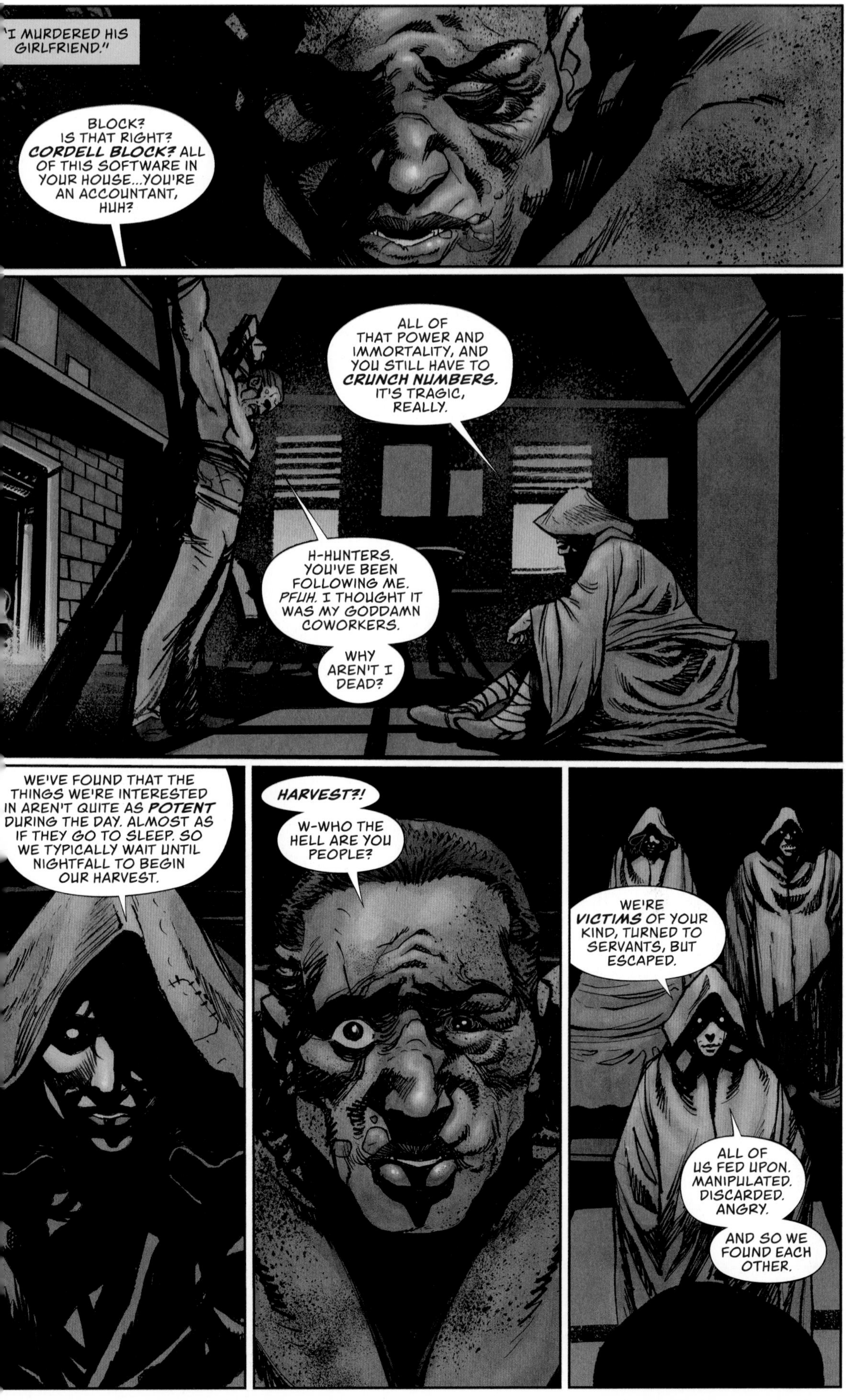
"I MURDERED HIS GIRLFRIEND."
BLOCK? IS THAT RIGHT? CORDELL BLOCK? ALL OF THIS SOFTWARE IN YOUR HOUSE...YOU'RE AN ACCOUNTANT, HUH?
ALL OF THAT POWER AND IMMORTALITY, AND YOU STILL HAVE TO CRUNCH NUMBERS. IT'S TRAGIC, REALLY.
H-HUNTERS. YOU'VE BEEN FOLLOWING ME. PFUH. I THOUGHT IT WAS MY GODDAMN COWORKERS.
WHY AREN'T I DEAD?
WE'VE FOUND THAT THE THINGS WE'RE INTERESTED IN AREN'T QUITE AS POTENT DURING THE DAY. ALMOST AS IF THEY GO TO SLEEP. SO WE TYPICALLY WAIT UNTIL NIGHTFALL TO BEGIN OUR HARVEST.
HARVEST?!
W-WHO THE HELL ARE YOU PEOPLE?
WE'RE VICTIMS OF YOUR KIND, TURNED TO SERVANTS, BUT ESCAPED.
ALL OF US FED UPON. MANIPULATED. DISCARDED. ANGRY.
AND SO WE FOUND EACH OTHER.

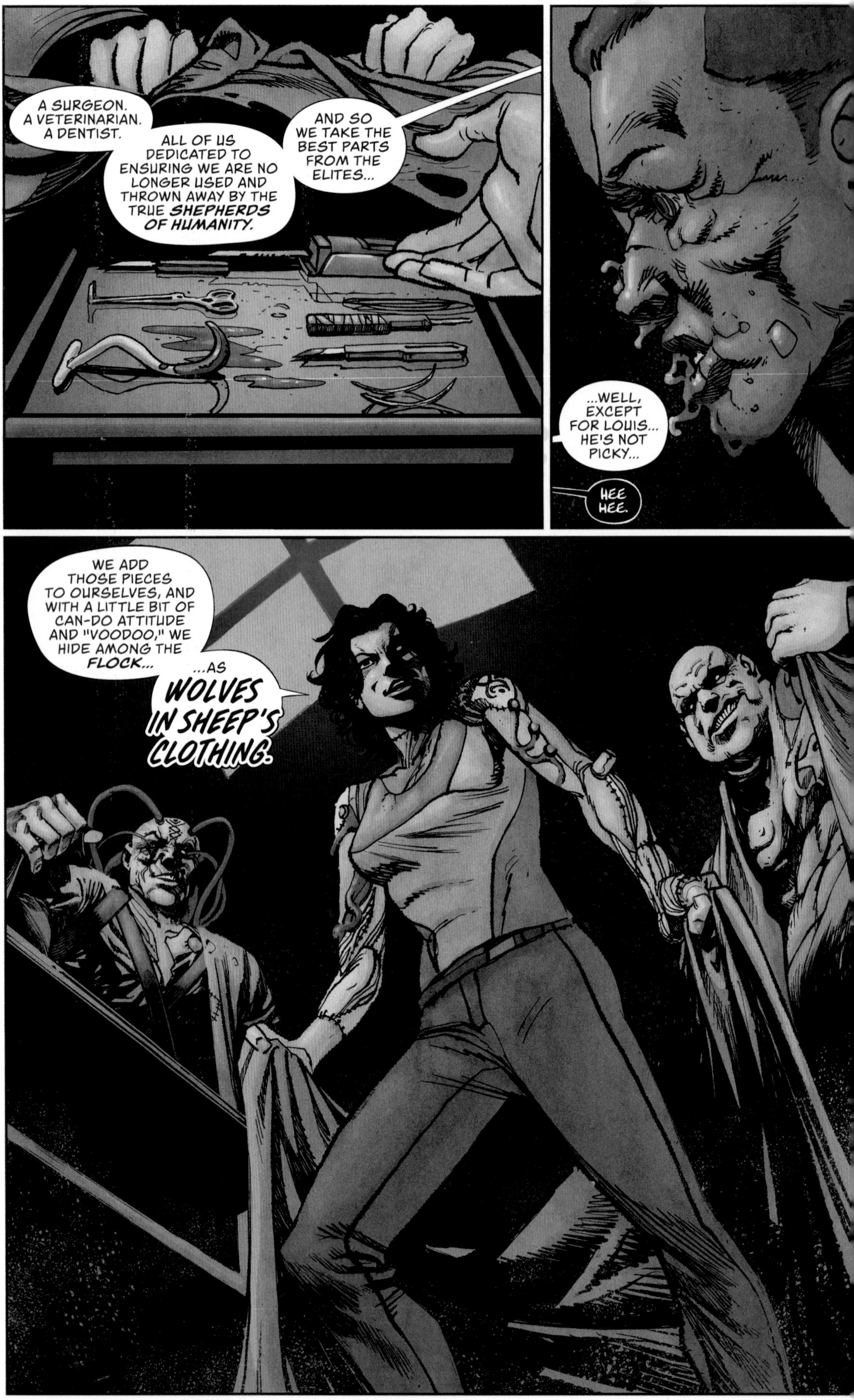
A SURGEON. A VETERINARIAN. A DENTIST.
ALL OF US DEDICATED TO ENSURING WE ARE NO LONGER USED AND THROWN AWAY BY THE TRUE SHEPHERDS OF HUMANITY.
AND SO WE TAKE THE BEST PARTS FROM THE ELITES...
...WELL, EXCEPT FOR LOUIS... HE'S NOT PICKY...
HEE HEE.
WE ADD THOSE PIECES TO OURSELVES, AND WITH A LITTLE BIT OF CAN-DO ATTITUDE AND "VOODOO," WE HIDE AMONG THE FLOCK...
...AS WOLVES IN SHEEP'S CLOTHING.

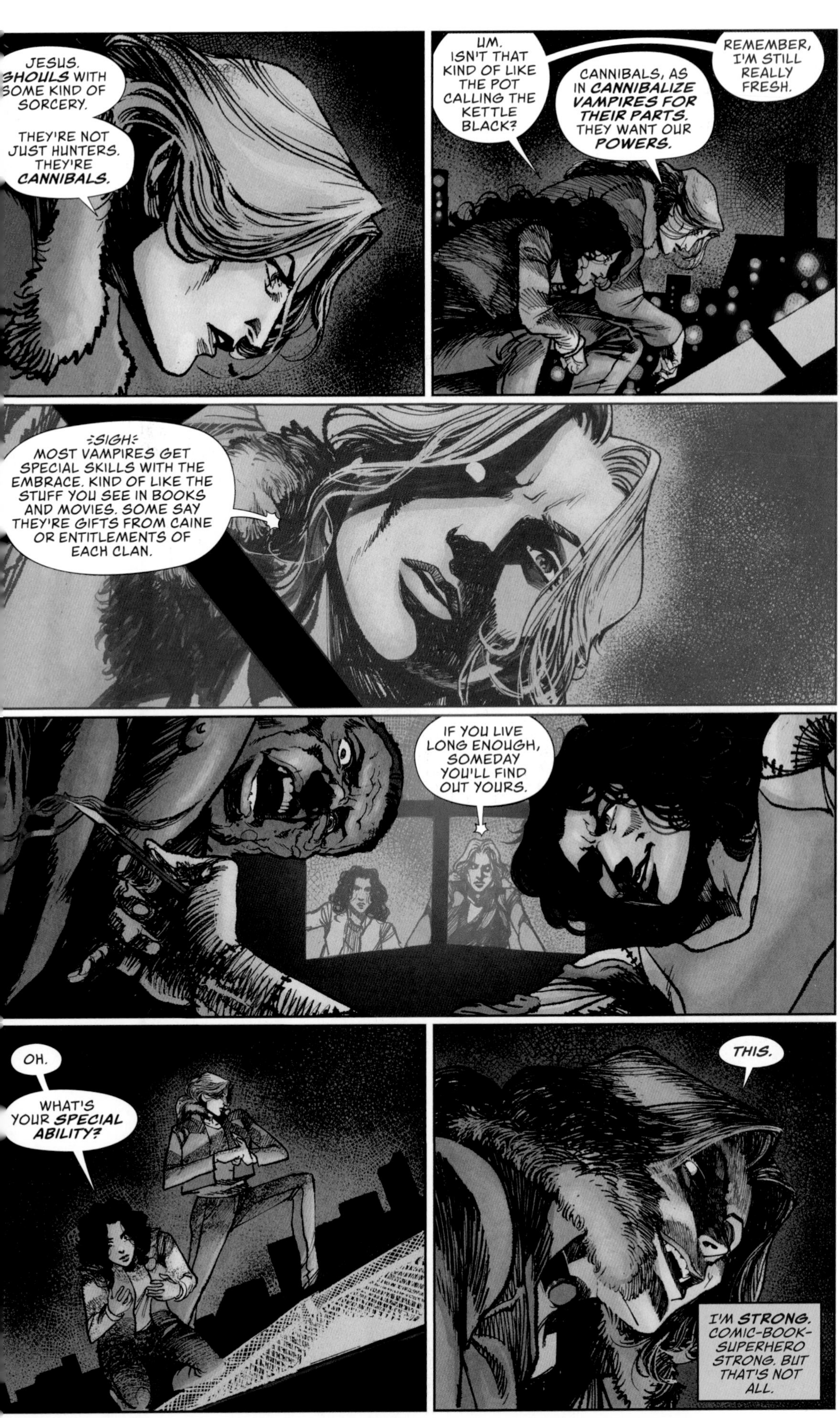

JESUS. GHOULS WITH SOME KIND OF SORCERY.
THEY'RE NOT JUST HUNTERS. THEY'RE CANNIBALS.
UM. ISN'T THAT KIND OF LIKE THE POT CALLING THE KETTLE BLACK?
REMEMBER, I'M STILL REALLY FRESH.
CANNIBALS, AS IN CANNIBALIZE VAMPIRES FOR THEIR PARTS. THEY WANT OUR POWERS.
SIGH
MOST VAMPIRES GET SPECIAL SKILLS WITH THE EMBRACE. KIND OF LIKE THE STUFF YOU SEE IN BOOKS AND MOVIES. SOME SAY THEY'RE GIFTS FROM CAINE OR ENTITLEMENTS OF EACH CLAN.
IF YOU LIVE LONG ENOUGH, SOMEDAY YOU'LL FIND OUT YOURS.
OH.
WHAT'S YOUR SPECIAL ABILITY?
THIS.
I'M STRONG. COMIC-BOOK-SUPERHERO STRONG. BUT THAT'S NOT ALL.

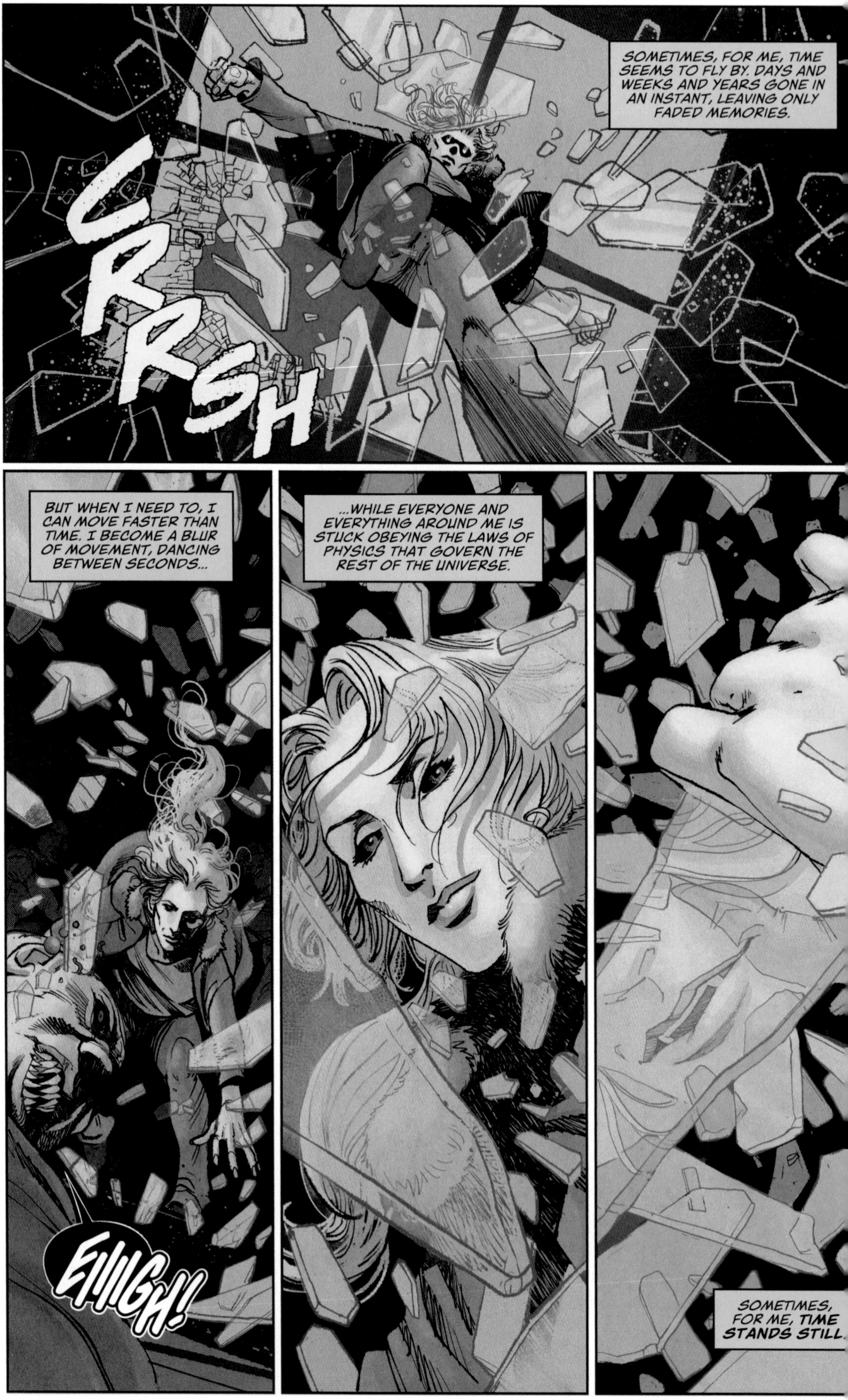

SOMETIMES, FOR ME, TIME SEEMS TO FLY BY. DAYS AND WEEKS AND YEARS GONE IN AN INSTANT, LEAVING ONLY FADED MEMORIES.
CRRSH
BUT WHEN I NEED TO, I CAN MOVE FASTER THAN TIME. I BECOME A BLUR OF MOVEMENT, DANCING BETWEEN SECONDS...
EIIIIGH!
...WHILE EVERYONE AND EVERYTHING AROUND ME IS STUCK OBEYING THE LAWS OF PHYSICS THAT GOVERN THE REST OF THE UNIVERSE.
SOMETIMES, FOR ME, TIME STANDS STILL.

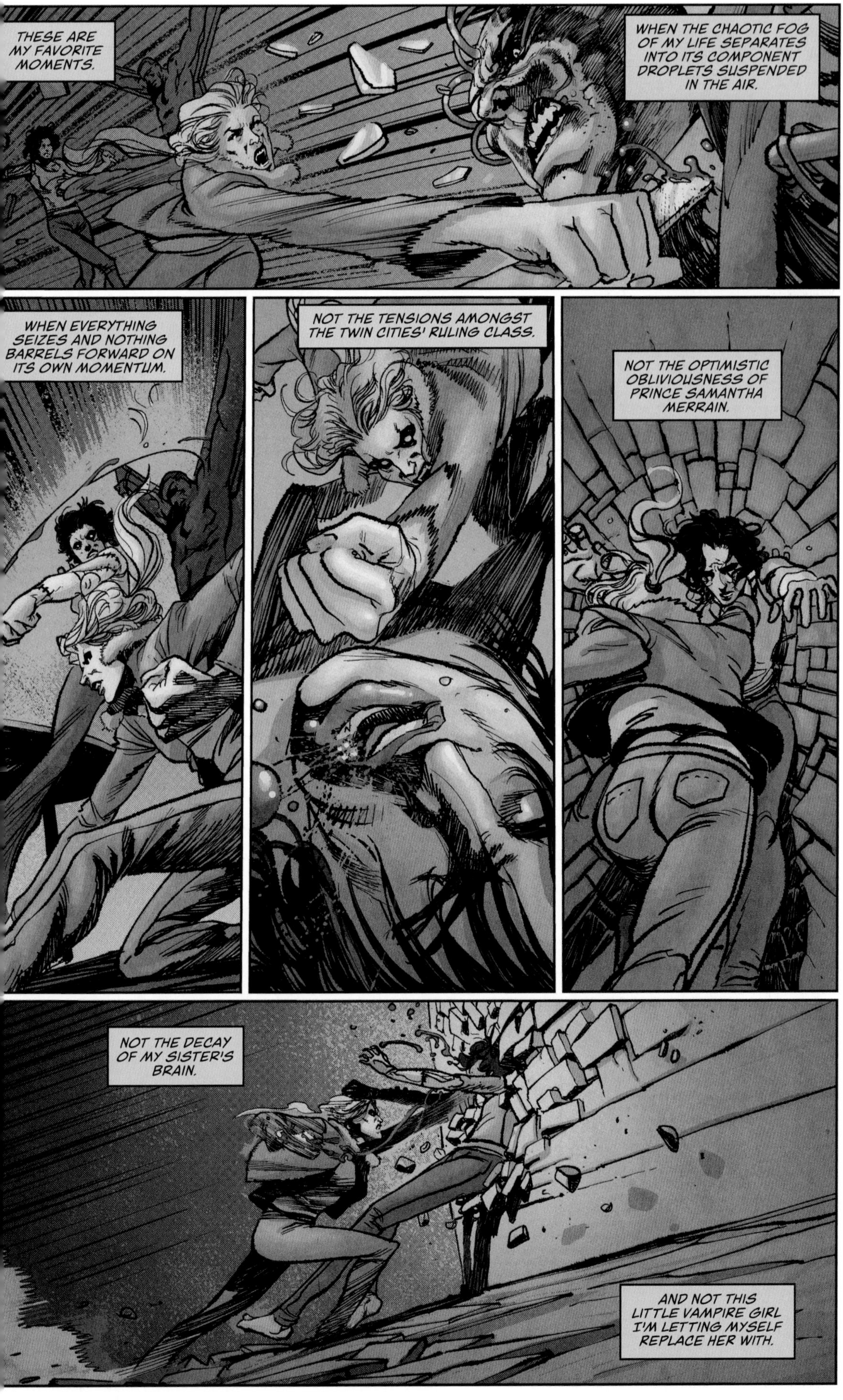
THESE ARE MY FAVORITE MOMENTS.
WHEN THE CHAOTIC FOG OF MY LIFE SEPARATES INTO ITS COMPONENT DROPLETS SUSPENDED IN THE AIR.
WHEN EVERYTHING SEIZES AND NOTHING BARRELS FORWARD ON ITS OWN MOMENTUM.
NOT THE TENSIONS AMONGST THE TWIN CITIES' RULING CLASS.
NOT THE OPTIMISTIC OBLIVIOUSNESS OF PRINCE SAMANTHA MERRAIN.
NOT THE DECAY OF MY SISTER'S BRAIN.
AND NOT THIS LITTLE VAMPIRE GIRL I'M LETTING MYSELF REPLACE HER WITH.

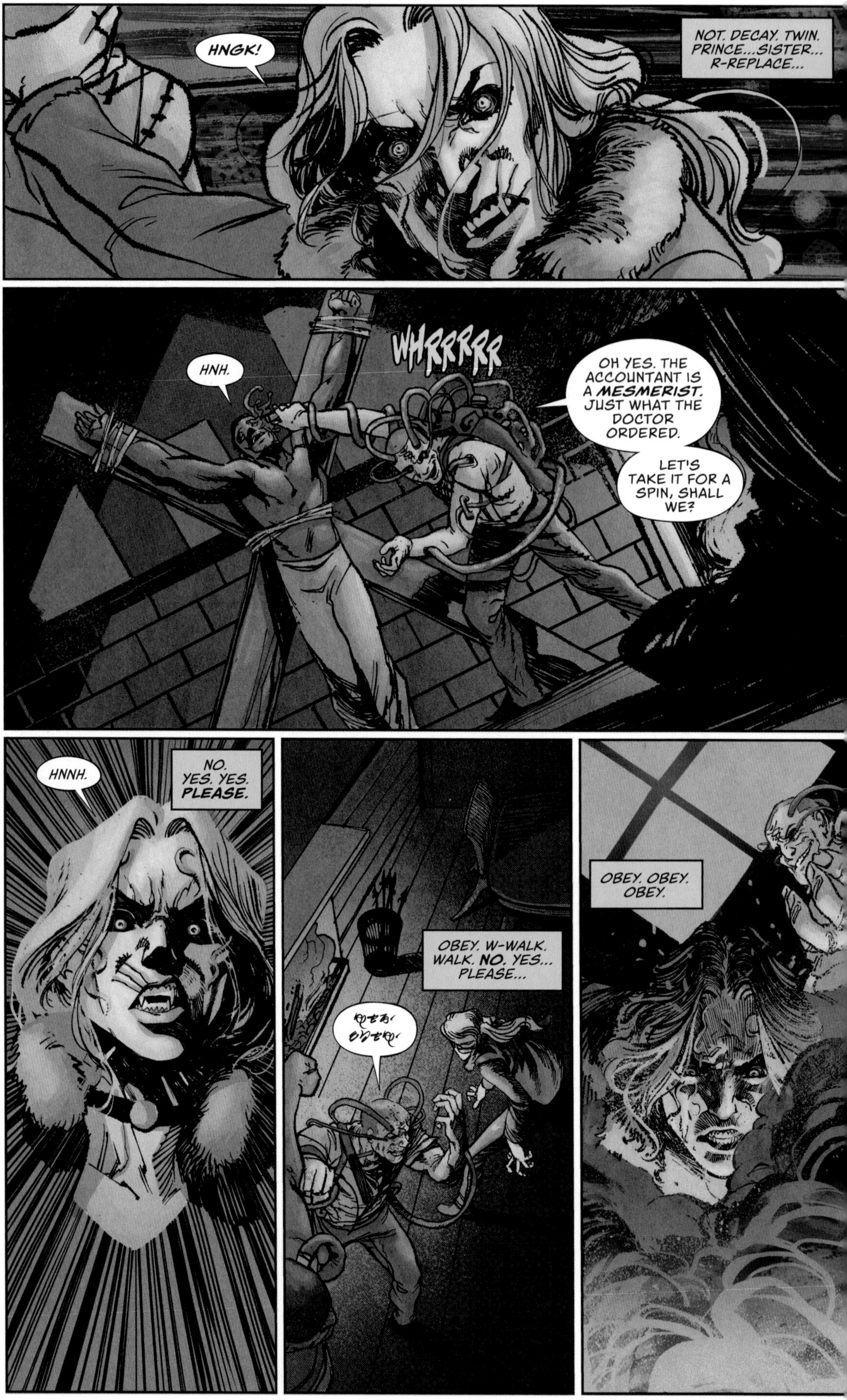
HNGK!
NOT. DECAY. TWIN. PRINCE...SISTER... R-REPLACE...
HNH.
WHRRRRR
OH YES. THE ACCOUNTANT IS A **MESMERIST.** JUST WHAT THE DOCTOR ORDERED.
LET'S TAKE IT FOR A SPIN, SHALL WE?
HNNH.
NO. YES. YES. **PLEASE.**
OBEY. W-WALK. WALK. **NO.** YES... PLEASE...
OBEY. OBEY. OBEY.

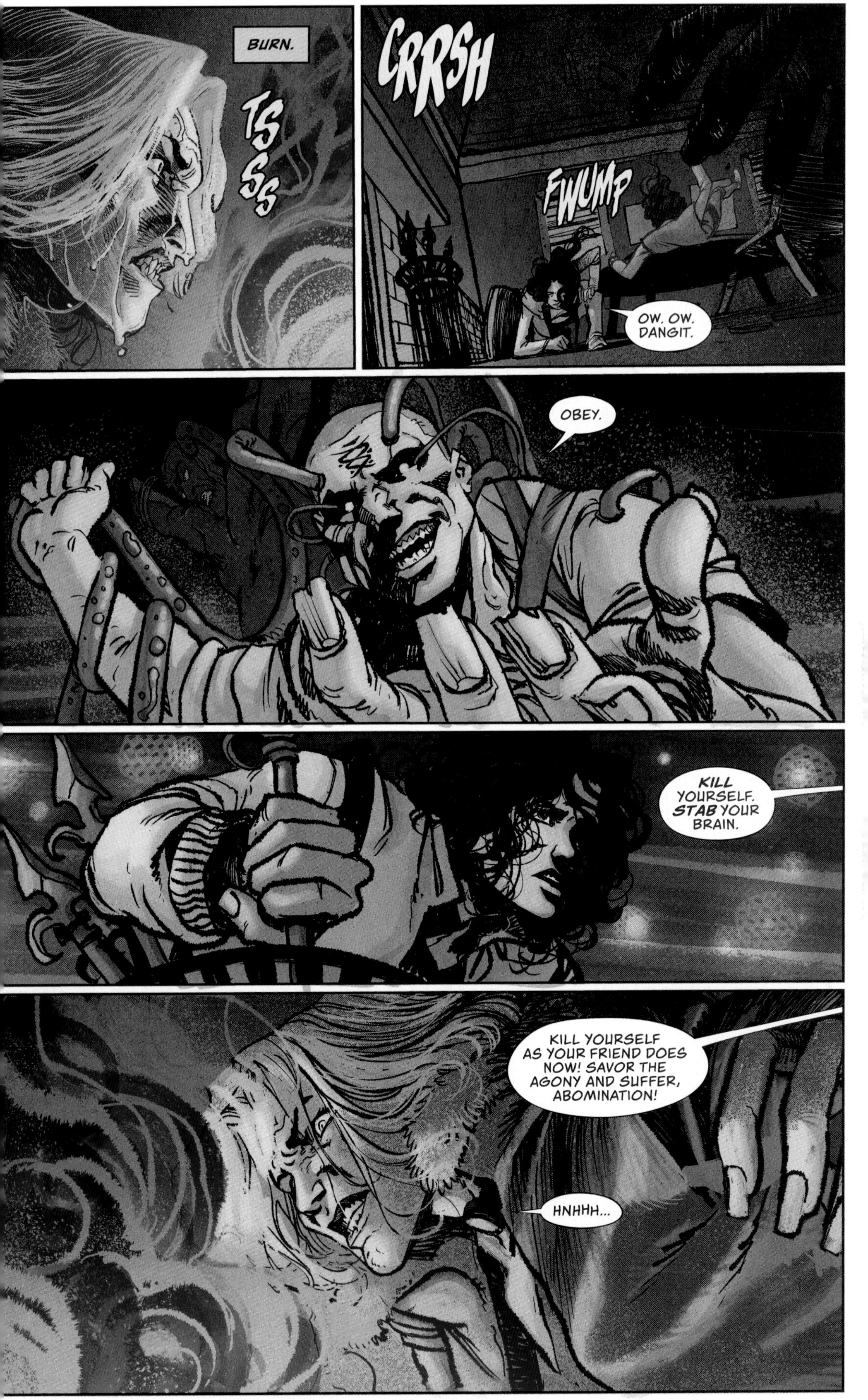

BURN.
TSSS
CRRSH
FWUMP
OW. OW. DANGIT.
OBEY.
KILL YOURSELF. STAB YOUR BRAIN.
KILL YOURSELF AS YOUR FRIEND DOES NOW! SAVOR THE AGONY AND SUFFER, ABOMINATION!
HNHHH...

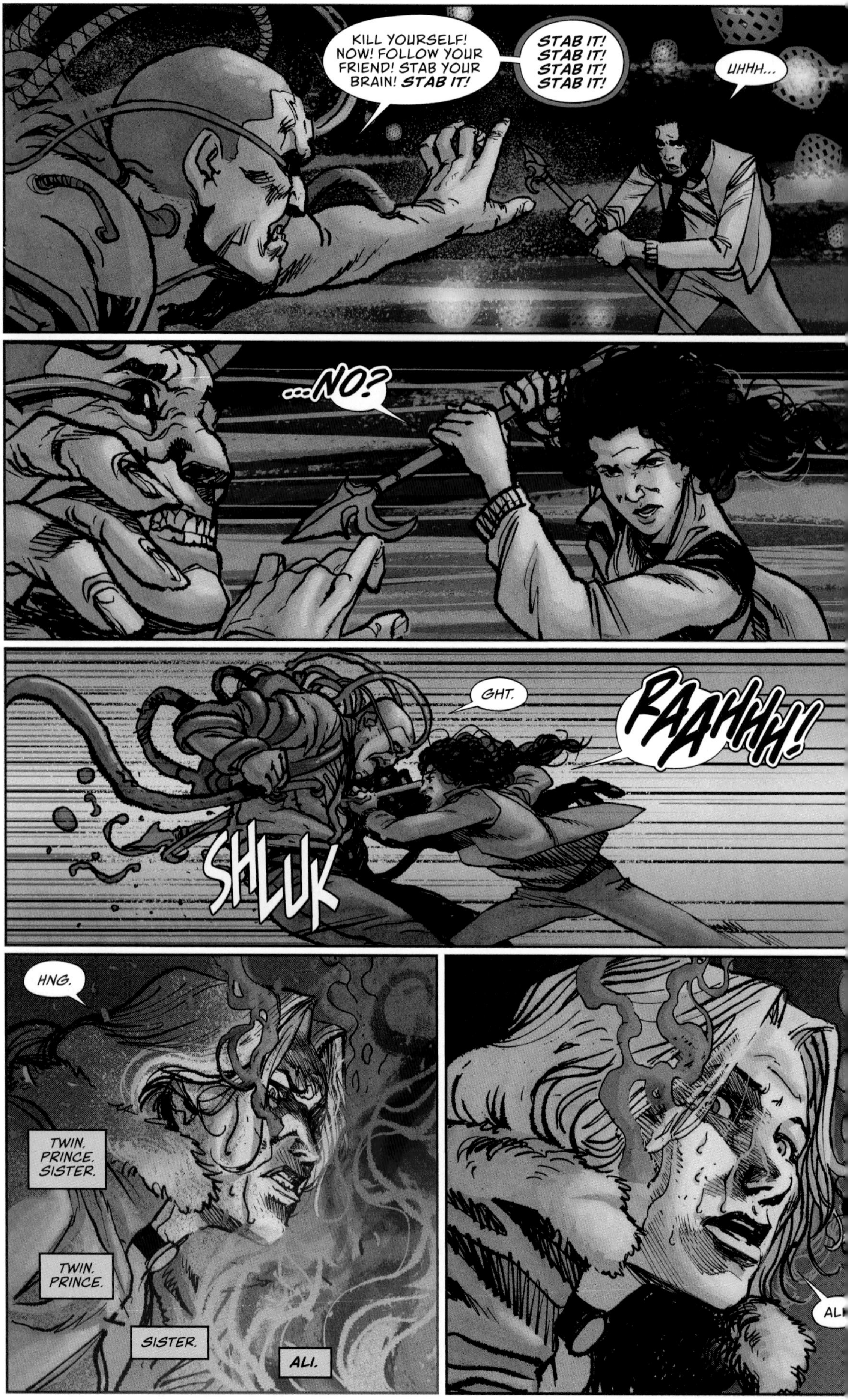
KILL YOURSELF! NOW! FOLLOW YOUR FRIEND! STAB YOUR BRAIN! STAB IT!
STAB IT! STAB IT! STAB IT! STAB IT!
UHHH...
...NO?
GHT.
RAAHHHH!
SHLUK
HNG.
TWIN. PRINCE. SISTER.
TWIN. PRINCE.
SISTER.
ALI.

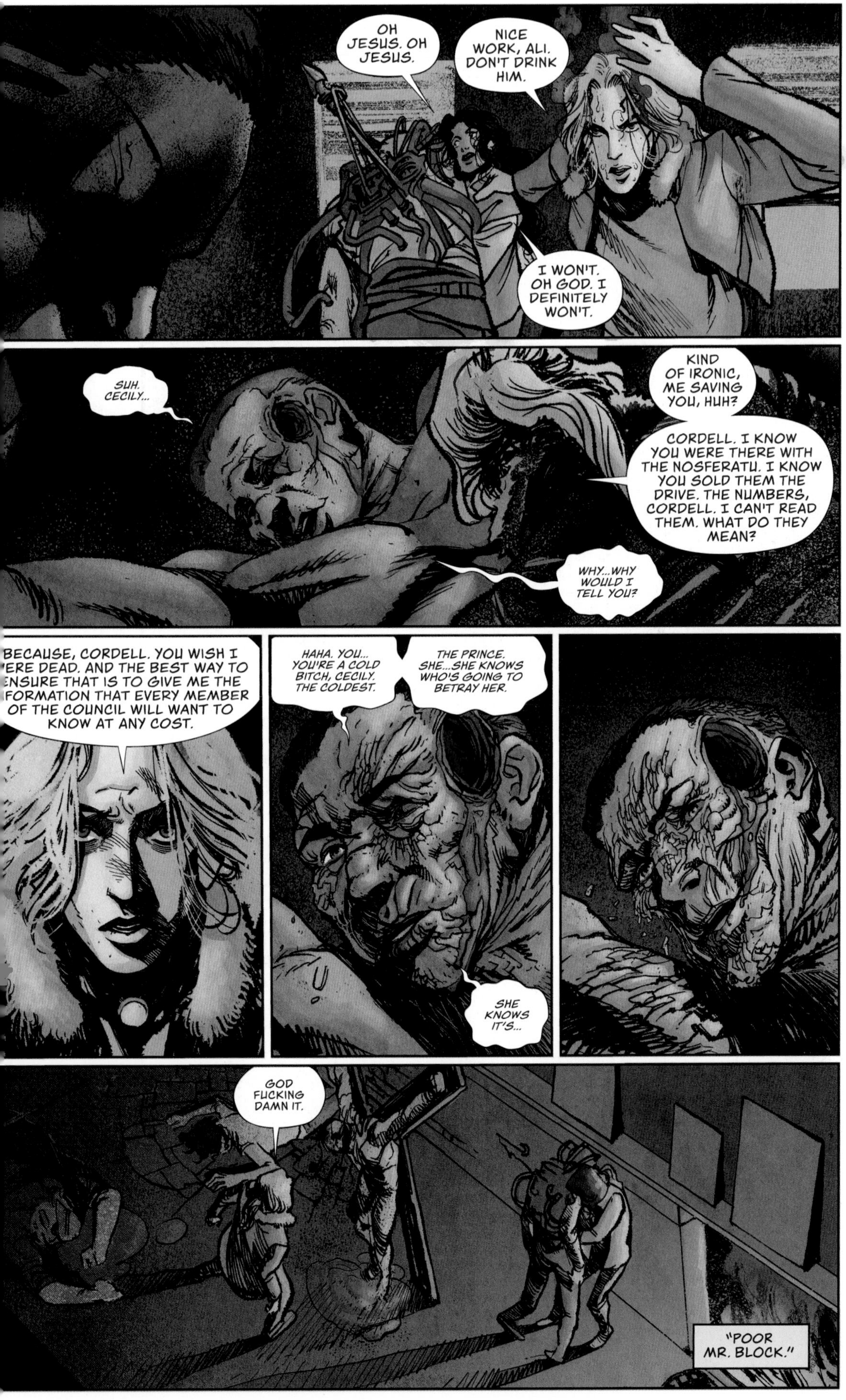
OH JESUS. OH JESUS.
NICE WORK, ALI. DON'T DRINK HIM.
I WON'T. OH GOD. I DEFINITELY WON'T.
SUH. CECILY...
KIND OF IRONIC, ME SAVING YOU, HUH?
CORDELL. I KNOW YOU WERE THERE WITH THE NOSFERATU. I KNOW YOU SOLD THEM THE DRIVE. THE NUMBERS, CORDELL. I CAN'T READ THEM. WHAT DO THEY MEAN?
WHY...WHY WOULD I TELL YOU?
BECAUSE, CORDELL. YOU WISH I ERE DEAD. AND THE BEST WAY TO NSURE THAT IS TO GIVE ME THE FORMATION THAT EVERY MEMBER OF THE COUNCIL WILL WANT TO KNOW AT ANY COST.
HAHA. YOU... YOU'RE A COLD BITCH, CECILY. THE COLDEST.
THE PRINCE. SHE...SHE KNOWS WHO'S GOING TO BETRAY HER.
SHE KNOWS IT'S...
GOD FUCKING DAMN IT.
"POOR MR. BLOCK."

GALTIER TOWERS.
SAINT PAUL.

FIRST HIS GIRLFRIEND, THEN HE'S UNLUCKY ENOUGH TO WALK BY SOME BODY HACKERS WHILE THEY'RE KNEE DEEP IN SEWER RAT.

EVEN WORSE, WE NEED TO FIND A **NEW ACCOUNTANT.**

THIS IS JUST THE KIND OF SECURITY ISSUE THE COUNCIL WOULD LOVE TO POUNCE ON AS A REASON TO SPLIT THE CITIES INTO TWO PRINCEDOMS.

I WATCH **PRIMOGEN WENDT** NONCHALANTLY SWIRL HIS FINGER IN THE BLOOD IN HIS THERMOS.

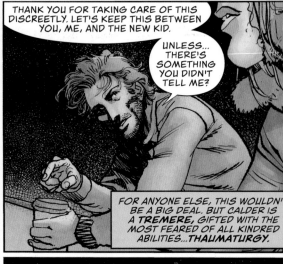

THANK YOU FOR TAKING CARE OF THIS DISCREETLY. LET'S KEEP THIS BETWEEN YOU, ME, AND THE NEW KID.

UNLESS... THERE'S SOMETHING YOU DIDN'T TELL ME?

FOR ANYONE ELSE, THIS WOULDN'T BE A BIG DEAL. BUT CALDER IS A **TREMERE,** GIFTED WITH THE MOST FEARED OF ALL KINDRED ABILITIES...**THAUMATURGY.**

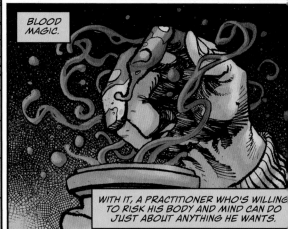

BLOOD MAGIC.

WITH IT, A PRACTITIONER WHO'S WILLING TO RISK HIS BODY AND MIND CAN DO JUST ABOUT ANYTHING HE WANTS.

HE CAN WARP FLESH AND SOULS. HE CAN MAKE A LIE INTO BELIEF. HE CAN OBSCURE THE TRUTH IN A RED SHROUD.

HE CAN PULL BACK THAT SHROUD AND REVEAL TRUTH.

I THINK OF ALI, A LOST CAITIFF I TOOK IN, BUT SAID WAS MY OWN CREATION. ALI, MY BIG LIE. MY OWN RED SHROUD.

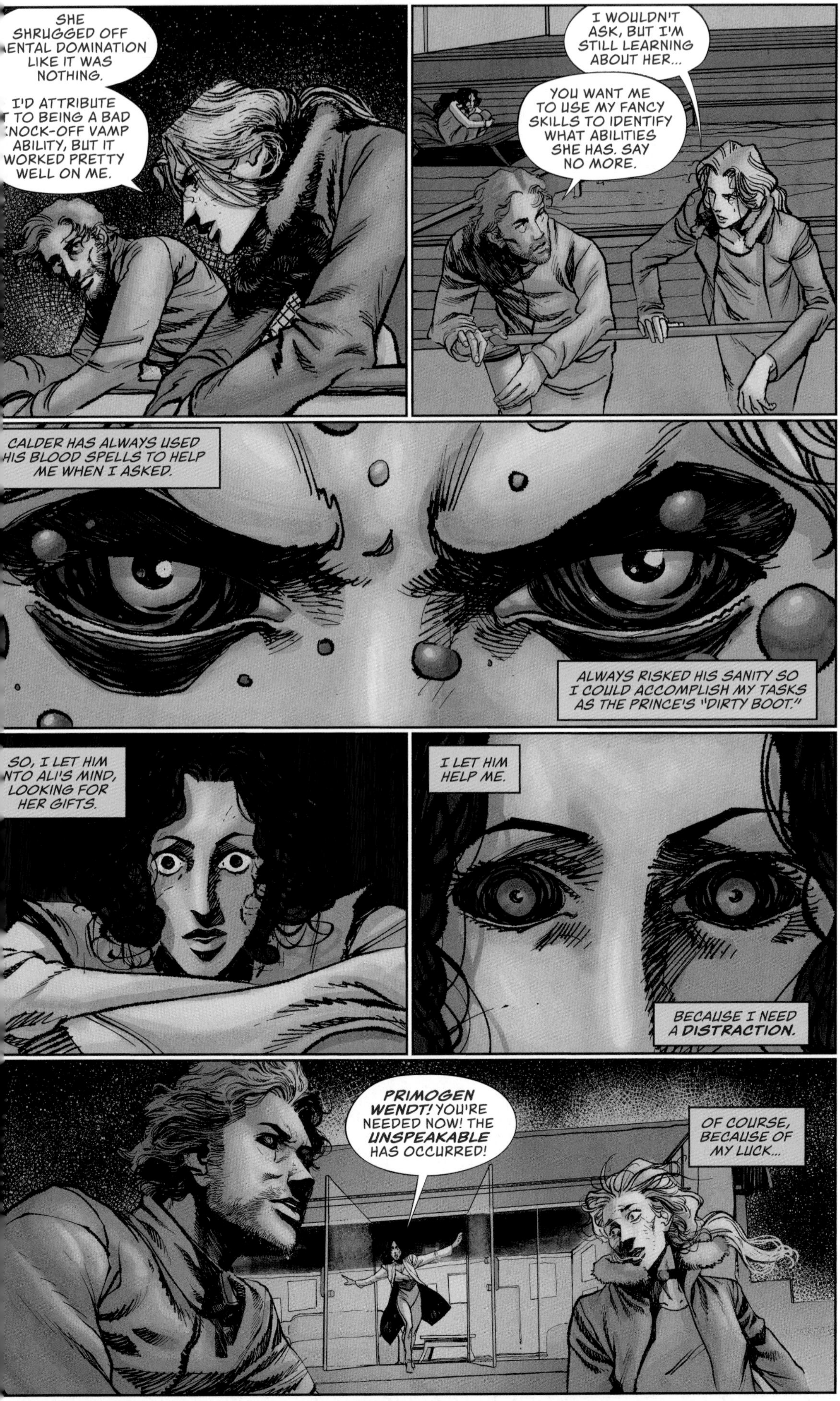
SHE SHRUGGED OFF MENTAL DOMINATION LIKE IT WAS NOTHING.
I'D ATTRIBUTE IT TO BEING A BAD KNOCK-OFF VAMP ABILITY, BUT IT WORKED PRETTY WELL ON ME.
I WOULDN'T ASK, BUT I'M STILL LEARNING ABOUT HER...
YOU WANT ME TO USE MY FANCY SKILLS TO IDENTIFY WHAT ABILITIES SHE HAS. SAY NO MORE.
CALDER HAS ALWAYS USED HIS BLOOD SPELLS TO HELP ME WHEN I ASKED.
ALWAYS RISKED HIS SANITY SO I COULD ACCOMPLISH MY TASKS AS THE PRINCE'S "DIRTY BOOT."
SO, I LET HIM INTO ALI'S MIND, LOOKING FOR HER GIFTS.
I LET HIM HELP ME.
BECAUSE I NEED A DISTRACTION.
PRIMOGEN WENDT! YOU'RE NEEDED NOW! THE UNSPEAKABLE HAS OCCURRED!
OF COURSE, BECAUSE OF MY LUCK...

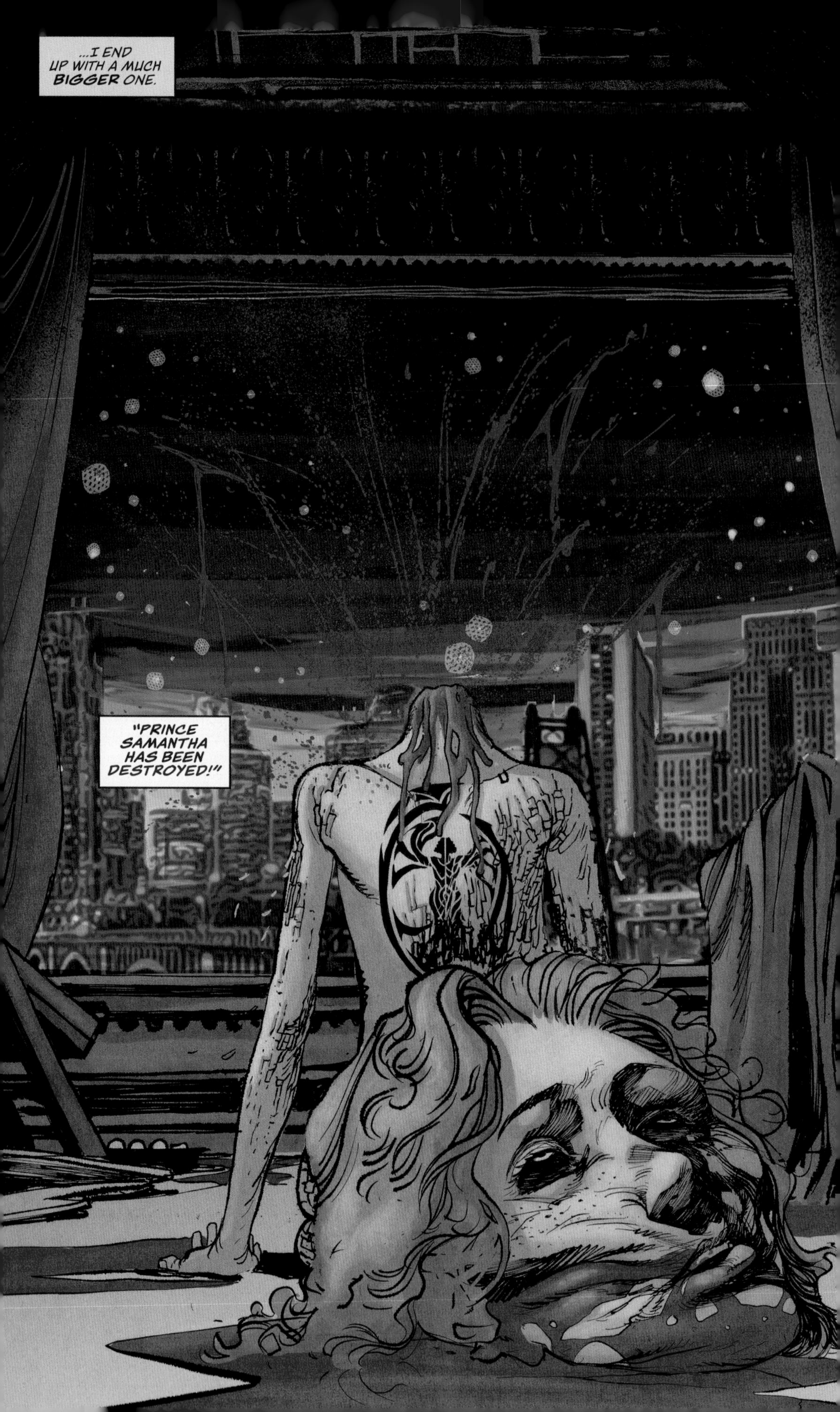
...I END UP WITH A MUCH BIGGER ONE.
"PRINCE SAMANTHA HAS BEEN DESTROYED!"

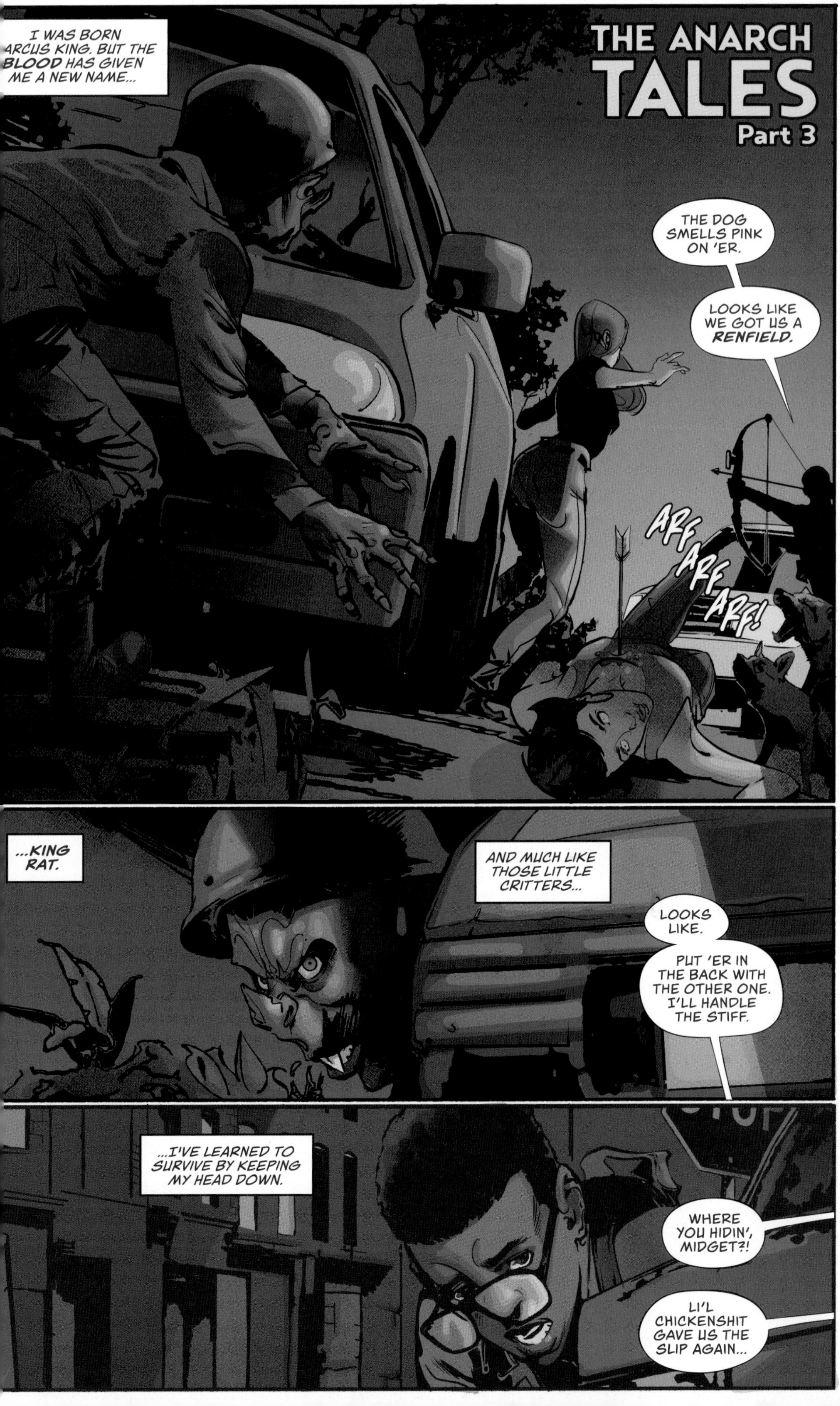
I WAS BORN ARCUS KING. BUT THE BLOOD HAS GIVEN ME A NEW NAME...
THE ANARCH TALES Part 3
THE DOG SMELLS PINK ON 'ER.
LOOKS LIKE WE GOT US A RENFIELD.
ARF ARF ARF!
...KING RAT.
AND MUCH LIKE THOSE LITTLE CRITTERS...
LOOKS LIKE.
PUT 'ER IN THE BACK WITH THE OTHER ONE. I'LL HANDLE THE STIFF.
...I'VE LEARNED TO SURVIVE BY KEEPING MY HEAD DOWN.
WHERE YOU HIDIN', MIDGET?!
LI'L CHICKENSHIT GAVE US THE SLIP AGAIN...

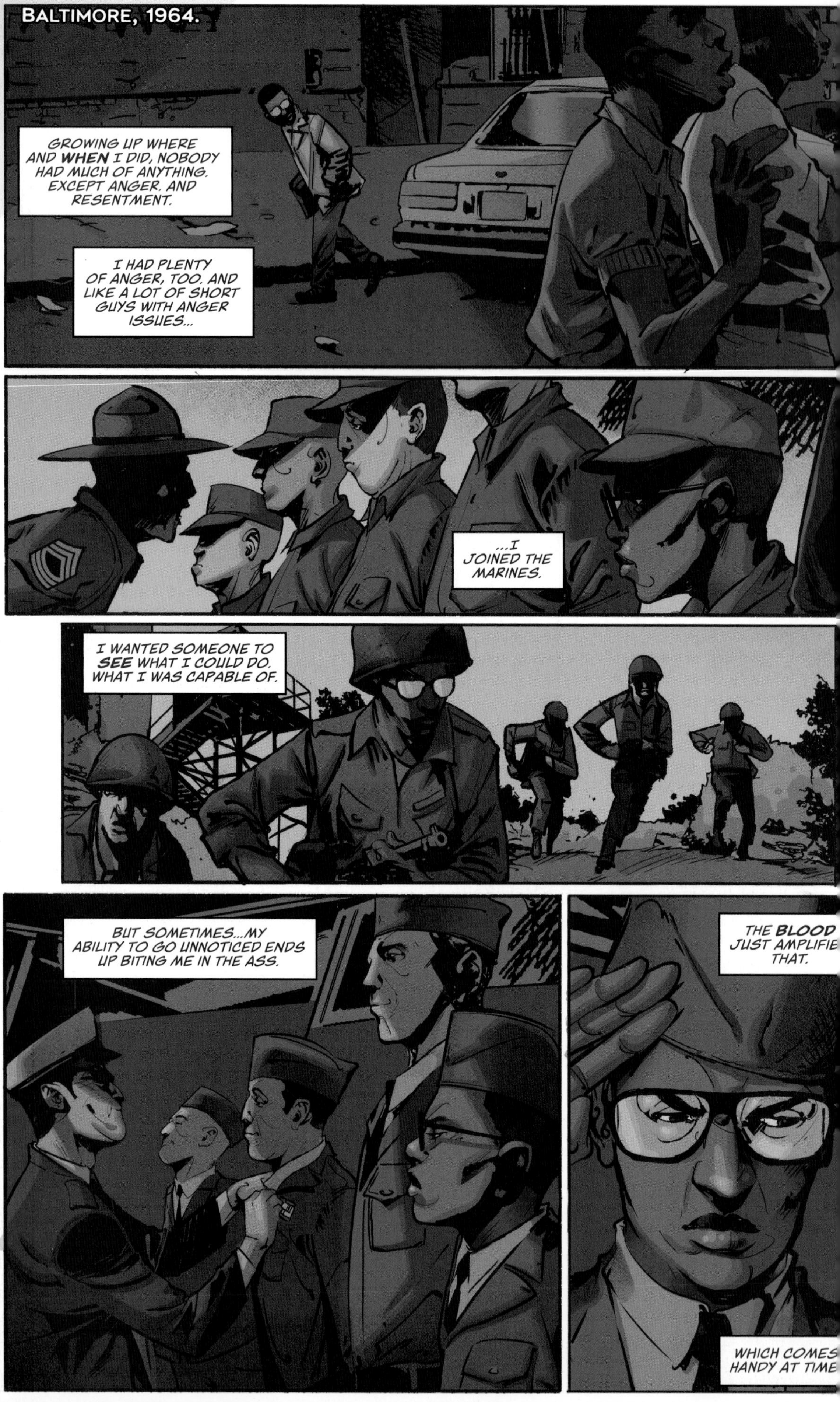
BALTIMORE, 1964.
GROWING UP WHERE AND WHEN I DID, NOBODY HAD MUCH OF ANYTHING. EXCEPT ANGER. AND RESENTMENT.
I HAD PLENTY OF ANGER, TOO. AND LIKE A LOT OF SHORT GUYS WITH ANGER ISSUES...
...I JOINED THE MARINES.
I WANTED SOMEONE TO SEE WHAT I COULD DO. WHAT I WAS CAPABLE OF.
BUT SOMETIMES...MY ABILITY TO GO UNNOTICED ENDS UP BITING ME IN THE ASS.
THE BLOOD JUST AMPLIFIE THAT.
WHICH COMES HANDY AT TIME

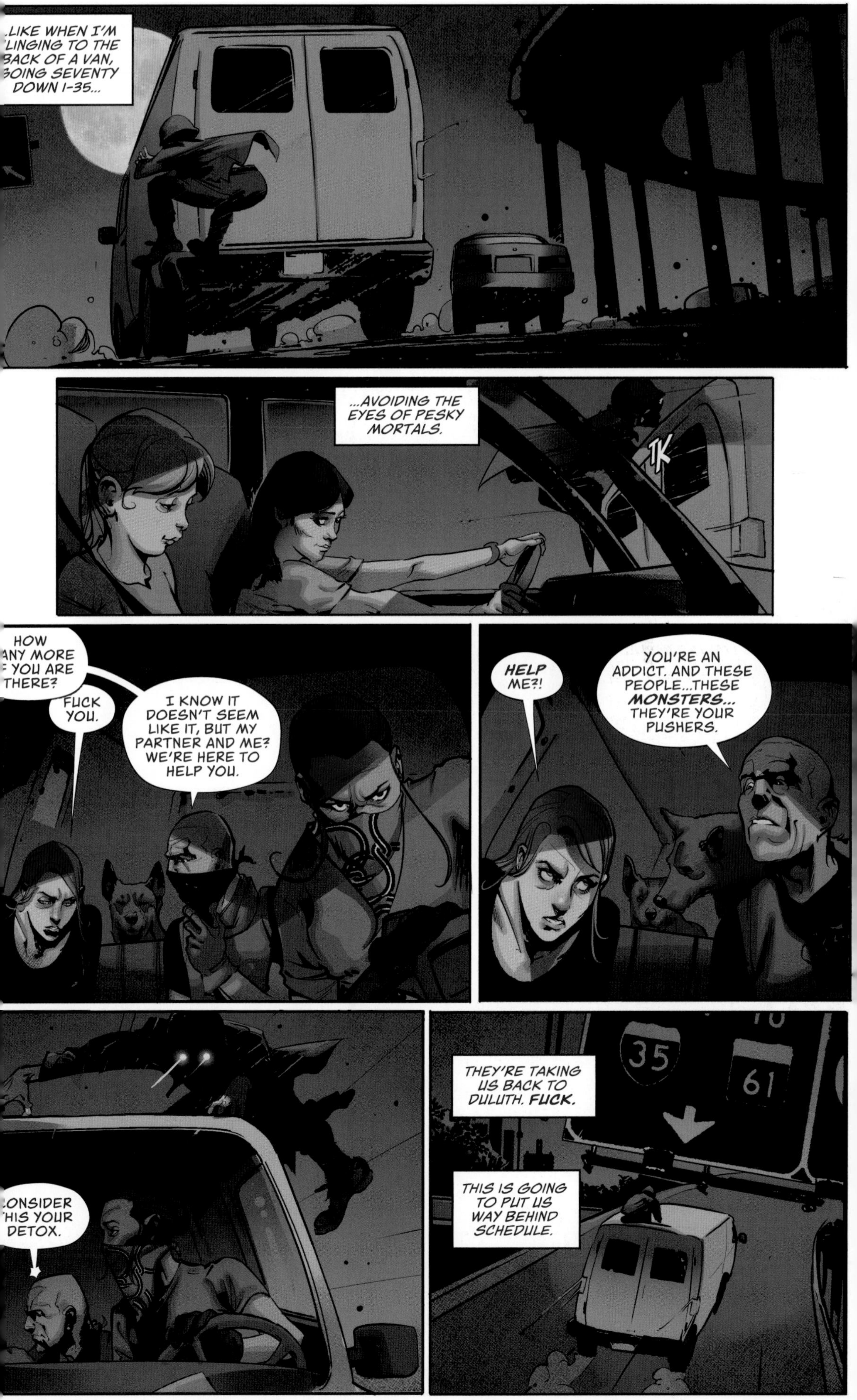
...LIKE WHEN I'M CLINGING TO THE BACK OF A VAN, GOING SEVENTY DOWN I-35...
...AVOIDING THE EYES OF PESKY MORTALS.
TK
HOW MANY MORE OF YOU ARE THERE?
FUCK YOU.
I KNOW IT DOESN'T SEEM LIKE IT, BUT MY PARTNER AND ME? WE'RE HERE TO HELP YOU.
HELP ME?!
YOU'RE AN ADDICT. AND THESE PEOPLE...THESE MONSTERS... THEY'RE YOUR PUSHERS.
CONSIDER THIS YOUR DETOX.
35
61
THEY'RE TAKING US BACK TO DULUTH. FUCK.
THIS IS GOING TO PUT US WAY BEHIND SCHEDULE.

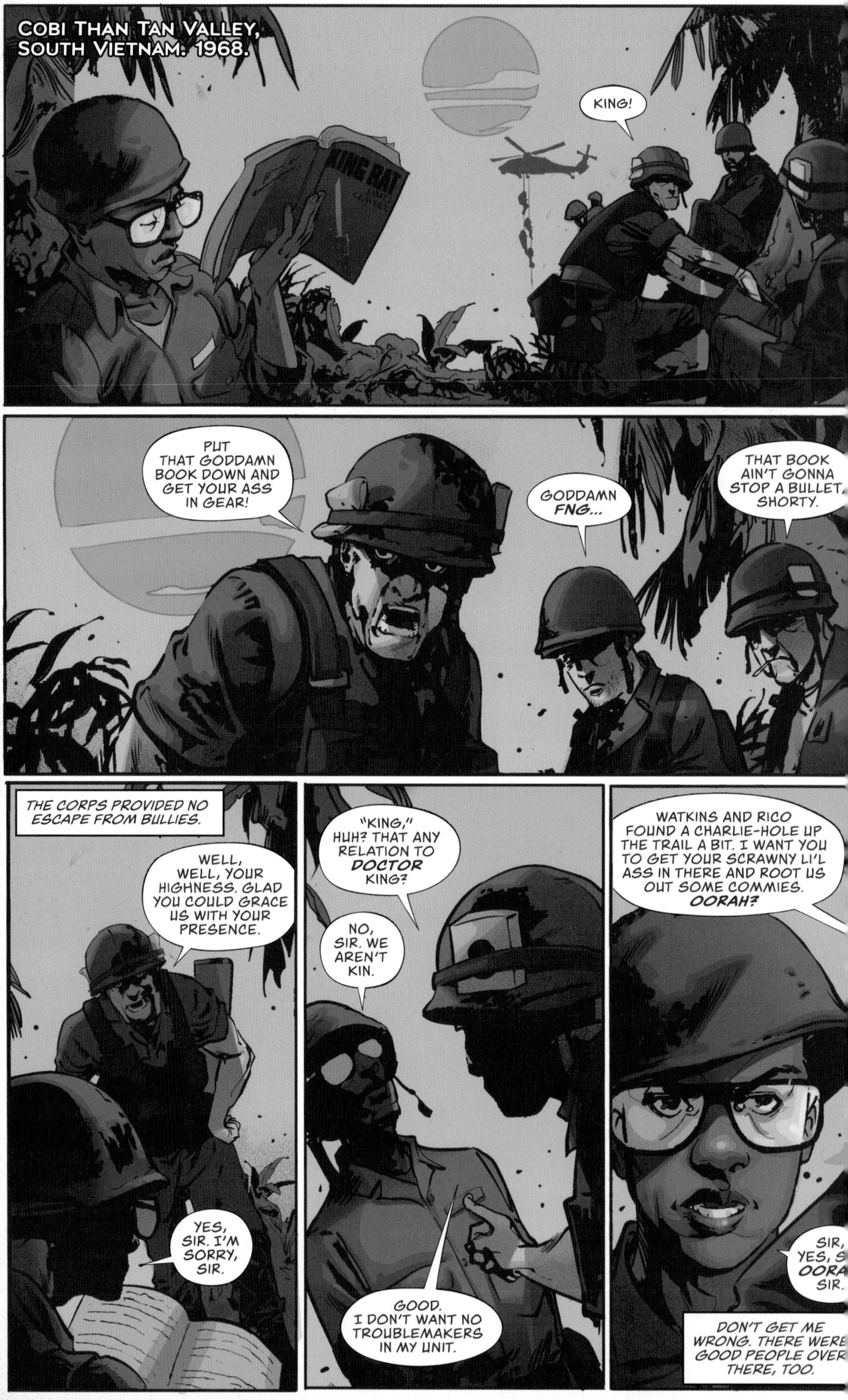
COBI THAN TAN VALLEY, SOUTH VIETNAM. 1968.
KING RAT
KING!
PUT THAT GODDAMN BOOK DOWN AND GET YOUR ASS IN GEAR!
GODDAMN FNG...
THAT BOOK AIN'T GONNA STOP A BULLET, SHORTY.
THE CORPS PROVIDED NO ESCAPE FROM BULLIES.
WELL, WELL, YOUR HIGHNESS. GLAD YOU COULD GRACE US WITH YOUR PRESENCE.
YES, SIR. I'M SORRY, SIR.
"KING," HUH? THAT ANY RELATION TO DOCTOR KING?
NO, SIR. WE AREN'T KIN.
GOOD. I DON'T WANT NO TROUBLEMAKERS IN MY UNIT.
WATKINS AND RICO FOUND A CHARLIE-HOLE UP THE TRAIL A BIT. I WANT YOU TO GET YOUR SCRAWNY LI'L ASS IN THERE AND ROOT US OUT SOME COMMIES. OORAH?
SIR, YES, S OORA SIR.
DON'T GET ME WRONG. THERE WERE GOOD PEOPLE OVER THERE, TOO.

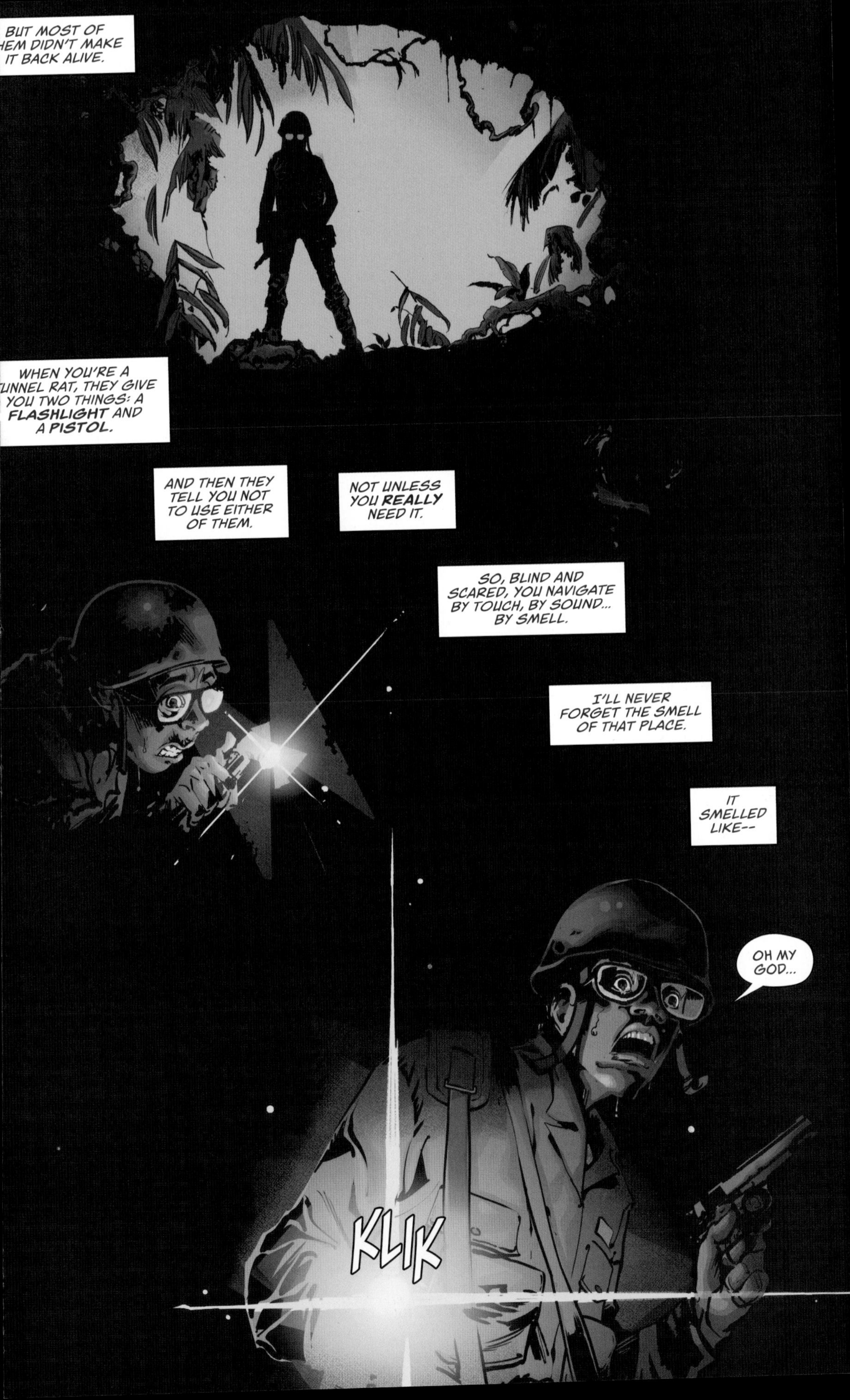
BUT MOST OF
HEM DIDN'T MAKE
IT BACK ALIVE.
WHEN YOU'RE A
UNNEL RAT, THEY GIVE
YOU TWO THINGS: A
FLASHLIGHT AND
A PISTOL.
AND THEN THEY
TELL YOU NOT
TO USE EITHER
OF THEM.
NOT UNLESS
YOU REALLY
NEED IT.
SO, BLIND AND
SCARED, YOU NAVIGATE
BY TOUCH, BY SOUND...
BY SMELL.
I'LL NEVER
FORGET THE SMELL
OF THAT PLACE.
IT
SMELLED
LIKE--
OH MY
GOD...
KLIK

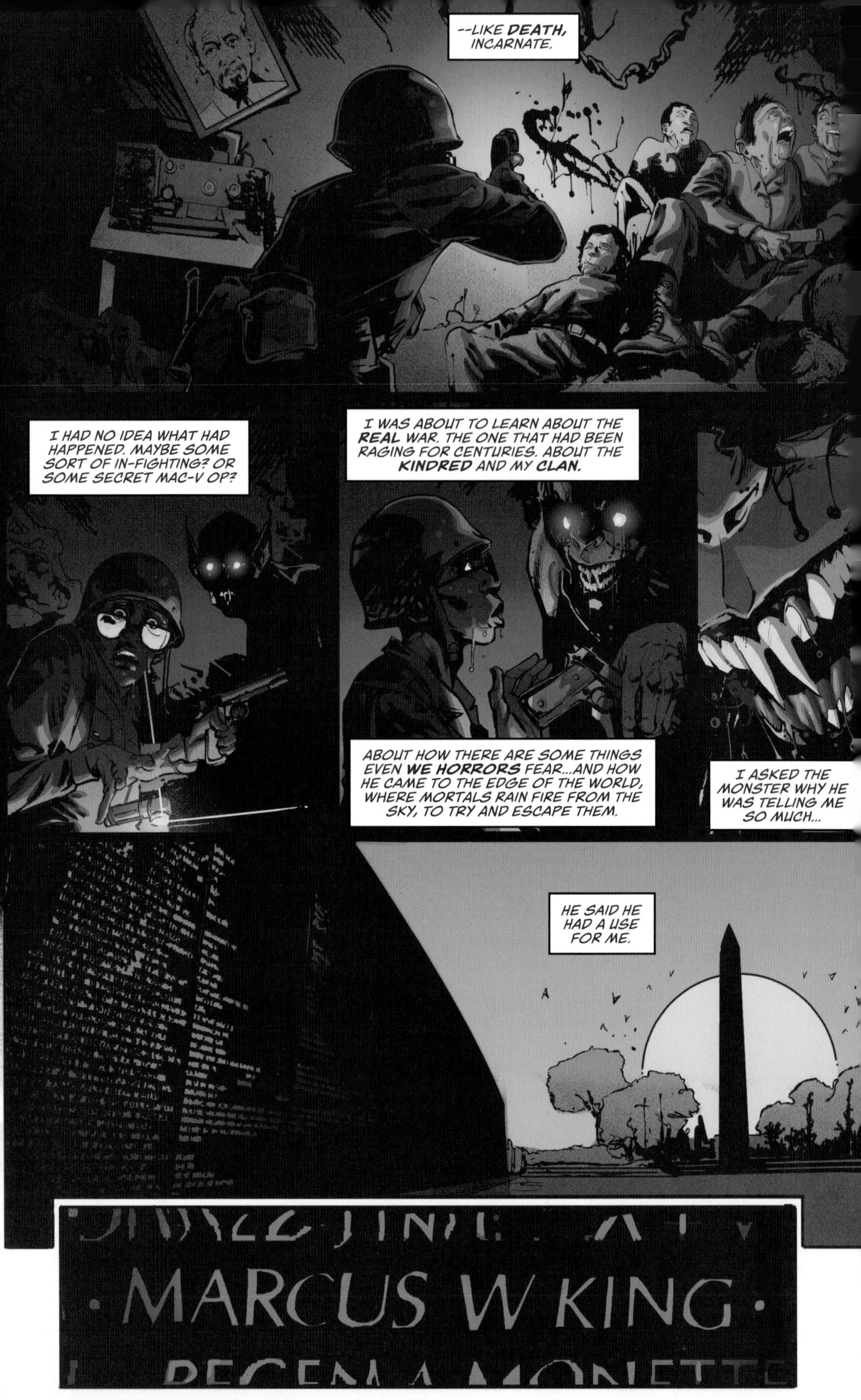
--LIKE DEATH, INCARNATE.
I HAD NO IDEA WHAT HAD HAPPENED. MAYBE SOME SORT OF IN-FIGHTING? OR SOME SECRET MAC-V OP?
I WAS ABOUT TO LEARN ABOUT THE REAL WAR. THE ONE THAT HAD BEEN RAGING FOR CENTURIES. ABOUT THE KINDRED AND MY CLAN.
ABOUT HOW THERE ARE SOME THINGS EVEN WE HORRORS FEAR...AND HOW HE CAME TO THE EDGE OF THE WORLD, WHERE MORTALS RAIN FIRE FROM THE SKY, TO TRY AND ESCAPE THEM.
I ASKED THE MONSTER WHY HE WAS TELLING ME SO MUCH...
HE SAID HE HAD A USE FOR ME.
MARCUS W KING

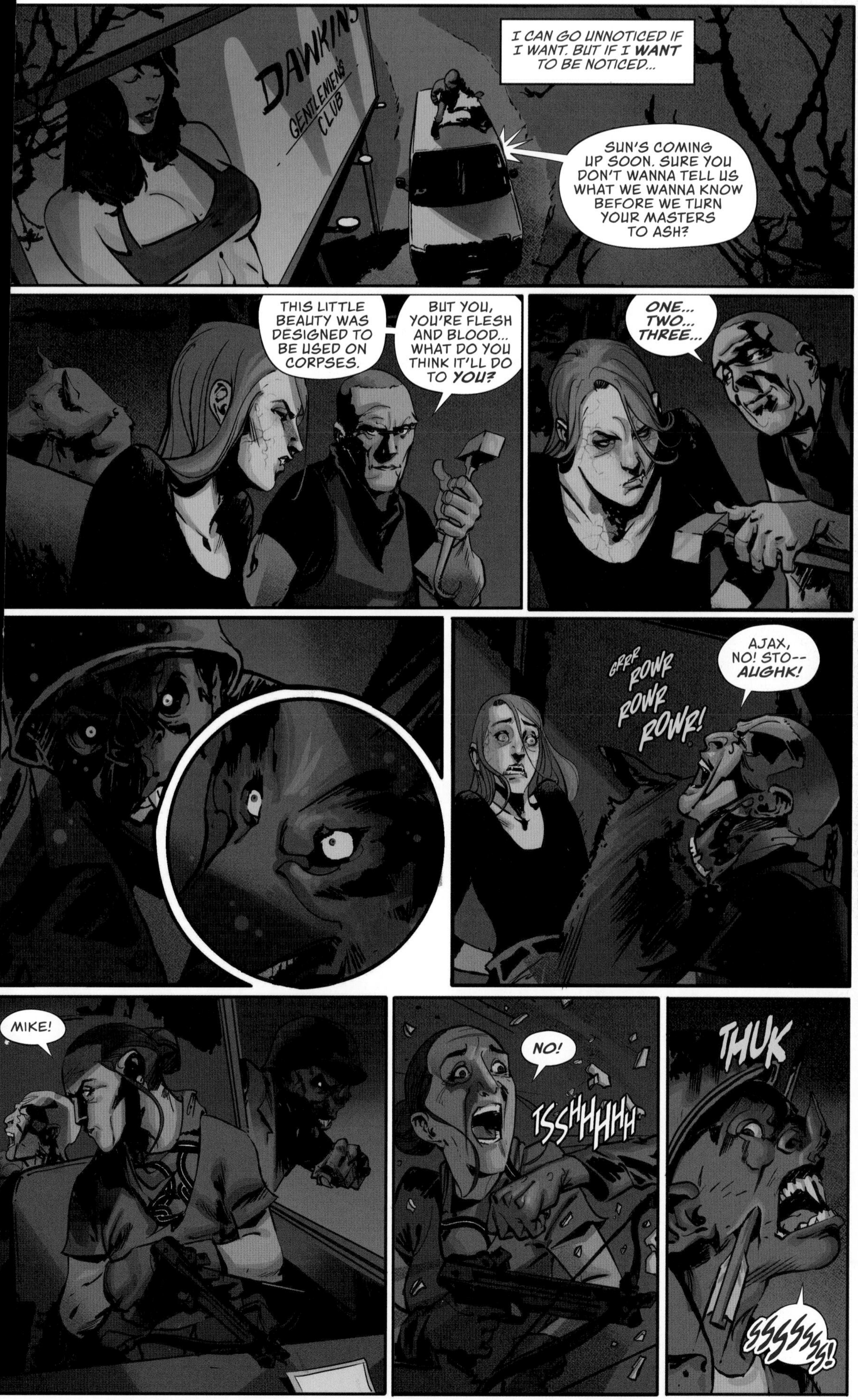
DAWKINS GENTLEMENS CLUB
I CAN GO UNNOTICED IF I WANT. BUT IF I WANT TO BE NOTICED...
SUN'S COMING UP SOON. SURE YOU DON'T WANNA TELL US WHAT WE WANNA KNOW BEFORE WE TURN YOUR MASTERS TO ASH?
THIS LITTLE BEAUTY WAS DESIGNED TO BE USED ON CORPSES.
BUT YOU, YOU'RE FLESH AND BLOOD... WHAT DO YOU THINK IT'LL DO TO YOU?
ONE... TWO... THREE...
GRRR ROWR ROWR ROWR!
AJAX, NO! STO-- AUGHK!
MIKE!
NO!
TSSHHHHH
THUK
SSSSSSS!

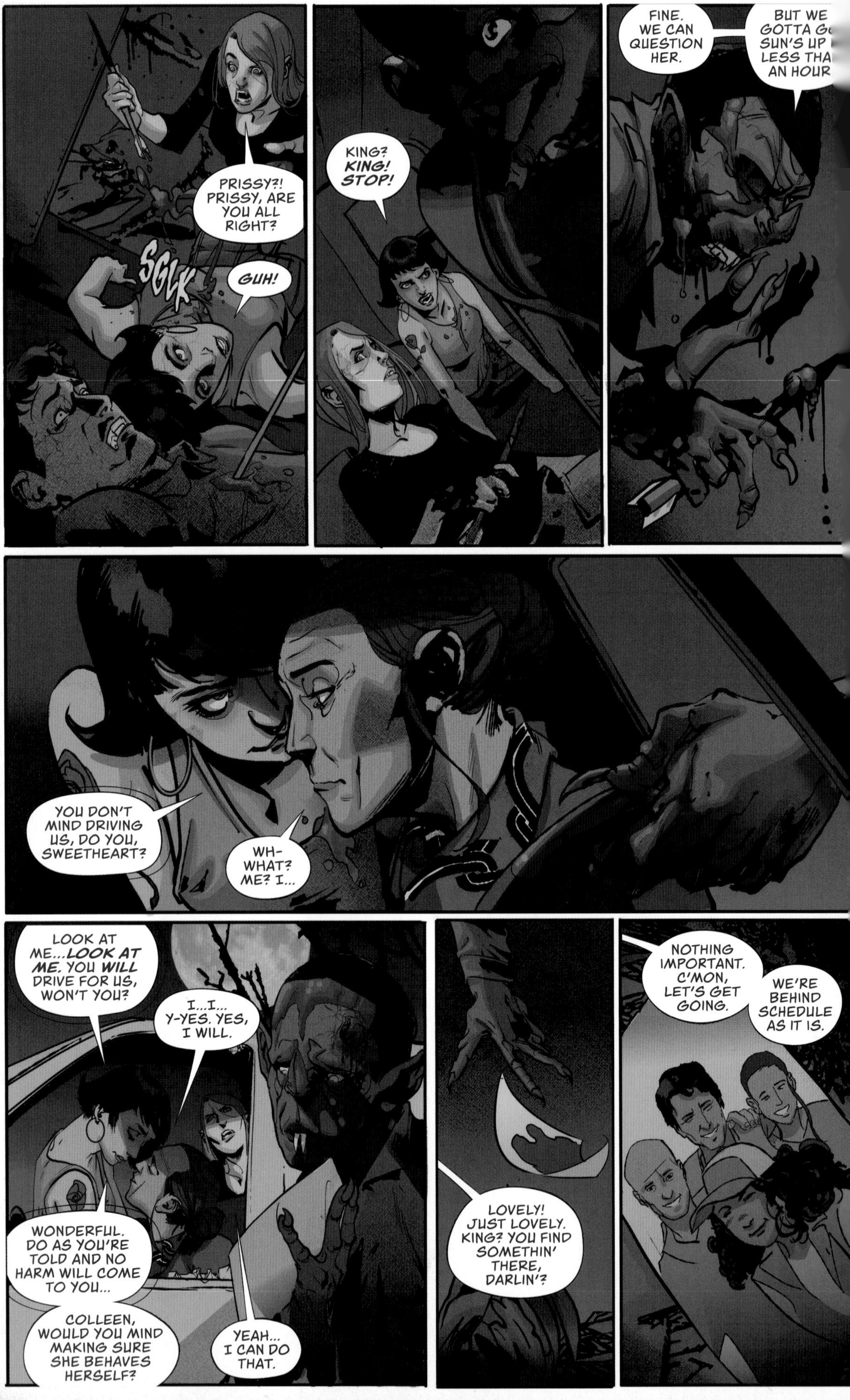
PRISSY?! PRISSY, ARE YOU ALL RIGHT?
SGLK
GUH!
KING? KING! STOP!
FINE. WE CAN QUESTION HER.
BUT WE GOTTA G SUN'S UP LESS THA AN HOUR
YOU DON'T MIND DRIVING US, DO YOU, SWEETHEART?
WH- WHAT? ME? I...
LOOK AT ME... LOOK AT ME. YOU WILL DRIVE FOR US, WON'T YOU?
I...I... Y-YES. YES, I WILL.
WONDERFUL. DO AS YOU'RE TOLD AND NO HARM WILL COME TO YOU...
COLLEEN, WOULD YOU MIND MAKING SURE SHE BEHAVES HERSELF?
YEAH... I CAN DO THAT.
LOVELY! JUST LOVELY. KING? YOU FIND SOMETHIN' THERE, DARLIN'?
NOTHING IMPORTANT. C'MON, LET'S GET GOING.
WE'RE BEHIND SCHEDULE AS IT IS.

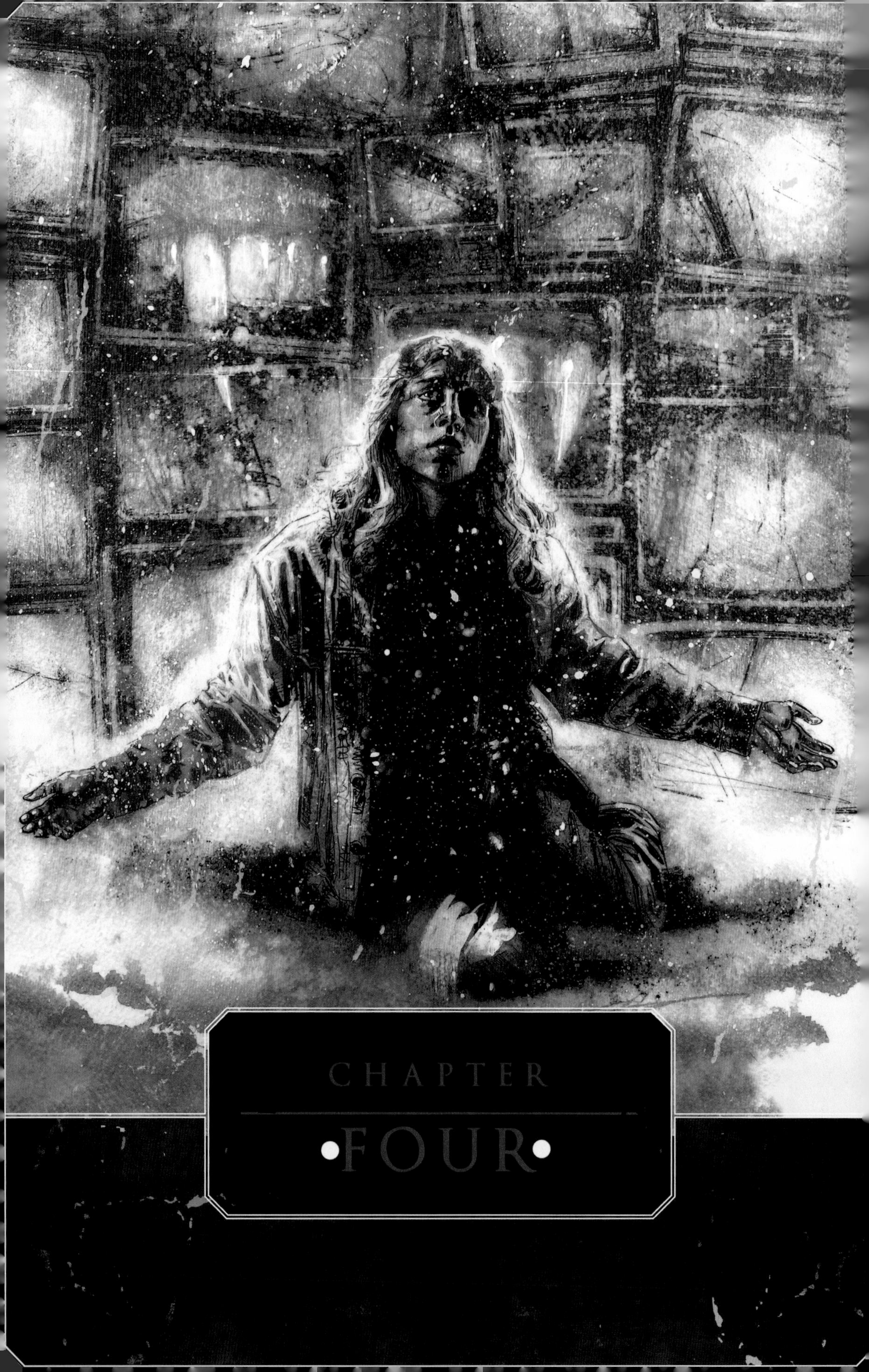

CHAPTER FOUR

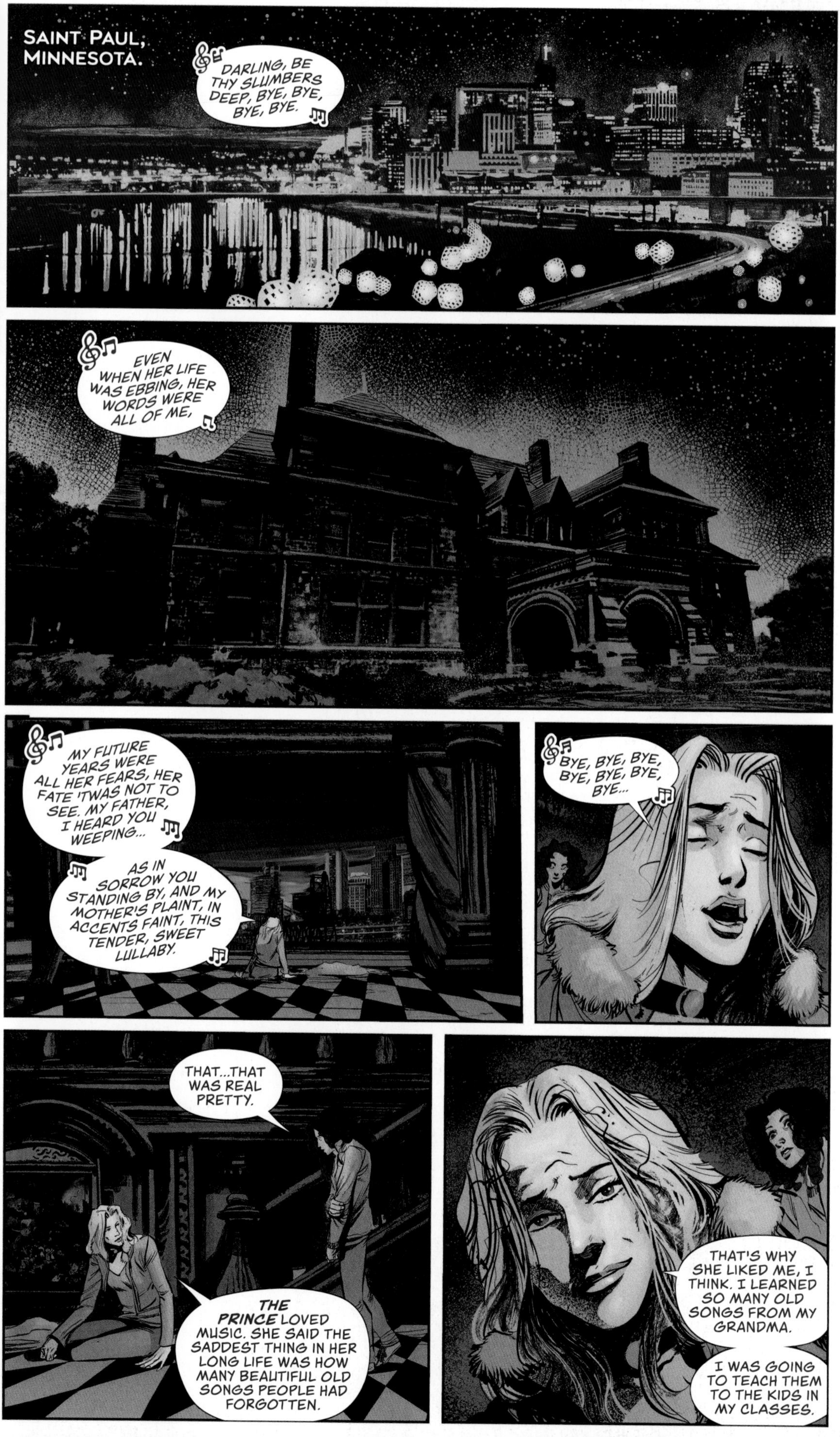
SAINT PAUL, MINNESOTA.
DARLING, BE THY SLUMBERS DEEP, BYE, BYE, BYE, BYE.
EVEN WHEN HER LIFE WAS EBBING, HER WORDS WERE ALL OF ME,
MY FUTURE YEARS WERE ALL HER FEARS, HER FATE 'TWAS NOT TO SEE. MY FATHER, I HEARD YOU WEEPING...
AS IN SORROW YOU STANDING BY, AND MY MOTHER'S PLAINT, IN ACCENTS FAINT, THIS TENDER, SWEET LULLABY.
BYE, BYE, BYE, BYE, BYE, BYE, BYE...
THAT...THAT WAS REAL PRETTY.
THE PRINCE LOVED MUSIC. SHE SAID THE SADDEST THING IN HER LONG LIFE WAS HOW MANY BEAUTIFUL OLD SONGS PEOPLE HAD FORGOTTEN.
THAT'S WHY SHE LIKED ME, I THINK. I LEARNED SO MANY OLD SONGS FROM MY GRANDMA.
I WAS GOING TO TEACH THEM TO THE KIDS IN MY CLASSES.

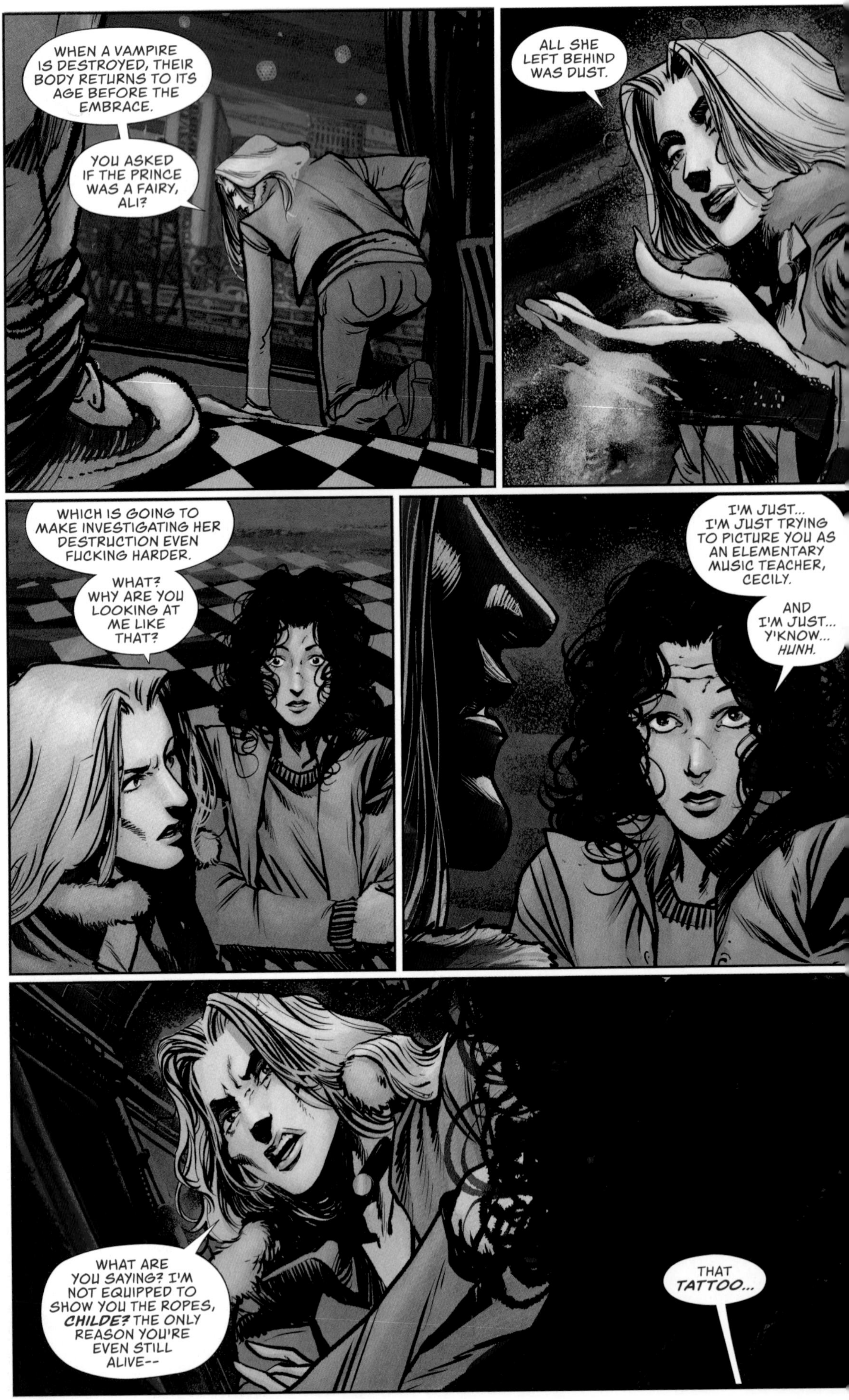
WHEN A VAMPIRE IS DESTROYED, THEIR BODY RETURNS TO ITS AGE BEFORE THE EMBRACE.
YOU ASKED IF THE PRINCE WAS A FAIRY, ALI?
ALL SHE LEFT BEHIND WAS DUST.
WHICH IS GOING TO MAKE INVESTIGATING HER DESTRUCTION EVEN FUCKING HARDER.
WHAT? WHY ARE YOU LOOKING AT ME LIKE THAT?
I'M JUST... I'M JUST TRYING TO PICTURE YOU AS AN ELEMENTARY MUSIC TEACHER, CECILY.
AND I'M JUST... Y'KNOW... *HUNH.*
WHAT ARE YOU SAYING? I'M NOT EQUIPPED TO SHOW YOU THE ROPES, ***CHILDE?*** THE ONLY REASON YOU'RE EVEN STILL ALIVE--
THAT ***TATTOO...***

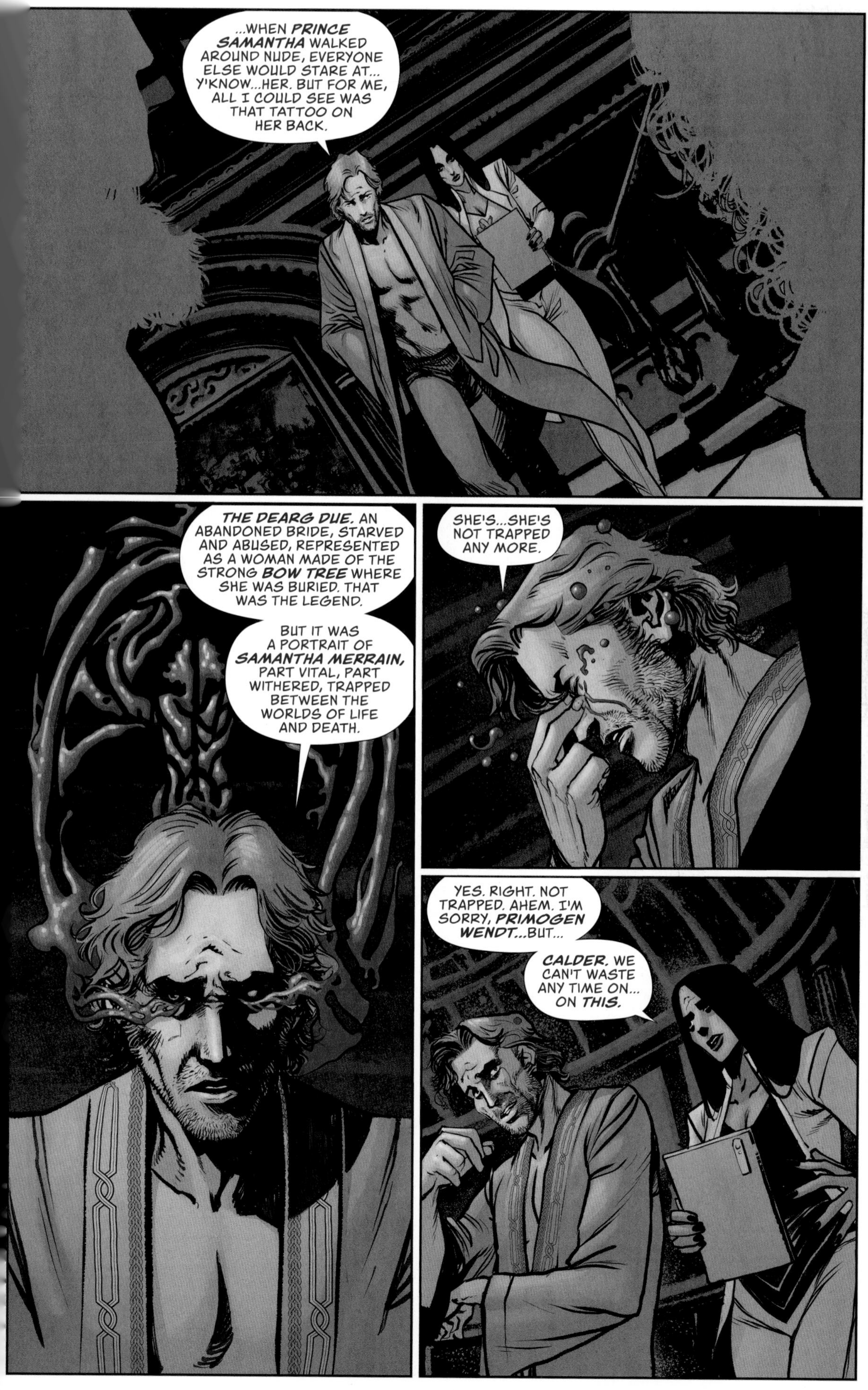
...WHEN PRINCE SAMANTHA WALKED AROUND NUDE, EVERYONE ELSE WOULD STARE AT... Y'KNOW...HER. BUT FOR ME, ALL I COULD SEE WAS THAT TATTOO ON HER BACK.
THE DEARG DUE. AN ABANDONED BRIDE, STARVED AND ABUSED, REPRESENTED AS A WOMAN MADE OF THE STRONG BOW TREE WHERE SHE WAS BURIED. THAT WAS THE LEGEND.
BUT IT WAS A PORTRAIT OF SAMANTHA MERRAIN, PART VITAL, PART WITHERED, TRAPPED BETWEEN THE WORLDS OF LIFE AND DEATH.
SHE'S...SHE'S NOT TRAPPED ANY MORE.
YES. RIGHT. NOT TRAPPED. AHEM. I'M SORRY, PRIMOGEN WENDT...BUT...
CALDER. WE CAN'T WASTE ANY TIME ON... ON THIS.

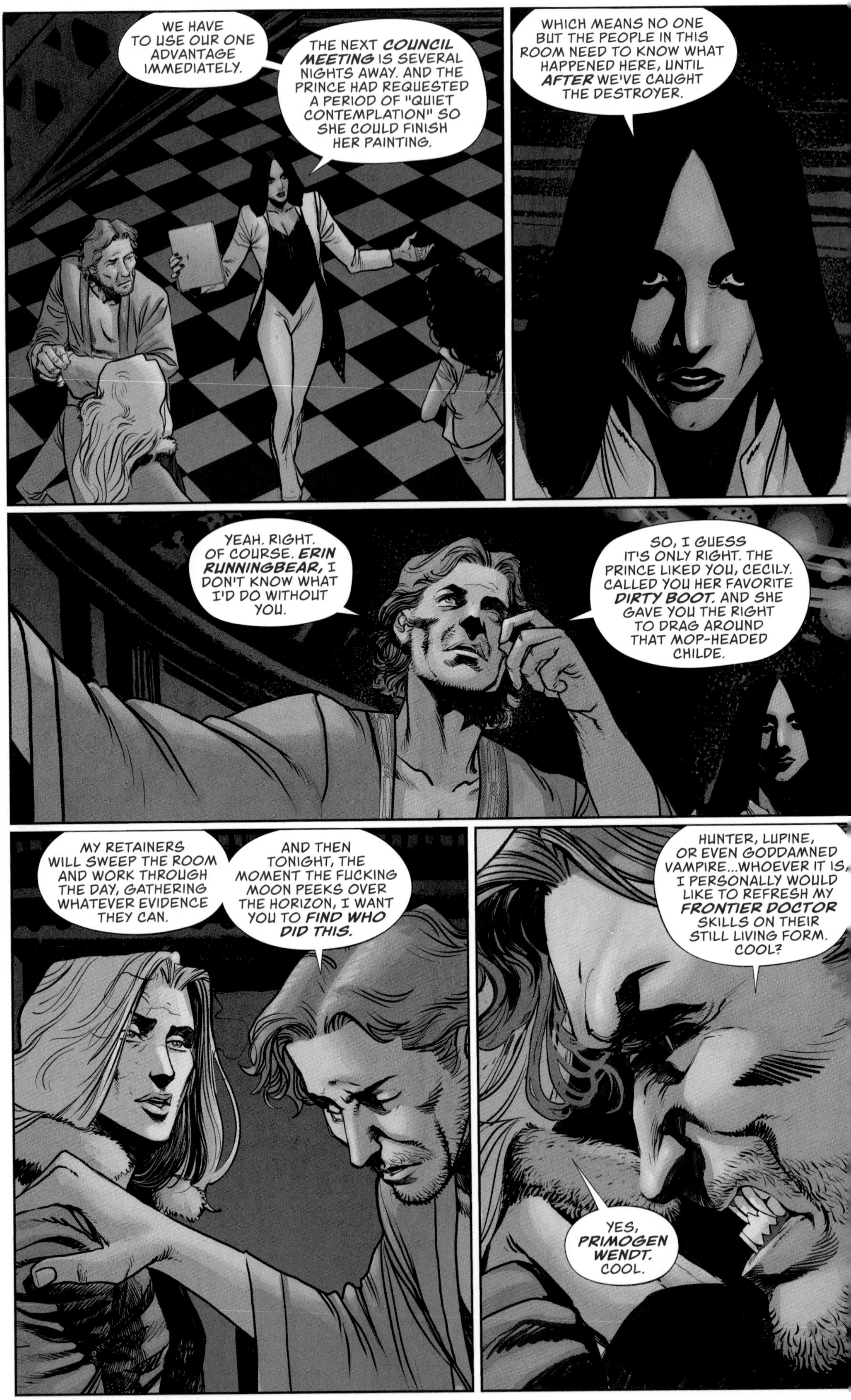
WE HAVE TO USE OUR ONE ADVANTAGE IMMEDIATELY.
THE NEXT **COUNCIL MEETING** IS SEVERAL NIGHTS AWAY. AND THE PRINCE HAD REQUESTED A PERIOD OF "QUIET CONTEMPLATION" SO SHE COULD FINISH HER PAINTING.
WHICH MEANS NO ONE BUT THE PEOPLE IN THIS ROOM NEED TO KNOW WHAT HAPPENED HERE, UNTIL **AFTER** WE'VE CAUGHT THE DESTROYER.
YEAH. RIGHT. OF COURSE. **ERIN RUNNINGBEAR,** I DON'T KNOW WHAT I'D DO WITHOUT YOU.
SO, I GUESS IT'S ONLY RIGHT. THE PRINCE LIKED YOU, CECILY. CALLED YOU HER FAVORITE **DIRTY BOOT.** AND SHE GAVE YOU THE RIGHT TO DRAG AROUND THAT MOP-HEADED CHILDE.
MY RETAINERS WILL SWEEP THE ROOM AND WORK THROUGH THE DAY, GATHERING WHATEVER EVIDENCE THEY CAN.
AND THEN TONIGHT, THE MOMENT THE FUCKING MOON PEEKS OVER THE HORIZON, I WANT YOU TO **FIND WHO DID THIS.**
HUNTER, LUPINE, OR EVEN GODDAMNED VAMPIRE...WHOEVER IT IS, I PERSONALLY WOULD LIKE TO REFRESH MY **FRONTIER DOCTOR** SKILLS ON THEIR STILL LIVING FORM. COOL?
YES, **PRIMOGEN WENDT.** COOL.

THIS IS BAD, RIGHT? SO BAD? LIKE, WITHOUT THE PRINCE THE CLANS OF THE *TWIN CITIES* WILL PROBABLY GO TO *WAR* HOPING TO CARVE OUT THEIR OWN DOMAIN KINDA BAD?

YEAH. *BAD.*

BAD LIKE, A WAR MEANS THE DESTRUCTION OF TRUCES AND ALLIANCES. THE BREAKDOWN IN CRITICAL INFRASTRUCTURE. MAYBE THE LOSS OF SANCTIONED FEEDINGS AND BODY DISPOSALS.

BAD LIKE, MAYBE EVERY VAMPIRE IN THE TWIN CITIES RUNNING AROUND, STARVING, READY TO TEAR THE THROAT OUT OF WHOEVER WALKS BY WHETHER IT'S AN ABUSIVE BOYFRIEND OR A LITTLE GIRL PLAYING HOPSCOTCH ON THE SIDEWALK.

BUT YEAH, YOU GOT THE BASIC IDEA RIGHT. BAD.

I GUESS I'M CAPABLE OF TEACHING *SOMETHING.*

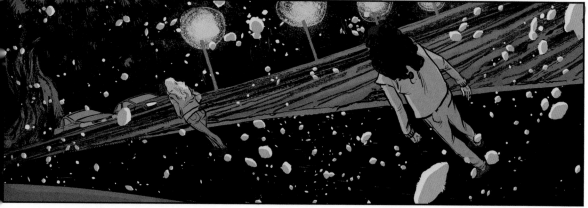

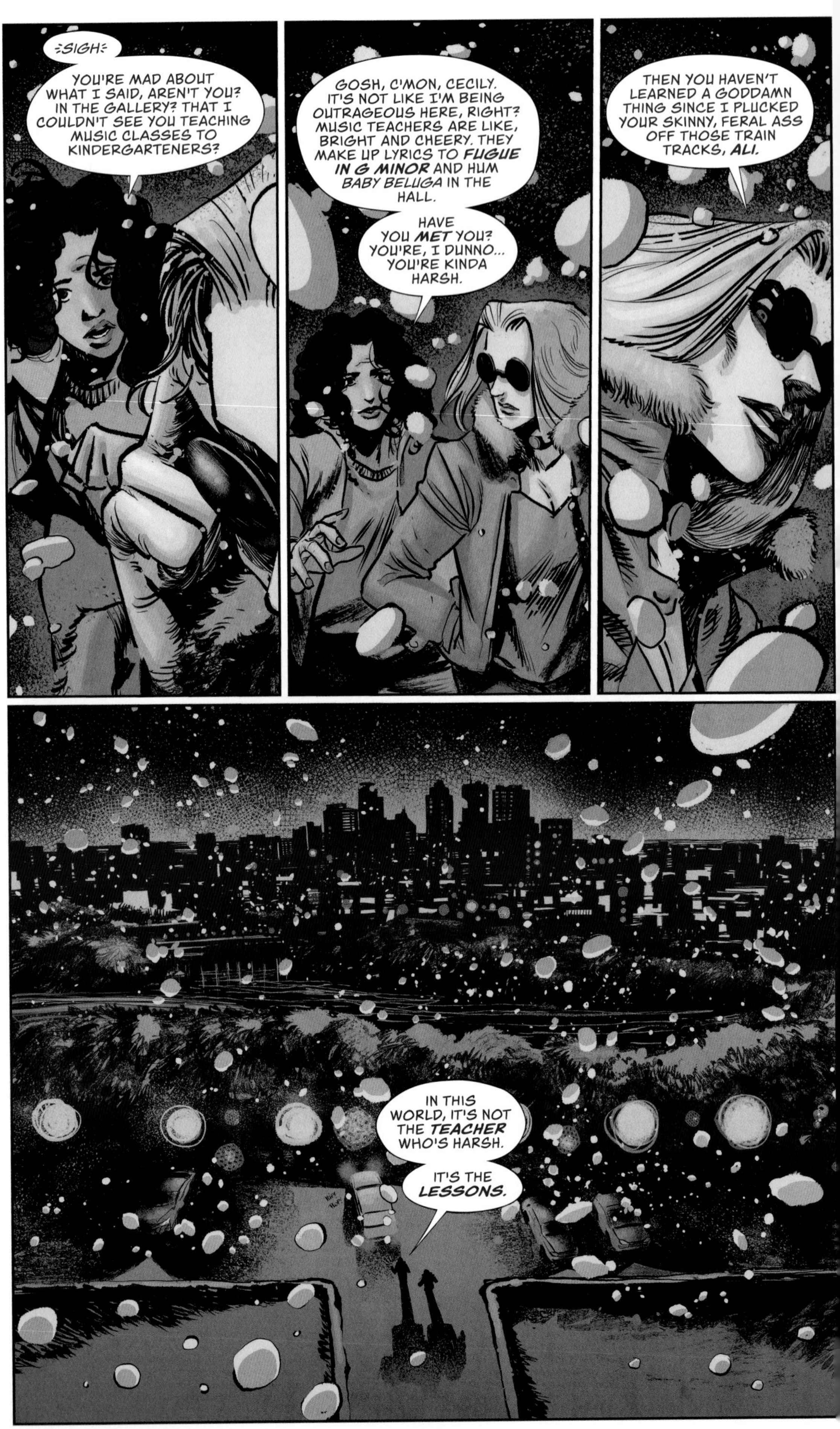
SIGH
YOU'RE MAD ABOUT WHAT I SAID, AREN'T YOU? IN THE GALLERY? THAT I COULDN'T SEE YOU TEACHING MUSIC CLASSES TO KINDERGARTENERS?
GOSH, C'MON, CECILY. IT'S NOT LIKE I'M BEING OUTRAGEOUS HERE, RIGHT? MUSIC TEACHERS ARE LIKE, BRIGHT AND CHEERY. THEY MAKE UP LYRICS TO FUGUE IN G MINOR AND HUM BABY BELUGA IN THE HALL.
HAVE YOU MET YOU? YOU'RE, I DUNNO... YOU'RE KINDA HARSH.
THEN YOU HAVEN'T LEARNED A GODDAMN THING SINCE I PLUCKED YOUR SKINNY, FERAL ASS OFF THOSE TRAIN TRACKS, ALI.
IN THIS WORLD, IT'S NOT THE TEACHER WHO'S HARSH.
IT'S THE LESSONS.

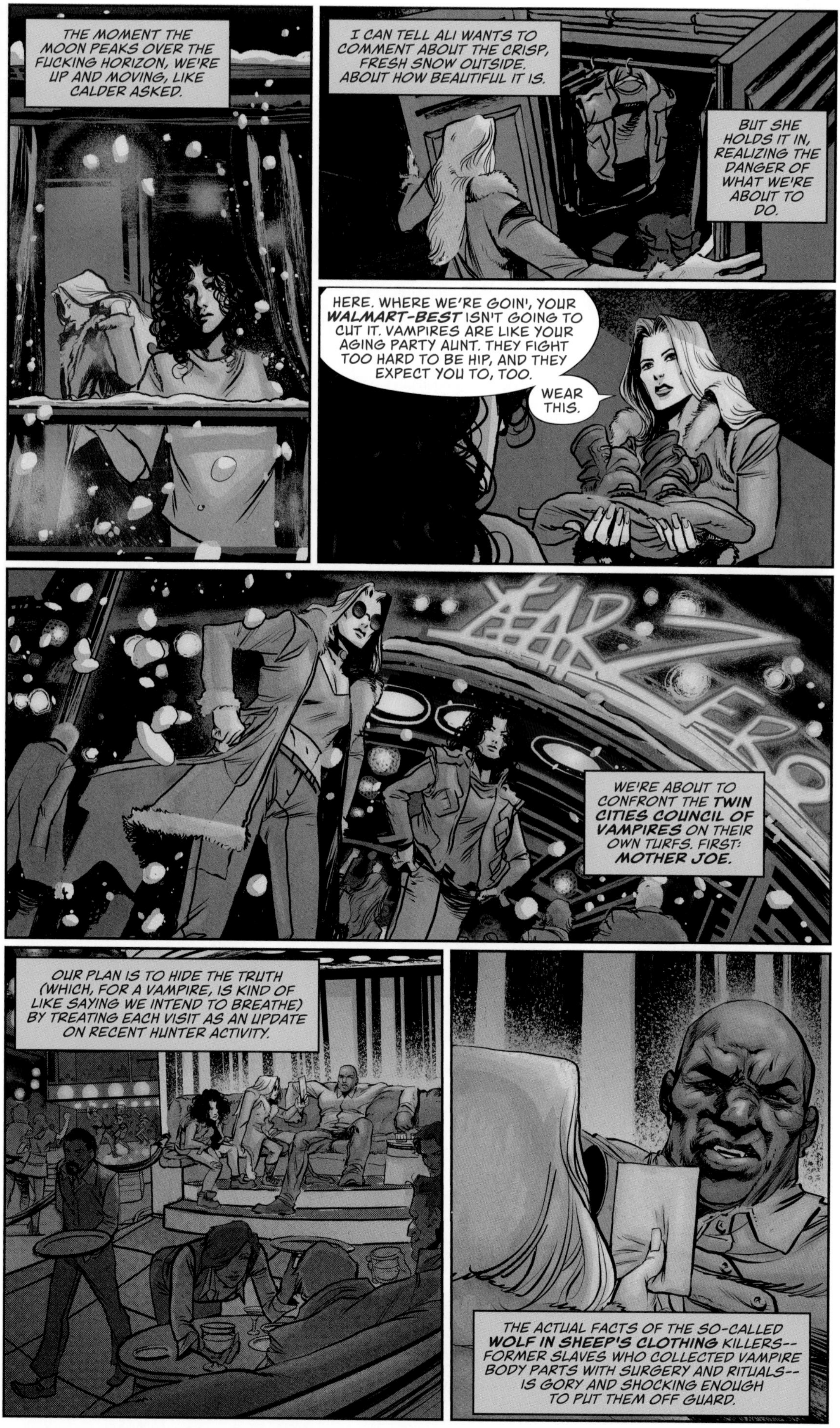

THE MOMENT THE MOON PEAKS OVER THE FUCKING HORIZON, WE'RE UP AND MOVING, LIKE CALDER ASKED.
I CAN TELL ALI WANTS TO COMMENT ABOUT THE CRISP, FRESH SNOW OUTSIDE. ABOUT HOW BEAUTIFUL IT IS.
BUT SHE HOLDS IT IN, REALIZING THE DANGER OF WHAT WE'RE ABOUT TO DO.
HERE. WHERE WE'RE GOIN', YOUR **WALMART-BEST** ISN'T GOING TO CUT IT. VAMPIRES ARE LIKE YOUR AGING PARTY AUNT. THEY FIGHT TOO HARD TO BE HIP, AND THEY EXPECT YOU TO, TOO.
WEAR THIS.
WE'RE ABOUT TO CONFRONT THE **TWIN CITIES COUNCIL OF VAMPIRES** ON THEIR OWN TURFS. FIRST: **MOTHER JOE.**
OUR PLAN IS TO HIDE THE TRUTH (WHICH, FOR A VAMPIRE, IS KIND OF LIKE SAYING WE INTEND TO BREATHE) BY TREATING EACH VISIT AS AN UPDATE ON RECENT HUNTER ACTIVITY.
THE ACTUAL FACTS OF THE SO-CALLED **WOLF IN SHEEP'S CLOTHING** KILLERS-- FORMER SLAVES WHO COLLECTED VAMPIRE BODY PARTS WITH SURGERY AND RITUALS-- IS GORY AND SHOCKING ENOUGH TO PUT THEM OFF GUARD.

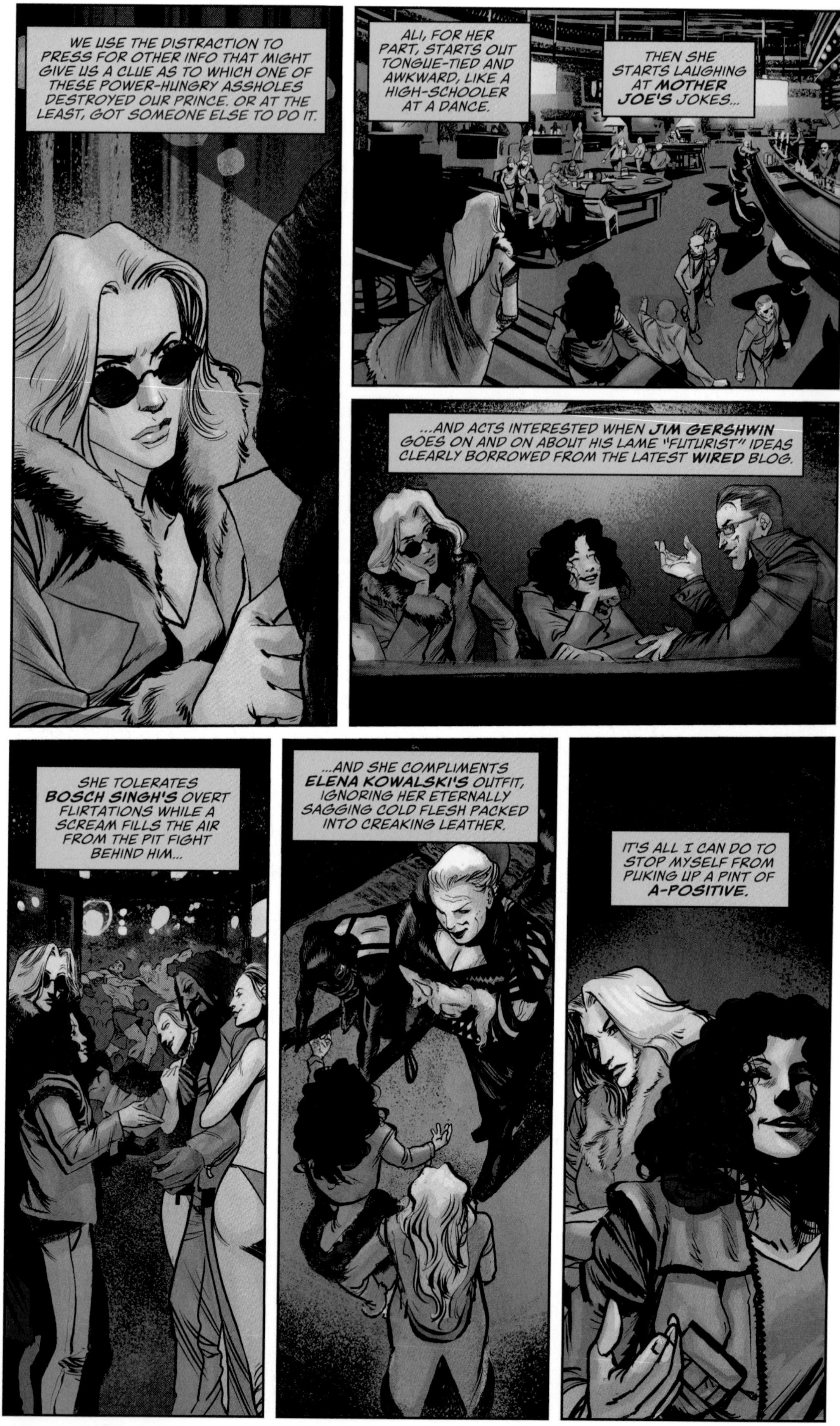
WE USE THE DISTRACTION TO PRESS FOR OTHER INFO THAT MIGHT GIVE US A CLUE AS TO WHICH ONE OF THESE POWER-HUNGRY ASSHOLES DESTROYED OUR PRINCE. OR AT THE LEAST, GOT SOMEONE ELSE TO DO IT.
ALI, FOR HER PART, STARTS OUT TONGUE-TIED AND AWKWARD, LIKE A HIGH-SCHOOLER AT A DANCE.
THEN SHE STARTS LAUGHING AT MOTHER JOE'S JOKES...
...AND ACTS INTERESTED WHEN JIM GERSHWIN GOES ON AND ON ABOUT HIS LAME "FUTURIST" IDEAS CLEARLY BORROWED FROM THE LATEST WIRED BLOG.
SHE TOLERATES BOSCH SINGH'S OVERT FLIRTATIONS WHILE A SCREAM FILLS THE AIR FROM THE PIT FIGHT BEHIND HIM...
...AND SHE COMPLIMENTS ELENA KOWALSKI'S OUTFIT, IGNORING HER ETERNALLY SAGGING COLD FLESH PACKED INTO CREAKING LEATHER.
IT'S ALL I CAN DO TO STOP MYSELF FROM PUKING UP A PINT OF A-POSITIVE.

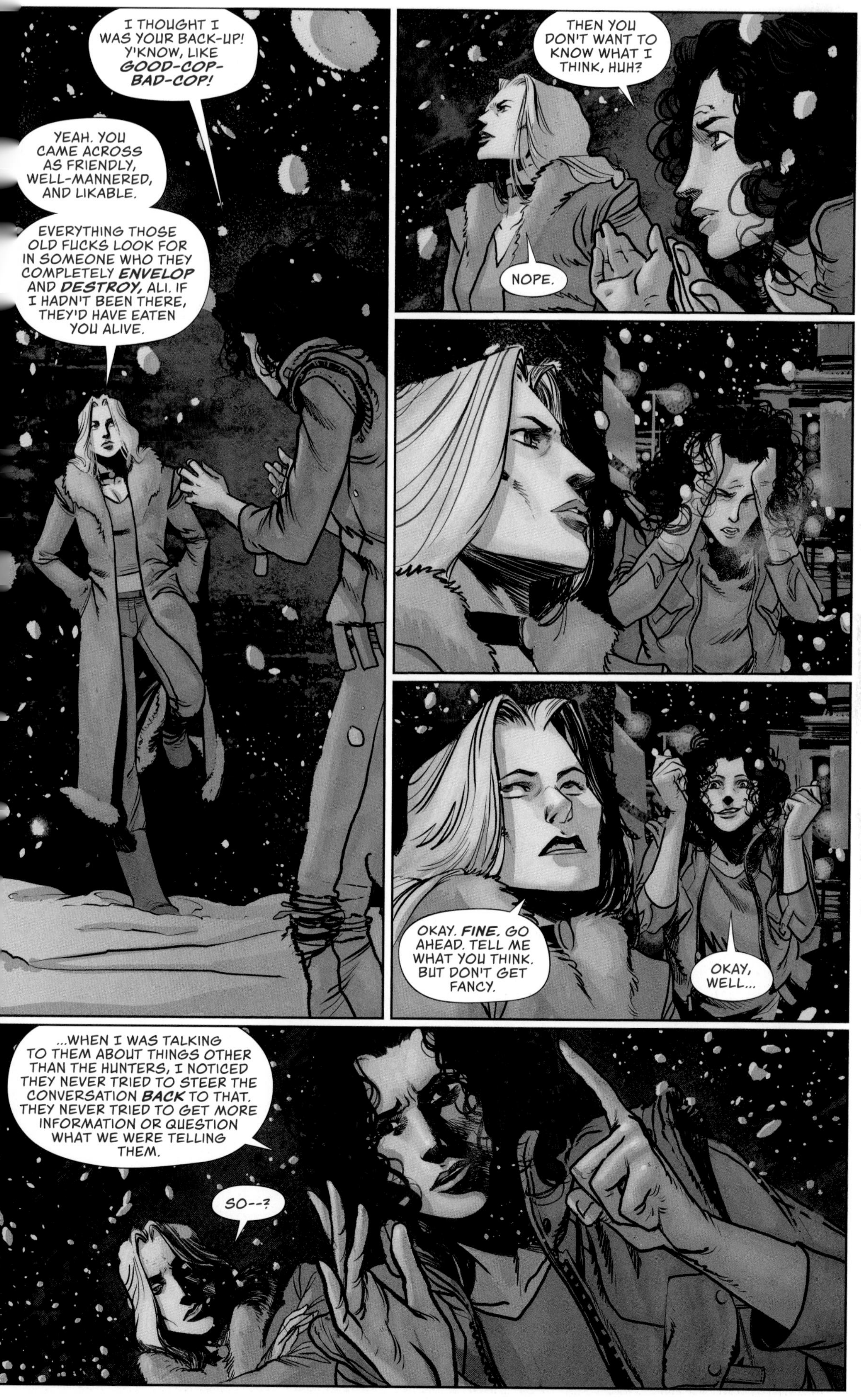
I THOUGHT I WAS YOUR BACK-UP! Y'KNOW, LIKE GOOD-COP-BAD-COP!
YEAH. YOU CAME ACROSS AS FRIENDLY, WELL-MANNERED, AND LIKABLE.
EVERYTHING THOSE OLD FUCKS LOOK FOR IN SOMEONE WHO THEY COMPLETELY ENVELOP AND DESTROY, ALI. IF I HADN'T BEEN THERE, THEY'D HAVE EATEN YOU ALIVE.
THEN YOU DON'T WANT TO KNOW WHAT I THINK, HUH?
NOPE.
OKAY. FINE. GO AHEAD. TELL ME WHAT YOU THINK. BUT DON'T GET FANCY.
OKAY, WELL...
...WHEN I WAS TALKING TO THEM ABOUT THINGS OTHER THAN THE HUNTERS, I NOTICED THEY NEVER TRIED TO STEER THE CONVERSATION BACK TO THAT. THEY NEVER TRIED TO GET MORE INFORMATION OR QUESTION WHAT WE WERE TELLING THEM.
SO--?

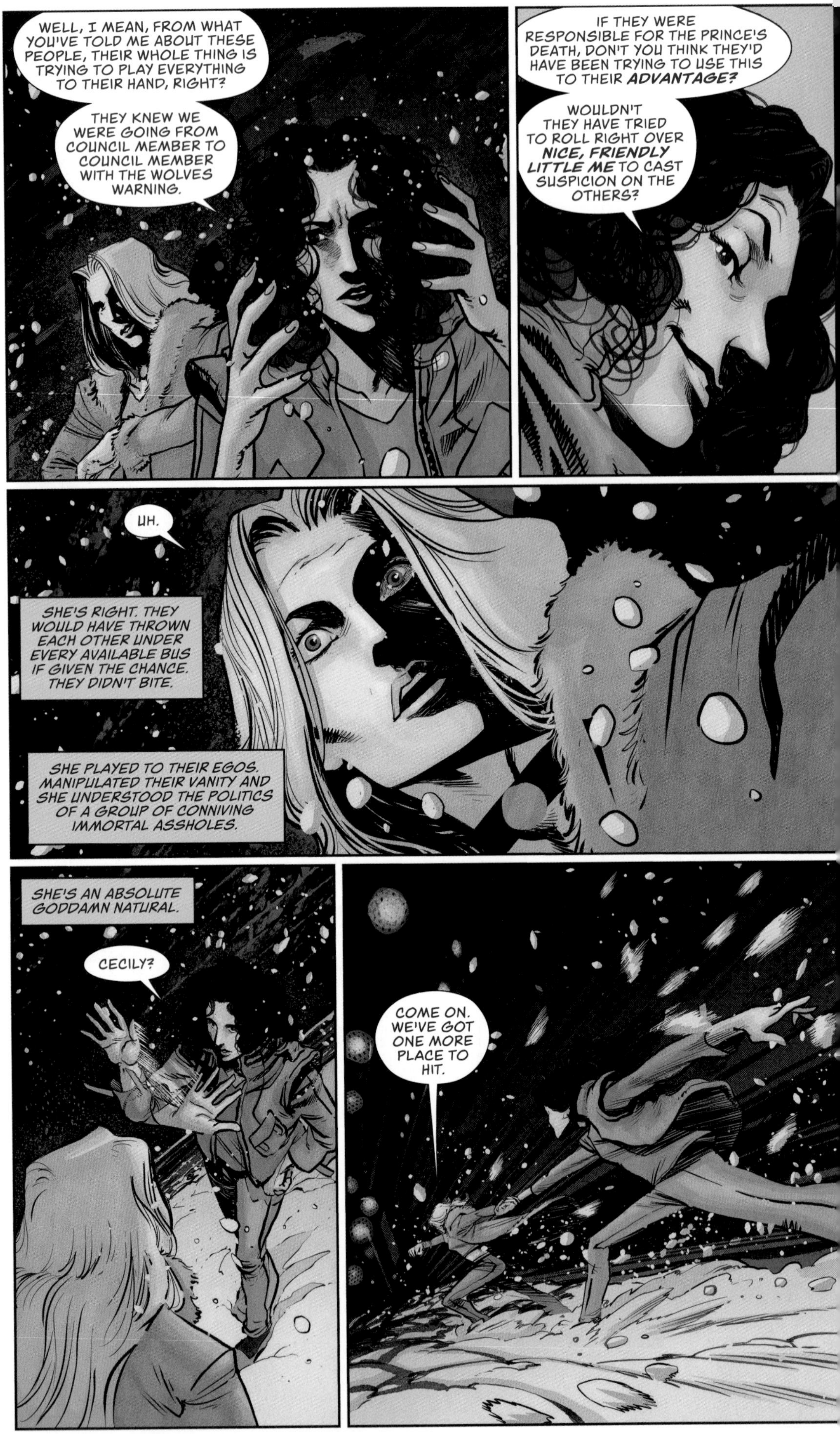
WELL, I MEAN, FROM WHAT YOU'VE TOLD ME ABOUT THESE PEOPLE, THEIR WHOLE THING IS TRYING TO PLAY EVERYTHING TO THEIR HAND, RIGHT?
THEY KNEW WE WERE GOING FROM COUNCIL MEMBER TO COUNCIL MEMBER WITH THE WOLVES WARNING.
IF THEY WERE RESPONSIBLE FOR THE PRINCE'S DEATH, DON'T YOU THINK THEY'D HAVE BEEN TRYING TO USE THIS TO THEIR ***ADVANTAGE?***
WOULDN'T THEY HAVE TRIED TO ROLL RIGHT OVER ***NICE, FRIENDLY LITTLE ME*** TO CAST SUSPICION ON THE OTHERS?
UH.
SHE'S RIGHT. THEY WOULD HAVE THROWN EACH OTHER UNDER EVERY AVAILABLE BUS IF GIVEN THE CHANCE. THEY DIDN'T BITE.
SHE PLAYED TO THEIR EGOS. MANIPULATED THEIR VANITY AND SHE UNDERSTOOD THE POLITICS OF A GROUP OF CONNIVING IMMORTAL ASSHOLES.
SHE'S AN ABSOLUTE GODDAMN NATURAL.
CECILY?
COME ON. WE'VE GOT ONE MORE PLACE TO HIT.

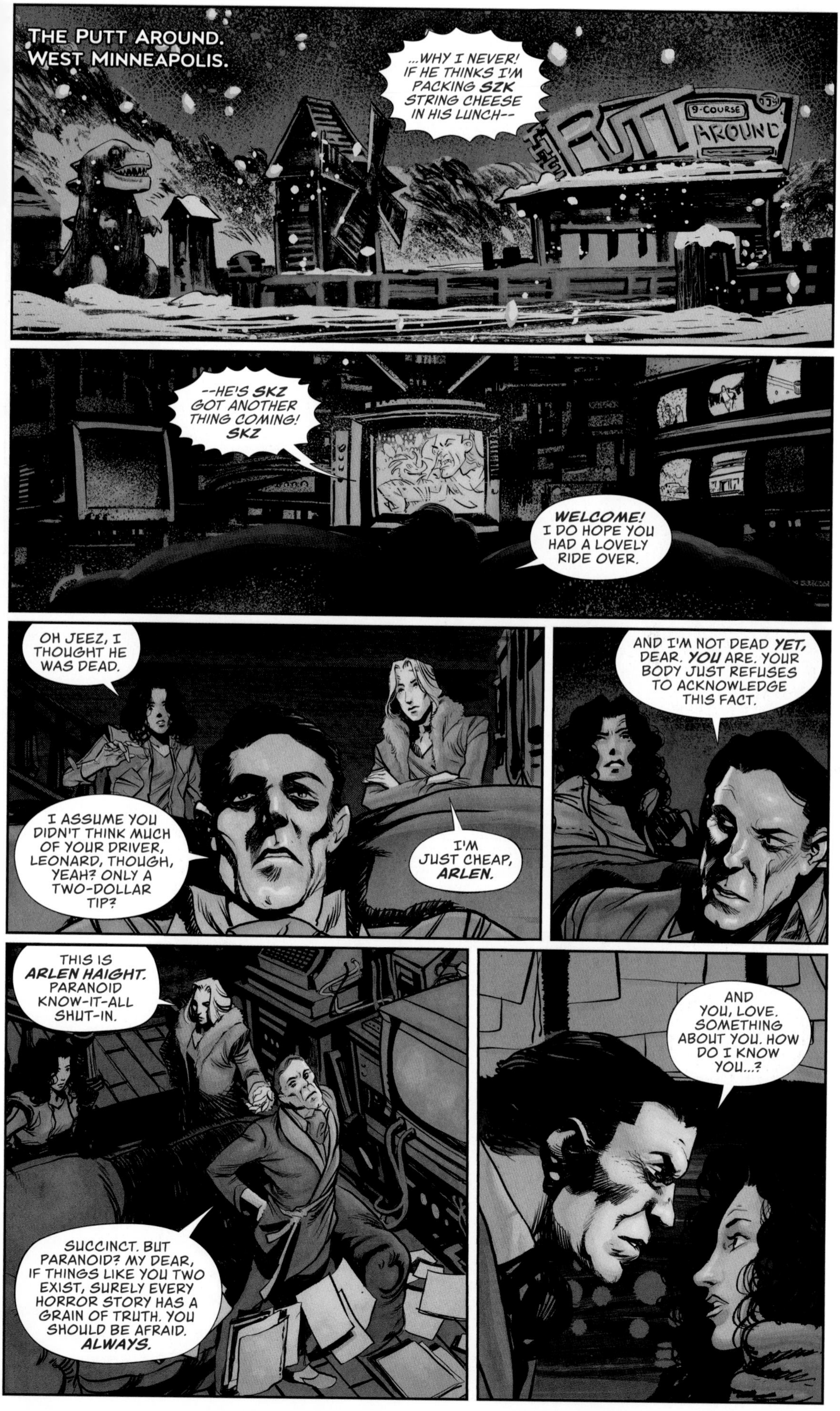
THE PUTT AROUND. WEST MINNEAPOLIS.
...WHY I NEVER! IF HE THINKS I'M PACKING SZK STRING CHEESE IN HIS LUNCH--
9-COURSE PUTT AROUND
--HE'S SKZ GOT ANOTHER THING COMING! SKZ
WELCOME! I DO HOPE YOU HAD A LOVELY RIDE OVER.
OH JEEZ, I THOUGHT HE WAS DEAD.
I ASSUME YOU DIDN'T THINK MUCH OF YOUR DRIVER, LEONARD, THOUGH, YEAH? ONLY A TWO-DOLLAR TIP?
I'M JUST CHEAP, ARLEN.
AND I'M NOT DEAD YET, DEAR. YOU ARE. YOUR BODY JUST REFUSES TO ACKNOWLEDGE THIS FACT.
THIS IS ARLEN HAIGHT. PARANOID KNOW-IT-ALL SHUT-IN.
SUCCINCT. BUT PARANOID? MY DEAR, IF THINGS LIKE YOU TWO EXIST, SURELY EVERY HORROR STORY HAS A GRAIN OF TRUTH. YOU SHOULD BE AFRAID. ALWAYS.
AND YOU, LOVE. SOMETHING ABOUT YOU. HOW DO I KNOW YOU...?

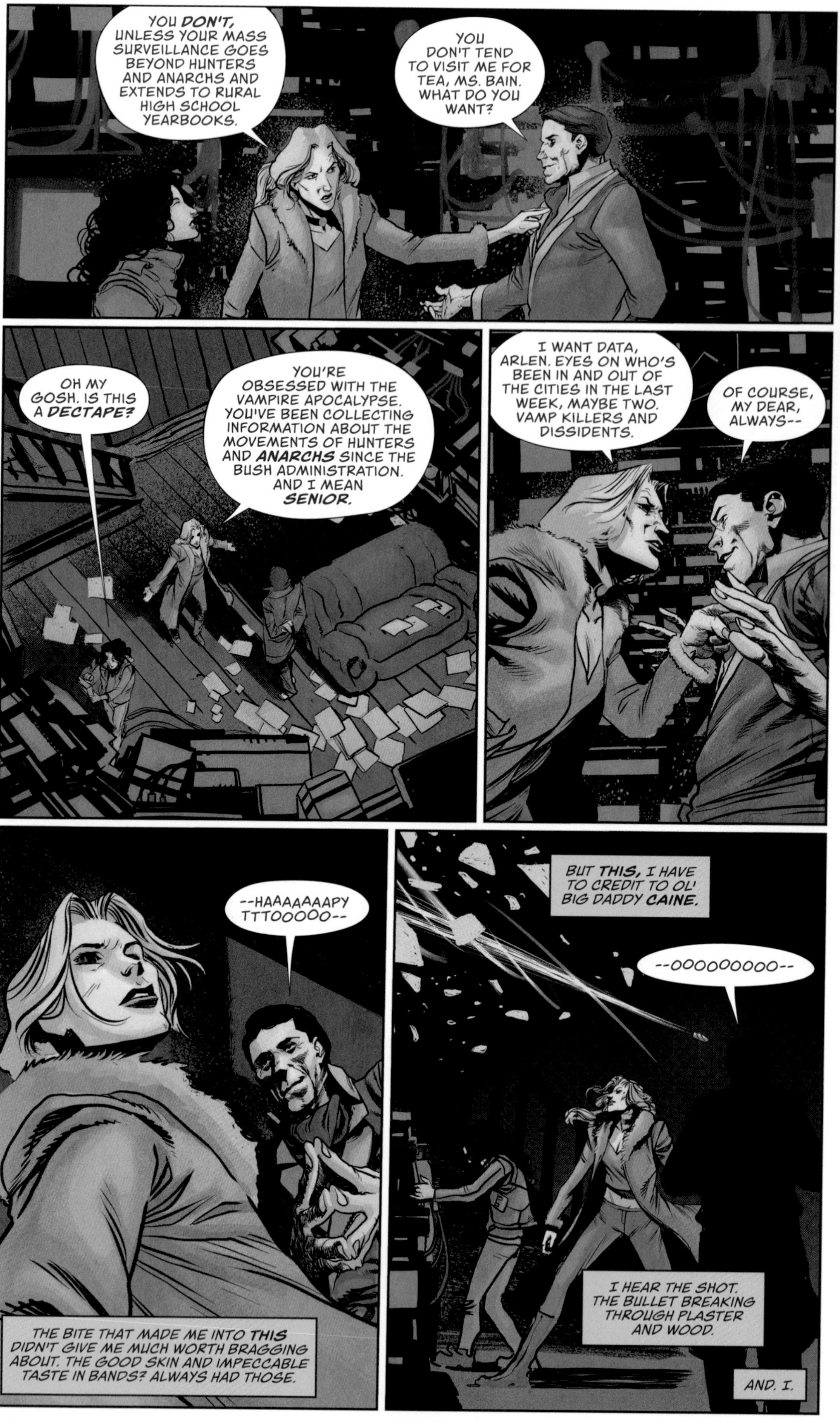

YOU **DON'T,** UNLESS YOUR MASS SURVEILLANCE GOES BEYOND HUNTERS AND ANARCHS AND EXTENDS TO RURAL HIGH SCHOOL YEARBOOKS.
YOU DON'T TEND TO VISIT ME FOR TEA, MS. BAIN. WHAT DO YOU WANT?
OH MY GOSH. IS THIS A ***DECTAPE?***
YOU'RE OBSESSED WITH THE VAMPIRE APOCALYPSE. YOU'VE BEEN COLLECTING INFORMATION ABOUT THE MOVEMENTS OF HUNTERS AND ***ANARCHS*** SINCE THE BUSH ADMINISTRATION. AND I MEAN ***SENIOR.***
I WANT DATA, ARLEN. EYES ON WHO'S BEEN IN AND OUT OF THE CITIES IN THE LAST WEEK, MAYBE TWO. VAMP KILLERS AND DISSIDENTS.
OF COURSE, MY DEAR, ALWAYS--
--HAAAAAAAPY TTTOOOOO--
THE BITE THAT MADE ME INTO **THIS** DIDN'T GIVE ME MUCH WORTH BRAGGING ABOUT. THE GOOD SKIN AND IMPECCABLE TASTE IN BANDS? ALWAYS HAD THOSE.
BUT **THIS,** I HAVE TO CREDIT TO OL' BIG DADDY **CAINE.**
--OOOOOOOOO--
I HEAR THE SHOT. THE BULLET BREAKING THROUGH PLASTER AND WOOD.
AND. I.

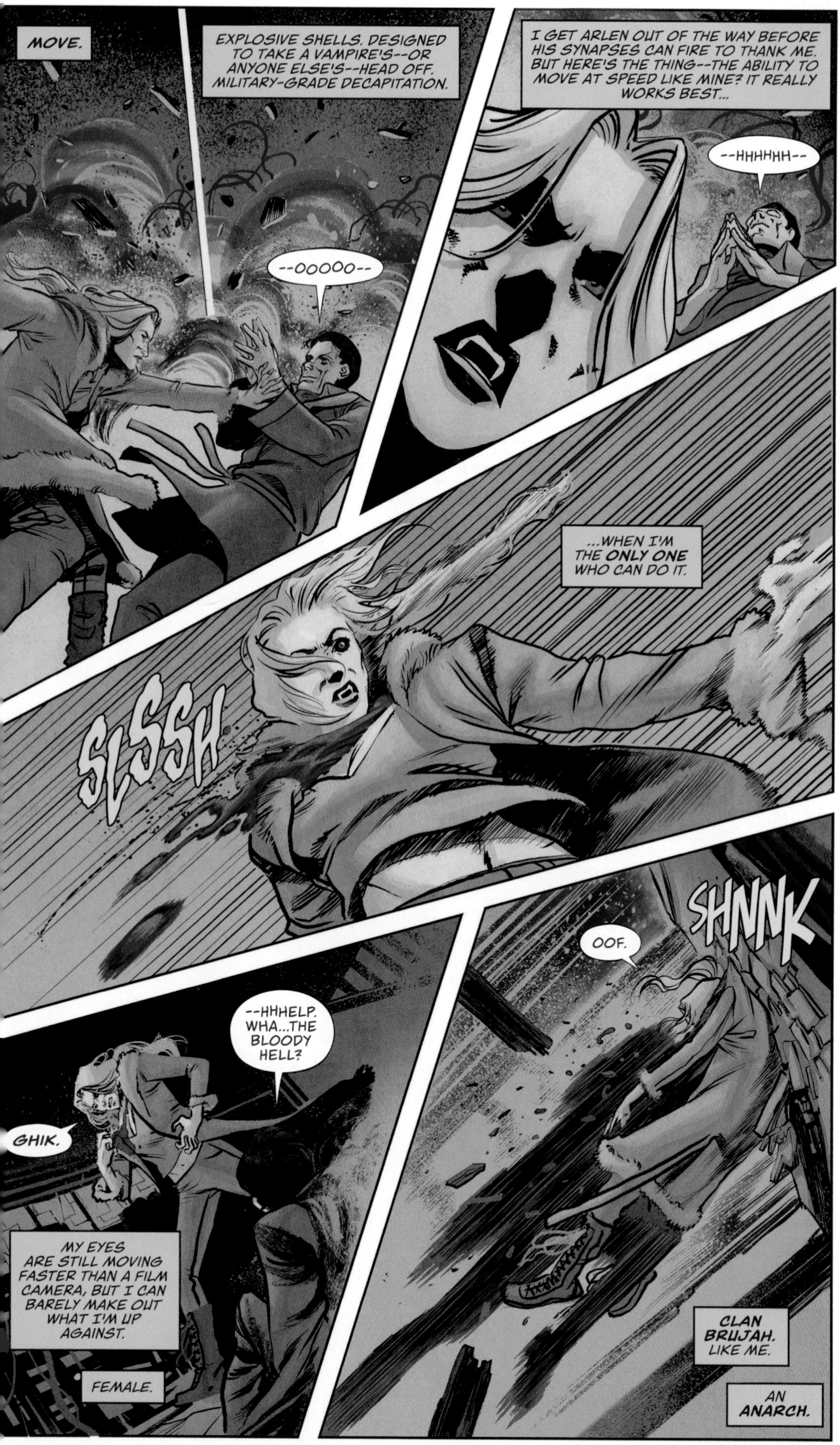
MOVE.
EXPLOSIVE SHELLS. DESIGNED TO TAKE A VAMPIRE'S--OR ANYONE ELSE'S--HEAD OFF. MILITARY-GRADE DECAPITATION.
--OOOOO--
I GET ARLEN OUT OF THE WAY BEFORE HIS SYNAPSES CAN FIRE TO THANK ME. BUT HERE'S THE THING--THE ABILITY TO MOVE AT SPEED LIKE MINE? IT REALLY WORKS BEST...
--HHHHHH--
...WHEN I'M THE **ONLY ONE** WHO CAN DO IT.
SLSSH
SHNNK
OOF.
--HHHELP. WHA...THE BLOODY HELL?
GHIK.
MY EYES ARE STILL MOVING FASTER THAN A FILM CAMERA, BUT I CAN BARELY MAKE OUT WHAT I'M UP AGAINST.
FEMALE.
CLAN BRUJAH. LIKE ME.
AN **ANARCH.**

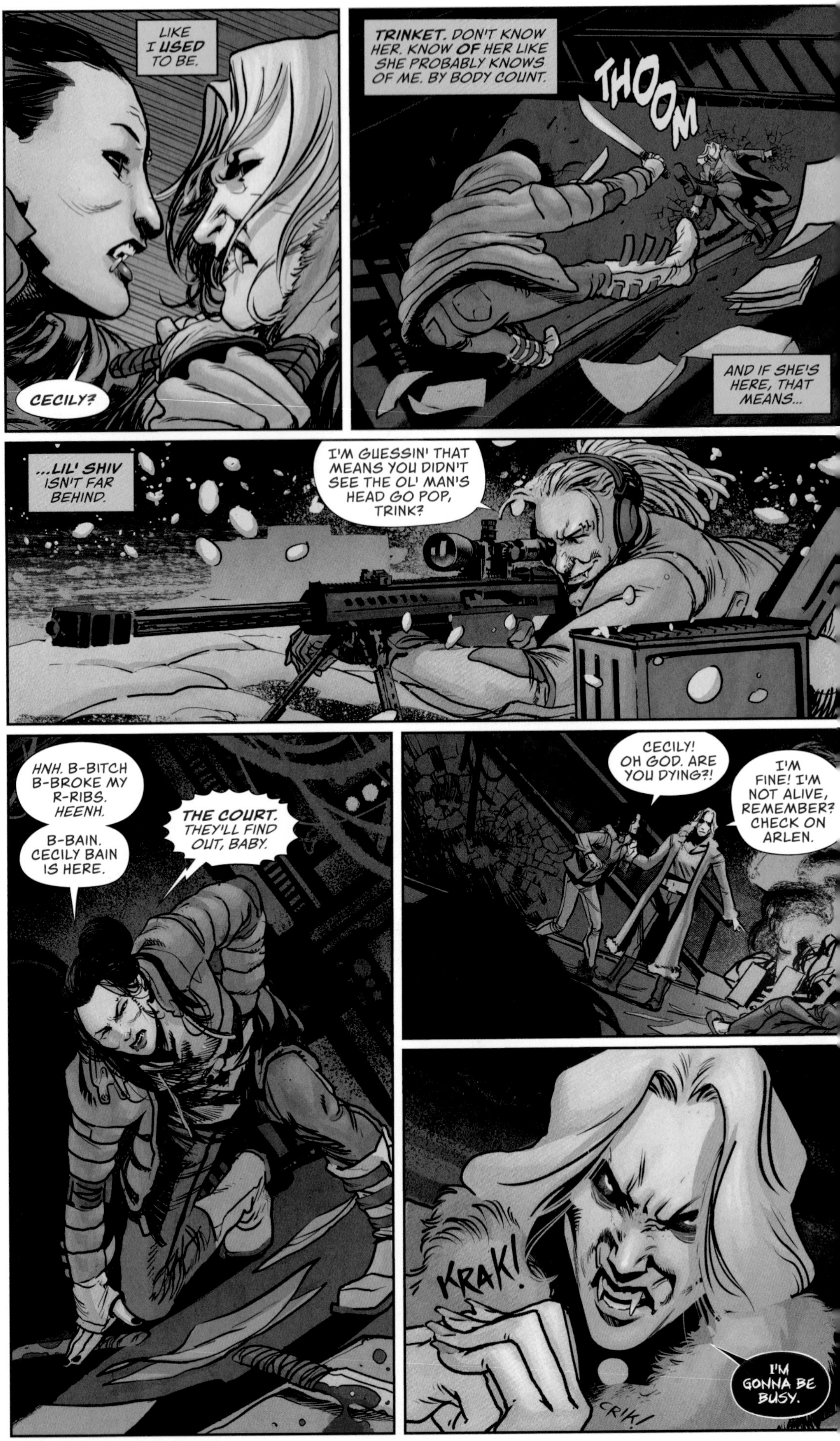

LIKE I USED TO BE.
CECILY?
TRINKET. DON'T KNOW HER. KNOW OF HER LIKE SHE PROBABLY KNOWS OF ME. BY BODY COUNT.
THOOM
AND IF SHE'S HERE, THAT MEANS...
...LIL' SHIV ISN'T FAR BEHIND.
I'M GUESSIN' THAT MEANS YOU DIDN'T SEE THE OL' MAN'S HEAD GO POP, TRINK?
HNH. B-BITCH B-BROKE MY R-RIBS. HEENH.
B-BAIN. CECILY BAIN IS HERE.
THE COURT. THEY'LL FIND OUT, BABY.
CECILY! OH GOD. ARE YOU DYING?!
I'M FINE! I'M NOT ALIVE, REMEMBER? CHECK ON ARLEN.
KRAK!
CRIK!
I'M GONNA BE BUSY.

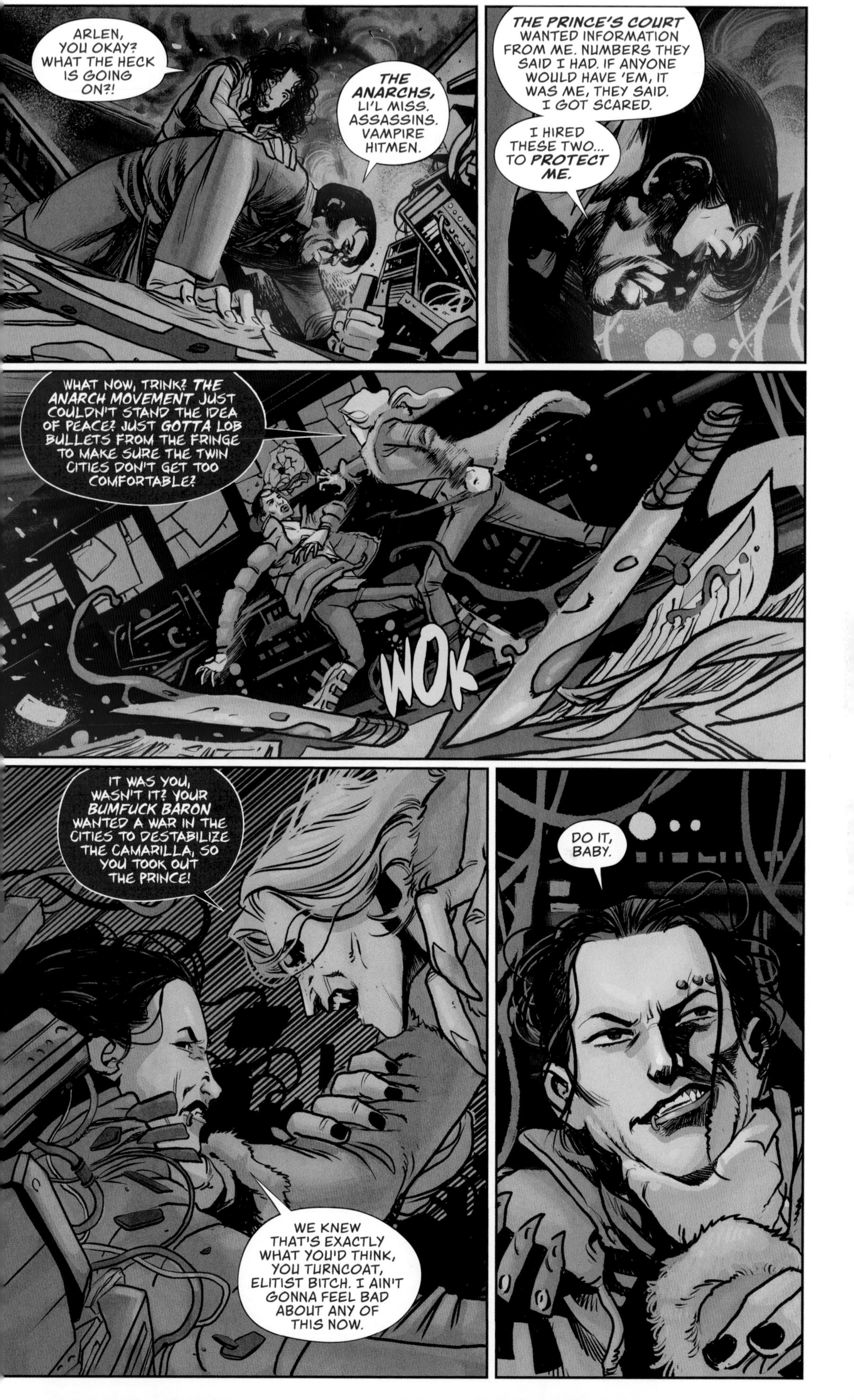
ARLEN, YOU OKAY? WHAT THE HECK IS GOING ON?!
THE ANARCHS, LI'L MISS. ASSASSINS. VAMPIRE HITMEN.
THE PRINCE'S COURT WANTED INFORMATION FROM ME. NUMBERS THEY SAID I HAD. IF ANYONE WOULD HAVE 'EM, IT WAS ME, THEY SAID. I GOT SCARED.
I HIRED THESE TWO... TO PROTECT ME.
WHAT NOW, TRINK? THE ANARCH MOVEMENT JUST COULDN'T STAND THE IDEA OF PEACE? JUST GOTTA LOB BULLETS FROM THE FRINGE TO MAKE SURE THE TWIN CITIES DON'T GET TOO COMFORTABLE?
WOK
IT WAS YOU, WASN'T IT? YOUR BUMFUCK BARON WANTED A WAR IN THE CITIES TO DESTABILIZE THE CAMARILLA, SO YOU TOOK OUT THE PRINCE!
WE KNEW THAT'S EXACTLY WHAT YOU'D THINK, YOU TURNCOAT, ELITIST BITCH. I AIN'T GONNA FEEL BAD ABOUT ANY OF THIS NOW.
DO IT, BABY.

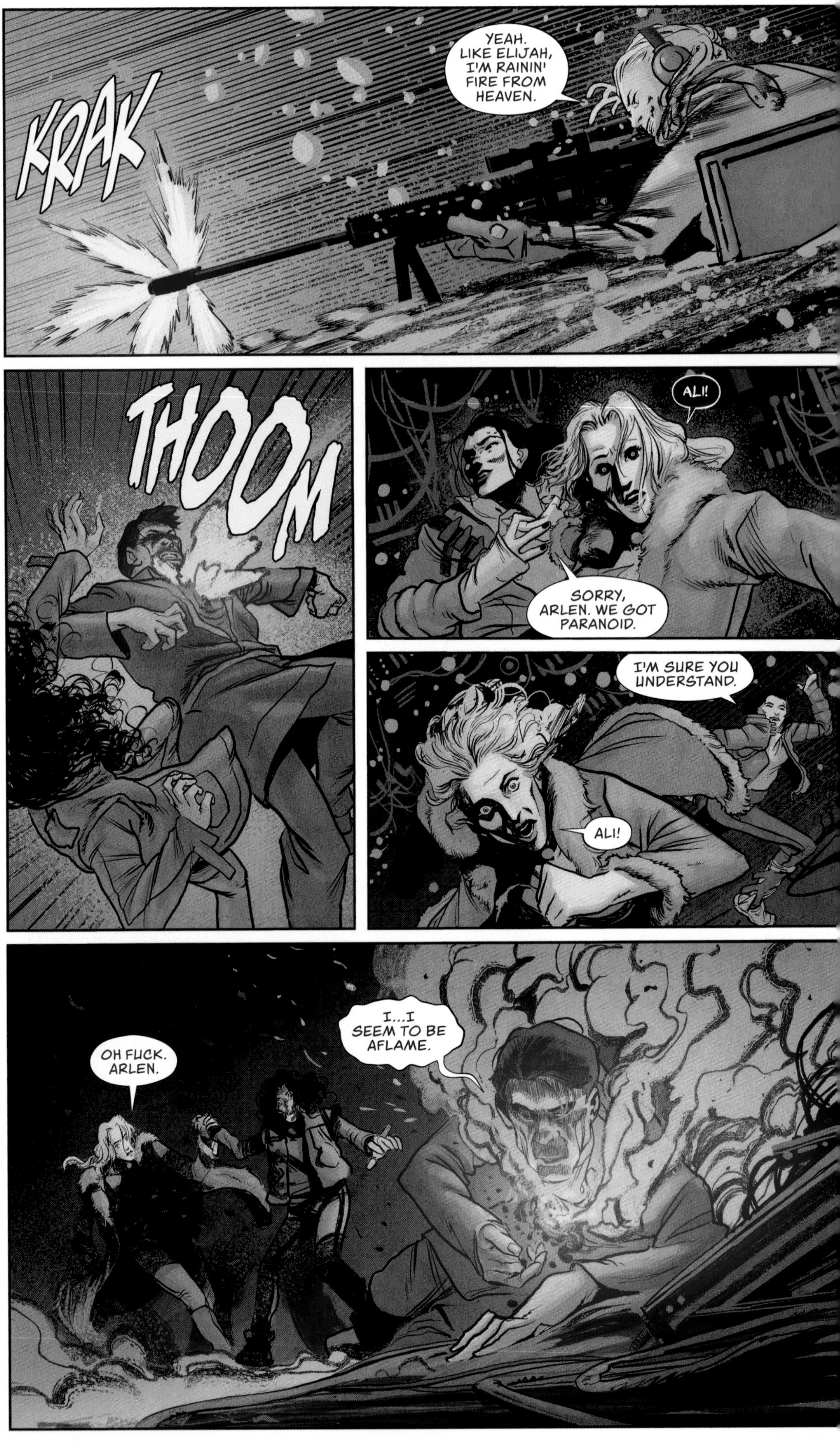
KRAK
YEAH. LIKE ELIJAH, I'M RAININ' FIRE FROM HEAVEN.
THOOM
ALI!
SORRY, ARLEN. WE GOT PARANOID.
I'M SURE YOU UNDERSTAND.
ALI!
OH FUCK. ARLEN.
I...I SEEM TO BE AFLAME.

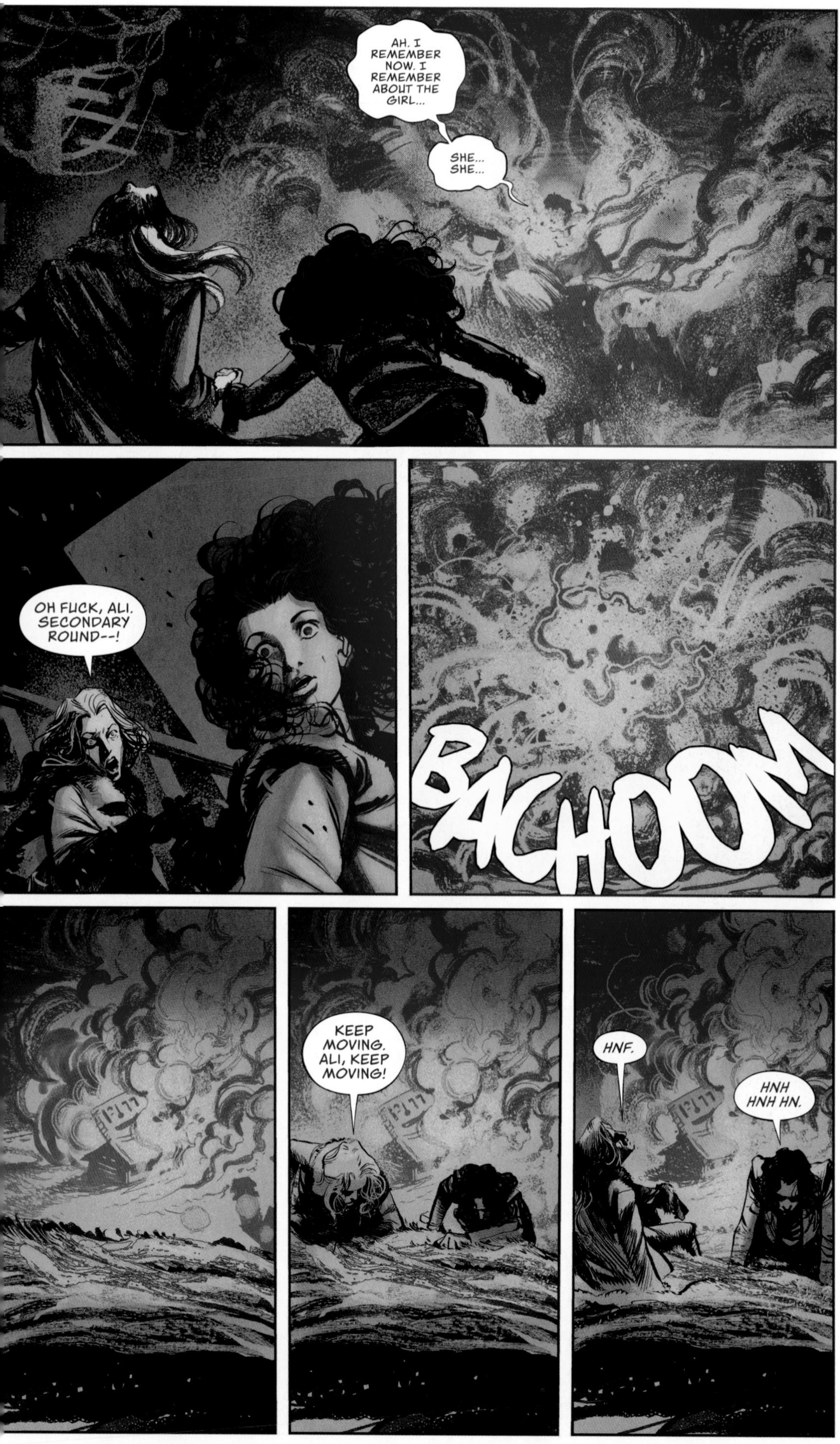
AH. I REMEMBER NOW. I REMEMBER ABOUT THE GIRL...
SHE... SHE...
OH FUCK, ALI. SECONDARY ROUND--!
BACHOOM
KEEP MOVING. ALI, KEEP MOVING!
HNF.
HNH HNH HN.

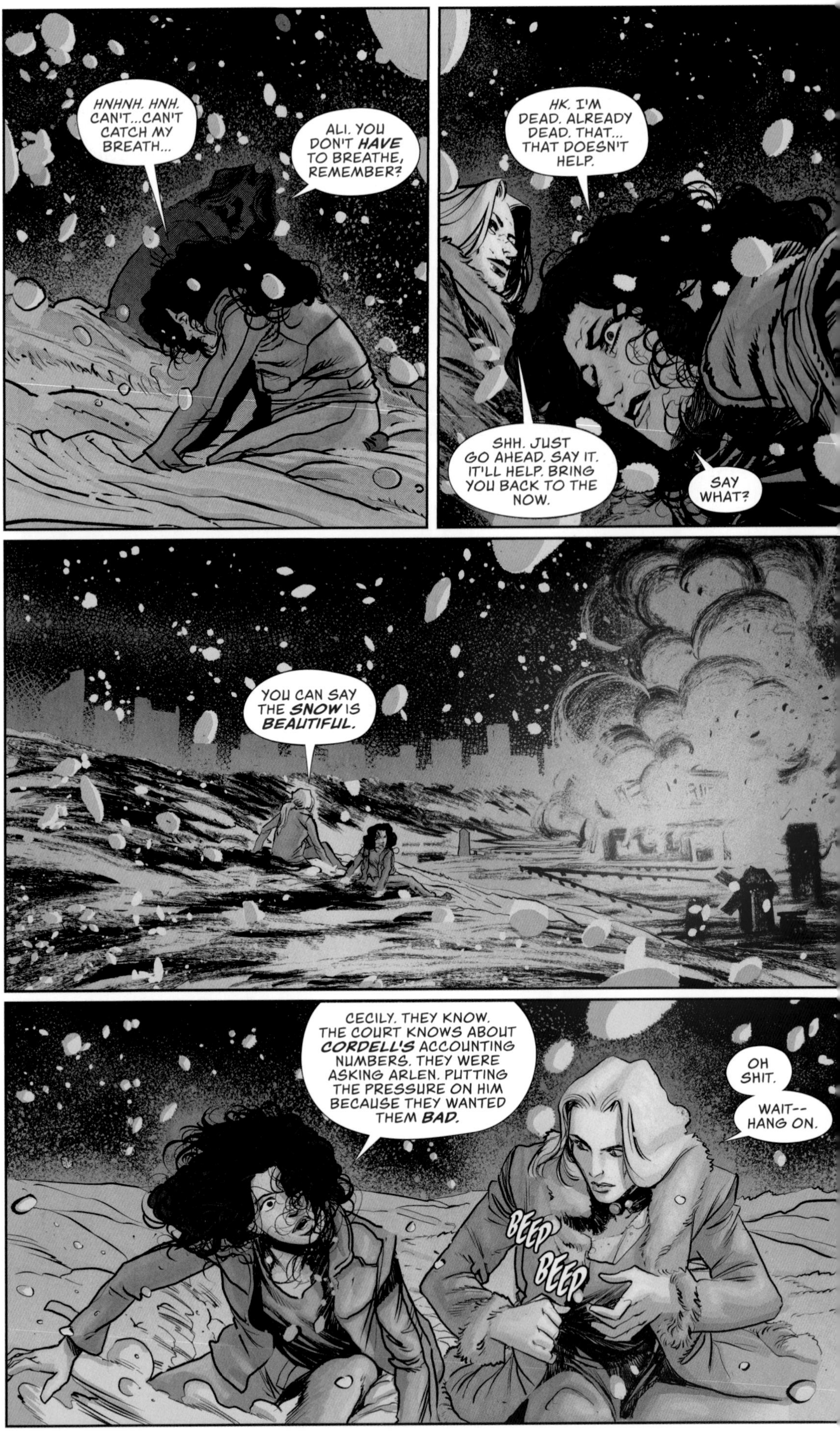
HNHNH. HNH. CAN'T...CAN'T CATCH MY BREATH...
ALI. YOU DON'T HAVE TO BREATHE, REMEMBER?
HK. I'M DEAD. ALREADY DEAD. THAT... THAT DOESN'T HELP.
SHH. JUST GO AHEAD. SAY IT. IT'LL HELP. BRING YOU BACK TO THE NOW.
SAY WHAT?
YOU CAN SAY THE SNOW IS BEAUTIFUL.
CECILY. THEY KNOW. THE COURT KNOWS ABOUT CORDELL'S ACCOUNTING NUMBERS. THEY WERE ASKING ARLEN. PUTTING THE PRESSURE ON HIM BECAUSE THEY WANTED THEM BAD.
BEEP
BEEP
OH SHIT.
WAIT-- HANG ON.

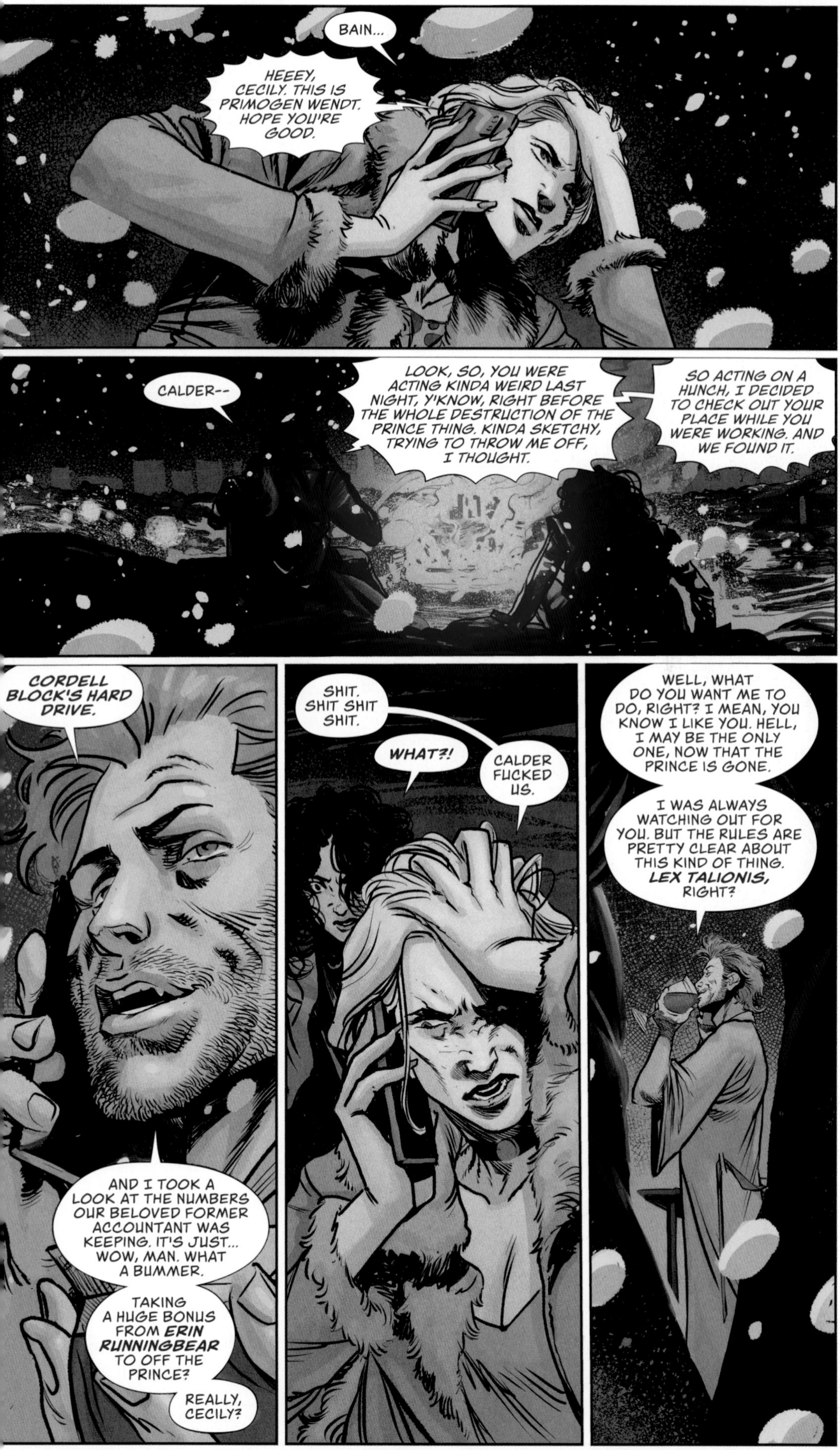
BAIN...
HEEEY, CECILY. THIS IS PRIMOGEN WENDT. HOPE YOU'RE GOOD.
CALDER--
LOOK, SO, YOU WERE ACTING KINDA WEIRD LAST NIGHT, Y'KNOW, RIGHT BEFORE THE WHOLE DESTRUCTION OF THE PRINCE THING. KINDA SKETCHY, TRYING TO THROW ME OFF, I THOUGHT.
SO ACTING ON A HUNCH, I DECIDED TO CHECK OUT YOUR PLACE WHILE YOU WERE WORKING. AND WE FOUND IT.
CORDELL BLOCK'S HARD DRIVE.
AND I TOOK A LOOK AT THE NUMBERS OUR BELOVED FORMER ACCOUNTANT WAS KEEPING. IT'S JUST... WOW, MAN. WHAT A BUMMER.
TAKING A HUGE BONUS FROM ERIN RUNNINGBEAR TO OFF THE PRINCE?
REALLY, CECILY?
SHIT. SHIT SHIT SHIT.
WHAT?!
CALDER FUCKED US.
WELL, WHAT DO YOU WANT ME TO DO, RIGHT? I MEAN, YOU KNOW I LIKE YOU. HELL, I MAY BE THE ONLY ONE, NOW THAT THE PRINCE IS GONE.
I WAS ALWAYS WATCHING OUT FOR YOU. BUT THE RULES ARE PRETTY CLEAR ABOUT THIS KIND OF THING. LEX TALIONIS, RIGHT?

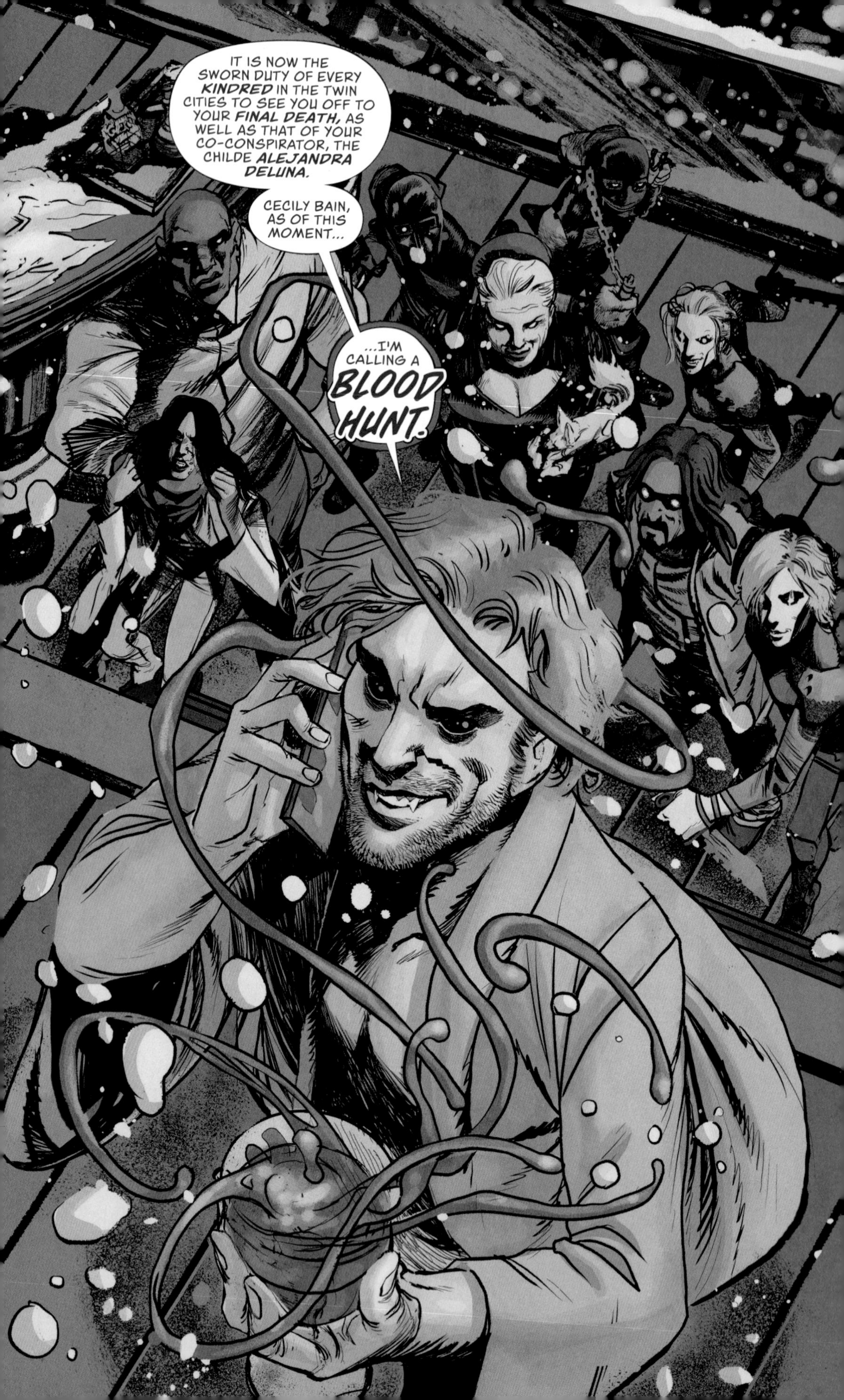
IT IS NOW THE SWORN DUTY OF EVERY **KINDRED** IN THE TWIN CITIES TO SEE YOU OFF TO YOUR **FINAL DEATH,** AS WELL AS THAT OF YOUR CO-CONSPIRATOR, THE CHILDE **ALEJANDRA DELUNA.**
CECILY BAIN, AS OF THIS MOMENT...
...I'M CALLING A **BLOOD HUNT.**

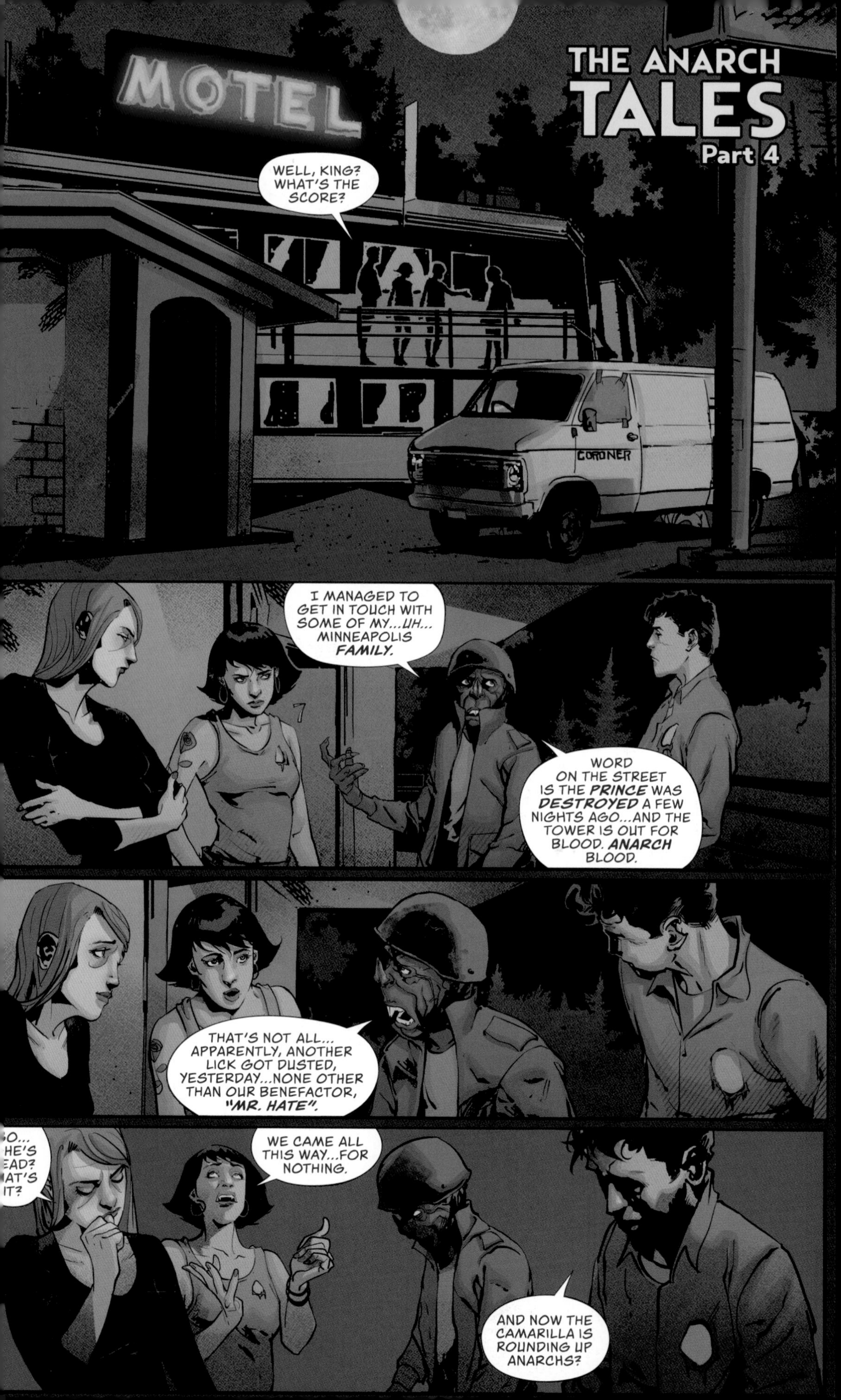
THE ANARCH TALES
Part 4
MOTEL
WELL, KING? WHAT'S THE SCORE?
CORONER
I MANAGED TO GET IN TOUCH WITH SOME OF MY...UH... MINNEAPOLIS FAMILY.
7
WORD ON THE STREET IS THE PRINCE WAS DESTROYED A FEW NIGHTS AGO...AND THE TOWER IS OUT FOR BLOOD. ANARCH BLOOD.
THAT'S NOT ALL... APPARENTLY, ANOTHER LICK GOT DUSTED, YESTERDAY...NONE OTHER THAN OUR BENEFACTOR, "MR. HATE".
WE CAME ALL THIS WAY...FOR NOTHING.
AND NOW THE CAMARILLA IS ROUNDING UP ANARCHS?

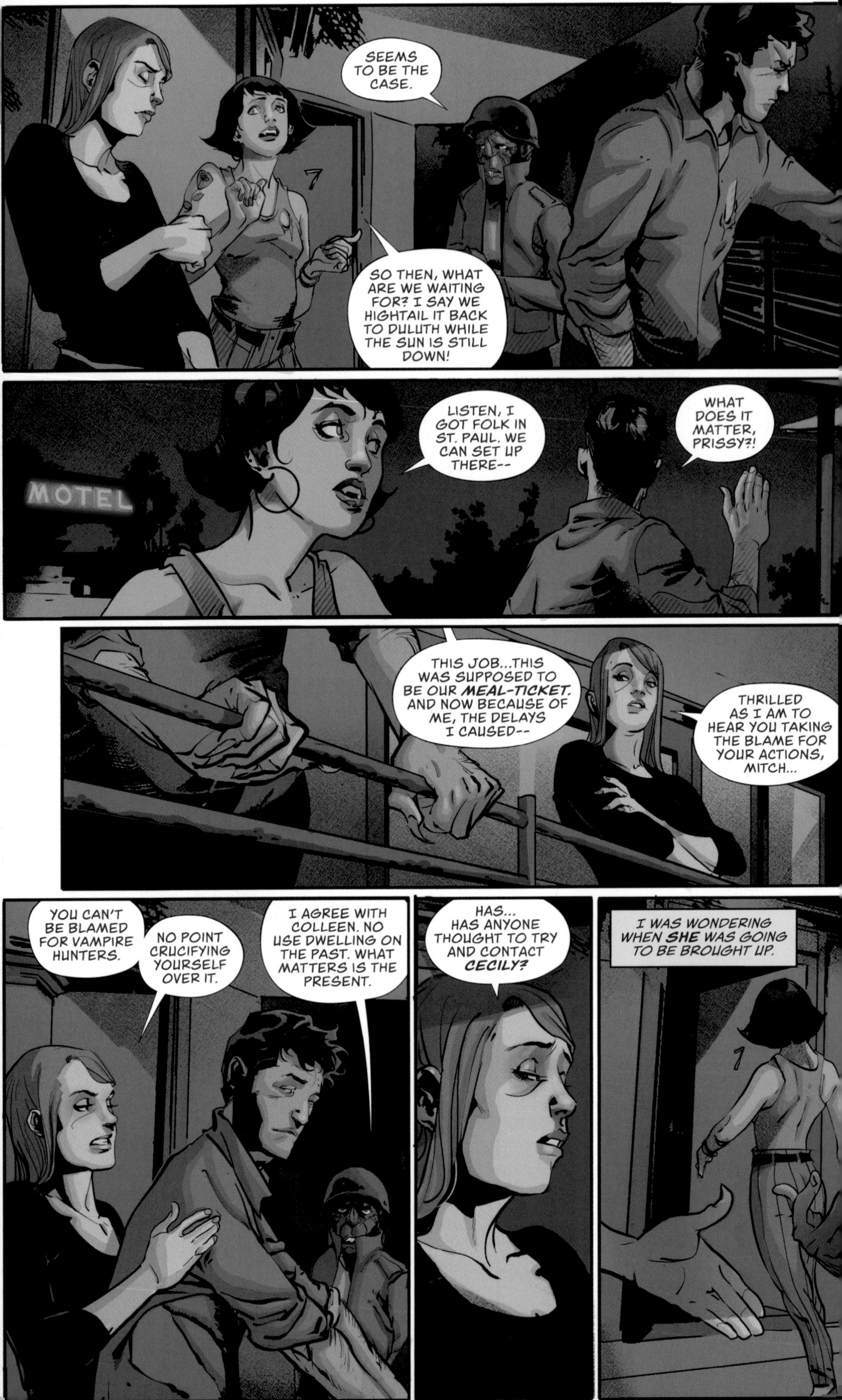
SEEMS TO BE THE CASE.
SO THEN, WHAT ARE WE WAITING FOR? I SAY WE HIGHTAIL IT BACK TO DULUTH WHILE THE SUN IS STILL DOWN!
MOTEL
LISTEN, I GOT FOLK IN ST. PAUL. WE CAN SET UP THERE--
WHAT DOES IT MATTER, PRISSY?!
THIS JOB...THIS WAS SUPPOSED TO BE OUR MEAL-TICKET. AND NOW BECAUSE OF ME, THE DELAYS I CAUSED--
THRILLED AS I AM TO HEAR YOU TAKING THE BLAME FOR YOUR ACTIONS, MITCH...
YOU CAN'T BE BLAMED FOR VAMPIRE HUNTERS.
NO POINT CRUCIFYING YOURSELF OVER IT.
I AGREE WITH COLLEEN. NO USE DWELLING ON THE PAST. WHAT MATTERS IS THE PRESENT.
HAS... HAS ANYONE THOUGHT TO TRY AND CONTACT CECILY?
I WAS WONDERING WHEN SHE WAS GOING TO BE BROUGHT UP.

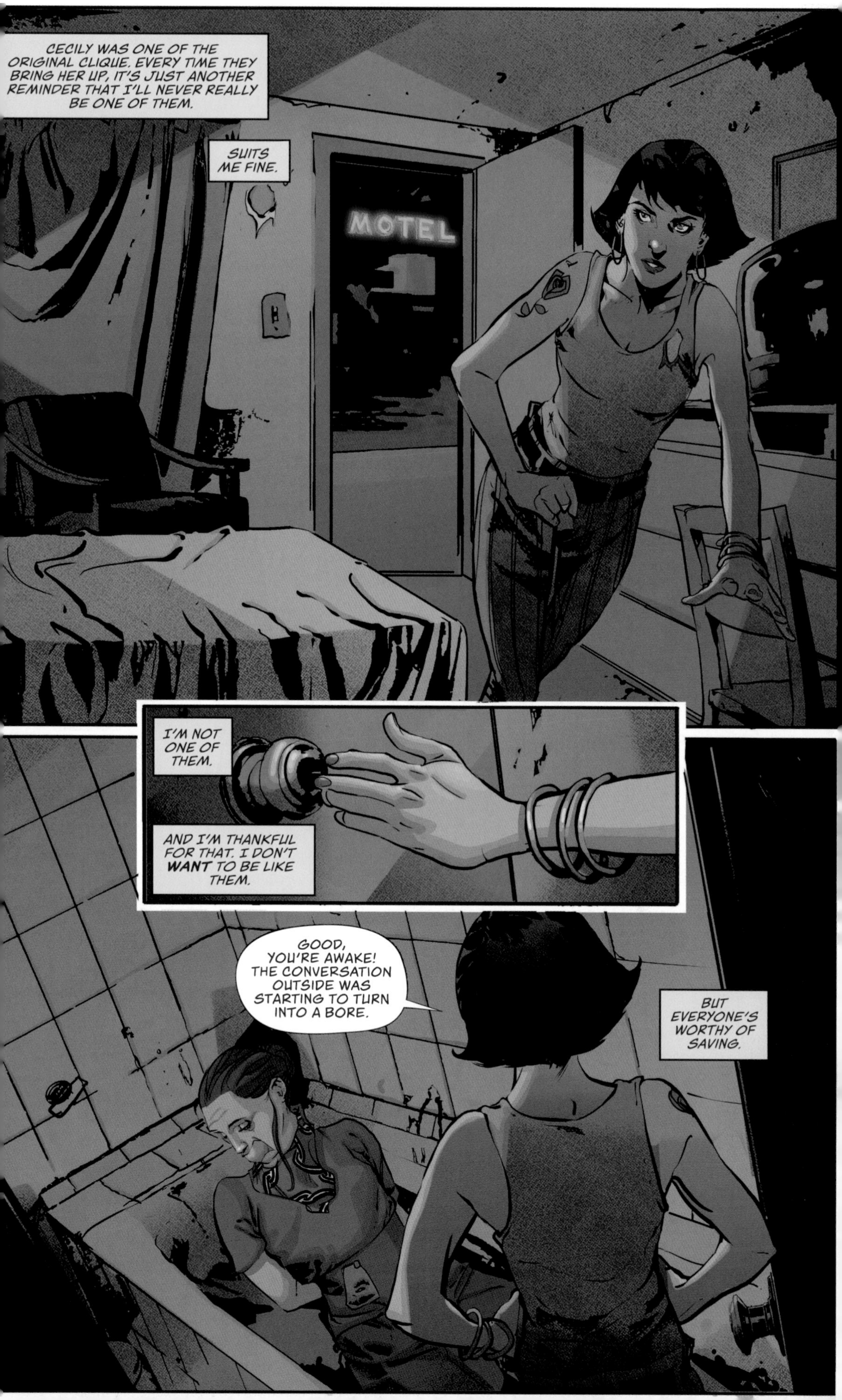
CECILY WAS ONE OF THE ORIGINAL CLIQUE. EVERY TIME THEY BRING HER UP, IT'S JUST ANOTHER REMINDER THAT I'LL NEVER REALLY BE ONE OF THEM.
SUITS ME FINE.
MOTEL
I'M NOT ONE OF THEM.
AND I'M THANKFUL FOR THAT. I DON'T **WANT** TO BE LIKE THEM.
GOOD, YOU'RE AWAKE! THE CONVERSATION OUTSIDE WAS STARTING TO TURN INTO A BORE.
BUT EVERYONE'S WORTHY OF SAVING.

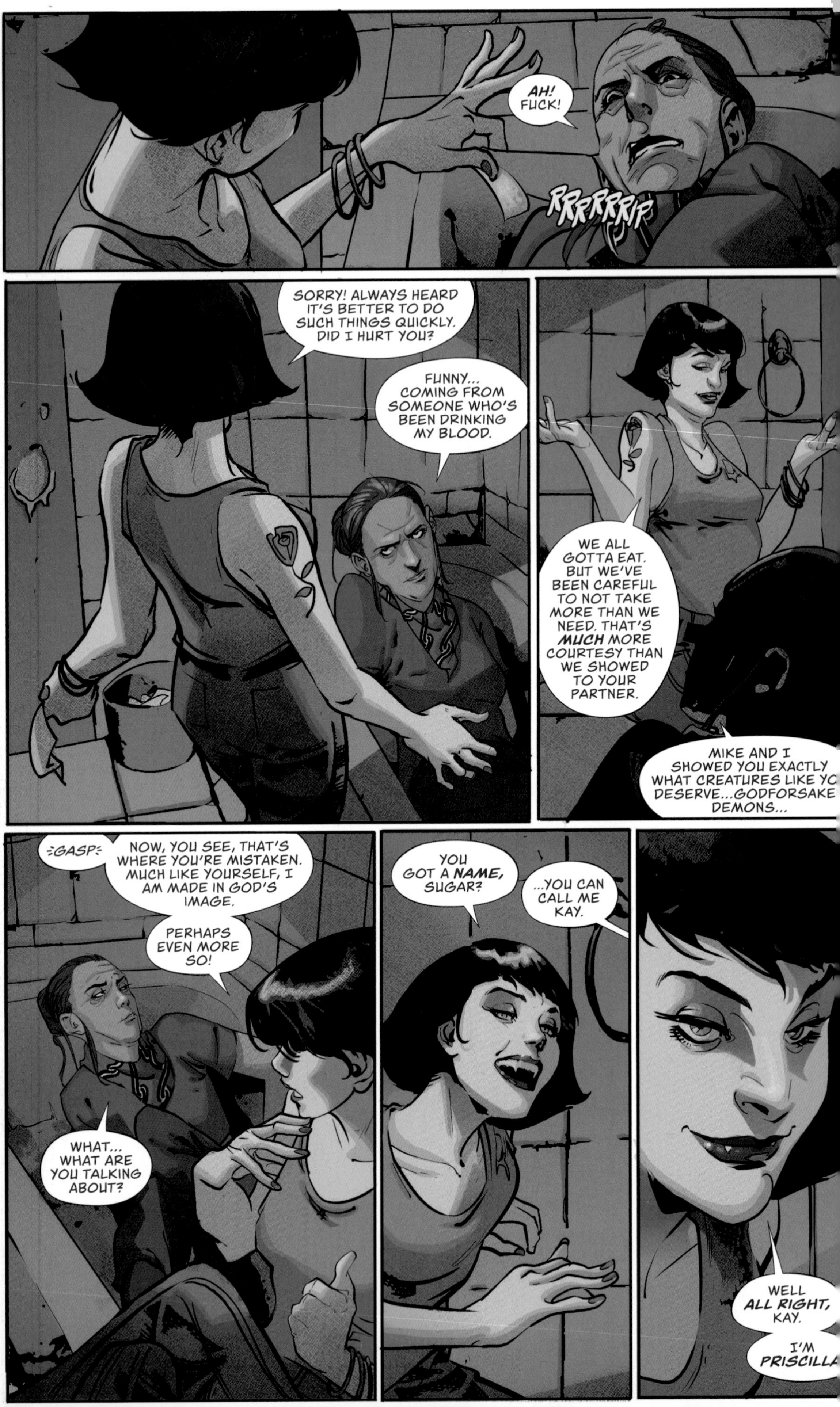
AH! FUCK!
RRRRRRIP
SORRY! ALWAYS HEARD IT'S BETTER TO DO SUCH THINGS QUICKLY. DID I HURT YOU?
FUNNY... COMING FROM SOMEONE WHO'S BEEN DRINKING MY BLOOD.
WE ALL GOTTA EAT. BUT WE'VE BEEN CAREFUL TO NOT TAKE MORE THAN WE NEED. THAT'S MUCH MORE COURTESY THAN WE SHOWED TO YOUR PARTNER.
MIKE AND I SHOWED YOU EXACTLY WHAT CREATURES LIKE YO DESERVE...GODFORSAKE DEMONS...
GASP
NOW, YOU SEE, THAT'S WHERE YOU'RE MISTAKEN. MUCH LIKE YOURSELF, I AM MADE IN GOD'S IMAGE.
PERHAPS EVEN MORE SO!
WHAT... WHAT ARE YOU TALKING ABOUT?
YOU GOT A NAME, SUGAR?
...YOU CAN CALL ME KAY.
WELL ALL RIGHT, KAY.
I'M PRISCILLA

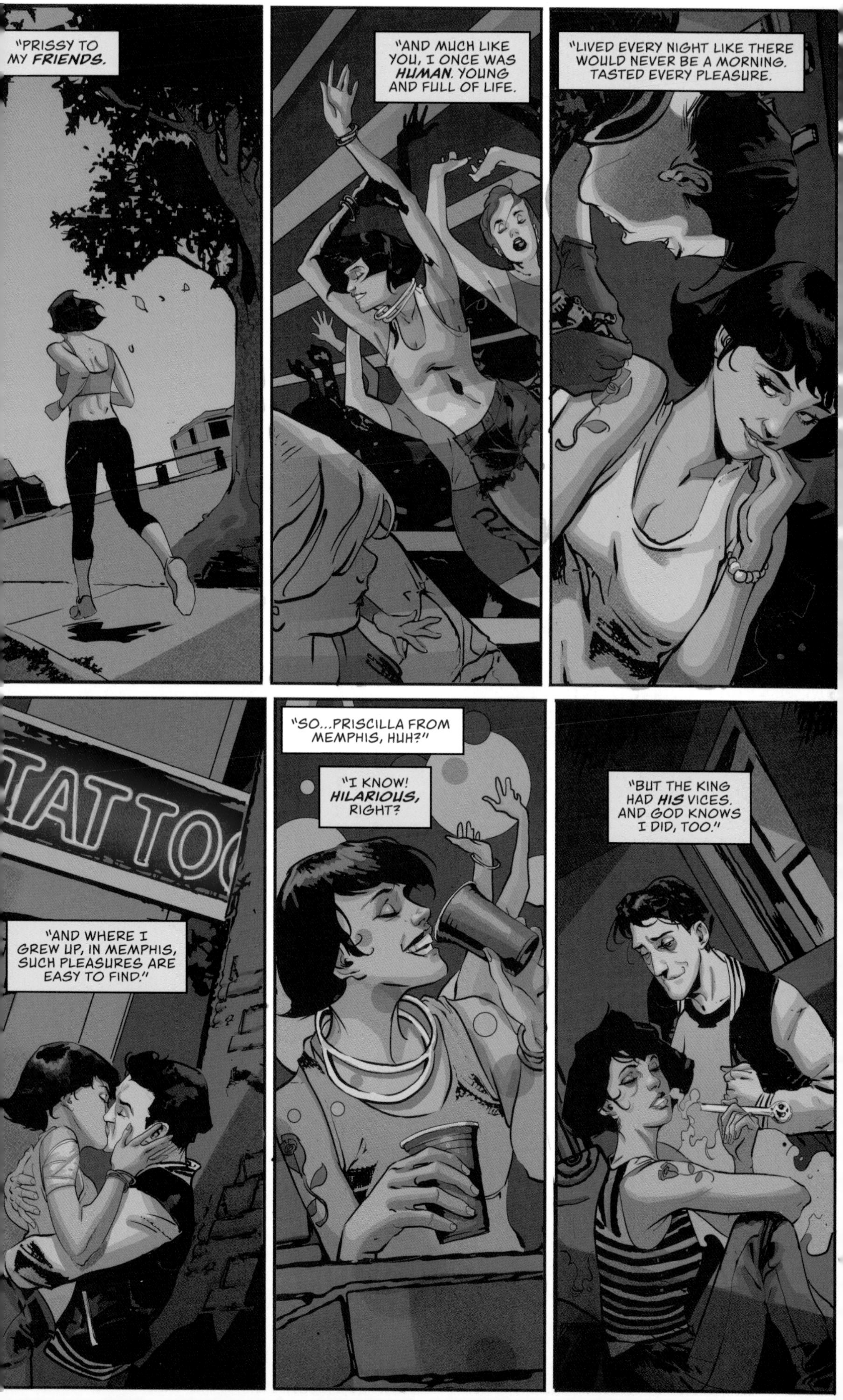
"PRISSY TO MY FRIENDS.
"AND MUCH LIKE YOU, I ONCE WAS HUMAN. YOUNG AND FULL OF LIFE.
"LIVED EVERY NIGHT LIKE THERE WOULD NEVER BE A MORNING. TASTED EVERY PLEASURE.
TATTOO
"AND WHERE I GREW UP, IN MEMPHIS, SUCH PLEASURES ARE EASY TO FIND."
"SO...PRISCILLA FROM MEMPHIS, HUH?"
"I KNOW! HILARIOUS, RIGHT?
"BUT THE KING HAD HIS VICES. AND GOD KNOWS I DID, TOO."

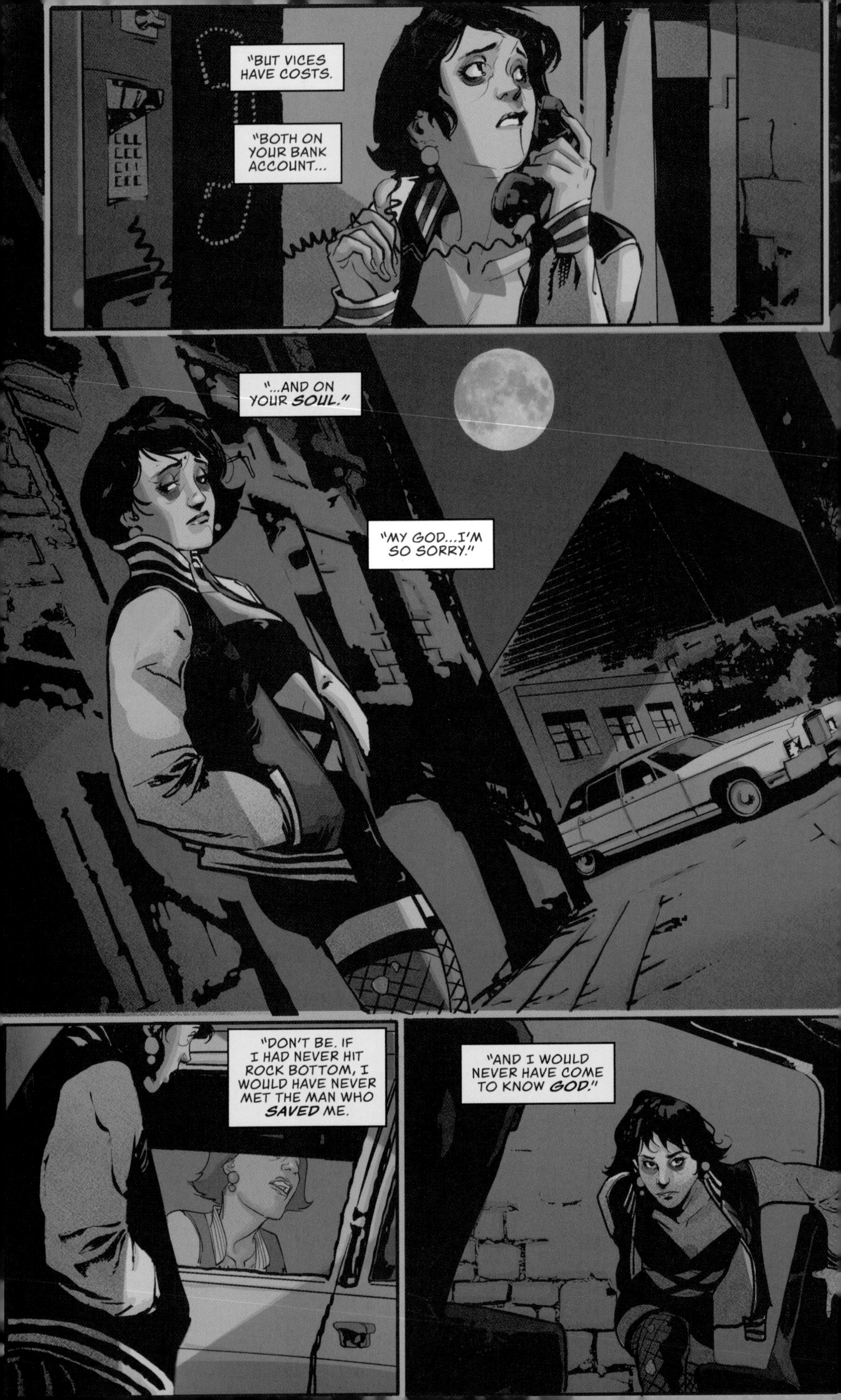
"BUT VICES HAVE COSTS.
"BOTH ON YOUR BANK ACCOUNT...
"...AND ON YOUR SOUL."
"MY GOD...I'M SO SORRY."
"DON'T BE. IF I HAD NEVER HIT ROCK BOTTOM, I WOULD HAVE NEVER MET THE MAN WHO SAVED ME.
"AND I WOULD NEVER HAVE COME TO KNOW GOD."

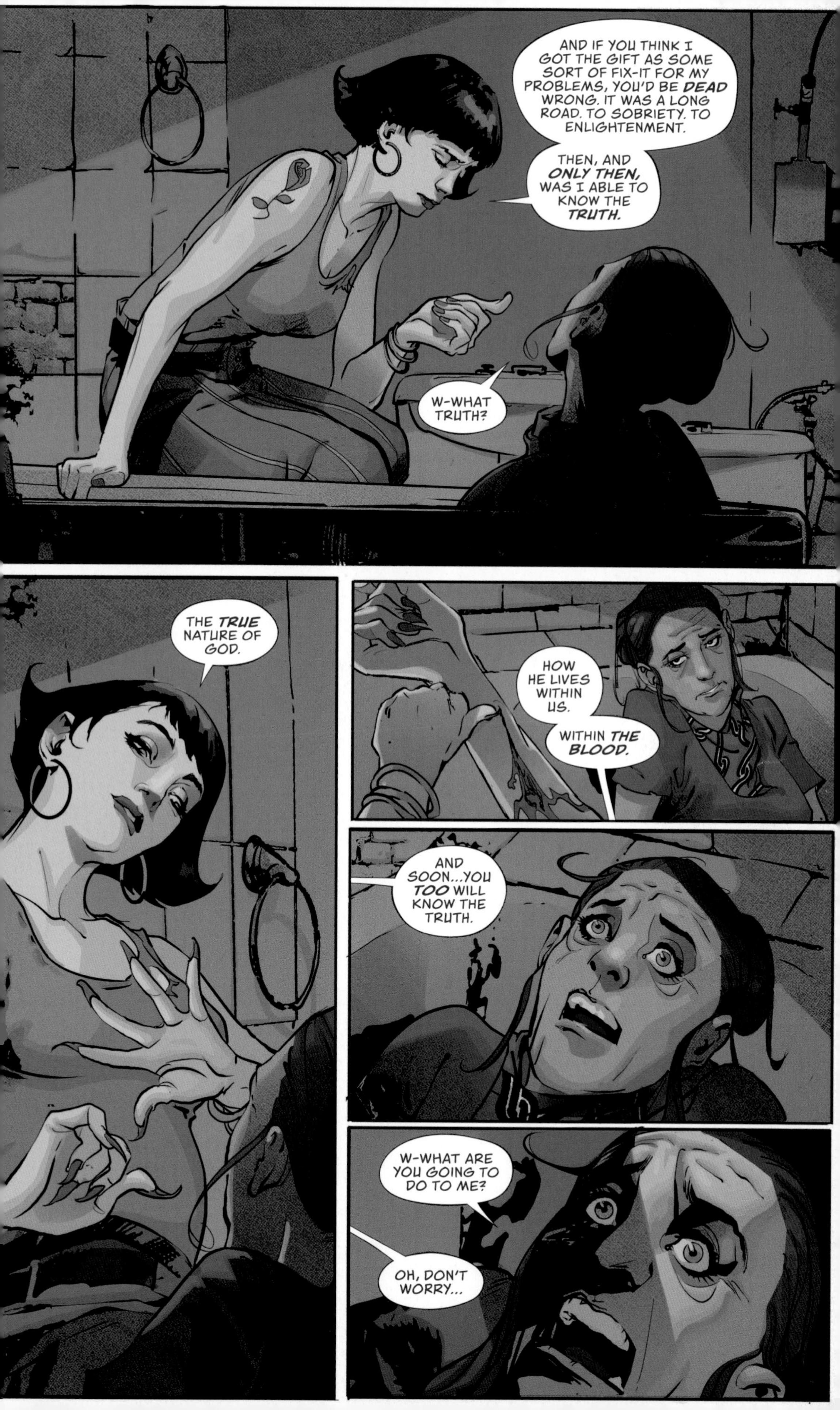
AND IF YOU THINK I GOT THE GIFT AS SOME SORT OF FIX-IT FOR MY PROBLEMS, YOU'D BE ***DEAD*** WRONG. IT WAS A LONG ROAD. TO SOBRIETY. TO ENLIGHTENMENT.
THEN, AND ***ONLY THEN,*** WAS I ABLE TO KNOW THE ***TRUTH.***
W-WHAT TRUTH?
THE ***TRUE*** NATURE OF GOD.
HOW HE LIVES WITHIN US.
WITHIN ***THE BLOOD.***
AND SOON...YOU ***TOO*** WILL KNOW THE TRUTH.
W-WHAT ARE YOU GOING TO DO TO ME?
OH, DON'T WORRY...

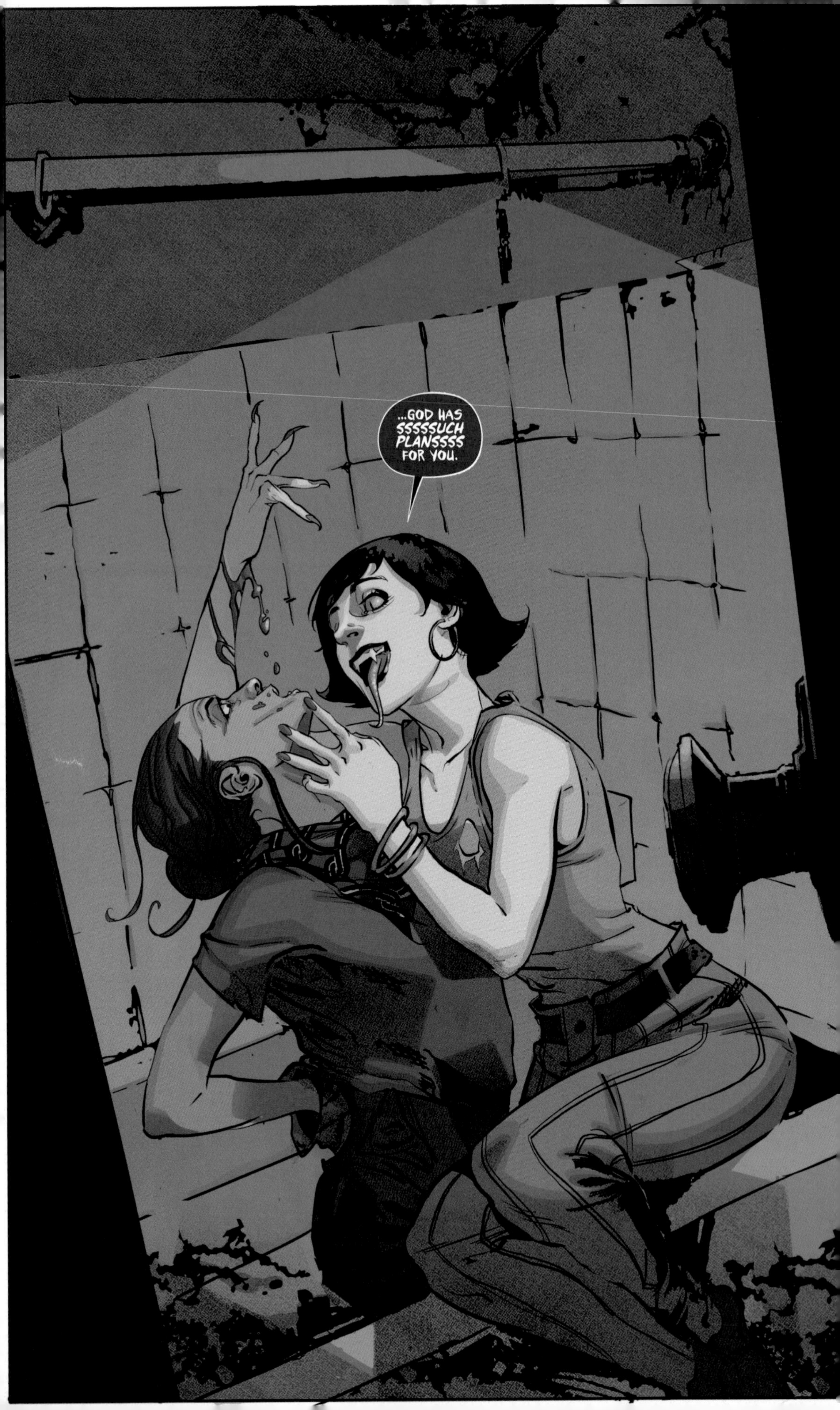
...GOD HAS SSSSSUCH PLANSSSS FOR YOU.

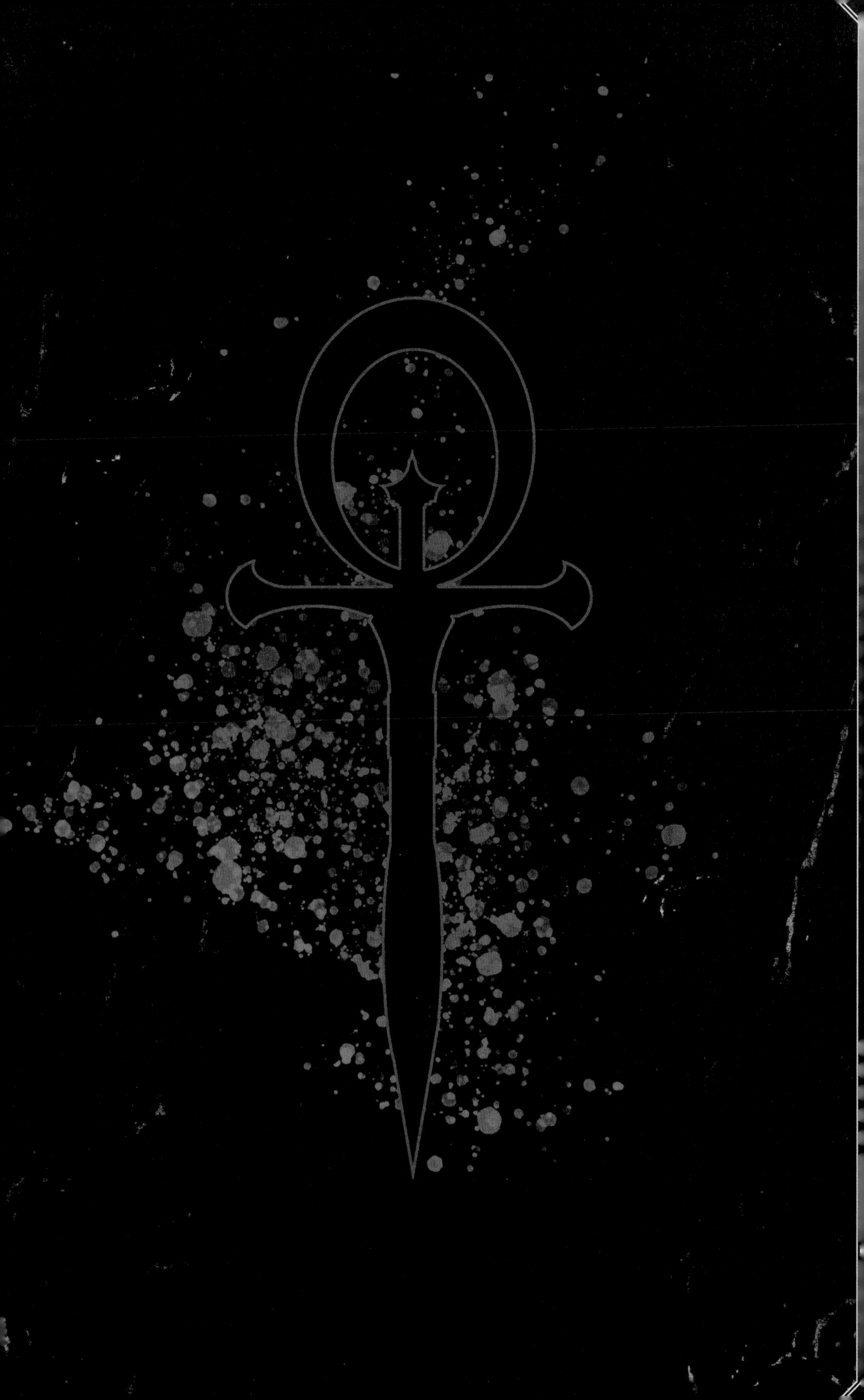

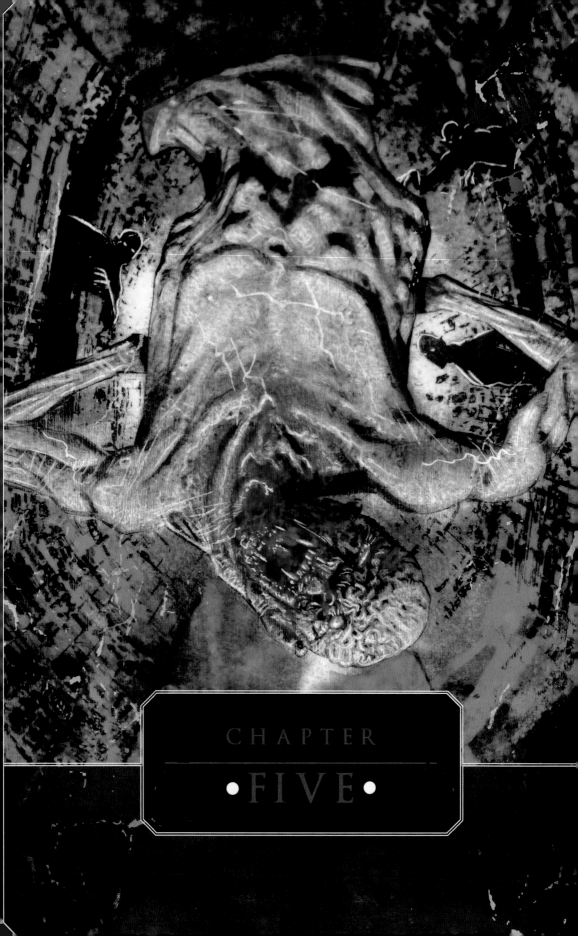

CHAPTER

• FIVE •

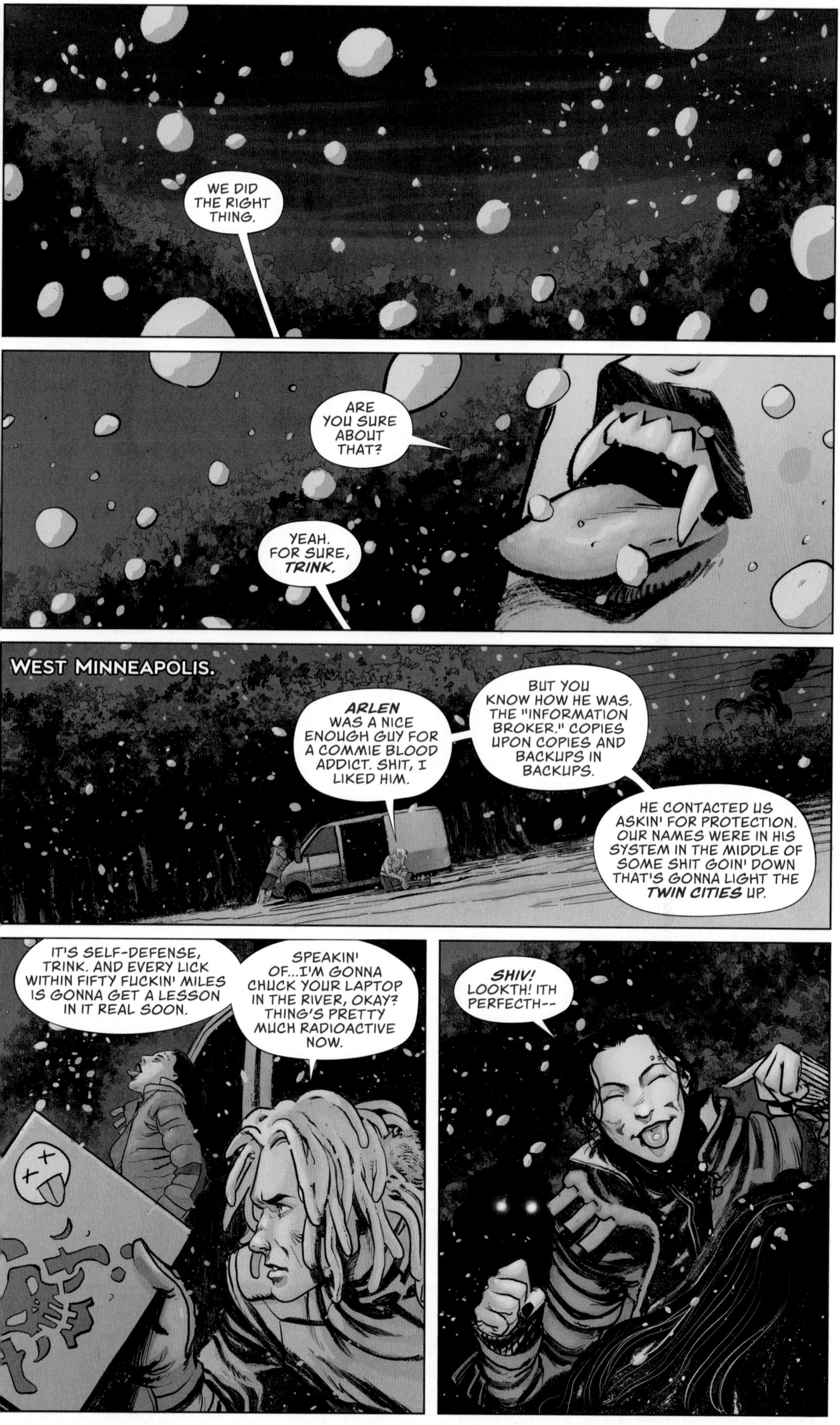

WE DID THE RIGHT THING.
ARE YOU SURE ABOUT THAT?
YEAH. FOR SURE, *TRINK.*
WEST MINNEAPOLIS.
ARLEN WAS A NICE ENOUGH GUY FOR A COMMIE BLOOD ADDICT. SHIT, I LIKED HIM.
BUT YOU KNOW HOW HE WAS. THE "INFORMATION BROKER." COPIES UPON COPIES AND BACKUPS IN BACKUPS.
HE CONTACTED US ASKIN' FOR PROTECTION. OUR NAMES WERE IN HIS SYSTEM IN THE MIDDLE OF SOME SHIT GOIN' DOWN THAT'S GONNA LIGHT THE *TWIN CITIES* UP.
IT'S SELF-DEFENSE, TRINK. AND EVERY LICK WITHIN FIFTY FUCKIN' MILES IS GONNA GET A LESSON IN IT REAL SOON.
SPEAKIN' OF...I'M GONNA CHUCK YOUR LAPTOP IN THE RIVER, OKAY? THING'S PRETTY MUCH RADIOACTIVE NOW.
SHIV! LOOKTH! ITH PERFECTH--

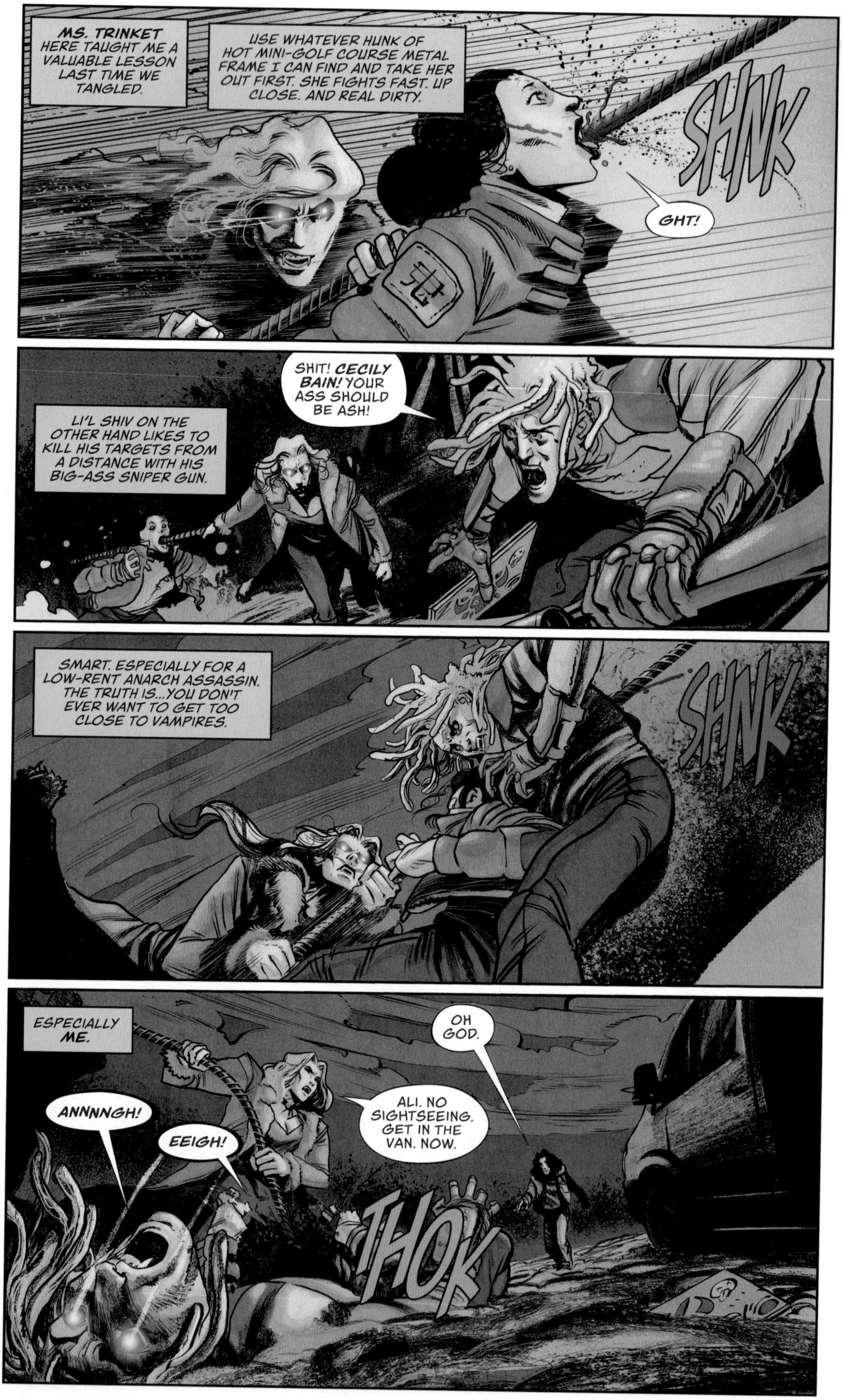
MS. TRINKET HERE TAUGHT ME A VALUABLE LESSON LAST TIME WE TANGLED.
USE WHATEVER HUNK OF HOT MINI-GOLF COURSE METAL FRAME I CAN FIND AND TAKE HER OUT FIRST. SHE FIGHTS FAST. UP CLOSE. AND REAL DIRTY.
SHNK
GHT!
LI'L SHIV ON THE OTHER HAND LIKES TO KILL HIS TARGETS FROM A DISTANCE WITH HIS BIG-ASS SNIPER GUN.
SHIT! CECILY BAIN! YOUR ASS SHOULD BE ASH!
SMART. ESPECIALLY FOR A LOW-RENT ANARCH ASSASSIN. THE TRUTH IS...YOU DON'T EVER WANT TO GET TOO CLOSE TO VAMPIRES.
SHNK
ESPECIALLY ME.
OH GOD.
ANNNNGH!
EEIGH!
ALI. NO SIGHTSEEING. GET IN THE VAN. NOW.
THOK

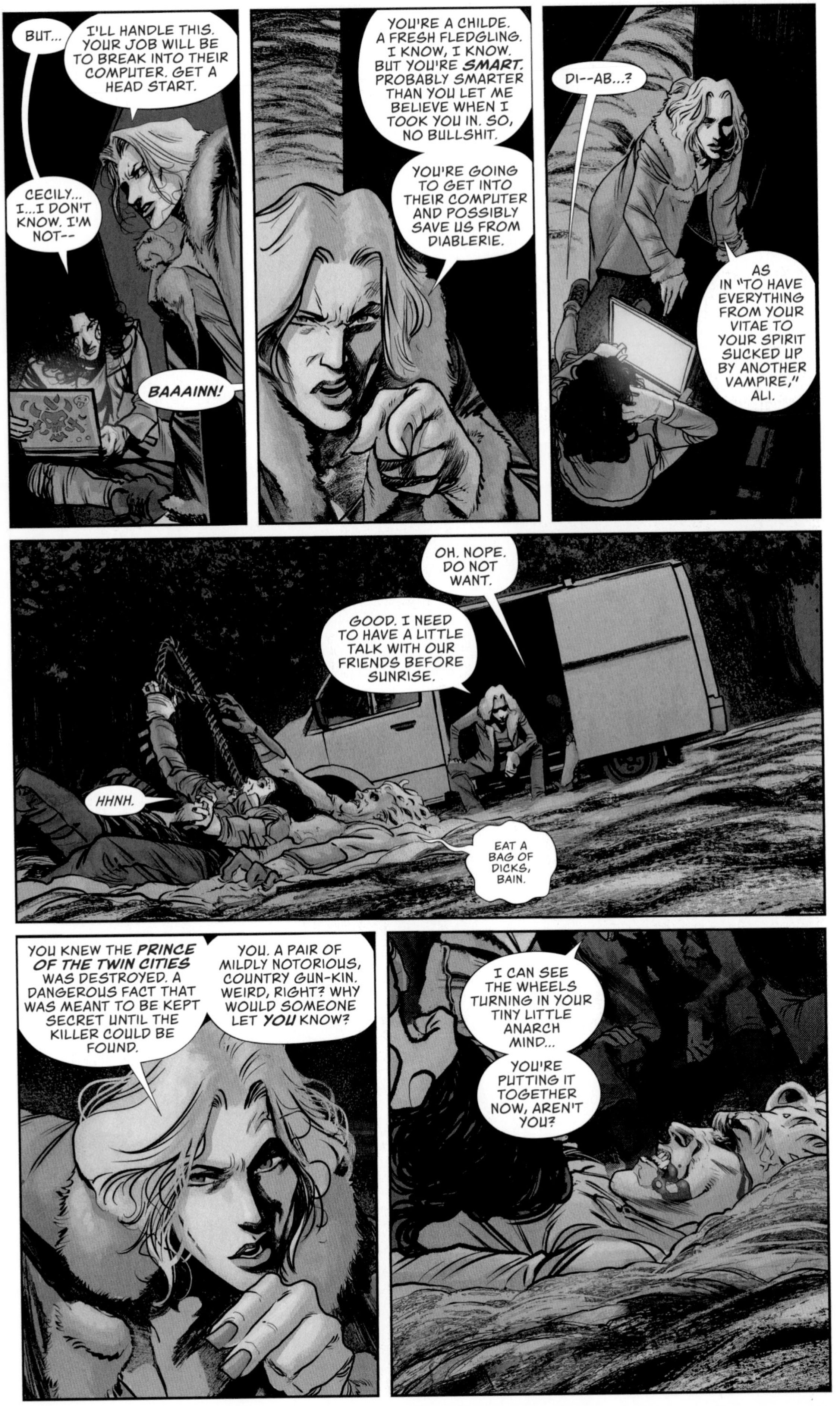
BUT...
I'LL HANDLE THIS. YOUR JOB WILL BE TO BREAK INTO THEIR COMPUTER. GET A HEAD START.
CECILY... I...I DON'T KNOW. I'M NOT--
BAAAINN!
YOU'RE A CHILDE. A FRESH FLEDGLING. I KNOW, I KNOW. BUT YOU'RE SMART. PROBABLY SMARTER THAN YOU LET ME BELIEVE WHEN I TOOK YOU IN. SO, NO BULLSHIT.
YOU'RE GOING TO GET INTO THEIR COMPUTER AND POSSIBLY SAVE US FROM DIABLERIE.
DI--AB...?
AS IN "TO HAVE EVERYTHING FROM YOUR VITAE TO YOUR SPIRIT SUCKED UP BY ANOTHER VAMPIRE," ALI.
OH. NOPE. DO NOT WANT.
GOOD. I NEED TO HAVE A LITTLE TALK WITH OUR FRIENDS BEFORE SUNRISE.
HHNH.
EAT A BAG OF DICKS, BAIN.
YOU KNEW THE PRINCE OF THE TWIN CITIES WAS DESTROYED. A DANGEROUS FACT THAT WAS MEANT TO BE KEPT SECRET UNTIL THE KILLER COULD BE FOUND.
YOU. A PAIR OF MILDLY NOTORIOUS, COUNTRY GUN-KIN. WEIRD, RIGHT? WHY WOULD SOMEONE LET YOU KNOW?
I CAN SEE THE WHEELS TURNING IN YOUR TINY LITTLE ANARCH MIND...
YOU'RE PUTTING IT TOGETHER NOW, AREN'T YOU?

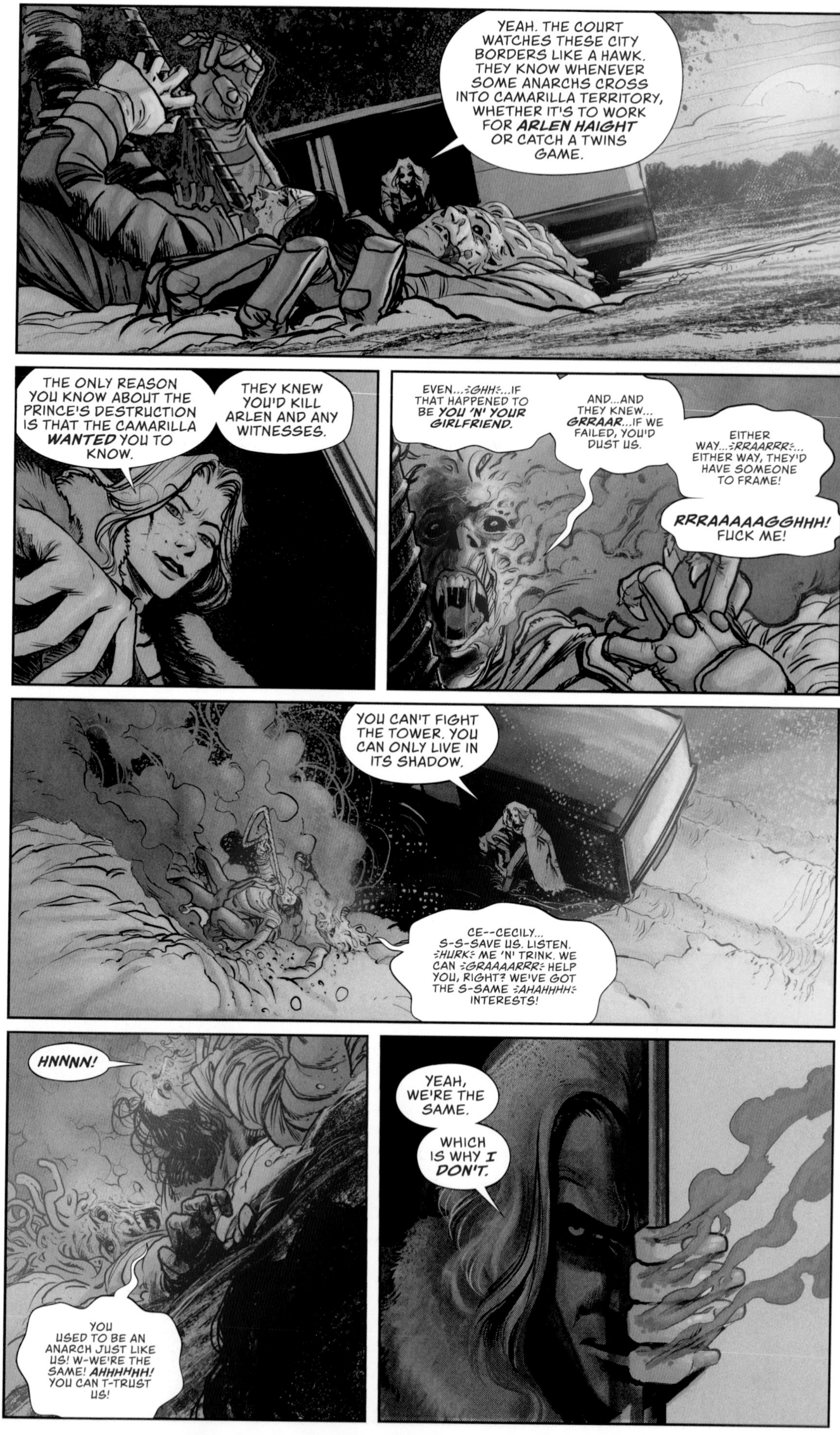

YEAH. THE COURT WATCHES THESE CITY BORDERS LIKE A HAWK. THEY KNOW WHENEVER SOME ANARCHS CROSS INTO CAMARILLA TERRITORY, WHETHER IT'S TO WORK FOR **ARLEN HAIGHT** OR CATCH A TWINS GAME.
THE ONLY REASON YOU KNOW ABOUT THE PRINCE'S DESTRUCTION IS THAT THE CAMARILLA **WANTED** YOU TO KNOW.
THEY KNEW YOU'D KILL ARLEN AND ANY WITNESSES.
EVEN...GHH...IF THAT HAPPENED TO BE ***YOU 'N' YOUR GIRLFRIEND.***
AND...AND THEY KNEW... ***GRRAAR***...IF WE FAILED, YOU'D DUST US.
EITHER WAY...RRAARRR... EITHER WAY, THEY'D HAVE SOMEONE TO FRAME!
RRRAAAAAGGHHH! FUCK ME!
YOU CAN'T FIGHT THE TOWER. YOU CAN ONLY LIVE IN ITS SHADOW.
CE--CECILY... S-S-SAVE US. LISTEN. HURK ME 'N' TRINK. WE CAN GRAAAARRR HELP YOU, RIGHT? WE'VE GOT THE S-SAME AHAHHHH INTERESTS!
HNNNN!
YOU USED TO BE AN ANARCH JUST LIKE US! W-WE'RE THE SAME! ***AHHHHHH!*** YOU CAN T-TRUST US!
YEAH, WE'RE THE SAME.
WHICH IS WHY ***I DON'T.***

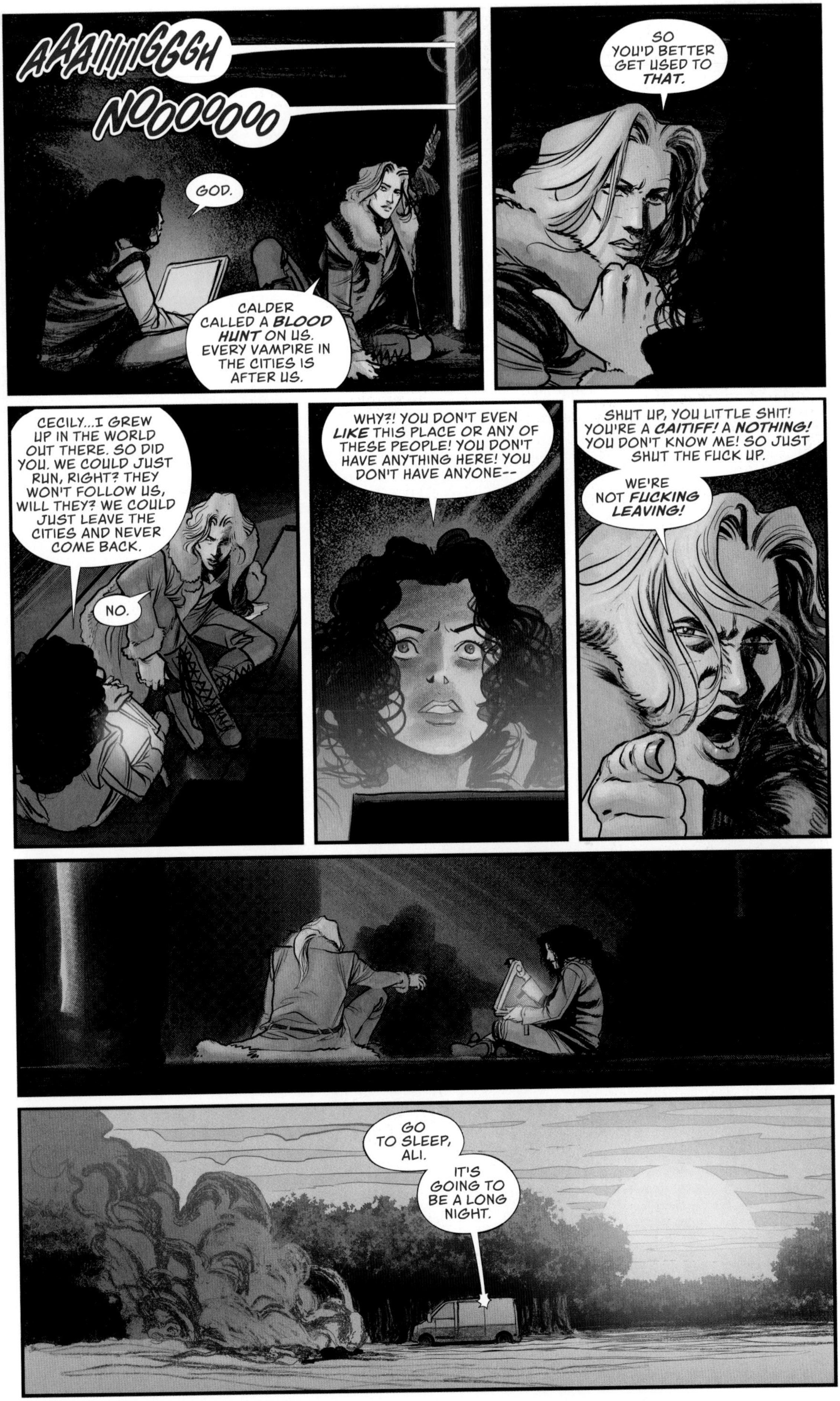
AAAIIIIIGGGH
NOOOOOOO
GOD.
CALDER CALLED A BLOOD HUNT ON US. EVERY VAMPIRE IN THE CITIES IS AFTER US.
SO YOU'D BETTER GET USED TO THAT.
CECILY...I GREW UP IN THE WORLD OUT THERE. SO DID YOU. WE COULD JUST RUN, RIGHT? THEY WON'T FOLLOW US, WILL THEY? WE COULD JUST LEAVE THE CITIES AND NEVER COME BACK.
NO.
WHY?! YOU DON'T EVEN LIKE THIS PLACE OR ANY OF THESE PEOPLE! YOU DON'T HAVE ANYTHING HERE! YOU DON'T HAVE ANYONE--
SHUT UP, YOU LITTLE SHIT! YOU'RE A CAITIFF! A NOTHING! YOU DON'T KNOW ME! SO JUST SHUT THE FUCK UP.
WE'RE NOT FUCKING LEAVING!
GO TO SLEEP, ALI.
IT'S GOING TO BE A LONG NIGHT.

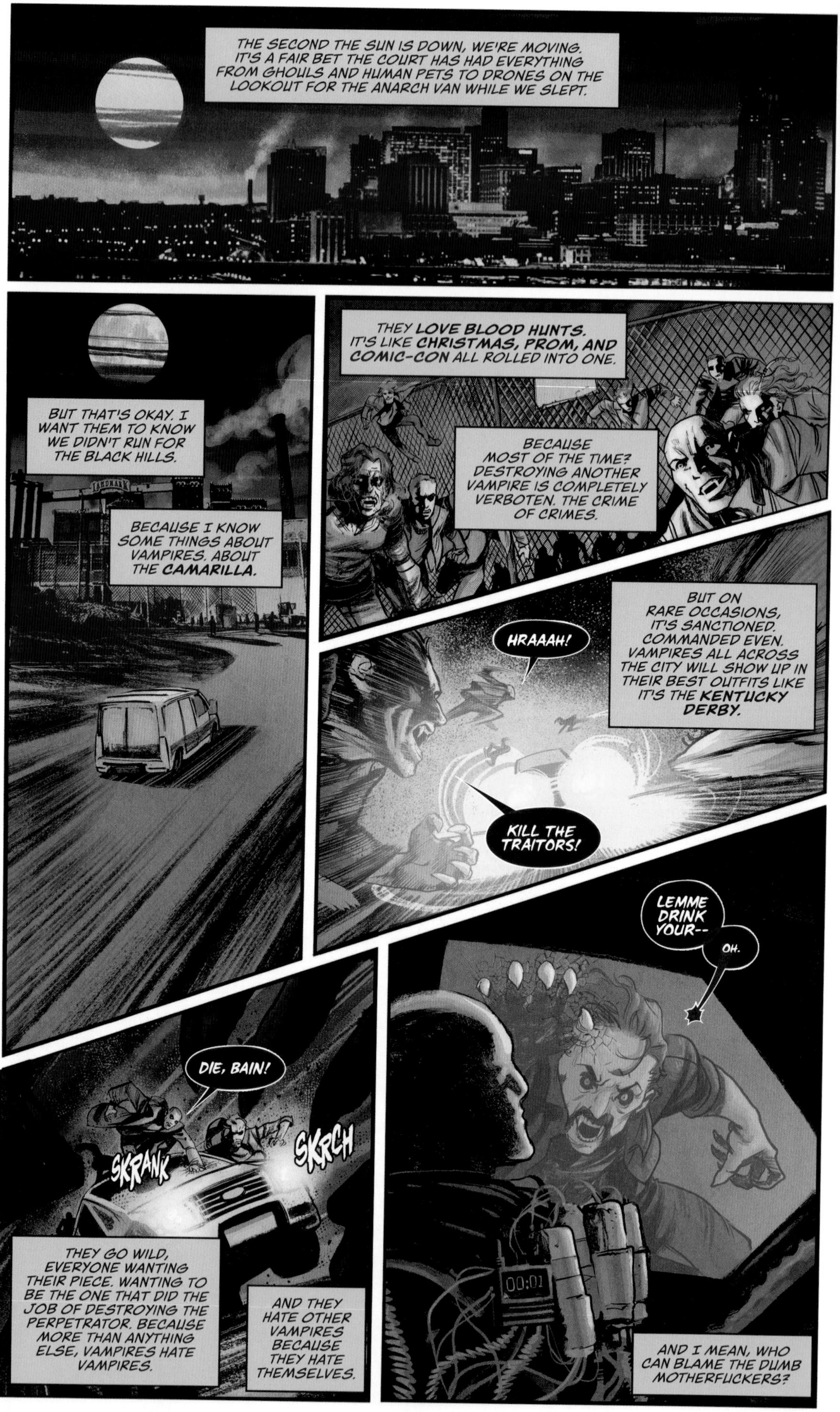
THE SECOND THE SUN IS DOWN, WE'RE MOVING. IT'S A FAIR BET THE COURT HAS HAD EVERYTHING FROM GHOULS AND HUMAN PETS TO DRONES ON THE LOOKOUT FOR THE ANARCH VAN WHILE WE SLEPT.
BUT THAT'S OKAY. I WANT THEM TO KNOW WE DIDN'T RUN FOR THE BLACK HILLS.
BECAUSE I KNOW SOME THINGS ABOUT VAMPIRES. ABOUT THE CAMARILLA.
THEY LOVE BLOOD HUNTS. IT'S LIKE CHRISTMAS, PROM, AND COMIC-CON ALL ROLLED INTO ONE.
BECAUSE MOST OF THE TIME? DESTROYING ANOTHER VAMPIRE IS COMPLETELY VERBOTEN. THE CRIME OF CRIMES.
BUT ON RARE OCCASIONS, IT'S SANCTIONED. COMMANDED EVEN. VAMPIRES ALL ACROSS THE CITY WILL SHOW UP IN THEIR BEST OUTFITS LIKE IT'S THE KENTUCKY DERBY.
HRAAAH!
KILL THE TRAITORS!
DIE, BAIN!
SKRANK
SKRCH
THEY GO WILD, EVERYONE WANTING THEIR PIECE. WANTING TO BE THE ONE THAT DID THE JOB OF DESTROYING THE PERPETRATOR. BECAUSE MORE THAN ANYTHING ELSE, VAMPIRES HATE VAMPIRES.
AND THEY HATE OTHER VAMPIRES BECAUSE THEY HATE THEMSELVES.
LEMME DRINK YOUR--
OH.
00:01
AND I MEAN, WHO CAN BLAME THE DUMB MOTHERFUCKERS?

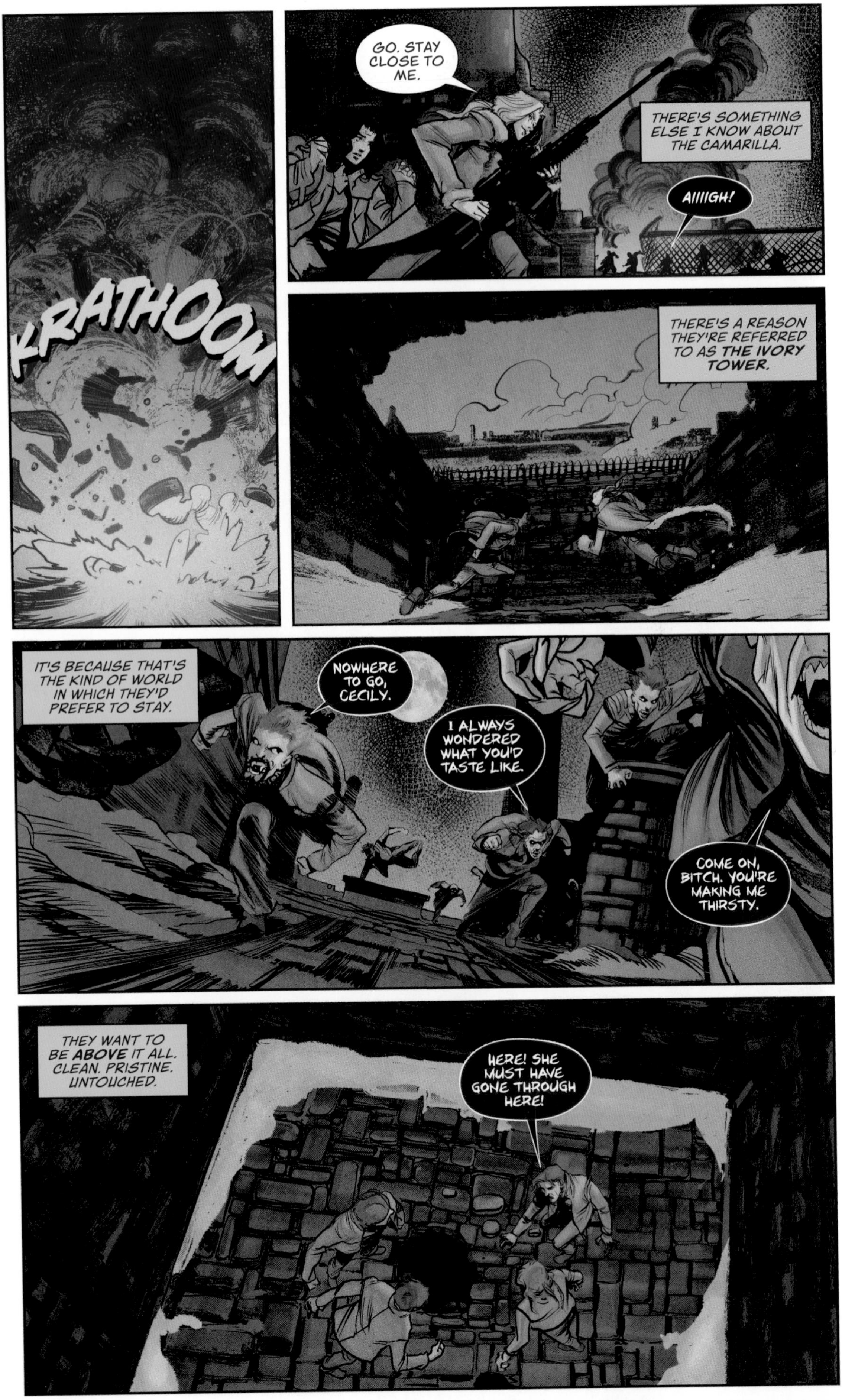
KRATHOOM
GO. STAY CLOSE TO ME.
THERE'S SOMETHING ELSE I KNOW ABOUT THE CAMARILLA.
AIIIIGH!
THERE'S A REASON THEY'RE REFERRED TO AS THE IVORY TOWER.
IT'S BECAUSE THAT'S THE KIND OF WORLD IN WHICH THEY'D PREFER TO STAY.
NOWHERE TO GO, CECILY.
I ALWAYS WONDERED WHAT YOU'D TASTE LIKE.
COME ON, BITCH. YOU'RE MAKING ME THIRSTY.
THEY WANT TO BE ABOVE IT ALL. CLEAN. PRISTINE. UNTOUCHED.
HERE! SHE MUST HAVE GONE THROUGH HERE!

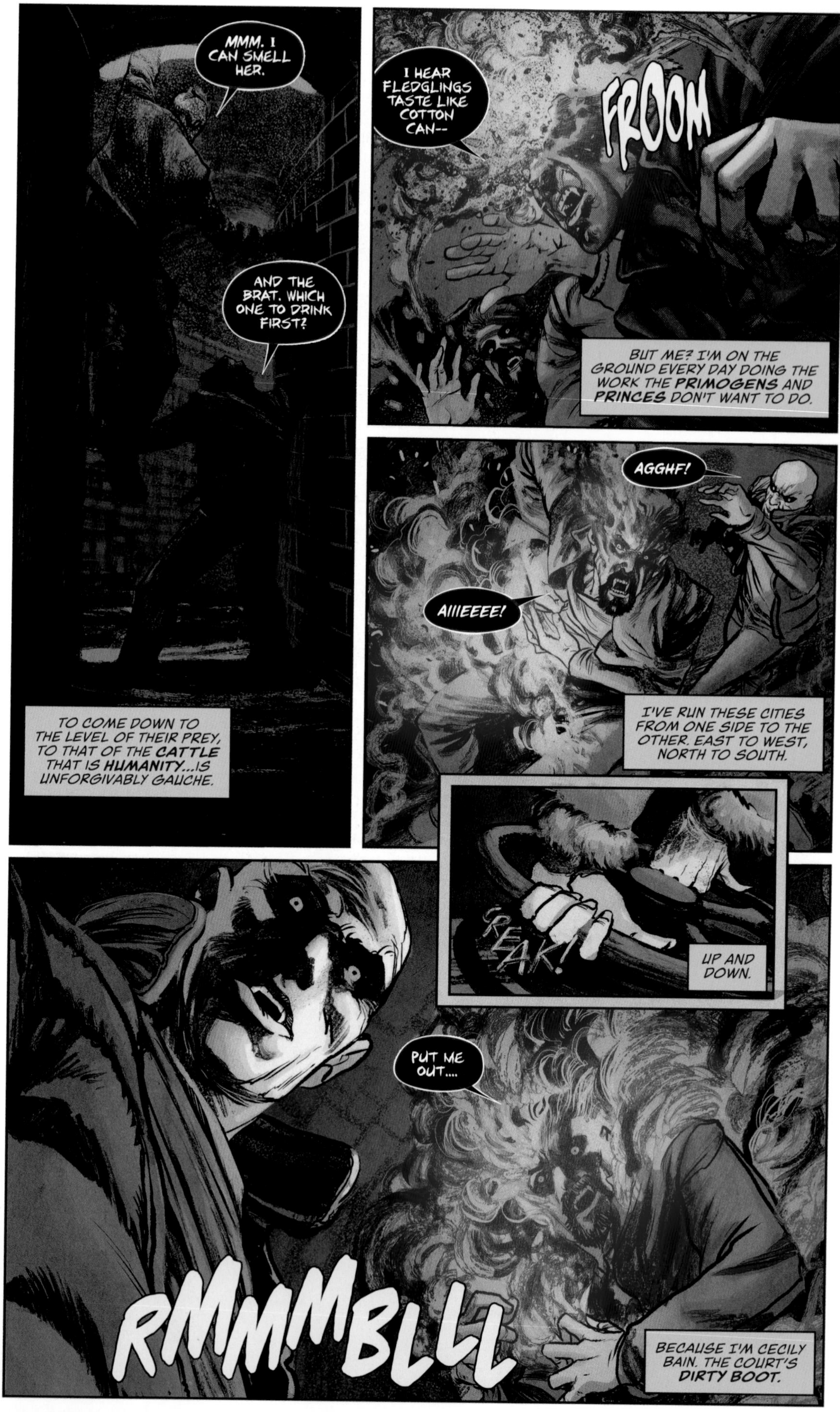
MMM. I CAN SMELL HER.
AND THE BRAT. WHICH ONE TO DRINK FIRST?
TO COME DOWN TO THE LEVEL OF THEIR PREY, TO THAT OF THE CATTLE THAT IS HUMANITY...IS UNFORGIVABLY GAUCHE.
I HEAR FLEDGLINGS TASTE LIKE COTTON CAN--
FROOM
BUT ME? I'M ON THE GROUND EVERY DAY DOING THE WORK THE PRIMOGENS AND PRINCES DON'T WANT TO DO.
AGGHF!
AIIIEEEE!
I'VE RUN THESE CITIES FROM ONE SIDE TO THE OTHER. EAST TO WEST, NORTH TO SOUTH.
CREAK!
UP AND DOWN.
PUT ME OUT....
RMMMBLLL
BECAUSE I'M CECILY BAIN. THE COURT'S DIRTY BOOT.

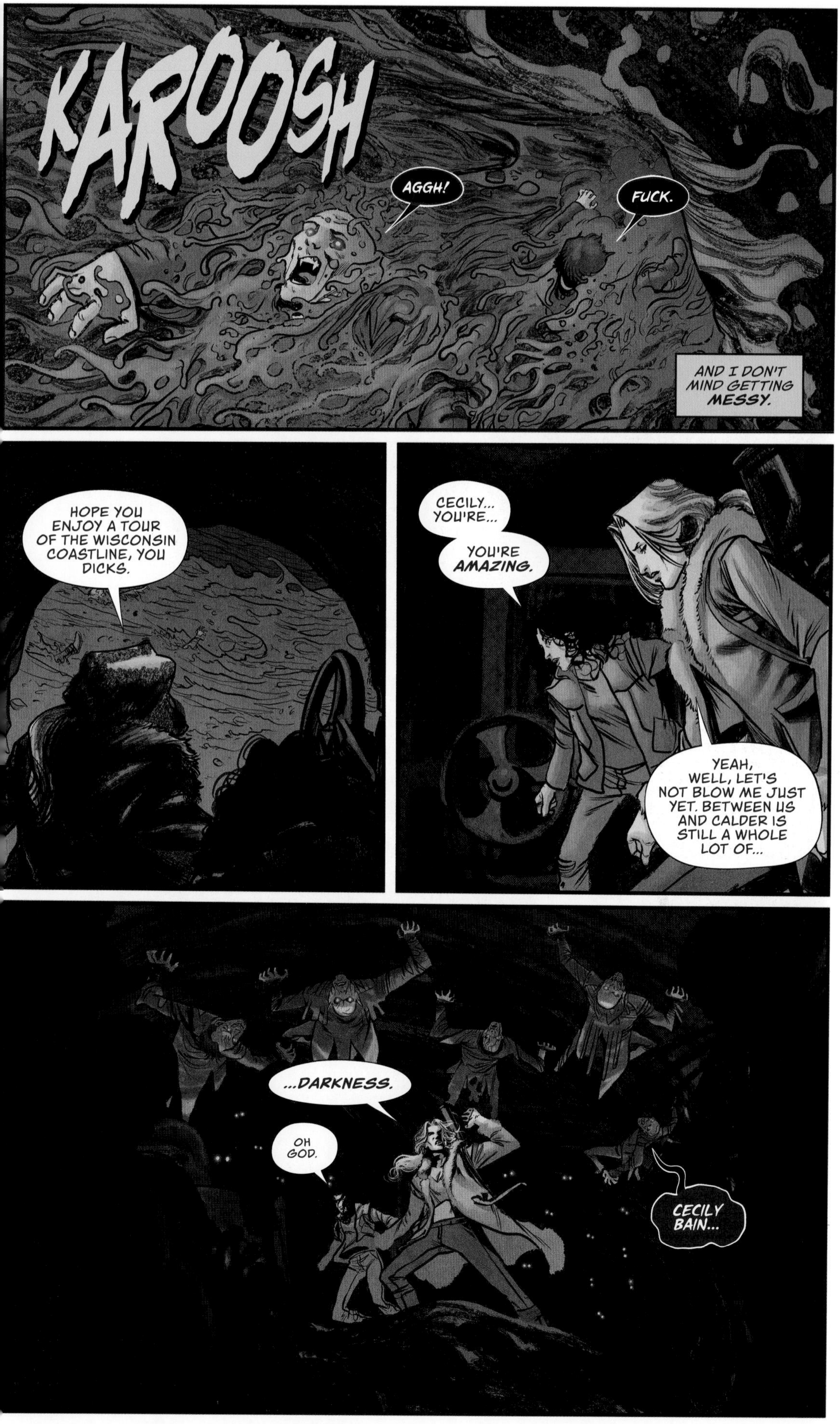
KAROOSH
AGGH!
FUCK.
AND I DON'T MIND GETTING MESSY.
HOPE YOU ENJOY A TOUR OF THE WISCONSIN COASTLINE, YOU DICKS.
CECILY... YOU'RE...
YOU'RE AMAZING.
YEAH, WELL, LET'S NOT BLOW ME JUST YET. BETWEEN US AND CALDER IS STILL A WHOLE LOT OF...
...DARKNESS.
OH GOD.
CECILY BAIN...

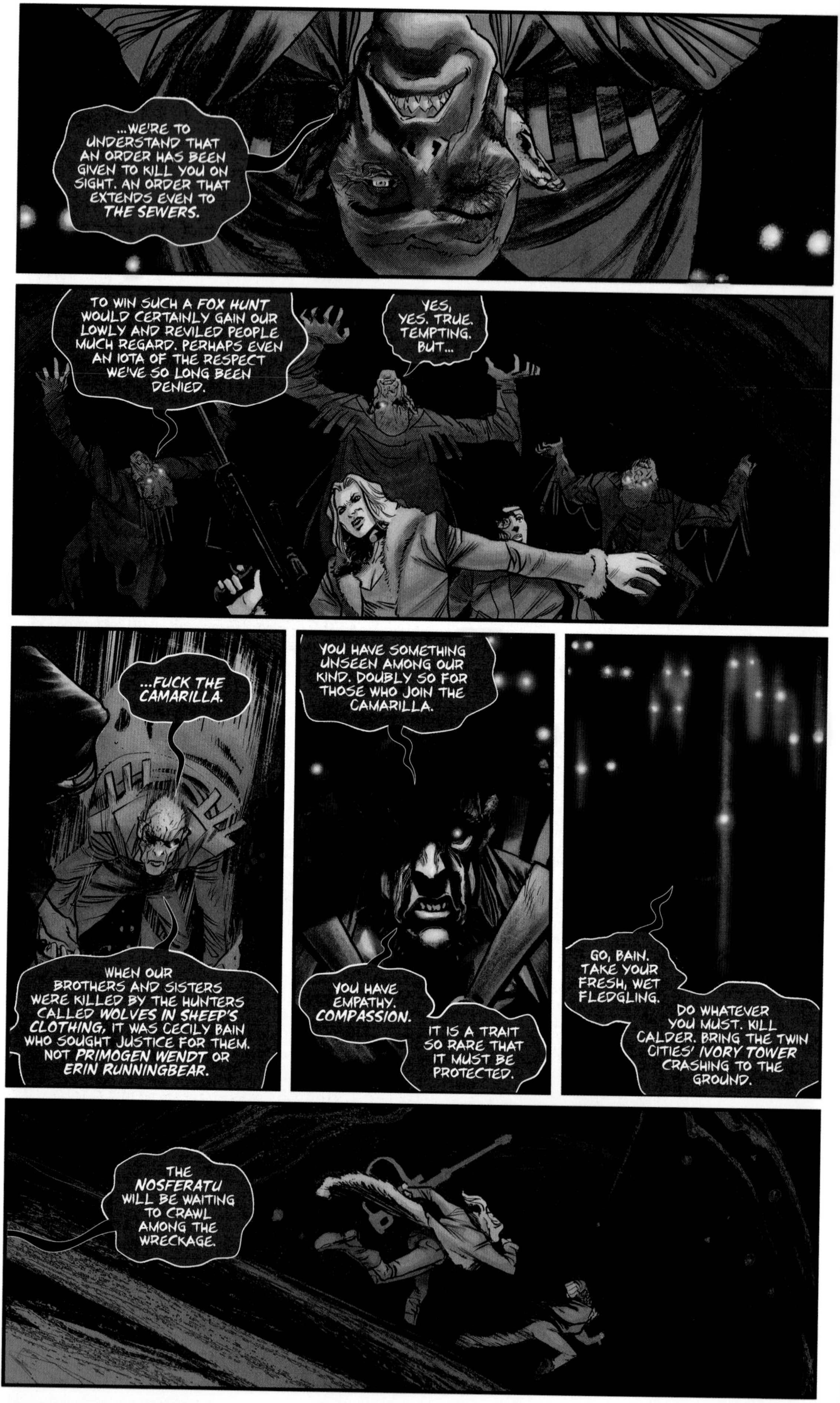
...WE'RE TO UNDERSTAND THAT AN ORDER HAS BEEN GIVEN TO KILL YOU ON SIGHT. AN ORDER THAT EXTENDS EVEN TO THE SEWERS.
TO WIN SUCH A FOX HUNT WOULD CERTAINLY GAIN OUR LOWLY AND REVILED PEOPLE MUCH REGARD. PERHAPS EVEN AN IOTA OF THE RESPECT WE'VE SO LONG BEEN DENIED.
YES, YES. TRUE. TEMPTING. BUT...
...FUCK THE CAMARILLA.
WHEN OUR BROTHERS AND SISTERS WERE KILLED BY THE HUNTERS CALLED WOLVES IN SHEEP'S CLOTHING, IT WAS CECILY BAIN WHO SOUGHT JUSTICE FOR THEM. NOT PRIMOGEN WENDT OR ERIN RUNNINGBEAR.
YOU HAVE SOMETHING UNSEEN AMONG OUR KIND. DOUBLY SO FOR THOSE WHO JOIN THE CAMARILLA.
YOU HAVE EMPATHY. COMPASSION.
IT IS A TRAIT SO RARE THAT IT MUST BE PROTECTED.
GO, BAIN. TAKE YOUR FRESH, WET FLEDGLING.
DO WHATEVER YOU MUST. KILL CALDER. BRING THE TWIN CITIES' IVORY TOWER CRASHING TO THE GROUND.
THE NOSFERATU WILL BE WAITING TO CRAWL AMONG THE WRECKAGE.

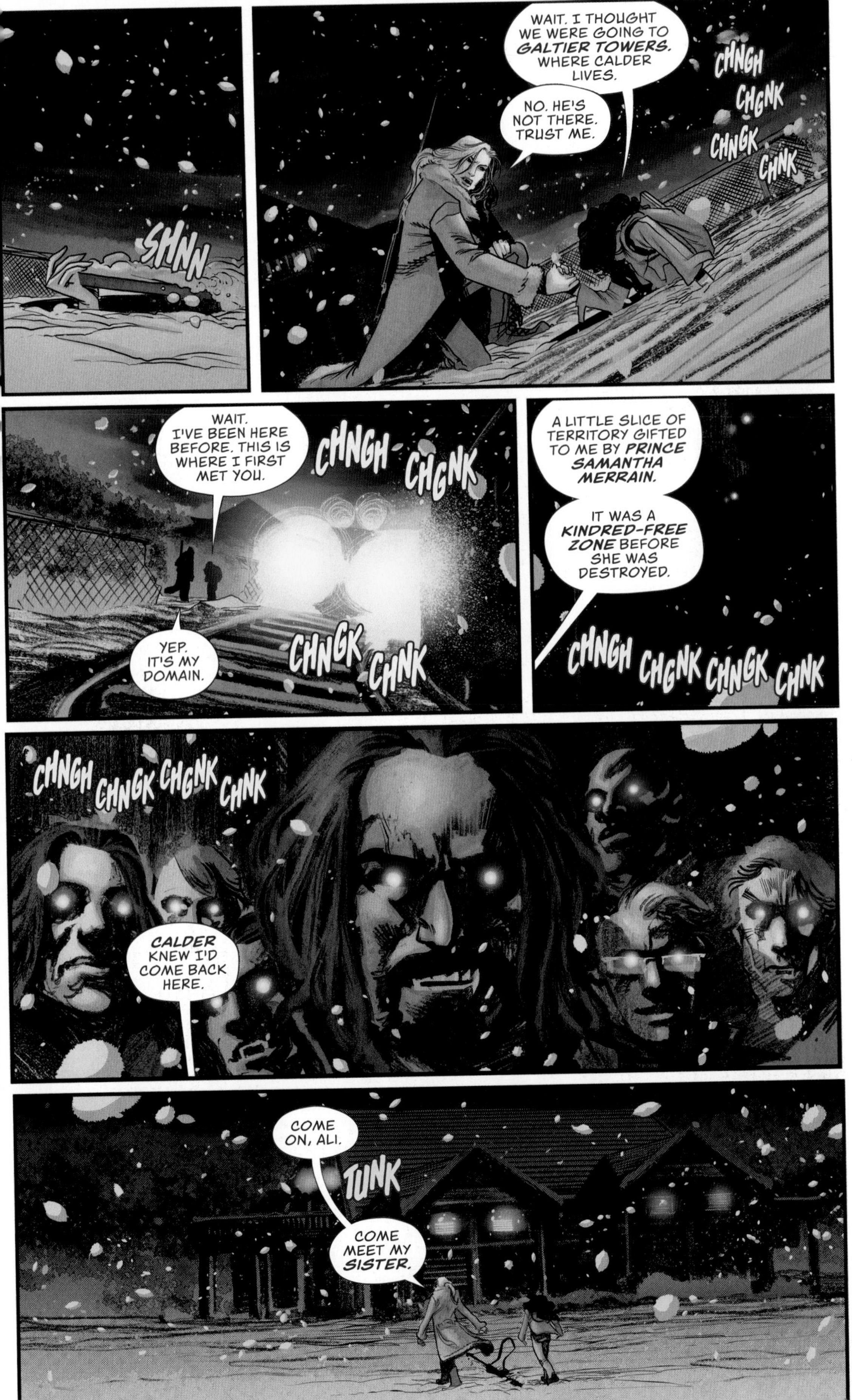
SHNN
WAIT. I THOUGHT WE WERE GOING TO GALTIER TOWERS. WHERE CALDER LIVES.
NO. HE'S NOT THERE. TRUST ME.
CHNGH
CHGNK
CHNGK
CHNK
WAIT. I'VE BEEN HERE BEFORE. THIS IS WHERE I FIRST MET YOU.
CHNGH
CHGNK
YEP. IT'S MY DOMAIN.
CHNGK
CHNK
A LITTLE SLICE OF TERRITORY GIFTED TO ME BY PRINCE SAMANTHA MERRAIN.
IT WAS A KINDRED-FREE ZONE BEFORE SHE WAS DESTROYED.
CHNGH CHGNK CHNGK CHNK
CHNGH CHNGK CHGNK CHNK
CALDER KNEW I'D COME BACK HERE.
COME ON, ALI.
TUNK
COME MEET MY SISTER.

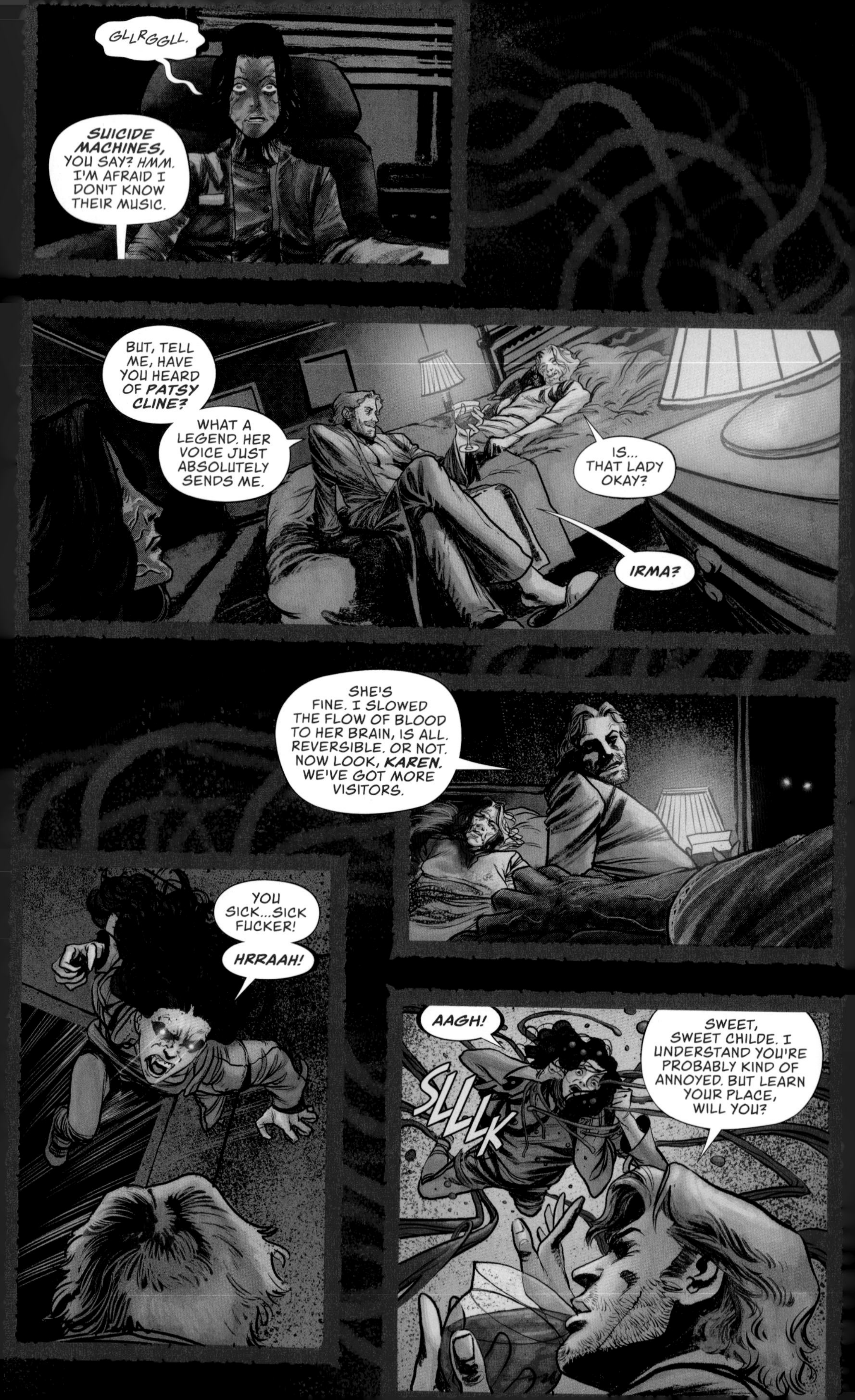
GLLRGGLL.
SUICIDE MACHINES, YOU SAY? HMM. I'M AFRAID I DON'T KNOW THEIR MUSIC.
BUT, TELL ME, HAVE YOU HEARD OF PATSY CLINE?
WHAT A LEGEND. HER VOICE JUST ABSOLUTELY SENDS ME.
IS... THAT LADY OKAY?
IRMA?
SHE'S FINE. I SLOWED THE FLOW OF BLOOD TO HER BRAIN, IS ALL. REVERSIBLE. OR NOT. NOW LOOK, KAREN. WE'VE GOT MORE VISITORS.
YOU SICK...SICK FUCKER!
HRRAAH!
AAGH!
SLLLK
SWEET, SWEET CHILDE. I UNDERSTAND YOU'RE PROBABLY KIND OF ANNOYED. BUT LEARN YOUR PLACE, WILL YOU?

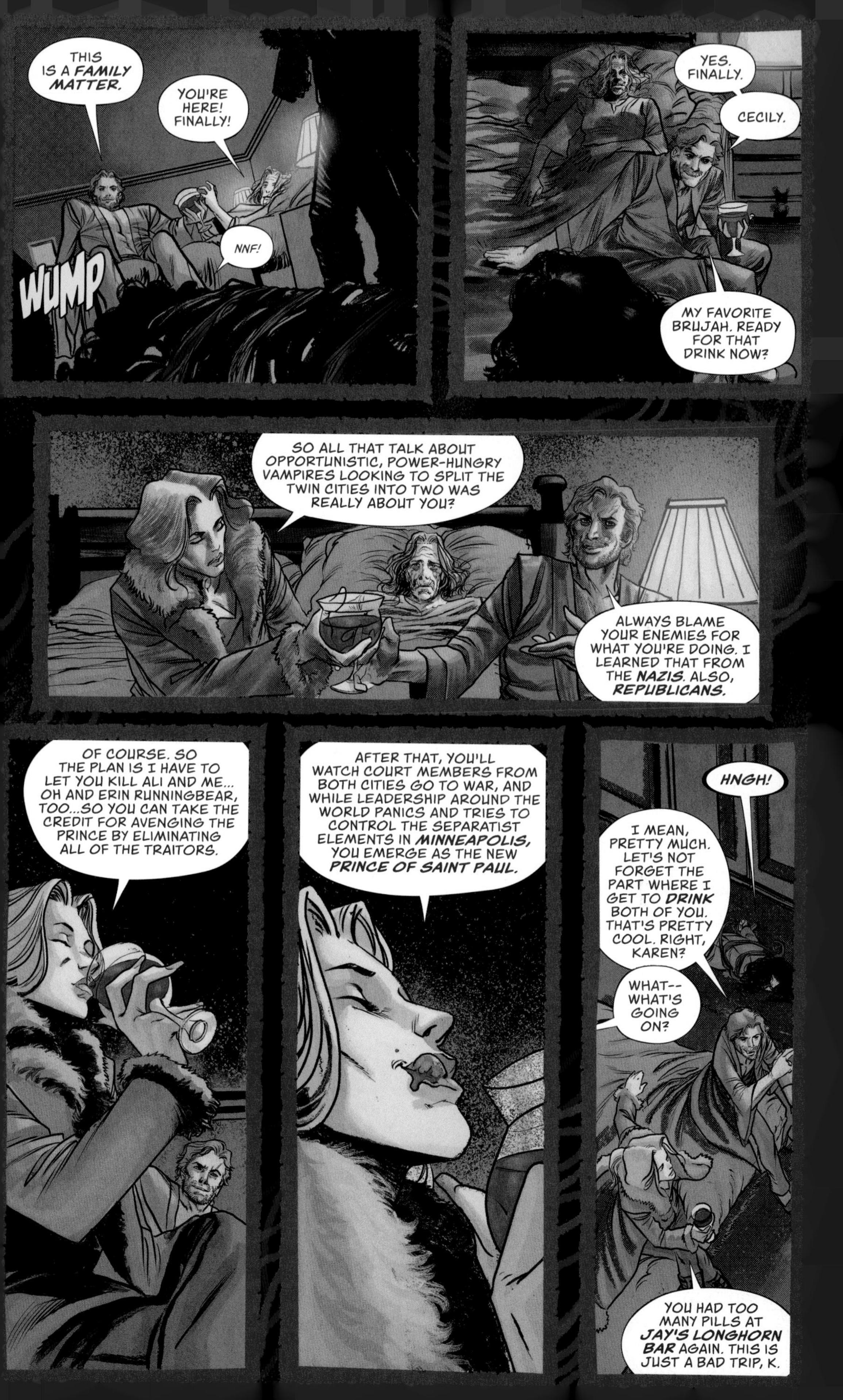
THIS IS A FAMILY MATTER.
YOU'RE HERE! FINALLY!
NNF!
WUMP
YES. FINALLY.
CECILY.
MY FAVORITE BRUJAH. READY FOR THAT DRINK NOW?
SO ALL THAT TALK ABOUT OPPORTUNISTIC, POWER-HUNGRY VAMPIRES LOOKING TO SPLIT THE TWIN CITIES INTO TWO WAS REALLY ABOUT YOU?
ALWAYS BLAME YOUR ENEMIES FOR WHAT YOU'RE DOING. I LEARNED THAT FROM THE NAZIS. ALSO, REPUBLICANS.
OF COURSE. SO THE PLAN IS I HAVE TO LET YOU KILL ALI AND ME... OH AND ERIN RUNNINGBEAR, TOO...SO YOU CAN TAKE THE CREDIT FOR AVENGING THE PRINCE BY ELIMINATING ALL OF THE TRAITORS.
AFTER THAT, YOU'LL WATCH COURT MEMBERS FROM BOTH CITIES GO TO WAR, AND WHILE LEADERSHIP AROUND THE WORLD PANICS AND TRIES TO CONTROL THE SEPARATIST ELEMENTS IN MINNEAPOLIS, YOU EMERGE AS THE NEW PRINCE OF SAINT PAUL.
HNGH!
I MEAN, PRETTY MUCH. LET'S NOT FORGET THE PART WHERE I GET TO DRINK BOTH OF YOU. THAT'S PRETTY COOL. RIGHT, KAREN?
WHAT-- WHAT'S GOING ON?
YOU HAD TOO MANY PILLS AT JAY'S LONGHORN BAR AGAIN. THIS IS JUST A BAD TRIP, K.

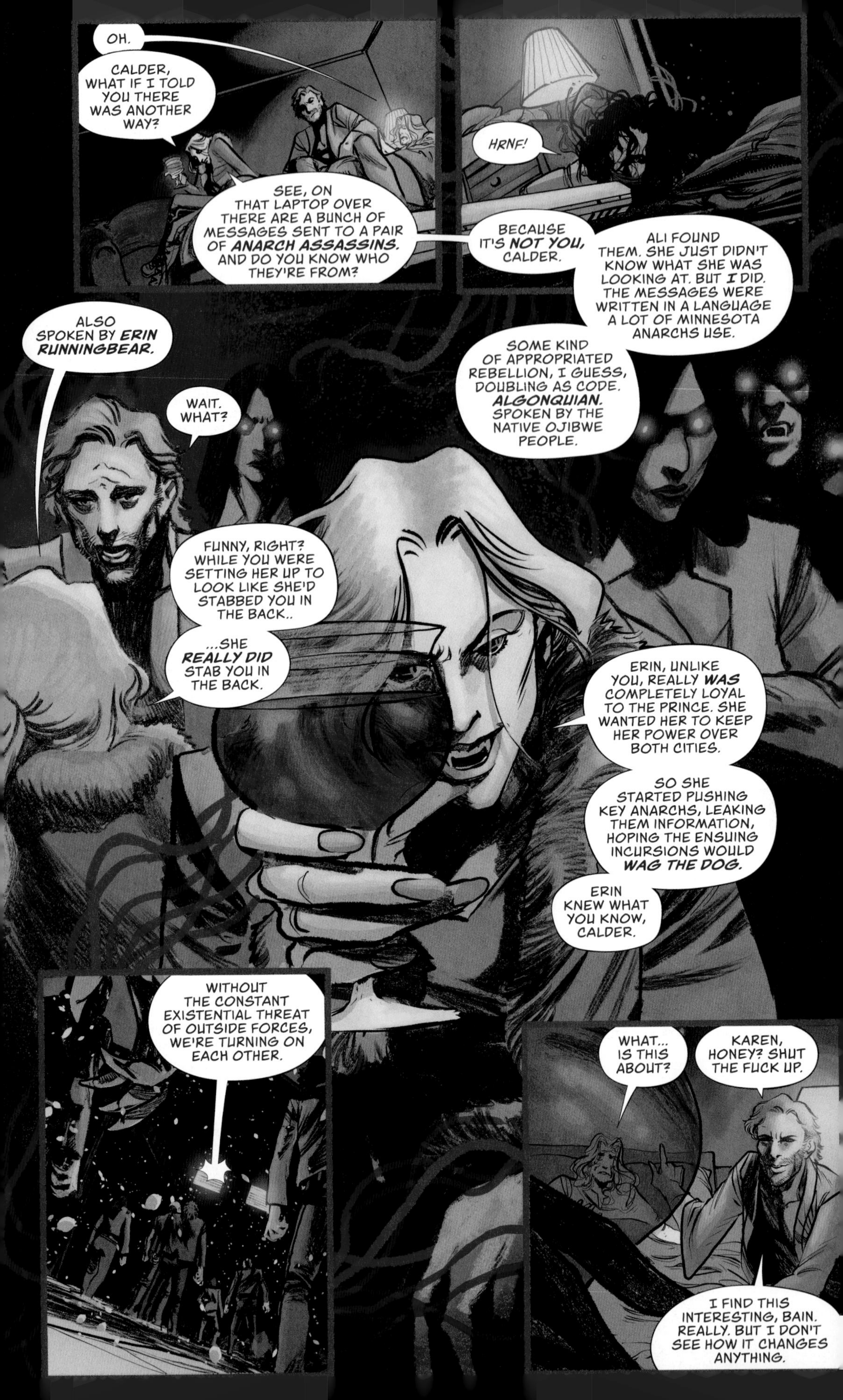
OH.
CALDER, WHAT IF I TOLD YOU THERE WAS ANOTHER WAY?
SEE, ON THAT LAPTOP OVER THERE ARE A BUNCH OF MESSAGES SENT TO A PAIR OF ANARCH ASSASSINS. AND DO YOU KNOW WHO THEY'RE FROM?
HRNF!
BECAUSE IT'S NOT YOU, CALDER.
ALI FOUND THEM. SHE JUST DIDN'T KNOW WHAT SHE WAS LOOKING AT. BUT I DID. THE MESSAGES WERE WRITTEN IN A LANGUAGE A LOT OF MINNESOTA ANARCHS USE.
SOME KIND OF APPROPRIATED REBELLION, I GUESS, DOUBLING AS CODE. ALGONQUIAN. SPOKEN BY THE NATIVE OJIBWE PEOPLE.
ALSO SPOKEN BY ERIN RUNNINGBEAR.
WAIT. WHAT?
FUNNY, RIGHT? WHILE YOU WERE SETTING HER UP TO LOOK LIKE SHE'D STABBED YOU IN THE BACK..
...SHE REALLY DID STAB YOU IN THE BACK.
ERIN, UNLIKE YOU, REALLY WAS COMPLETELY LOYAL TO THE PRINCE. SHE WANTED HER TO KEEP HER POWER OVER BOTH CITIES.
SO SHE STARTED PUSHING KEY ANARCHS, LEAKING THEM INFORMATION, HOPING THE ENSUING INCURSIONS WOULD WAG THE DOG.
ERIN KNEW WHAT YOU KNOW, CALDER.
WITHOUT THE CONSTANT EXISTENTIAL THREAT OF OUTSIDE FORCES, WE'RE TURNING ON EACH OTHER.
WHAT... IS THIS ABOUT?
KAREN, HONEY? SHUT THE FUCK UP.
I FIND THIS INTERESTING, BAIN. REALLY. BUT I DON'T SEE HOW IT CHANGES ANYTHING.

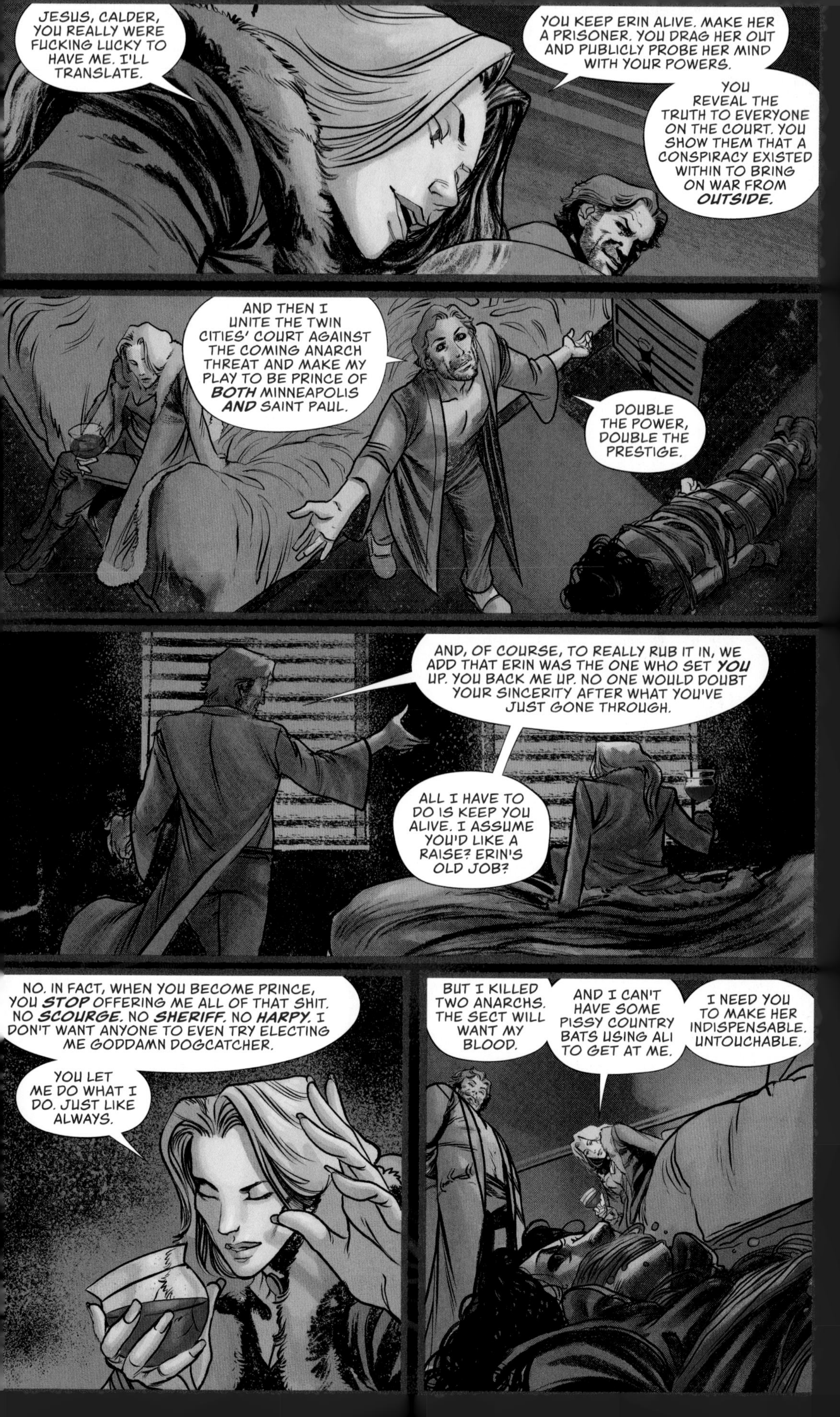
JESUS, CALDER, YOU REALLY WERE FUCKING LUCKY TO HAVE ME. I'LL TRANSLATE.
YOU KEEP ERIN ALIVE. MAKE HER A PRISONER. YOU DRAG HER OUT AND PUBLICLY PROBE HER MIND WITH YOUR POWERS.
YOU REVEAL THE TRUTH TO EVERYONE ON THE COURT. YOU SHOW THEM THAT A CONSPIRACY EXISTED WITHIN TO BRING ON WAR FROM ***OUTSIDE.***
AND THEN I UNITE THE TWIN CITIES' COURT AGAINST THE COMING ANARCH THREAT AND MAKE MY PLAY TO BE PRINCE OF ***BOTH*** MINNEAPOLIS ***AND*** SAINT PAUL.
DOUBLE THE POWER, DOUBLE THE PRESTIGE.
AND, OF COURSE, TO REALLY RUB IT IN, WE ADD THAT ERIN WAS THE ONE WHO SET ***YOU*** UP. YOU BACK ME UP. NO ONE WOULD DOUBT YOUR SINCERITY AFTER WHAT YOU'VE JUST GONE THROUGH.
ALL I HAVE TO DO IS KEEP YOU ALIVE. I ASSUME YOU'D LIKE A RAISE? ERIN'S OLD JOB?
NO. IN FACT, WHEN YOU BECOME PRINCE, YOU ***STOP*** OFFERING ME ALL OF THAT SHIT. NO ***SCOURGE.*** NO ***SHERIFF.*** NO ***HARPY.*** I DON'T WANT ANYONE TO EVEN TRY ELECTING ME GODDAMN DOGCATCHER.
YOU LET ME DO WHAT I DO. JUST LIKE ALWAYS.
BUT I KILLED TWO ANARCHS. THE SECT WILL WANT MY BLOOD.
AND I CAN'T HAVE SOME PISSY COUNTRY BATS USING ALI TO GET AT ME.
I NEED YOU TO MAKE HER INDISPENSABLE. UNTOUCHABLE.

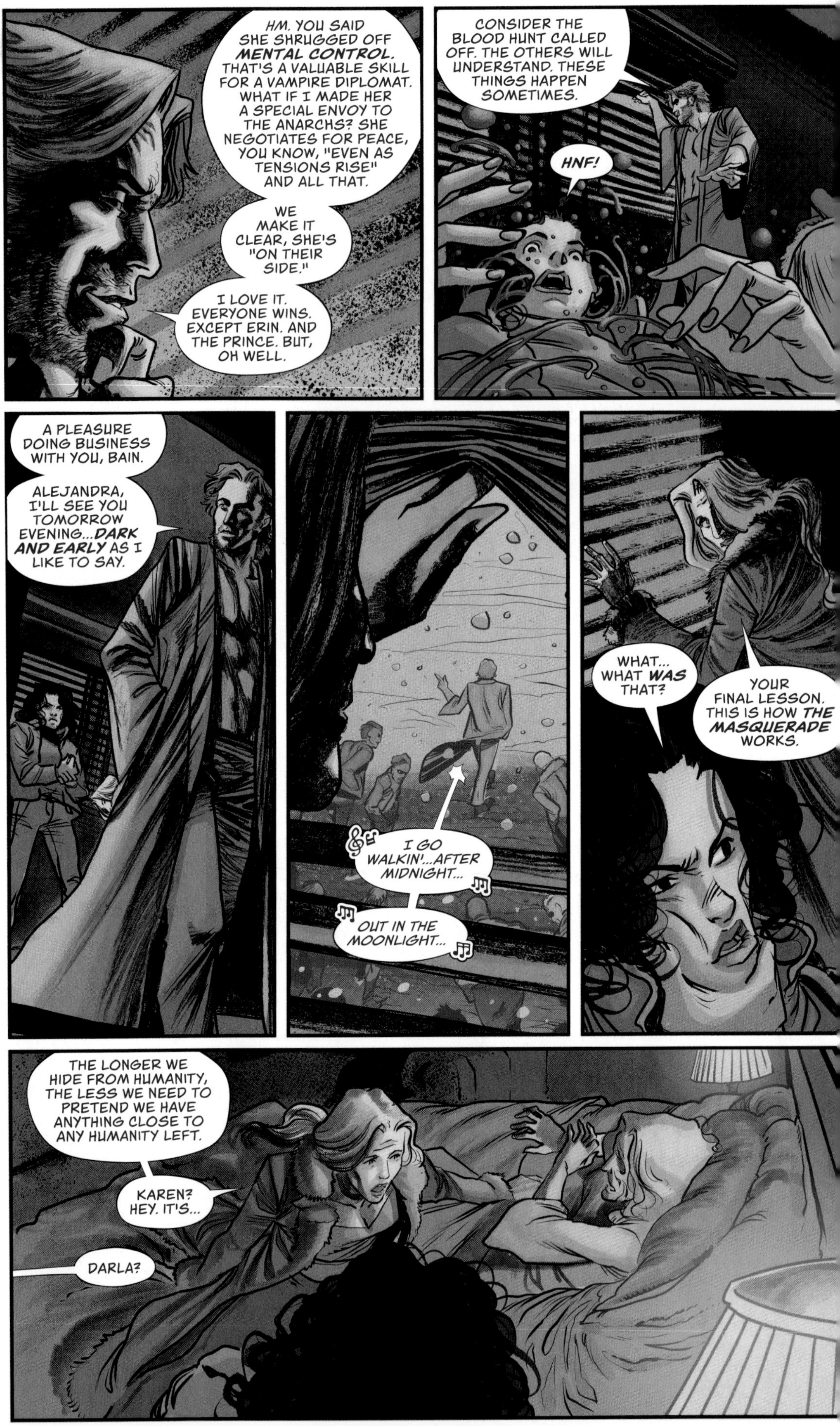

HM. YOU SAID SHE SHRUGGED OFF **MENTAL CONTROL.** THAT'S A VALUABLE SKILL FOR A VAMPIRE DIPLOMAT. WHAT IF I MADE HER A SPECIAL ENVOY TO THE ANARCHS? SHE NEGOTIATES FOR PEACE, YOU KNOW, "EVEN AS TENSIONS RISE" AND ALL THAT.
WE MAKE IT CLEAR, SHE'S "ON THEIR SIDE."
I LOVE IT. EVERYONE WINS. EXCEPT ERIN. AND THE PRINCE. BUT, OH WELL.
CONSIDER THE BLOOD HUNT CALLED OFF. THE OTHERS WILL UNDERSTAND. THESE THINGS HAPPEN SOMETIMES.
HNF!
A PLEASURE DOING BUSINESS WITH YOU, BAIN.
ALEJANDRA, I'LL SEE YOU TOMORROW EVENING...**DARK AND EARLY** AS I LIKE TO SAY.
I GO WALKIN'...AFTER MIDNIGHT...
OUT IN THE MOONLIGHT...
WHAT... WHAT **WAS** THAT?
YOUR FINAL LESSON. THIS IS HOW **THE MASQUERADE** WORKS.
THE LONGER WE HIDE FROM HUMANITY, THE LESS WE NEED TO PRETEND WE HAVE ANYTHING CLOSE TO ANY HUMANITY LEFT.
KAREN? HEY. IT'S...
DARLA?

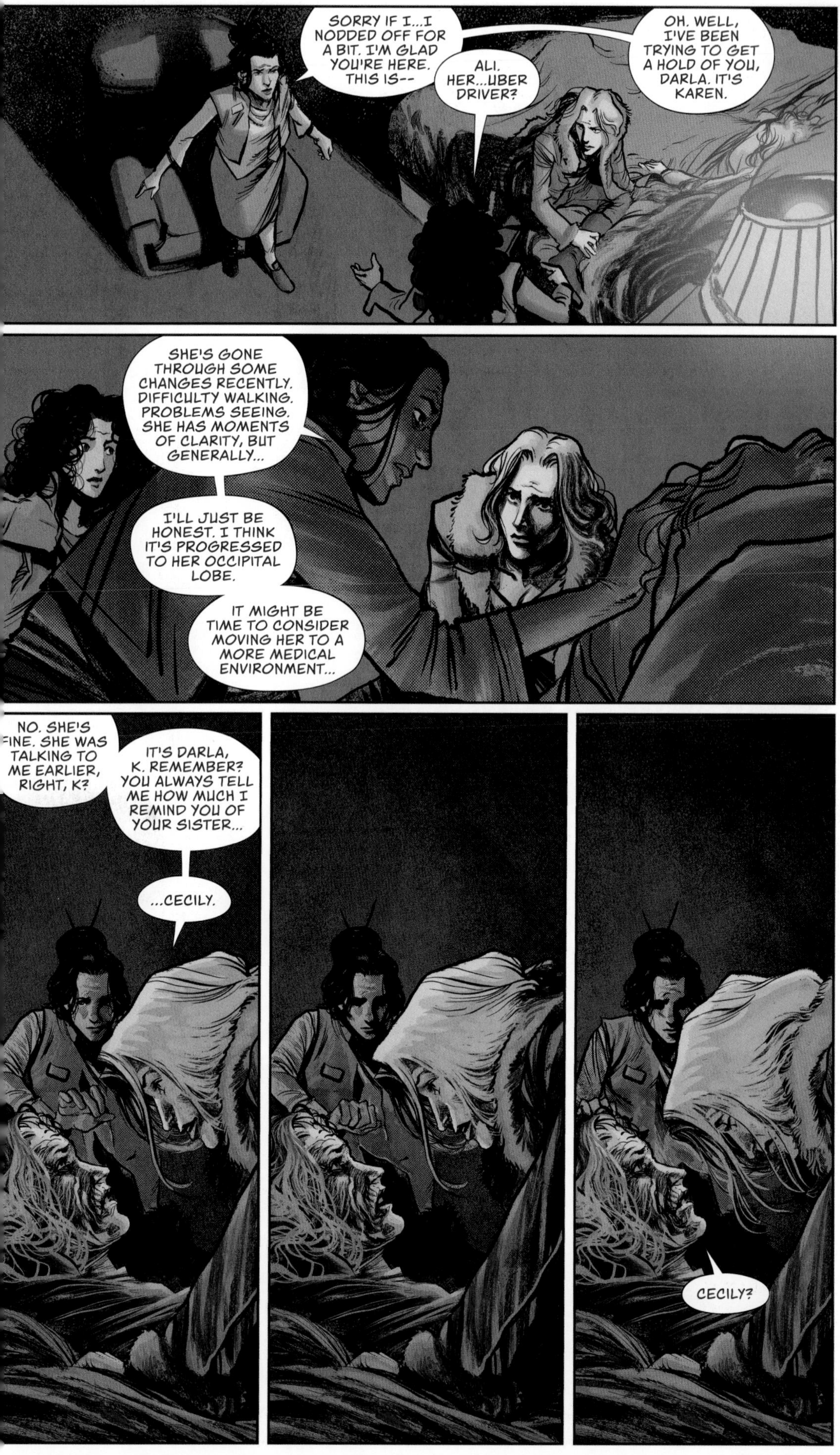
SORRY IF I...I NODDED OFF FOR A BIT. I'M GLAD YOU'RE HERE. THIS IS--
ALI. HER...UBER DRIVER?
OH. WELL, I'VE BEEN TRYING TO GET A HOLD OF YOU, DARLA. IT'S KAREN.
SHE'S GONE THROUGH SOME CHANGES RECENTLY. DIFFICULTY WALKING. PROBLEMS SEEING. SHE HAS MOMENTS OF CLARITY, BUT GENERALLY...
I'LL JUST BE HONEST. I THINK IT'S PROGRESSED TO HER OCCIPITAL LOBE.
IT MIGHT BE TIME TO CONSIDER MOVING HER TO A MORE MEDICAL ENVIRONMENT...
NO. SHE'S FINE. SHE WAS TALKING TO ME EARLIER, RIGHT, K?
IT'S DARLA, K. REMEMBER? YOU ALWAYS TELL ME HOW MUCH I REMIND YOU OF YOUR SISTER...
...CECILY.
CECILY?

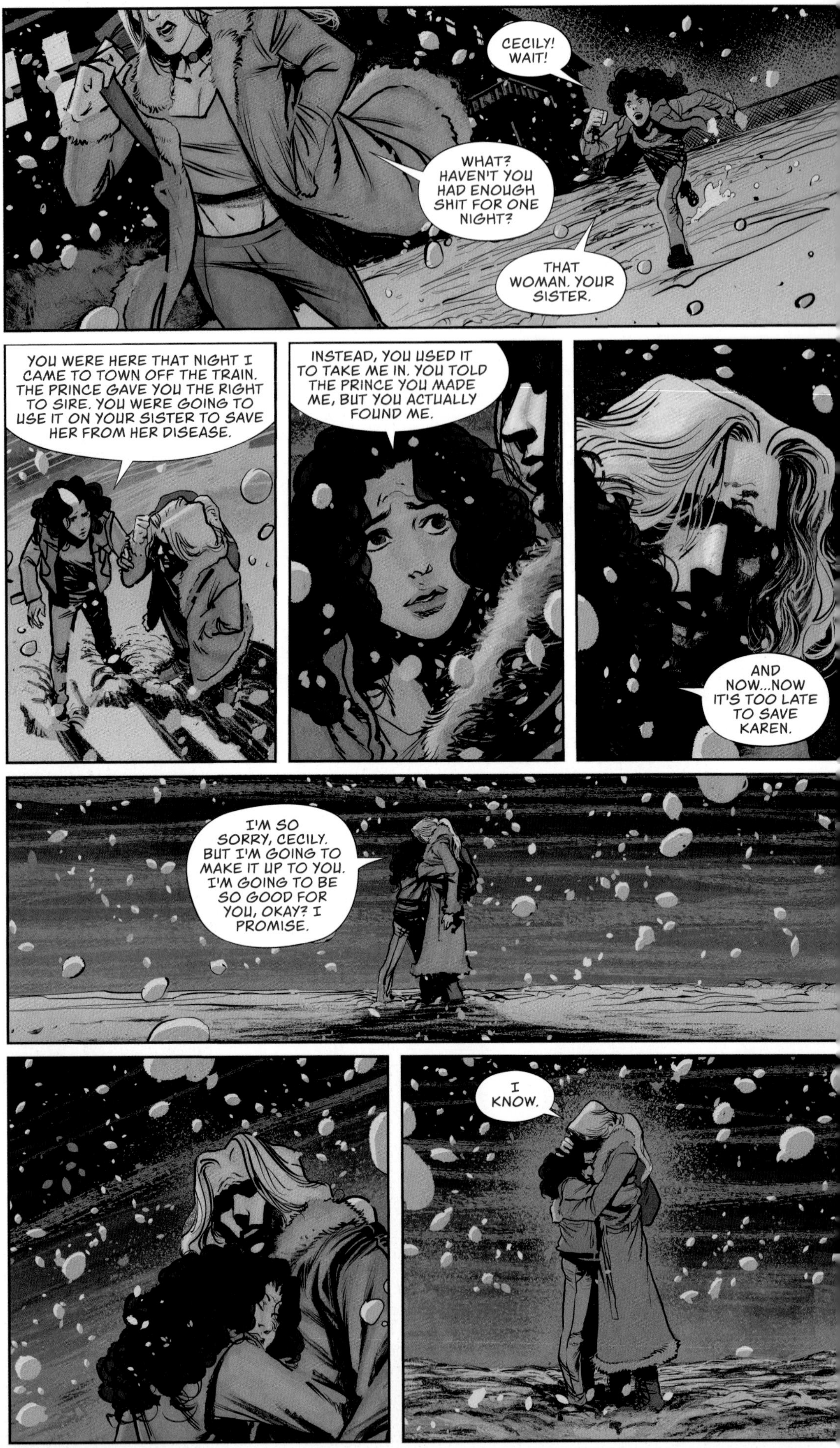

CECILY! WAIT!
WHAT? HAVEN'T YOU HAD ENOUGH SHIT FOR ONE NIGHT?
THAT WOMAN. YOUR SISTER.
YOU WERE HERE THAT NIGHT I CAME TO TOWN OFF THE TRAIN. THE PRINCE GAVE YOU THE RIGHT TO SIRE. YOU WERE GOING TO USE IT ON YOUR SISTER TO SAVE HER FROM HER DISEASE.
INSTEAD, YOU USED IT TO TAKE ME IN. YOU TOLD THE PRINCE YOU MADE ME, BUT YOU ACTUALLY FOUND ME.
AND NOW...NOW IT'S TOO LATE TO SAVE KAREN.
I'M SO SORRY, CECILY. BUT I'M GOING TO MAKE IT UP TO YOU. I'M GOING TO BE SO GOOD FOR YOU, OKAY? I PROMISE.
I KNOW.

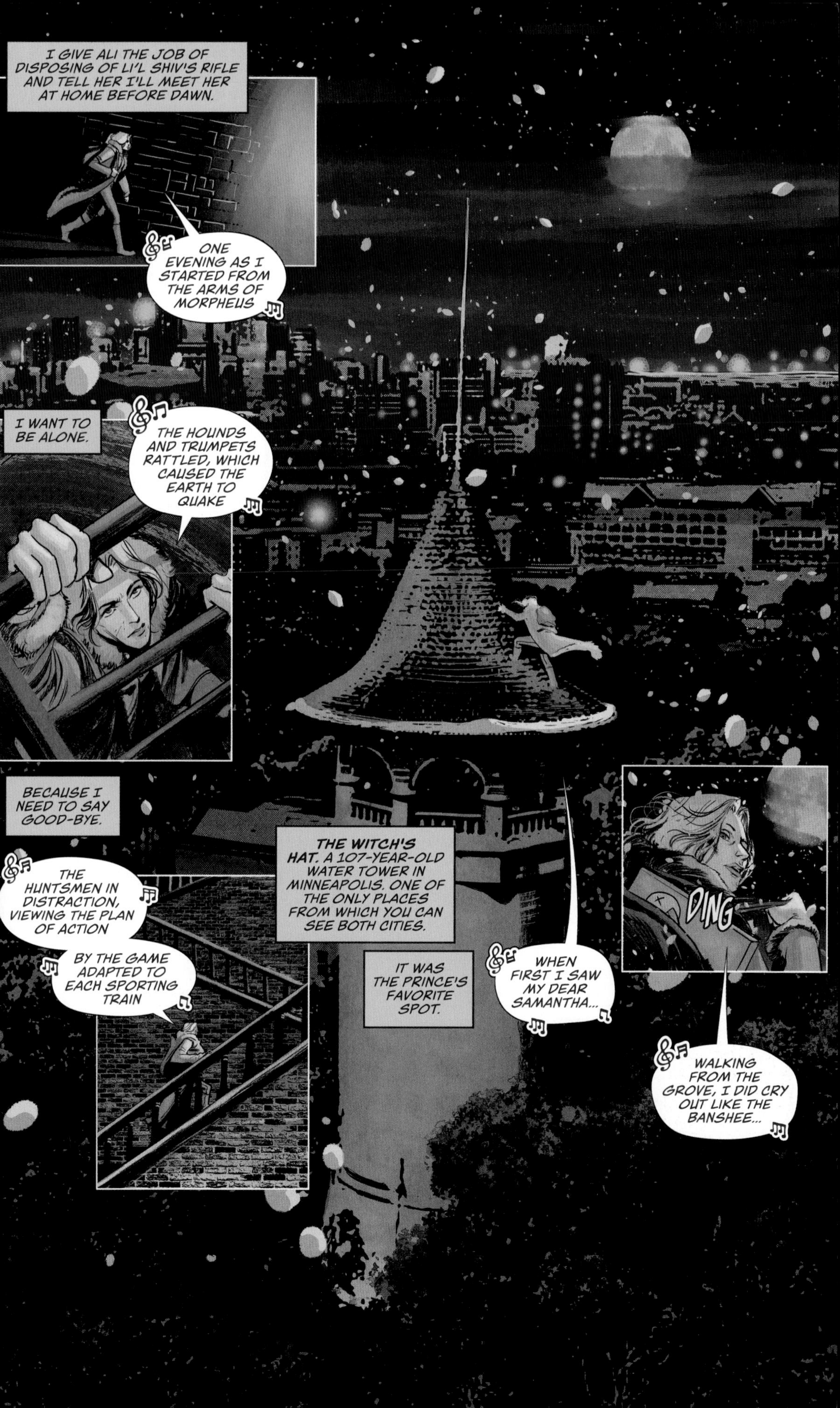

I GIVE ALI THE JOB OF DISPOSING OF LI'L SHIV'S RIFLE AND TELL HER I'LL MEET HER AT HOME BEFORE DAWN.
ONE EVENING AS I STARTED FROM THE ARMS OF MORPHEUS
I WANT TO BE ALONE.
THE HOUNDS AND TRUMPETS RATTLED, WHICH CAUSED THE EARTH TO QUAKE
BECAUSE I NEED TO SAY GOOD-BYE.
THE HUNTSMEN IN DISTRACTION, VIEWING THE PLAN OF ACTION
BY THE GAME ADAPTED TO EACH SPORTING TRAIN
THE WITCH'S HAT. A 107-YEAR-OLD WATER TOWER IN MINNEAPOLIS. ONE OF THE ONLY PLACES FROM WHICH YOU CAN SEE BOTH CITIES.
IT WAS THE PRINCE'S FAVORITE SPOT.
WHEN FIRST I SAW MY DEAR SAMANTHA...
DING
WALKING FROM THE GROVE, I DID CRY OUT LIKE THE BANSHEE...

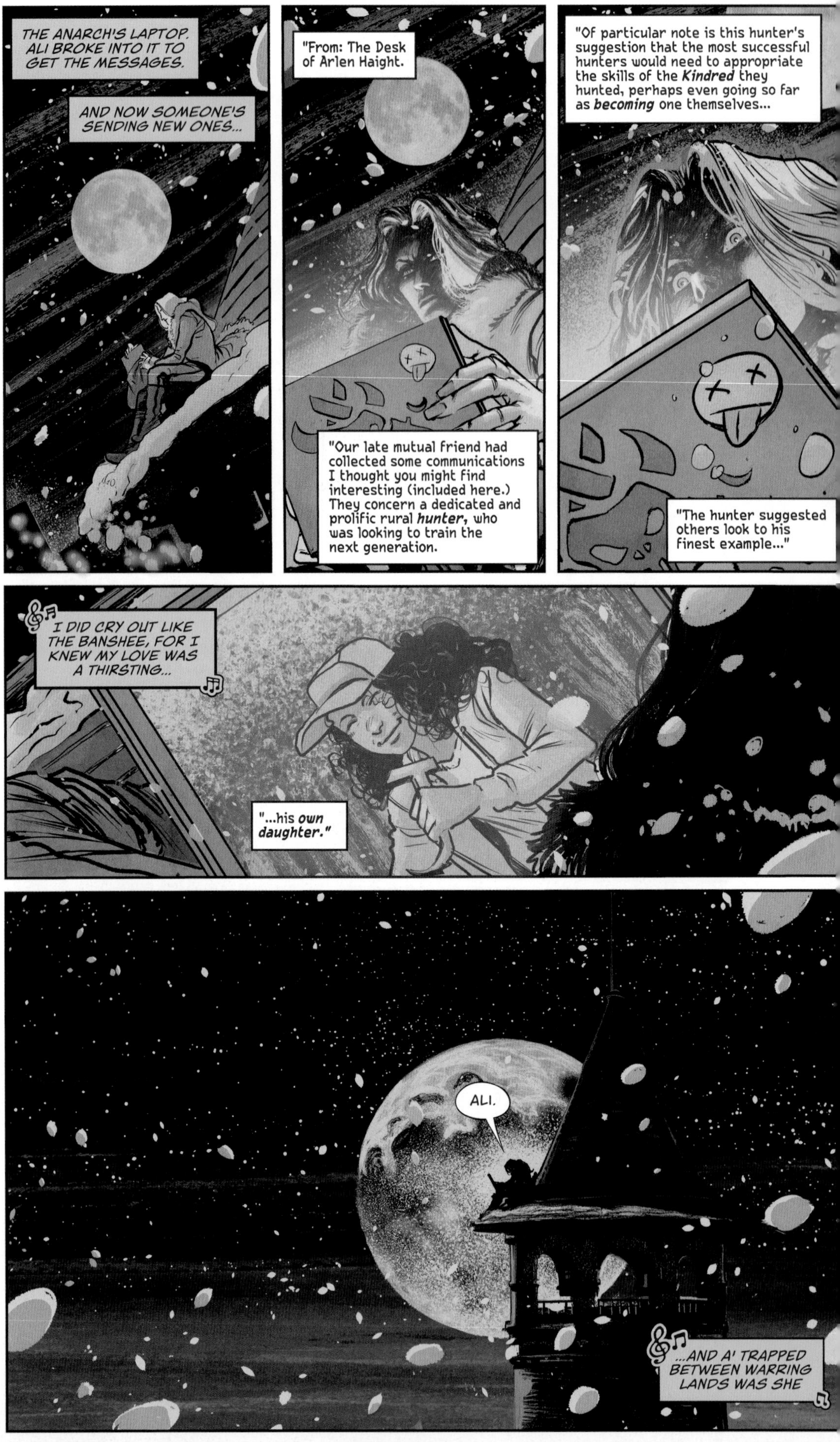
THE ANARCH'S LAPTOP. ALI BROKE INTO IT TO GET THE MESSAGES.
AND NOW SOMEONE'S SENDING NEW ONES...
"From: The Desk of Arlen Haight.
"Our late mutual friend had collected some communications I thought you might find interesting (included here.) They concern a dedicated and prolific rural *hunter*, who was looking to train the next generation.
"Of particular note is this hunter's suggestion that the most successful hunters would need to appropriate the skills of the *Kindred* they hunted, perhaps even going so far as *becoming* one themselves...
"The hunter suggested others look to his finest example..."
I DID CRY OUT LIKE THE BANSHEE, FOR I KNEW MY LOVE WAS A THIRSTING...
"...his *own daughter.*"
ALI.
...AND A' TRAPPED BETWEEN WARRING LANDS WAS SHE

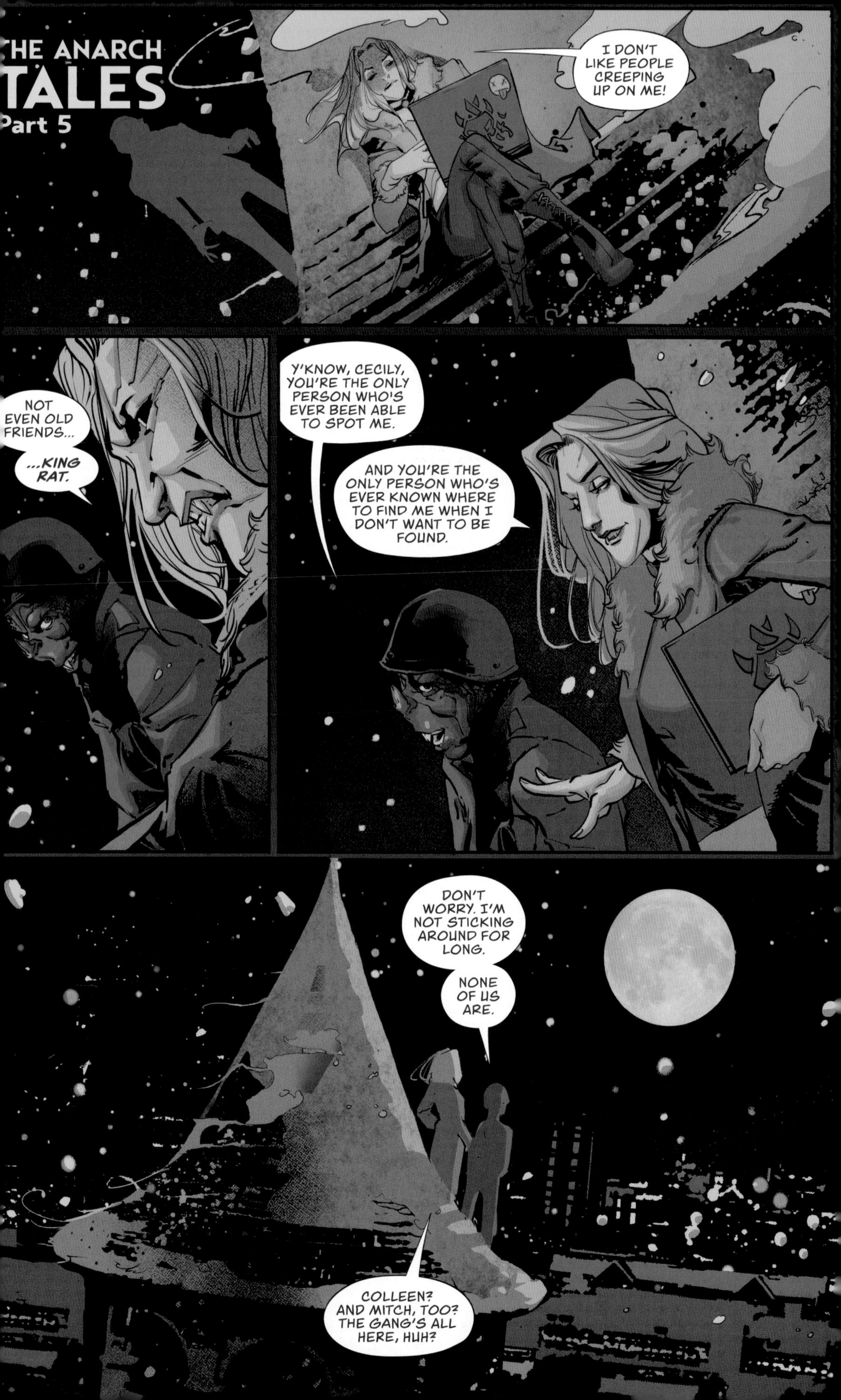

THE ANARCH TALES
Part 5
I DON'T LIKE PEOPLE CREEPING UP ON ME!
NOT EVEN OLD FRIENDS...
...KING RAT.
Y'KNOW, CECILY, YOU'RE THE ONLY PERSON WHO'S EVER BEEN ABLE TO SPOT ME.
AND YOU'RE THE ONLY PERSON WHO'S EVER KNOWN WHERE TO FIND ME WHEN I DON'T WANT TO BE FOUND.
DON'T WORRY. I'M NOT STICKING AROUND FOR LONG.
NONE OF US ARE.
COLLEEN? AND MITCH, TOO? THE GANG'S ALL HERE, HUH?

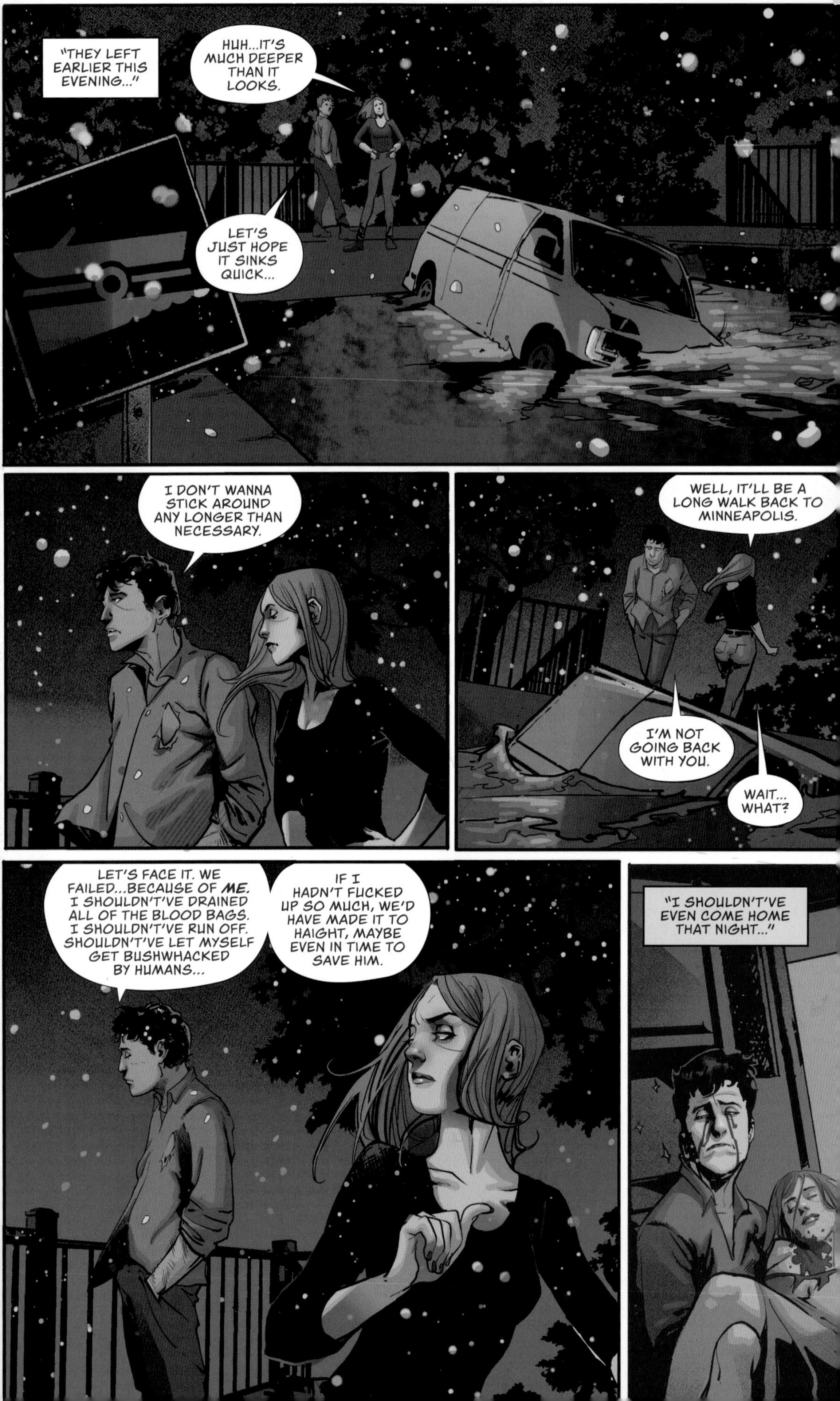
"THEY LEFT EARLIER THIS EVENING..."
HUH...IT'S MUCH DEEPER THAN IT LOOKS.
LET'S JUST HOPE IT SINKS QUICK...
I DON'T WANNA STICK AROUND ANY LONGER THAN NECESSARY.
WELL, IT'LL BE A LONG WALK BACK TO MINNEAPOLIS.
I'M NOT GOING BACK WITH YOU.
WAIT... WHAT?
LET'S FACE IT. WE FAILED...BECAUSE OF *ME.* I SHOULDN'T'VE DRAINED ALL OF THE BLOOD BAGS. I SHOULDN'T'VE RUN OFF. SHOULDN'T'VE LET MYSELF GET BUSHWHACKED BY HUMANS...
IF I HADN'T FUCKED UP SO MUCH, WE'D HAVE MADE IT TO HAIGHT, MAYBE EVEN IN TIME TO SAVE HIM.
"I SHOULDN'T'VE EVEN COME HOME THAT NIGHT..."

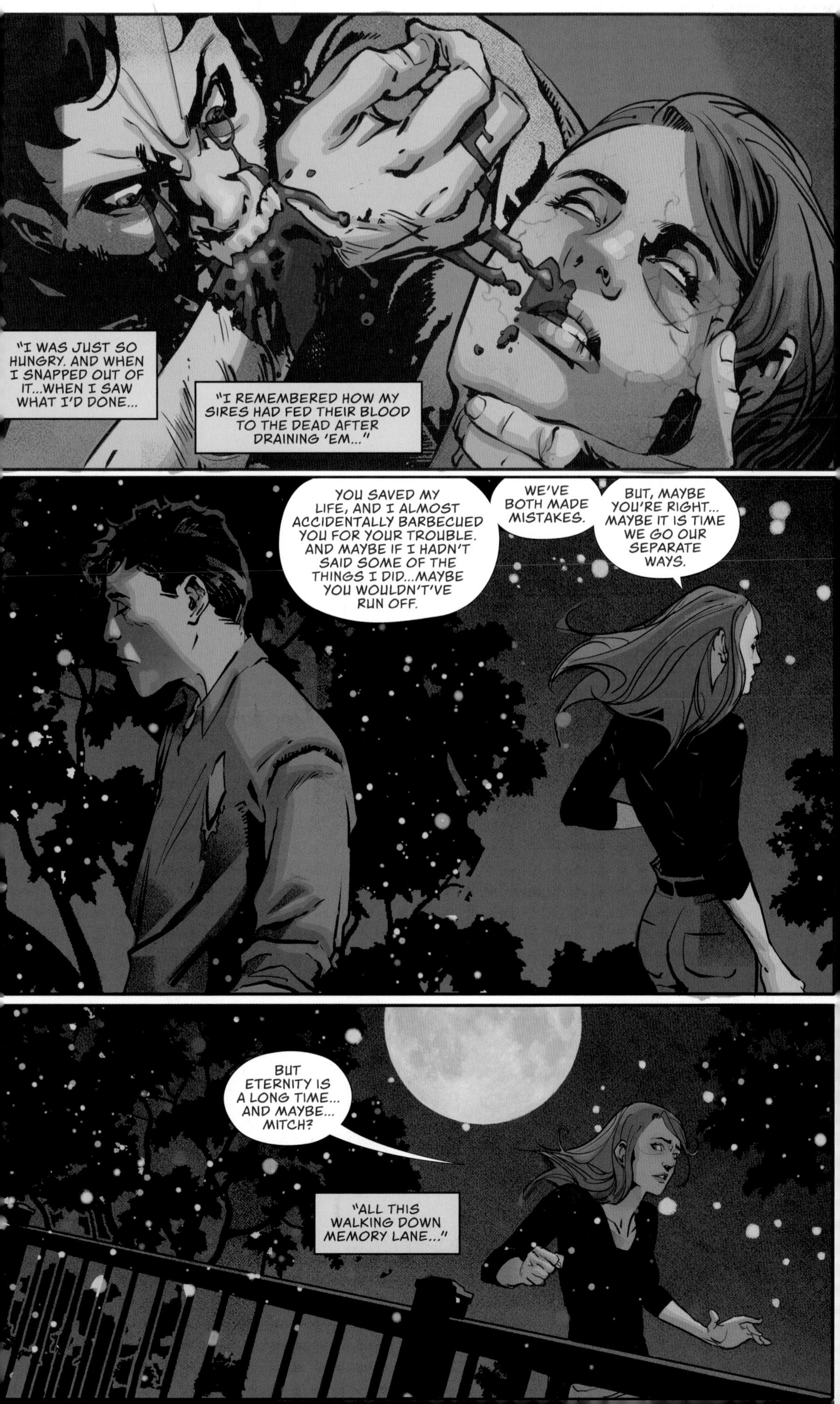
"I WAS JUST SO HUNGRY. AND WHEN I SNAPPED OUT OF IT...WHEN I SAW WHAT I'D DONE...
"I REMEMBERED HOW MY SIRES HAD FED THEIR BLOOD TO THE DEAD AFTER DRAINING 'EM..."
YOU SAVED MY LIFE, AND I ALMOST ACCIDENTALLY BARBECUED YOU FOR YOUR TROUBLE. AND MAYBE IF I HADN'T SAID SOME OF THE THINGS I DID...MAYBE YOU WOULDN'T'VE RUN OFF.
WE'VE BOTH MADE MISTAKES.
BUT, MAYBE YOU'RE RIGHT... MAYBE IT IS TIME WE GO OUR SEPARATE WAYS.
BUT ETERNITY IS A LONG TIME... AND MAYBE... MITCH?
"ALL THIS WALKING DOWN MEMORY LANE..."

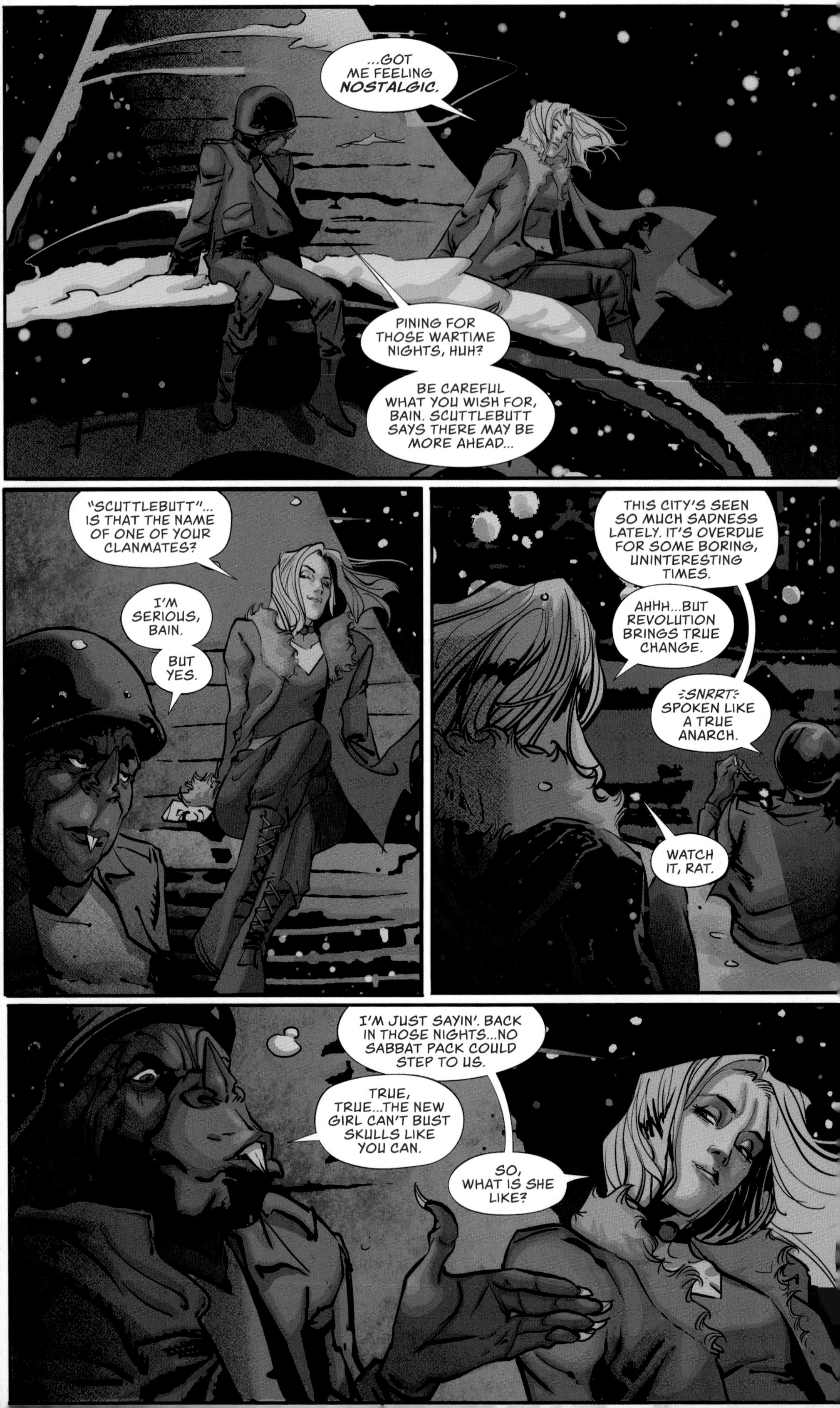
...GOT ME FEELING NOSTALGIC.
PINING FOR THOSE WARTIME NIGHTS, HUH?
BE CAREFUL WHAT YOU WISH FOR, BAIN. SCUTTLEBUTT SAYS THERE MAY BE MORE AHEAD...
"SCUTTLEBUTT"... IS THAT THE NAME OF ONE OF YOUR CLANMATES?
I'M SERIOUS, BAIN.
BUT YES.
THIS CITY'S SEEN SO MUCH SADNESS LATELY. IT'S OVERDUE FOR SOME BORING, UNINTERESTING TIMES.
AHHH...BUT REVOLUTION BRINGS TRUE CHANGE.
=SNRRT= SPOKEN LIKE A TRUE ANARCH.
WATCH IT, RAT.
I'M JUST SAYIN'. BACK IN THOSE NIGHTS...NO SABBAT PACK COULD STEP TO US.
TRUE, TRUE...THE NEW GIRL CAN'T BUST SKULLS LIKE YOU CAN.
SO, WHAT IS SHE LIKE?

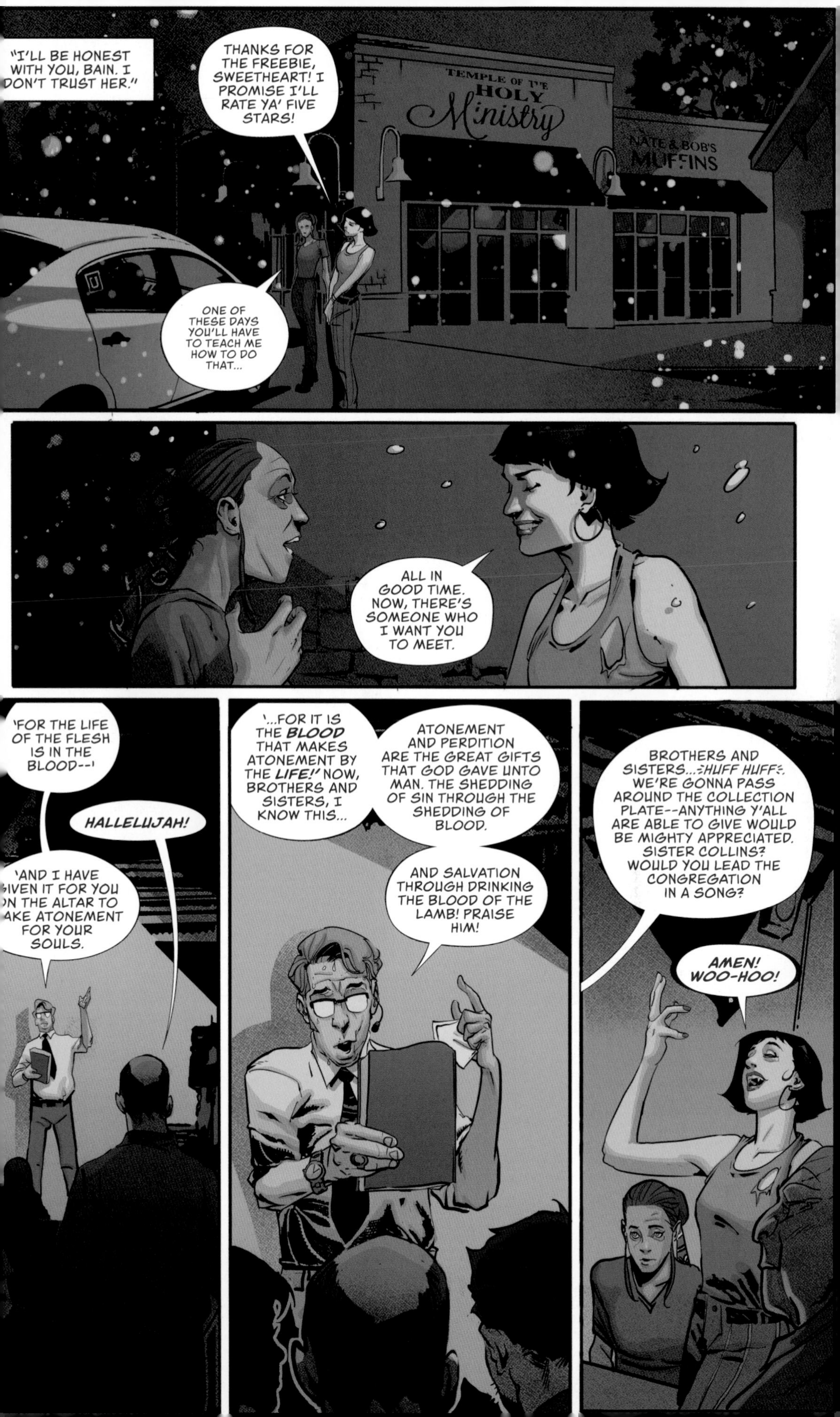
"I'LL BE HONEST WITH YOU, BAIN. I DON'T TRUST HER."
THANKS FOR THE FREEBIE, SWEETHEART! I PROMISE I'LL RATE YA' FIVE STARS!
TEMPLE OF THE HOLY Ministry
NATE & BOB'S MUFFINS
ONE OF THESE DAYS YOU'LL HAVE TO TEACH ME HOW TO DO THAT...
ALL IN GOOD TIME. NOW, THERE'S SOMEONE WHO I WANT YOU TO MEET.
'FOR THE LIFE OF THE FLESH IS IN THE BLOOD--'
HALLELUJAH!
'AND I HAVE GIVEN IT FOR YOU ON THE ALTAR TO MAKE ATONEMENT FOR YOUR SOULS.
'...FOR IT IS THE BLOOD THAT MAKES ATONEMENT BY THE LIFE!' NOW, BROTHERS AND SISTERS, I KNOW THIS...
ATONEMENT AND PERDITION ARE THE GREAT GIFTS THAT GOD GAVE UNTO MAN. THE SHEDDING OF SIN THROUGH THE SHEDDING OF BLOOD.
AND SALVATION THROUGH DRINKING THE BLOOD OF THE LAMB! PRAISE HIM!
BROTHERS AND SISTERS... HUFF HUFF. WE'RE GONNA PASS AROUND THE COLLECTION PLATE--ANYTHING Y'ALL ARE ABLE TO GIVE WOULD BE MIGHTY APPRECIATED. SISTER COLLINS? WOULD YOU LEAD THE CONGREGATION IN A SONG?
AMEN! WOO-HOO!

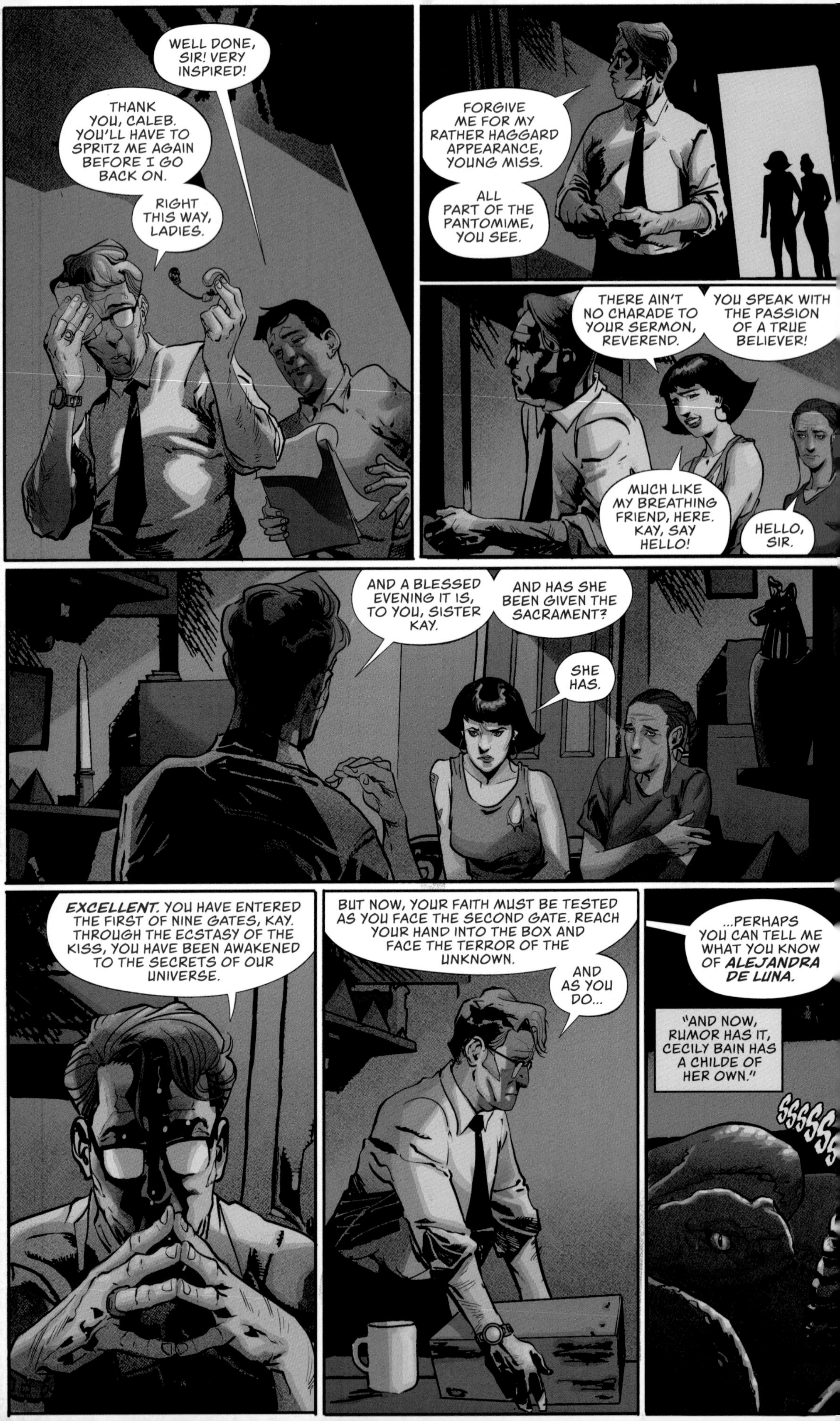

WELL DONE, SIR! VERY INSPIRED!
THANK YOU, CALEB. YOU'LL HAVE TO SPRITZ ME AGAIN BEFORE I GO BACK ON.
RIGHT THIS WAY, LADIES.
FORGIVE ME FOR MY RATHER HAGGARD APPEARANCE, YOUNG MISS.
ALL PART OF THE PANTOMIME, YOU SEE.
THERE AIN'T NO CHARADE TO YOUR SERMON, REVEREND.
YOU SPEAK WITH THE PASSION OF A TRUE BELIEVER!
MUCH LIKE MY BREATHING FRIEND, HERE. KAY, SAY HELLO!
HELLO, SIR.
AND A BLESSED EVENING IT IS, TO YOU, SISTER KAY.
AND HAS SHE BEEN GIVEN THE SACRAMENT?
SHE HAS.
EXCELLENT. YOU HAVE ENTERED THE FIRST OF NINE GATES, KAY. THROUGH THE ECSTASY OF THE KISS, YOU HAVE BEEN AWAKENED TO THE SECRETS OF OUR UNIVERSE.
BUT NOW, YOUR FAITH MUST BE TESTED AS YOU FACE THE SECOND GATE. REACH YOUR HAND INTO THE BOX AND FACE THE TERROR OF THE UNKNOWN.
AND AS YOU DO...
...PERHAPS YOU CAN TELL ME WHAT YOU KNOW OF ALEJANDRA DE LUNA.
"AND NOW, RUMOR HAS IT, CECILY BAIN HAS A CHILDE OF HER OWN."
SSSSSS

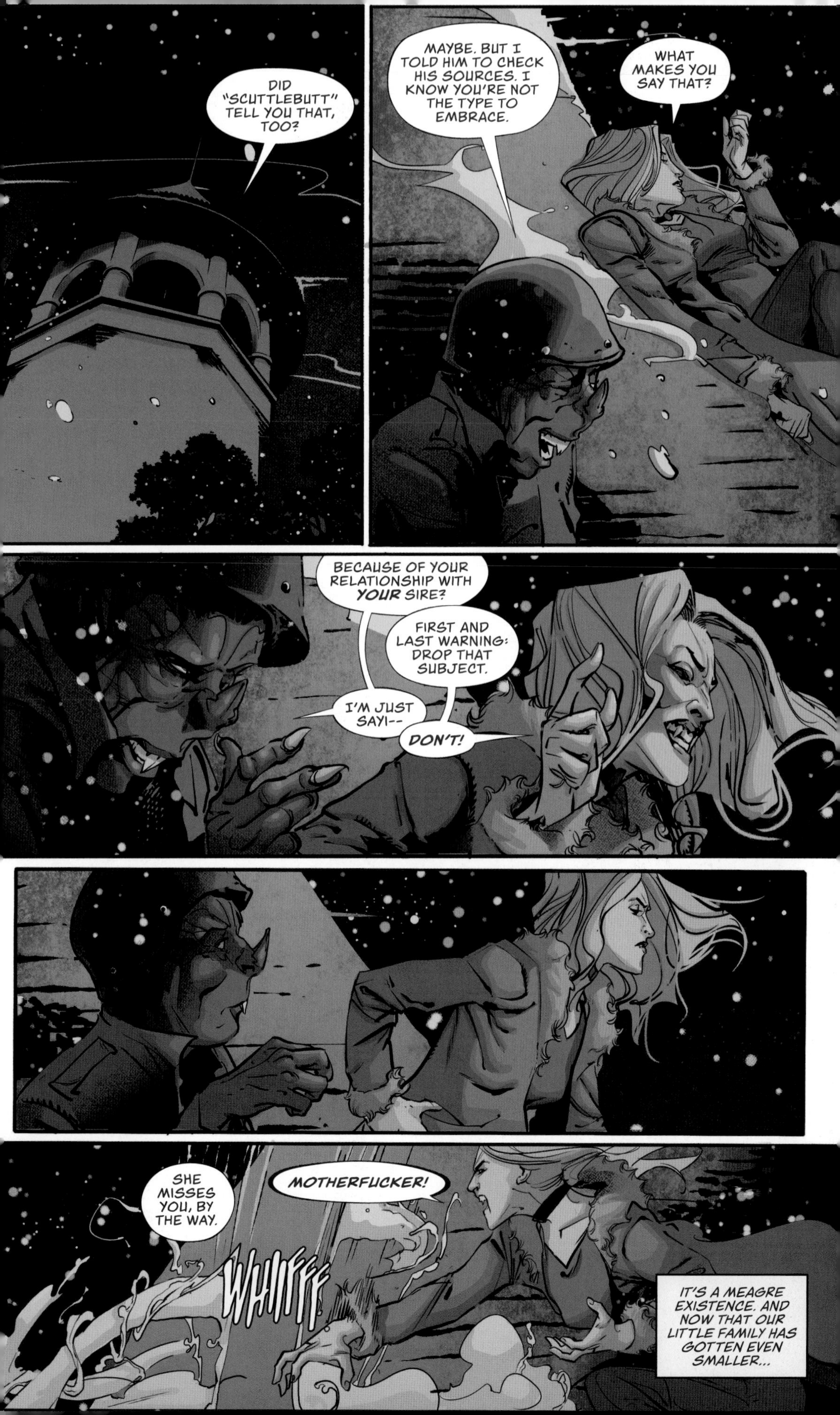
DID "SCUTTLEBUTT" TELL YOU THAT, TOO?
MAYBE. BUT I TOLD HIM TO CHECK HIS SOURCES. I KNOW YOU'RE NOT THE TYPE TO EMBRACE.
WHAT MAKES YOU SAY THAT?
BECAUSE OF YOUR RELATIONSHIP WITH *YOUR* SIRE?
FIRST AND LAST WARNING: DROP THAT SUBJECT.
I'M JUST SAYI--
DON'T!
SHE MISSES YOU, BY THE WAY.
MOTHERFUCKER!
WHIIFFF
IT'S A MEAGRE EXISTENCE. AND NOW THAT OUR LITTLE FAMILY HAS GOTTEN EVEN SMALLER...

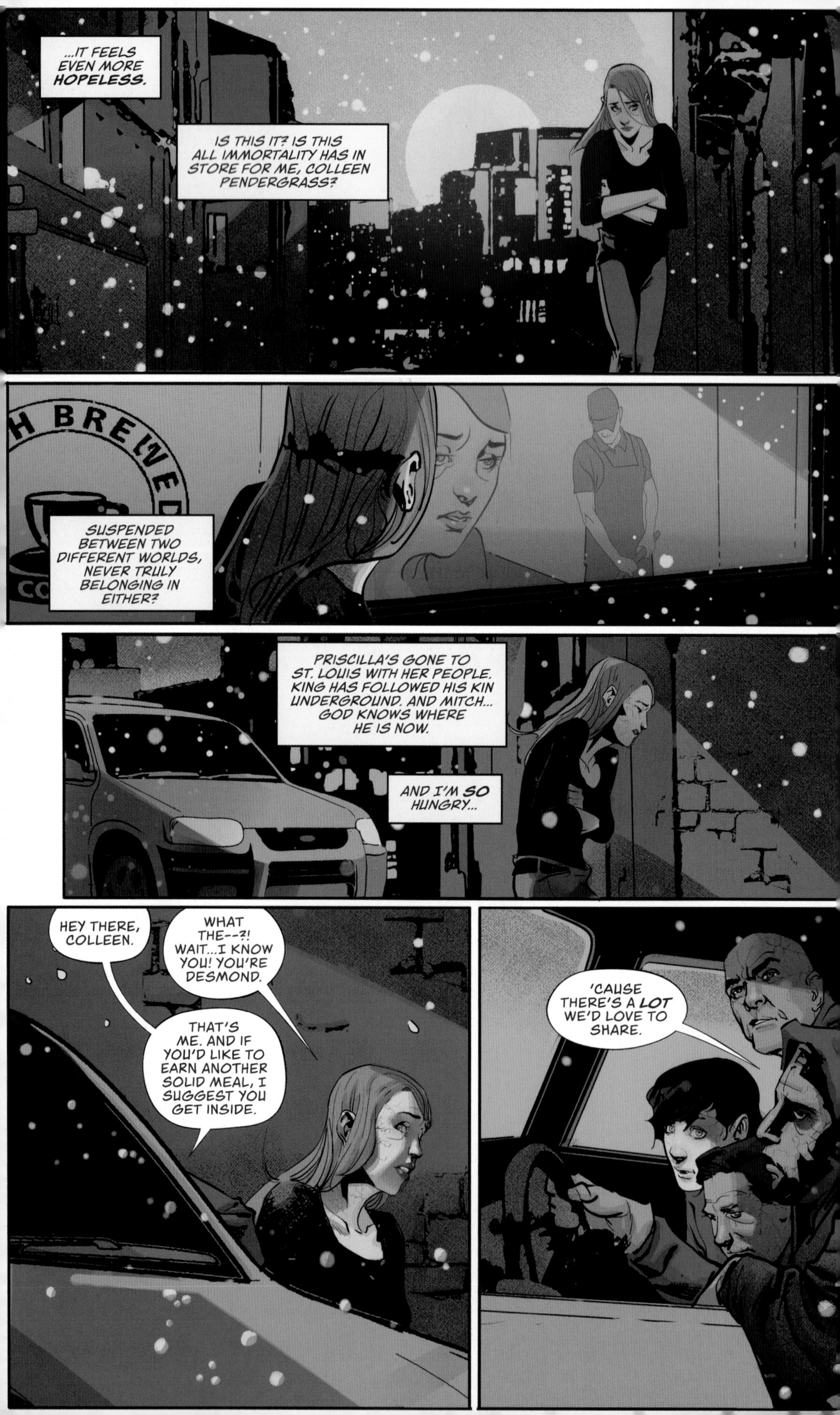
...IT FEELS EVEN MORE HOPELESS.
IS THIS IT? IS THIS ALL IMMORTALITY HAS IN STORE FOR ME, COLLEEN PENDERGRASS?
SUSPENDED BETWEEN TWO DIFFERENT WORLDS, NEVER TRULY BELONGING IN EITHER?
PRISCILLA'S GONE TO ST. LOUIS WITH HER PEOPLE. KING HAS FOLLOWED HIS KIN UNDERGROUND. AND MITCH... GOD KNOWS WHERE HE IS NOW.
AND I'M SO HUNGRY...
HEY THERE, COLLEEN.
WHAT THE--?! WAIT...I KNOW YOU! YOU'RE DESMOND.
THAT'S ME. AND IF YOU'D LIKE TO EARN ANOTHER SOLID MEAL, I SUGGEST YOU GET INSIDE.
'CAUSE THERE'S A LOT WE'D LOVE TO SHARE.

END OF BOOK ONE

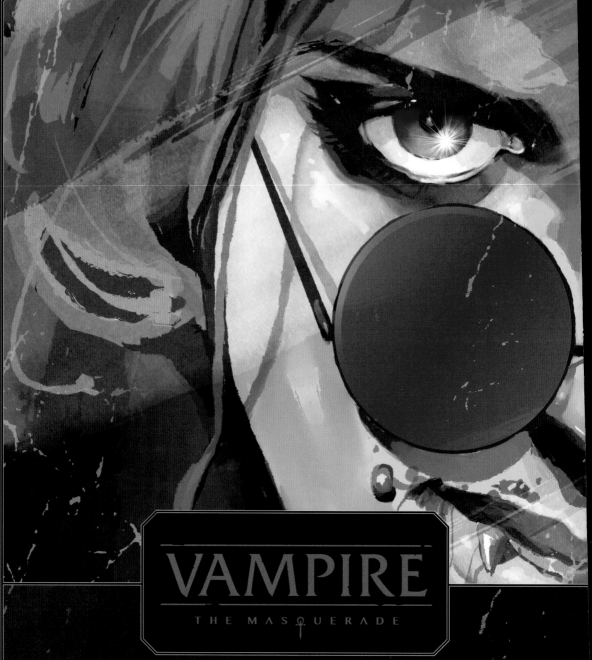

VAMPIRE
THE MASQUERADE

ROLEPLAYING SUPPLEMENTS

INCLUDING LORE SHEETS FOR PLAYABLE CHARACTERS FEATURED IN THE NEW SERIES FROM VAULT COMICS

MINNEAPOLIS
ST. PAUL

CECILY BAIN
COLLEEN PENDERGRASS

TABLE OF CONTENTS

THE NICTUKU
WOLVES IN SHEEP'S CLOTHING

THE COURT OF SAMANTHA
BOSCHE SINGH
ELENA KOWALSKI
JIM GERSHWIN

VAMPIRE

THE MASQUERADE

WINTER'S TEETH

MINNEAPOLIS

While St. Paul may claim the distinction of age over her twin sister city, Minneapolis has her beat on both size and population. Beginning life as a milling outpost along the Mississippi river, Minneapolis has swung back and forth on the pendulum of progress in nights since.

Skyscrapers loom proudly over the downtown district while soft, yellow streetlights illuminate the fine dining of the riverfront. Between the city's expansive sculpture garden and the Minneapolis Institute of Art, an appreciation for the fine arts has been blended into the city's soul. Outside of New York City, Minneapolis boasts the largest number of theaters per capita in the United States. Even pop culture has been shaped by the City of Lakes, who can claim famed musicians such as Bob Dylan and Prince as native sons.

When the Camarilla arrived in Minneapolis, they had already laid claim to the sister city of St. Paul. Despite Anarch protestations, Prince Samantha Merrain has claimed praxis over both of the Twin Cities and considers all Kindred dwelling within to be her subjects. However, cooler heads within the Camarilla of the domains are wary to directly support her reign, having grown fearful of uprisings in similarly fractured domains, such as Berlin. Some within the Anarch movement have also noticed certain similarities to those of their German brethren, and rumors of a possible revolt have begun to propagate the night...

———————●———————

• THE NOD LOT

This unofficial district located in the northwest of the city is known among the local Kindred as the "Nod Lot." Though the hunting there is just as bountiful as it is in more posh locales such as the Rack, the population of the Nod Lot consists of the discarded, forgotten, and despairing. You have cultivated a small Herd (••), whose blood resonance varies from the melancholic to completely absent. Add this to end: Additionally, feeding from such victims presents a high-risk of transferring blood-borne pathogens, potentially poisoning the well. You must take the Flaw Addiction (•) or Dark Secret - Plague Bearer (•).

•• THE ARTIST FORMERLY KNOWN AS...

You are one of the lucky few who has managed to make a name for themselves within the music industry as a performing artist. Unfortunately, since your Embrace, ➤

your renown has become a double-edged sword, especially after the highly publicized reports of your death. You gain Fame (•••), however, must also take the flaw Mask (Known Corpse).

••• THE REVOLUTION

Minneapolis, like many American cities, is plagued with a history of racism and societal injustice, whose wounds still bleed well into the modern nights. However, Minneapolis also has a strong tradition of those who fight for equal rights and representation. Perhaps you were once an active force for change within your community, or have otherwise become familiar to those who are, currently. You gain four dots to spend among Allies, Contacts, or Influence, to represent your affiliation with prominent grassroots movements, local leaders, or institutions. This activism among mortals has made you a target among your elite Camarilla enemies, however -- you must take the Flaw Status: Shunned - Camarilla (•).

•••• THE RIVER RATS

The Kindred of Clan Nosferatu infest the city of Minneapolis from the sewers and the riverfront, to the dark corners of the skywalk and the ruins of ancient flour mills. While many object to their loathsome presence, few can deny the invaluable intel that information brokers within the Clan of the Hidden will provide for the right price. You have somehow managed to ingratiate yourself to this cabal of secret-seekers; you may distribute three dots between Contacts and Mawla (Nosferatu Mawla only), and, once per story, you may gain one valuable piece of information (at storyteller's discretion) relevant to your characters Ambition.

••••• THE MINNEAPOLIS SIX

In 2003, a riot stemming from a University of Minneapolis hockey victory was blamed on the Anarch community. Prince Merrain capitalized upon the opportunity to cripple Minneapolis' Anarch leadership, and had three of the six perpetrators put to Final Death. The remaining three were forcibly blood bound to the Prince to ensure their continued loyalty. You are one of the surviving three. Your blood bond has broken, and now, you and your kin hunger for retribution. Once per chronicle, you may evoke the memory of the Minneapolis Six in order to sway the Anarch community to your cause, at the discretion of the Storyteller.

ST. PAUL

Built upon native Dakota land, the kine have their various pseudonyms for it: Imnizaska, the Saintly City, the "Pig's Eye," and the Last City of the East. That final nickname is particularly true for the city's Kindred, who view St. Paul as the last bastion of American Camarilla power before one reaches the lupine-dominated Rockies and the chaotic battlegrounds of the so-called Anarch Free States. Of late, even its sister city of Minneapolis has become more and more defiant of Camarilla authority. Nevertheless, those who claim praxis over St. Paul tend to claim the title happily: "Prince of the Twin Cities."

To many within the Ivory Tower, St. Paul is little more than a bourgeois pretender; an up-jumped satellite domain to the realm of Chicago. But for those who have dwelled there through decades and centuries, St. Paul represents everything that Clan Toreador holds dear. From its Gallic origins, to the thriving (if humble) local arts scene, the Clan of the Rose fancy themselves as the bringers of culture and civilization to a raucous American frontier.

For the past century, the monarch of St. Paul has been Prince Samantha Merrain—a Toreador elder of seemingly ancient origins. Though her true age and generation are a closely guarded secret, Merrain has seemingly avoided the siren call of the Beckoning. A beloved protector of arts and culture to some—a spoiled, vapid tyrant to others—Merrain's direct influence over Minneapolis has waxed and waned with the tenacity of the local Anarch movement, yet her hold over St. Paul is all but absolute.

●

• DIRTY BOOT

If there is anything that Prince Samantha values, it's talent. Those who are useful for furthering the Prince's goals often find themselves awash in superficial praises from Merrain and her court. However, word travels fast between the Twin Cities, and those who may find themselves celebrated in St. Paul may be marked with suspicion elsewhere. You gain one rank (••) of Status (Camarilla) within the domain of St. Paul, however, you gain the Flaw Shunned (Anarchs) when in the borders of Minneapolis.

•• THE CAVES

An open secret to locals, the man-made caves located underneath the otherwise innocuous Wabasha Street have played host to miners, mushroom farmers, bootleggers, and nightclubs throughout the years. Suffice it to say, their subterranean location has made them the ideal haven for Kindred, and many an Elysium has been held in the spacious, sandstone dancehall carved into the underground tunnels. As one of the denizens of the caves, you gain Haven (••) with the merits Postern (•) and Luxury (•).

••• CRIMINAL HISTORY

Though the age of Prohibition and gangsters may be over, organized crime still finds a foothold in St. Paul. From Babyface Nelson, to John Dillinger, to Machine Gun Kelly, you represent a heritage of underworld culture that lives on to the modern nights. You gain a +2 dice bonus to all Streetwise rolls made to gather information on local criminal activity, and a specialty of your choice in Larceny.

•••• COURTIER

Those who know how to cater to a Toreador Prince's whims have learned to make themselves not only little worker bees, but beautiful social butterflies. You gain the specialty Etiquette (High Society) and may add +2 dice to any Social Conflict roll made within an Elysium or Courtly setting once per session.

••••• DUAL CITIZENSHIP

Perhaps your service to Prince Merrain has been so subtle as to not attract the ire of your fellow Kindred across the river. Or, perhaps you've become so well-embedded as an Anarch within St. Paul that none would dare question your presence in either city. You gain a cover identity, in the form of Mask (••), for the purposes of undercover travelling within whichever Twin City you do not reside. That identity may also gain two ranks of Status with either the Camarilla (for St. Paul) or the Anarchs (for Minneapolis.) Once per story, any egregious breaking of the Masquerade (or that city's Traditions) may be blamed upon that false identity (and, by extension, that Sect), leaving you to suffer little to no consequences. This is an ideal strategy for both infiltrators and Agents Provocateur within both sects.

CECILY BAIN

Epitaph: Lone Wolf Without a Cub

Quote: "We are the vampires of the Twin Cities...and we are desperately in need of some fucking public transportation."

Clan: Brujah

MORTAL DAYS:
Cecily Bain was born Cecily Banashefski in 1952 in Pinewood, Minnesota, a small rural farming community outside Bemidji. When she was thirteen, her father was severely injured in a farming accident, and her uncle came to stay with the family to help run the farm. At seventeen, Cecily discovered her uncle had been abusing her eight-year-old sister, Karen, and told her mother, who, desperate not to disrupt the status quo, ignored the warnings. Cecily sought help from someone outside her household, making her way to the home of a neighbor rumored to be a witch. Instead, Cecily was introduced to her first Kindred, an Anarch woman who offered her the power to right wrongs herself.

KINDRED NIGHTS:
Upon her Embrace, Cecily killed her uncle and mother, and euthanized her suffering father. Her sister, unaware of what had transpired, joined Cecily in escaping to the Twin Cities. Cecily regularly used her ability to cloud minds to keep her sister unaware of reality, which she believes eventually contributed to her susceptibility to dementia. While Cecily and Karen spent most nights engulfed in the Minneapolis hardcore punk music scene, Cecily was also secretly feeding on its members. Cecily became affiliated with the Anarch movement of the Cities, and actively resisted the Camarilla's attempt at urban domination, headed by Primogen Calder Wendt. Eventually though, Cecily saw the writing on the wall, and realizing she needed some kind of stability to aid her ailing sister, joined the Ivory Tower as one of Prince Samantha Merrain's "dirty boot" enforcers.

PLOTS AND SCHEMES:
Beholden to None: Cecily actively resists any and all offers to become an official part of the local Camarilla's complicated ruling structure, instead demanding independence in return for her flawlessly executed services. (Status: Camarilla 3)

DOMAIN AND HAVEN:
In the late-90s, Cecily secured a warehouse space above the LOVELAND 24-hour sex shop, reasoning no one would question her coming and going at all hours, while occasionally providing a drunken snack showing up, confused, lost and horny on her doorstep. The neighborhood has gentrified around her and the shop, and she regularly wonders when Loveland will be replaced with a brewery or coffee shop. (Haven Rating: 2. Haven Merits: Location, Palisade)

THRALLS AND TOOLS:
Street-Level Informants (Contacts 2) In conducting her work as protector of the Masquerade, Cecily often relies upon information provided by individuals savvy about the criminal underworld of the Twin Cities. If there's a favored spot for dumping bodies, or fencing stolen goods, it's a safe bet Cecily knows a guy who knows a guy.

Dwindling Goth Scene (Herd 1) Bela Lugosi may truly be dead; a far-cry from the Halcyon days of the late-80s/early-90s, the Goth-Punk subculture of the Twin Cities has considerably waned. To Cecily Bain, however, true taste is about quality, not quantity.

KINDRED RELATIONSHIPS:
Primogen Calder Wendt (Confidant) Cecily likes that Calder never pretends to be anything more than what he is...a survivor who gets by because he's charming and smart. She appreciates that he finds her past as an enemy of the Camarilla an asset. She favors clothing that appears soft and frivolous, masking her job as a physical enforcer.

Prince Samantha Merrain (Respect) Cecily has seen the worst of Kindred kind but sees in Merrain someone who has genuine affection for her adopted home. She knows that Merrain is genuine, and that it'll be her doom.

WHISPERS:
Dangerous Liaisons: Nobody knows of Cecily's sister, Karen. And Cecily aims to keep it that way. Regardless, rumors have begun to circulate about just who the enigmatic Cecily Bain might be visiting, night after night — current consensus seems to speculate a favored Blood Doll.

VAMPIRE

THE MASQUERADE
WINTER'S TEETH

CECILY BAIN

MASK AND MIEN:
Cecily makes use of a number of aliases and identities whenever the situation calls for it. None of them are particularly ironclad, and their largely disposable nature means most will not hold up to high-level scrutiny. (Mask 1)

Cecily has purposely changed her clothing to reflect the urban chic of the Camarilla, abandoning her old punk costume with her Anarch affiliation. She knows that the Court will accept someone who dresses the part, no matter that Kindred's history, because surface appearance is all most Camarilla Kindred are interested in.

ATTRIBUTES:	SECONDARY ATTRIBUTES:
Strength 3	Health 9
Dexterity 3	Willpower 6
Stamina 4	
Charisma 3	
Manipulation 2	
Composure 2	
Intelligence 3	
Wits 2	
Resolve 4	

SKILLS:	DISCIPLINES:
Athletics 3	Celerity 3
Brawl 3	Dominate 1
Drive 3	Fortitude 2
Firearms 3	Potence 3
Larceny 1	Presence 2
Melee 3	
Stealth 2	
Survival 2	
Intimidation 3	
Leadership 2	
Performance (Singing) 2	
Persuasion 2	
Streetwise 3	
Subterfuge 2	
Academics 2	
Awareness 3	
Investigation 3	
Occult 2	
Politics 3	
Technology 2	

SIRE: ASHA CHRISTESON

EMBRACED: 1979

AMBITION: TO SURVIVE. PREFERABLY ALONE.

HUMANITY: 6

CONVICTIONS: "SOME SECRETS ARE WORTH PROTECTING."

TOUCHSTONES: CECILY REGULARLY VISITS HER SISTER, KAREN, WHO SUFFERS FROM DEMENTIA ASSOCIATED WITH ALZHEIMER'S.

GENERATION: 11

BLOOD POTENCY: 3

VAMPIRE
THE MASQUERADE
ANARCH TALES

COLLEEN PENDERGRASS

Epitaph: Beleaguered Thin-Blood, Duskborn Den Mother

Quote: "I'm exhausted... all of the time..."

Clan: Thin-blood

MORTAL DAYS:
Colleen Pendergrass (née Halstead) was born in 1976, the fourth of six children in a lower middle-class family. At eighteen, Colleen had met Mitch Pendergrass, a high school dropout who had started working for her father's HVAC company as a technician. Though four years older than her, Mitch and Colleen formulated a mutual attraction to one another, much to her father's frustration. After two years of dating, Mitch and Colleen were married and, using the money saved from working at her father's company, moved to Duluth and bought their first home.

Mitch found work at a towing company while Colleen set out to complete her RN training at community college, yet it seemed that every attempt at progress was met with setback after setback. Colleen eventually dropped out of college after becoming pregnant with her first child, Kady. Their son, Luke, would be born shortly after.

Money, stress and wasted opportunity all began to take their toll on the young couple, and as frustrations gave way to resentment, Mitch and Colleen's relationship soon became perilously rocky.

One night, after venturing on a late-night call, Mitch disappeared. With Mitch missing, Colleen was suddenly filled with intense regret over the negativity with which she'd viewed her husband these past several months, and had promised herself to try and make it work, if only her spouse would return to her.

KINDRED NIGHTS:
Two nights after vanishing without a trace, Mitch returned just as mysteriously and suddenly as he had gone. Pale, cold and dirty, Colleen ushered her husband back into their home, when suddenly, he lunged upon her, sinking his teeth into her throat and draining the blood from her body. When Colleen awoke, she found herself lying in her bed, with Mitch's lifeless corpse lying next to her.

Confused, and possessed of a consuming hunger, Colleen got out of bed and pulled the blankets serving as makeshift curtains from the bedroom windows. As daylight poured in from the outside, Mitch's corpse suddenly burst into flames – Colleen, herself, remained unburned. Acting on pure instinct, her emergency training kicked in and she covered the burning body with the heavy comforter, dousing the flames as best as she could. Though Mitch would eventually recover from the brush with Final Death, the pair learned a valuable lesson – the nature of their curse was different for each of them.

Though initially Colleen attempted to nurture and care for her children, the Beast within her meant that her children would always be in danger so long as she and Mitch were part of their lives. After ten months of heartbreaking effort, Kady and Luke were remanded to the care of Colleen's older sister, Meghan, under the cover that Colleen and Mitch were entering a long-term care facility for drug abuse. The shame of this abandonment would become so severe that Colleen could never bear to bring herself to see her family again.

However, Mitch and Colleen soon found their own social group, as they formed a close bond with a band of local Kindred, all leaning upon one another for survival. Though her thin-blood nature makes her the most vulnerable member of her Coterie, it also makes her uniquely capable to handle daylight tasks. As a result, she has taken on the mantle of 'provider,' and spends most of her daytime solidarity hunting down the Coterie's next bagged lunch.

PLOTS AND SCHEMES:
"On My Own." Colleen and Mitch were on the fast track to divorce even before their respective Embraces, and, in her mind, has only been temporarily sidelined. The pair are in a mutually codependent relationship, but Colleen is constantly looking for the opportunity to make a clean break.

DOMAIN AND HAVEN:
Colleen and her Coterie all spend their days in the home Mitch and Colleen bought for themselves as newlyweds. Though it has fallen into disrepair due to lack of consistent maintenance, the two-story house, which rests in the shadow of the Duluth Ore Docks, has plenty of space for the errant Kindred needing somewhere to lay their head.

VAMPIRE

THE MASQUERADE

ANARCH TALES

KINDRED RELATIONSHIPS:

Mitch Pendergrass (Contempt) Her Sire and her estranged husband. Colleen and Mitch spend as much time as possible apart from one another -- a remarkably easy task considering that Mitch spends the day in torpor while Colleen tends to her own solitary errands.

Priscilla (Confidant) The coterie's newest member, Priscilla, has brought a much-needed feminine presence to the gang of bloodsuckers. Priscilla, for her part, is more than eager to provide an ear for Colleen's gripes, gushings and gossip.

King Rat (Charming) Perhaps it is King Rat's smaller stature, or his loathsome appearance, but Colleen views the Nosferatu as a proxy for her own children. Though King is quite capable of taking care of himself, Colleen can usually be trusted to dote upon the young man with all of the fuss of an overbearing mother.

WHISPERS:

Untapped Potential. As a Thin-Blood, Colleen has exhibited no propensity at any particular discipline, nor is she versed in the practice of Duskborn alchemy. However, like many of the Thin-Bloods populating the Modern Nights, the only thing that can be expected of them is the unexpected.

MASK AND MIEN:

Colleen Pendergrass still possesses all of her credentials from her lifetime and attempts to keep them active and up-to-date. Her haggard and exhausted appearance assists in selling the illusion of her being twenty years older than she'd otherwise appear.

Colleen is a slender woman of 5'6, who appears anywhere from her late twenties to her early forties. Bright, poker-straight red hair falls to her mid-back, and her pale green eyes compliment her equally pale, lightly freckled cheeks. Colleen has no real sense of style or fashion and can usually be found wearing what's clean or available.

COLLEEN PENDERGRASS

SIRE: MITCH PENDERGRASS

EMBRACED: 2004

AMBITION: TO SEE HER CHILDREN, AGAIN.

CONVICTIONS:
"INNOCENTS SHOULD BE SHIELDED FROM HORROR."
"ADAPT TO SURVIVE."

HUMANITY: 8

TOUCHSTONES: KADY (20) AND LUKE (18),
HER DAUGHTER AND SON.

GENERATION: 14

BLOOD POTENCY: 0

ATTRIBUTES:

Strength 2
Dexterity 2
Stamina 2
Charisma 2
Manipulation 3
Composure 3
Intelligence 2
Wits 4
Resolve 3

SECONDARY ATTRIBUTES:
Health 5
Willpower 6

SKILLS:

Insight 2
Leadership 1
Persuasion 2
Subterfuge 2
Awareness 1
Finance 2
Medicine 2
Technology 2

Athletics 1
Craft (Domestic Crafts) 3
Drive 2
Larceny 2
Stealth 4
Survival 2
Animal Ken 2
Etiquette 3

DISCIPLINES:
None

THIN-BLOOD MERITS:
Day Drinker, Lifelike

THIN-BLOOD FLAWS:
Baby Teeth

THE NICTUKU
(Nosferatu Characters Only)

In the underground tunnels of the Clan of the Hidden, there are whispered legends and cautionary tales shared among the Sewer Rats. Sires warn their childer of dangers lurking in the darkest corners of night, and of monstrosities that would chill the vitae of even the most hideous of horrors.

Nictuku.

That single word is enough to spread like wildfire throughout the ranks of the Nosferatu rumor mill, sending neonates and elders alike scuttling back to their warrens in paranoid dread. To some, they are believed to be the vengeful offspring of the clan progenitor – a vindictive and cannibalistic bloodline whose thirst can only be sated by the blood of the Antediluvian's lesser childer. To others, it is the colorful sobriquet applied to those Nosferatu who have succumbed to their Beasts – a less existential, if similarly harrowing, threat – and now stalk the caverns and catacombs of the world, hunting their own kind. Even others maintain that it is a title taken by the eldest of the clan, merely another mask adopted to feed upon their own.

Whatever the truth may be, no Kindred currently active in the modern nights knows for sure, and those who are unlucky enough to actually encounter one of the Nictuku are certain never to survive to tell about it. You, however, have managed to piece together key pieces of knowledge that may, one night, save your unlife.

===== ● =====

• SIGNAL-TO-NOISE
More than one mysterious death or disappearance has been attributed, by conspiracy-minded Sewer Rats, to be the work of the dreaded Nictuku. Whether it's a scouting party that has vanished beneath the streets of Manhattan, or a warren in St. Louis suddenly going dark, time and resources are often wasted on wild goose chases. Once per story, by examining the tell-tale signs (or lack thereof), you may definitively know whether such a crime was committed by your ancestral enemy, or some other circumstance.

•• MORBID CURIOSITY
Whether through legend, gossip, or indirect exposure, you have grown obsessed with the concept of these ancestral nemeses and have devoted your unlife to the study of the Nictuku. When making an **Occult** or **Investigation** roll regarding the Nictuku you may add +2 dice to the roll.

••• BLINDSPOT
Most Nosferatu believe the most powerful weapon in their arsenal is the Discipline of Obfuscate. However, while this may make them all but imperceptible to humans, Kindred and other supernatural beings have senses that extend beyond mortal means. In keeping with their name, the Hidden have had to hone their skills to counter not only the perceptive Tremere regent on whom they are spying, but also the unknown shadows that haunt their every step. Once per session, when contesting against a power such as **Sense the Unseen**, you may add two dice to your **Obfuscate** roll.

•••• DEATHMARK
Just because you're paranoid doesn't mean they're not out to get you. You've managed to attract the attention of one of the Nictuku (or something that appears as one), and now it is but a matter of time before they catch up with you. You gain **Adversary (••••)**; however, you may spend an equal number of points on haven merits relating to the added security measures taken against your phantom nemesis. Once per story, you may permanently sacrifice up to three dots in Backgrounds to make a clean getaway, at the Storyteller's discretion.

••••• HUNTED-BECOMES-HUNTER
You have developed skills of survival and combat against more than just the Nictuku. Indeed, you have managed to hone yourself into a defensive weapon against any Kindred who would seek to consume the vitae within you. You gain the specialization **Brawl (Kindred)** and may add an additional +2 dice to all conflicted rolls against cannibalistic Kindred (diablerists, Blood Leeches, and the like.)

VAMPIRE
THE MASQUERADE
WINTER'S TEETH

WOLVES IN SHEEP'S CLOTHING

Discarded and disenfranchised ghouls forming themselves into confederations and cults is no new phenomenon. Animosity between servant and master is a tale as old as the practice of servitude itself, and woe to the vampire who carelessly abuses his faithful retainer. More than one city in the modern nights are plagued with bands of independent ghouls, stalking their former dominitors to feast upon the vitae that fuels their unearthly addiction – using the gifts bestowed upon them to bite the hand that feeds.

Though this practice is hardly novel, the cabal that calls itself the Wolves in Sheep's Clothing has personalized this poetic justice in unique and perverse ways. The Wolves use their augmented blood coupled with a strange and blasphemous form of mortal Hedge Magic, to technomantically graft preserved kindred body-parts onto themselves. By harvesting, say, the eyes of a Kindred, they may, in turn, temporarily harness a semblance of that Kindred's ability to control the minds of others through eye-contact, or to see into the depths of the soul.

No one truly knows from where these reprehensible mongrels first gained their taste of vitae, (though their passing familiarity with some form of necromancy implies a possible connection to a certain family of the Hecata) and any Kindred found responsible for such a plunder would surely find themselves upon the Red List. It is only their relatively small number and covert activities that keep them from being perceived as a bigger threat – instead, they are merely another faction of dangerous mortals to watch out for in the modern nights.

●

WHAT BIG TEETH YOU HAVE!

As their names suggest, the Wolves in Sheep's Clothing are deadly simply because, as ghouled mortals, Kindred have a tendency to underestimate them – allowing them to get in close enough to strike with lethal precision. You have learned to recognize the tell-tale signs of these abominations as your Beast instinctively finds itself agitated around these callous usurpers.

● HUNTSMAN

You have engaged in a deadly game of cat-and-mouse with the Wolves in Sheep's Clothing for years. The lines between predator and prey have ➤ become blurred as you seek out these deadly foes while simultaneously ensuring your own safety during daylight hours. You gain an extra die to all **Investigation** rolls made to track down or investigate the Wolves in Sheep's Clothing, in addition to gaining an extra die to all rolls made to act during the daytime.

●●● CARRION PRESERVATION

You have managed to replicate the way in which the Wolves harvest vampiric body parts without them immediately decaying into dust. While you are certain to not gain the benefits they do by grafting such parts onto yourself, such a talent can nevertheless prove useful when it comes to preserving evidence, or grisly keepsakes. By dousing the organ or extremity into one Rouse Check's worth of vitae and succeeding at a Resolve + Occult roll (diff. 3), the vampire may embalm the object for a year, at which time the preservation needs to be renewed. Final Death of the caster, however, immediately renders this preservation null.

●●●● A WOLF IN THE FOLD

You have been victimized by the Wolves in Sheep's Clothing, though have managed to escape. To this night, some up-jumped ghoul stalks the streets, wielding pieces of your body as their own. While this may serve them for now, you have managed to turn this plunder into a Trojan Horse. Once per Chronicle, you may attempt to inhabit the perception of your assailant, as per the Auspex power **Share the Senses** (**using Resolve + Insight.**) Should you already possess **Share the Senses**, you instead reduce the difficulty of the roll by two.

●●●●● THE SHEPHERD

You have made yourself a mysterious benefactor to the Wolves in Sheep's Clothing to such a degree that they have become your loyal, if ignorant, hounds. You gain Allies (●●●●) representing a cell of these redoubtable ghouls. Once per Chronicle, you may send this cell to dispatch a Kindred enemy. However, should the Wolves discover your true nature, said Allies may very easily become Enemies (●●●●) instead, not to mention any objections your local Camarilla may take to those who willingly aid and abet anathemas such as these.

●

NEXT ➤
SAMPLE: WOLF IN SHEEP'S CLOTHING
(DEADLY MORTAL)

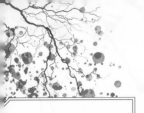

SAMPLE WOLF IN SHEEP'S CLOTHING (DEADLY MORTAL)

Attributes: Strength 2, Dexterity 2, Stamina 4, Charisma 2, Manipulation 2, Composure, 3, Intelligence 4, Wits 3, Resolve 5.

Secondary Attributes: Health 7, Willpower 8

Skills: Academics 4, Awareness 3, Medicine 4, Occult (Hedge Magic) 5, Science 3, Technology 4, Athletics 2, Brawl 3, Craft 3, Drive 2, Firearms 2, Melee 2, Stealth 2, Insight 3, Intimidation 2.

Disciplines: Oblivion 1, Special*

Special: In addition to the single Discipline power gained from being a ghoul, the Wolves in Sheep's Clothing may have up to additional three dots in Disciplines, representing powers gained through grafting vampiric anatomy. Those powers must be chosen from the following: Auspex, Dominate, Fortitude, Potence, Protean. (Note that these powers can exhibit a lot of variation from regular Disciplines, and the Storyteller is free to come up with new, unique, powers and variants.)

Note: The Wolf may have up to three dots, spent however they please. Example: One Wolf may have Auspex 3, while another possesses Fortitude 2, Potence 1, and yet a third has Auspex 1, Dominate 1, Protean 1, etc.

NEW POWERS

ANIMALISM
Level 2
Atavism
By subtly projecting their Beast into a mortal animal, the vampire may cause it to revert to its most base and primal of instincts. Loyal guard dogs suddenly become ravenous, slathering curs and prized thoroughbreds throw their riders as they champ and buck in mad panic.

- **Cost:** One Rouse Check
- **Dice Pools:** Composure + Animalism
- **System:** The target must be able to sense (smell, hear, or see) the user in question to use this power. Roll Com posure + Animalism vs. Difficulty 1-4, depending on type of animal, its training, and whether or not it is a ghoul A win against the target allows the user to choose one of two primal responses: Fight or Flight. If Fight is chosen, the creature reacts in kind, lashing out at the closest perceived threat or prey. If Flight, the creature instead flies into a panic, trying to escape its surroundings at any cost to their safety. Well-trained and faithful animals tend to shake off this reaction quickly, and so, clever users tend to time their uses of this power in order to create maximum effect. **Duration:** A number of rounds equal to the test margin plus one, or the entire Scene in the case of a critical win.

BLOOD SORCERY
Level 1
Shape the Sanguine Sacrament

Learned only by the most ostentatious of Tremere, this power is used to manipulate blood or vitae into finely crafted images – whether entertaining your fellows at Elysium with gaudy magician's tricks or diverting flowing rivulets into painstakingly precise Hermetic sigils.

- **Cost:** Free (or One Rouse Check if using own Blood)
- **Dice Pools:** Manipulation + Blood Sorcery
- **System:** Using a measure of blood or vampiric vitae, the user may channel their mastery of Blood Sorcery to influence the very essence of the blood itself, to obey the user's whim. By making a successful Manipulation + Blood Sorcery roll, the user may craft the blood into any shape or image they desire. Complexity of the image varies by difficulty – a simple message of "Help!" or a basic polygonal shape may only be at Difficulty 2, while a lengthy diatribe or an intricate sculpture may be Difficulty 4 or higher. Failure on this roll means the blood fails to form the desired shape or does not respond at all – a Critical Success not only forms the desired image, but negates the need for any further rolls to change its shape for the duration of the scene.
- **Duration:** For the remainder of the scene, unless dispelled by the user.

FORTITUDE
Level 2
Obdurate
Amalgam: Potence 2

Though the Discipline of Fortitude allows a Kindred to resist damage from bullets, blades, and even burning fire and sunlight. It does little, however, to keep the forces of physics at bay and an overwhelming blow can still stagger or knock prone the unprepared vampire. By shoring up their physical hardiness with vampiric **Potence**, the Kindred may maintain a steady footing when struck by a massive force.

Cost: One Rouse Check.
Dice Pools: Wits + Survival
System: When activated, a vampire may use this power to become a sturdy and strong immovable object. Vampires falling from great heights find themselves able to literally hit the ground running. Vampires struck by moving vehicles won't budge an inch while the car crumples like aluminum. Users may consciously activate this ability in advance or may instinctively activate it by making a successful Stamina + Survival check at Difficulty 3. Any superficial damage received from falling or collisions is reduced by the user's Fortitude score, before being halved.
Duration: One scene.

PRESENCE
Level 4
Magnum Opus
Amalgam: Auspex 3

A favored power of the Roses, with this ability, the user may sublimate and infuse the powers of the blood into their works of art – capable of rendering sculptures so beautiful as to make the viewer fall in love with them, or paintings of such ghastly disquiet they make even the most visceral Caravaggio seem facile by comparison. This masterwork is merely an illusion, however -- a flash-in-the-pan beauty that does not withstand deep scrutiny.

Cost: One or more Rouse Checks.
Dice Pools: Charisma, Manipulation + Crafts
System: Before embarking on a **Project Roll** to create a work of art the user must make One Rouse Check for each roll made. The difficulty of the project must be 10 or higher. Upon successful completion of the project, the user finds that residual traces of their **Presence** linger within the work itself. When your artwork is on display, audiences must roll **Composure + Resolve** (Difficulty equal to the user's Presence rank) or succumb to the rough equivalent of either **Awe** or **Daunt** exuding from the piece. A Critical Success on the resistance roll renders the subject immune to further influence by the piece. Note: By integrating Disciplines into its creation, the work of art has no true staying power, aside from the initial exposure. Critics and observers may find themselves suddenly able to critique flaws or imperfections once they have left the immediate area.
Duration: N/A

VAMPIRE

THE MASQUERADE

WINTER'S TEETH

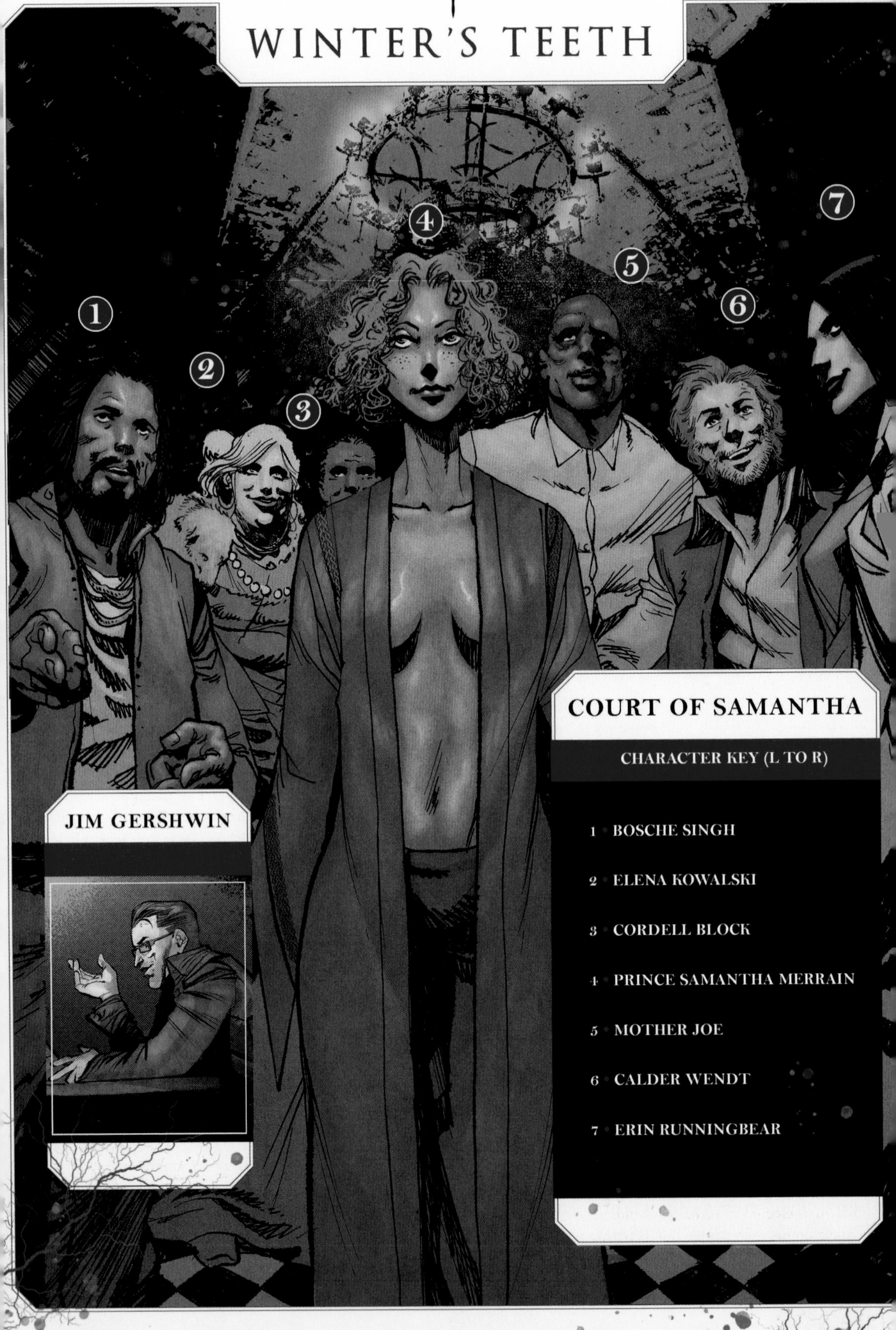

1
2
3
4
5
6
7
JIM GERSHWIN
COURT OF SAMANTHA
CHARACTER KEY (L TO R)
1 BOSCHE SINGH
2 ELENA KOWALSKI
3 CORDELL BLOCK
4 PRINCE SAMANTHA MERRAIN
5 MOTHER JOE
6 CALDER WENDT
7 ERIN RUNNINGBEAR

VAMPIRE

THE MASQUERADE

WINTER'S TEETH

THE COURT OF PRINCE SAMANTHA (PART I)

BOSCHE SINGH
Epitaph: The Great Tiger
Quote: "It is only when we are battling for survival that we are truly alive."
Clan: Gangrel

MORTAL DAYS:

Bosche Singh was born descended from a long line of Rajput — his family taking great pride in their warrior-caste. In the early 19th-Century, Bosche joined the Bengal Army, under the purview of the East India Trading Company. Though commanded by British officers, Singh was pleased to find that the majority of his comrades-in-arms were Rajput such as he, or Brahmin of high esteem. In 1839, Singh and his company were deployed to Kabul, taking part in the First Anglo-Afghan War. It was here, in the dusty mountains, that Singh took a grievous wound before his company was routed by an ambush from Afghan partisans. As he lay, bleeding out, he watched the sun set around him as twilight gave way to the dark of night. As the sleep of death threatened to overtake him, he raged against his imminent demise with a low and feral roar of fury.

KINDRED NIGHTS:

It was then that Singh was approached by that which he least expected and had never considered. A white man, in a poorly-fitting British officer's uniform silently approached Singh's dying body. Seeing him lash out like a cornered beast, the man revealed his true self -- a wandering Kindred named Sir Charles Stromwell. Stromwell gave Singh no choice as he hungrily supped at what little blood remained within his body, before forcing him to imbibe Stromwell's own. As Singh was reborn, the two travelled the world by night, taking part in various conflicts as hired mercenaries, or simply unaffiliated interlopers. In the 1860s, the duo crossed the Atlantic where they revelled in the wanton bloodshed of the American Civil War. Eventually, the pair settled out West for a time, where Stromwell served as Primogen within the Twin Cities. Three years ago, Stromwell left the United States toward the conflict of the Gehenna Crusade. And while he did not feel the unshakeable, ancestral Beckoning, he was nevertheless summoned by the prospect of a great battle of immortals. Singh, having grown weary of his wanderlust, elected to remain behind, where he could hope to develop his own power not as Stromwell's childe, but as a powerful Kindred in his own right.

PLOTS AND SCHEMES:

Khan Ascendent: Bosche is uneasy with not being the top predator within his territory. While more than a match for most Kindred, when it comes to battles of claw and fang, Bosche lacks the critical influence required to not only claim praxis over a city, but to hold it. It is, however, something he is actively working toward changing.

DOMAIN AND HAVEN:

In his effort to exert a wider control over his own niche of the city, Singh has taken to procuring a number of gymnasiums and sporting venues as both his personal hunting grounds and his havens. Singh's Gangrel blood rebels at the idea of staying in one place for too long, and so varies his resting place, night after night. (Various level 1 Havens)

THRALLS AND TOOLS:

Combat Junkies: Bosche has no interest in those who attend his gym purely for exercise or "bettering themselves." Those that catch his eye tend to be the ones who step into the octagon with the desire to cause pain and achieve victory. (Allies 2, Retainers 2)

The Menagerie: Bosche has managed to infiltrate the staff of the Minnesota Zoo, located in nearby Apple Valley to the south. There, Singh has managed to cultivate a small herd from the humble collective of Bengal tigers currently held in captivity. While not his preference, Singh believes that feeding from these beasts of his homeland fill him with a sort of shamanic power, transferring their essence unto him. (Herd 1)

KINDRED RELATIONSHIPS:
- **Elena Kowalski (Disdain)** "A useless sycophant who caters to both her own ego, and that of the Prince's."
- **Jim Gershwin (Fool)** "There are few things more pathetic than an aged songbird desperately attempting to preen their molting plumage."
- **Mother Joe (Useful)** "A warrior, to be sure. But a blunt instrument. One that could possibly be wielded to greater effect."

MORE ►
THE COURT OF
PRINCE SAMANTHA (PART I)

VAMPIRE

THE MASQUERADE

WINTER'S TEETH

WHISPERS:

Patricide: Some doubt Singh's tale of his sire's venture to the Middle East. Many believe that the Great Tiger, hungry for power, commit diablerie on his creator.

MASK AND MIEN:

Singh dresses in bright and ostentatious pastels and colors. However, this display is not that of the strutting peacock, but rather the attention-grabbing coloration of a venomous creature: I'm here, and I'm dangerous. Take note of me. Beneath his clothing, Bosche's torso bears strange, striated discolorations -- a lasting influence from the frenzying Beast within him. In dealing with mortals, primarily as a means of promoting fights (both of legal exhibitions and underground "street level" scuffles,) Bosche operates under a number of pseudonyms -- never sticking with one for a long enough time to create a true mask around it.

ATTRIBUTES:

Strength 3
Dexterity 4
Stamina 3
Charisma 3
Manipulation 3
Composure 4
Intelligence 2
Wits 3
Resolve 3

SECONDARY ATTRIBUTES:

Health 8
Willpower 7

SKILLS:

Athletics 3
Brawl 4 (Grappling)
Craft (Smithing) 2
Drive 1
Firearms 2
Melee 4
Stealth 4
Survival 3 (Find Shelter)
Animal Ken 3 (Dressage)
Etiquette 2

Insight 3
Intimidation 3
Streetwise 2
Subterfuge 2
Academics (Geography) 2
Awareness 4
Finances 2
Investigation 2
Politics 2
Technology 1

BOSCHE SINGH

SIRE: SIR CHARLES STROMWELL

EMBRACED: 1841

AMBITION: TO BECOME PRINCE OF THE TWIN CITIES.

CONVICTIONS: "ALL ARE WORTHY OF SURVIVAL, BUT ONLY THE STRONG MAY THRIVE."

TOUCHSTONES: SINGH HAS TAKEN NOTE OF A YOUNG MMA FIGHTER, SANDY NGO, WHO EXHIBITS
A TRUE WARRIOR SPIRIT. HE HAS BEGUN GROOMING HER FOR COMPETITION AND HAS NOT ENTIRELY RULED OUT THE POSSIBILITY OF THE EMBRACE.

HUMANITY: 4

GENERATION: 8

BLOOD POTENCY: 3

DISCIPLINES:

Animalism 3
Protean 4
Fortitude 2
Celerity 1
Potence 1

VAMPIRE

THE MASQUERADE

WINTER'S TEETH

THE COURT OF PRINCE SAMANTHA (PART II)

ELENA KOWALSKI (KOWALSKA)
Epitaph: The Long Con
Quote: "The portrait? My great-grandmother. Why yes, the resemblance is striking!"
Clan: Ventrue

MORTAL DAYS:
Elena Kowalska was the daughter of an affluent Polish-Lithuanian family within Prague. As was often the custom with the daughters of the aristocracy, Elena was educated within a nunnery from the age of nine. By the time the young lady became a debutante at age eighteen, her family had already betrothed her to a kind and promising suitor.

Elena would never make her grand re-entry into high society, however, nor would she ever even lay eyes upon her groom-to-be. For none within the convent knew that their greatest patron, a wealthy Prussian widow by the name of Countess Gretel von Flemming, had taken a great interest in the youthful Elena, and took her under her wing to complete her true education.

Under the tutelage of Countess von Flemming, Elena learned that everything she had been taught of piety and prudence were simply pre-cursors. "One must first learn the rules of polite society," Gretel had said, "before they can be broken for our benefit." Gretel trained Elena in how to navigate the world of nobility where her sex would not be viewed as a hinderance, but instead as her greatest weapon. For decades, the duo traveled the courts of Europe, and as Elena grew older and wiser, she had become molded into the Countess' own image. Elena became the Countess' prized pupil, and later, all but an equal in partnership. It was then that she was also schooled upon the secrets of everlasting life.

KINDRED NIGHTS:
Upon her Baptism into the night, Elena Kowalska was presented with an opportunity after the disastrous Napoleonic conflicts which tore Poland asunder. With her family having been utterly decimated and left without an heir, it was then that the prodigal "missing heiress" returned, filled with fanciful tales of an abduction and captivity by dreadful Russian agents, a daring escape, and a life spent in exile. ▶

So taken were the executors of the familial estate with the magnificent tale that they immediately took her at her word, and Elena soon found her family's vast inheritance to be all hers. With a trove of gold and riches but no home to speak of, she took her vast fortune and set out for more hospitable climes.

Across the centuries Elena has put up her tent posts in various different cities and countries, having spent the last several decades within the American midwest as a darling of the Court of Prince Samantha Merrain.

PLOTS AND SCHEMES:
None. Unlike a great many of the Kindred that surround her, Elena is quite content to simply live out her unlife in relative comfort and luxury. She wants for nothing, because she has it all. In Elena's mind, it is no shame to serve rather than to rule, for heavy is the head that wears the crown.

DOMAIN AND HAVEN:
Elena and her (current) husband occupy a large and historic mansion in St. Paul's Summit Avenue, located in the wealthy Macalaster-Groveland neighborhood. Lightly armed security, electronic alarm systems, and closed-circuit surveillance allow Elena to relax within the safety of her haven with general peace of mind. (Resources 4, Haven Rating: 2. Haven Merits: Location, Luxury, Security, Watchmen.)

THRALLS AND TOOLS:
Blackfire Security: While Elena may be a formidable undead monster, she prefers to keep her hands unsullied with the sordid acts that often come from the Eternal Struggle. As an unscrupulous member of the one percent, Elena has no qualms with hiring the services of disreputable firms such as that of Blackfire Security. While, for the most part, her small security detail is tasked with ensuring her personal safety, Blackfire contractors seldom ask too many questions when it comes to pre-emptive strikes. (Allies 3)
Junior: Elena has ghouled many people over her long life, though few manage to remain in her service for long. Lately, Elena has conscripted the services of a middle-aged man whom she simply refers to as "Junior." Silent, sturdy and secretive, Junior serves as Elena's chauffeur, daytime courier, and all-around toadie. (Retainer 2)

MORE ▶
THE COURT OF PRINCE SAMANTHA (PART II)

VAMPIRE
THE MASQUERADE
WINTER'S TEETH

KINDRED RELATIONSHIPS:

Bosche Singh (Ignorance): "I see him at Elysium often enough, and I know we've been introduced. But for the life of me I can't seem to put the name to the face..."

Jim Gershwin (Plaything): "Darling James gets ever so passionate about such trivial things. It is quite precious to observe."

Mother Joe (Revulsion): "You mean that great big brute with the slack jaw? What Kindred would waste their vitae making something like that immortal?"

WHISPERS:

Hints of Cruelty: As was ingrained in her from the moment of her Embrace, Elena has learned how to keep her true self buried deep, deep down. Elena is far from the shrinking violet she purports herself to be, and more than one of her victims have learned, first-hand, the true depths of her sadism. Such individuals do not often live to spread such rumors, however.

Messy Eater: Throughout the years, Elena has masqueraded as various scions of her own family -- using the mystique and the influence to infiltrate high-class social circles around the world. A brief marriage here, an inheritance there, and Elena has accrued such a vast amount of wealth that any deep scrutiny into her personal finances would reveal that she has not been vigilant about discretion. As the Second Inquisition nips at the heels of Kindred resources, such a flagrant money trail could spell her doom.

Tool of Another: Countess von Flemming still lives within the modern nights. She has nearly half-a-dozen childer to her name, all with the same training and tutelage as Elena. Is the venerable Ventrue perhaps setting her pawns, strategically, across the board?

MASK AND MIEN:

Elena's was preserved not as a comely young maiden but as an accomplished grown woman. As such, though her face may be careworn and her skin not as supple as the convent girl she had been so many ages ago, she still carries herself with a poise and a dignity that is utterly majestic. (**Looks: Beautiful**)

Elena dresses herself in exquisite finery, though often it may seem slightly out-of-fashion. Exquisite furs and boas -- long opera gloves and strings of pearls -- Elena knows the value of a first impression and wishes for all who look upon her to recognize her wealth and privilege. She is not without her eccentricities, however, and recently has taken to keeping exotic pets. In recent nights, she does not travel to social occasions without her pet Fennec fox cradled within her arms.

Elena has acquired the services of the best identity launderers that money can buy and uses them to great effect. Throughout her long life, Elena has adopted many identities - "Helen Smith," "Ellen Carmichael," and even the subtle, yet slightly more Americanized "Elena Kowalski".

ELENA KOWALSKI

SIRE: COUNTESS GRETEL VON FLEMMING

EMBRACED: 1796

AMBITION: TO LIVE FOREVER, IN STYLE.

CONVICTIONS: "NEVER LET ANYONE KNOW WHAT YOU'RE TRULY CAPABLE OF."

TOUCHSTONES: EUGENE RUTHERFORD LANG (67). THE CFO OF HERRICK'S FOODS, A NATIONAL GROCERY STORE CHAIN. EUGENE IS THE LATEST IN A LONG LINE OF UNWARY MORTALS WHOM ELENA HAS CLEAVED HERSELF UNTO FOR THE PURPOSES OF EXPANDING HER REVENUE.

HUMANITY: 3

GENERATION: 9

BLOOD POTENCY: 2

ATTRIBUTES:
Strength 1
Dexterity 2
Stamina 3
Charisma 4
Manipulation 4
Composure 5
Intelligence 3
Wits 3
Resolve 3

SECONDARY ATTRIBUTES:
Health 6
Willpower 8

DISCIPLINES:
Animalism 1
Dominate 3
Presence 3

SKILLS:
Craft (Needlework) 2
Drive 2
Larceny 1
Stealth 2
Animal Ken 2
Etiquette 5 (High Society)
Insight 4
Leadership 3
Performance (Storytelling) 4
Persuasion 4
Subterfuge 4
Academics (Seminary) 3
Awareness 2
Finance 4
Technology 3

THE COURT OF PRINCE SAMANTHA (PART III)

JIM GERSHWIN

Epitaph: The Dilatant Poseur

Quote: "They call it 'Virtual Realism'. Possibly the most exciting thing since the kinetoscope!"

Clan: Toreador

———————————————●———————————————

MORTAL DAYS:

When James Gershwin was a young man, the world was in an unprecedented state of progress and innovation. As a child, he witnessed the proliferation of the steam locomotive, the exponential growth of factories, and the industrialization of civilization. As a young man, James (or "Jim," to his friends) saw the future ahead of him and knew that there was no real limit to the possibilities of human ingenuity. Despite his fascination with engines and other such machinery, Jim had no education in engineering, and was a gentleman of leisure. He did, however, use his family's riches to sponsor the efforts of actual inventors. Though most of the projects he supported were complete failures, Jim viewed his efforts as a labor of love rather than venture capitalism.

KINDRED NIGHTS:

One evening, Gershwin attended an exhibition in Southampton, showcasing a marvelous new machine referred to as the "horseless steam carriage," created by the shipwright firm, Summer, Ogle & Co. The showcase featured a twelve-passenger bus that ran on steam locomotion, but on an inlaid track, but on the same streets and roads as any other carriage. The northbound excursion from Southampton to London was proclaimed to last only five hours, beginning shortly after sundown, and was attended by numerous members of Europe's futurist minds, including Charles Babbage. Also in attendance was the French Toreador socialite, Henrietta L'Abadie, who was utterly taken with Gershwin's impassioned gesticulations and contagious anticipation for all things novel. As the carriage arrived in London, shortly before midnight, Henrietta invited James to her lodgings, where they spent the evening speaking, until the sun rose and both of them fell into slumber. For an entire week, James and Henrietta spent every moment in each other's company, sharing in Gershwin's predictions of the future and Henrietta's eyewitness accounts of ages past. By the end of the week, Jim was pleading with Henrietta for the Embrace. No matter how dark the shadow of night, the brightness of the future would surely drown it out. Henrietta's unbeating heart was moved, and so, obliged him.

But hope for the future ran out for Henrietta. At the turn of the twentieth century, humanity's love of innovation and invention was harnessed for industrialized warfare, and her beloved France was ripped asunder. Leaving her Childe with a blood-tear stained letter, Henrietta walked into the sunrise. Devastated by the loss of his Sire, Gershwin followed his beloved's letter, and sailed across the Atlantic in search of Samantha Merrain, a fellow rose named by Henrietta. "Proclaim yourself of my Blood, and Merrain shall know I've come to claim my boon." Indeed, Merrain held true to whatever pact the two had made, and so she took Jim under her wing.

Since then, Gershwin has acted as Prince Samantha's Harpy -- ensuring that the record of prestation in Prince Samantha's domain is well-documented, and that those of strong reputation are rewarded or rebuked, accordingly. He has also acted as the Prince's link to the modern world -- a notion rather vexing to many Camarilla neonates and fledglings, as Gershwin's own grasp on what is "new" or "relevant" is not always prescient.

PLOTS AND SCHEMES:

Endorse "The Next Big Thing": Despite the unforgettable experience of the steam-carriage, Gershwin failed to capitalize on the opportunity, and dismissed it as merely an attraction -- had he known about the ubiquity of cars throughout the modern nights, he might have thought better of it. In Gershwin's mind, were it not for his apathy, the name of Summer, Ogle & Co. might be as well known as the name Ford. Because of this perceived failure, Gershwin is obsessed with keeping an ear to the ground in the realm of bleeding-edge technology. In spite of this, Gershwin's instincts are relatively poor, and he has passed over such opportunities as the radio, personal computer, and cellular phone, in favor of the carpet sweeper, 8-track, and 1-800 numbers.

Embarrass Calder Wendt: Jim is displeased by the favor in which Tremere Primogen Calder Wendt has curried with Prince Samantha.

———————————————●———————————————

MORE ➤
THE COURT OF
PRINCE SAMANTHA (PART III)

THE COURT OF PRINCE SAMANTHA (PART III)

PLOTS AND SCHEMES (con't):

He believes that the Warlock's intentions are impure, and that he is merely ingratiating himself to Merrain for the sole purpose of betraying her. In light of Prince Merrain's death, Gershwin has begun to suspect that Wendt must have played some part in it, though he lacks the evidence to prove it. He seeks to leverage his position as Harpy (while it lasts) in order to irrevocably destroy Calder's standing in the city.

DOMAIN AND HAVEN:

In 1977, Gershwin became the proprietor of a nightclub known as Disco USA. By 1982, it was completely remodeled and renamed Hank's, reflecting a more Country-Western vibe. In 1997, Hank's became Hankies, Minneapolis' newest gay bar. By 2005, Hankies had reverted back to the now nostalgic Disco USA, until the novelty wore off and it was closed in 2007. After six years in reinventive torpor, the venue finally reopened as Rhapsody in Blue, a hipster cocktail and piano bar. Here, patrons may sip gin and tonics from mason jars at absurd mark-ups in exchange for chill vibes and an exclusive environment, uninviting to outsiders. Since the initial venue's opening, Jim has directly overseen operations from his apartment, located upstairs. And while his pseudonym is no longer on the lease, not a single drink is poured behind the bar without Jim knowing about it. (**Haven Rating: 2, Haven Benefits: Location, Luxury, Postern, Security.**)

Gershwin's feeding ground extends to the entirety of Northloop and the trendy Warehouse District of Minneapolis. Jim is not particularly draconian when it comes to hunting and feeding rights and tends to look the other way whenever a group of Anarchs wants to snack on a few bar-hoppers or sports fans -- provided that they don't leave a mess. (**Herd 3, Resources 3**)

THRALLS AND TOOLS:

Start-Up Incubators: While Minneapolis-St. Paul may not be the mecca for advancements in digital-space that Silicon Valley is, affordable housing and leasing has led many nascent tech companies to set up shop in the Twin Cities. Predictably, Jim Gershwin has ensured that many forward-thinking enterprises receive the funding necessary. (**Contacts 4, Influence 3**) ➤

Twin Cities Camarilla: As Prince Samantha's Harpy, Gershwin understand that there are any number of ambitious fledglings and neonates willing to serve as his catspaw if it means moving up the social ladder. (**Status: Camarilla 4, Mawla 2**)

KINDRED RELATIONSHIPS:

Bosche Singh (Blackguard) "A pugnacious pugilist without an ounce of subtlety! Still, I'd like to meet his tailor."

Elena Kowalski (Rakehell) "Isn't the Clan of Kings known for desiring thrones? Why waste immortality by simply existing?"

Mother Joe (Mooncalf) "The chap has a lethal uppercut, to be sure -- but I'm uncertain if he can lace his own boots."

WHISPERS:

Digital Footprint: In flagrant defiance of the Camarilla's recent eschewing of modern technology, as a means of avoiding detection from the Second Inquisition, Jim Gershwin still keeps a very active social media presence -- typically through dummy accounts and assorted false identities. However, as savvy as Jim purports himself to be, his sense of privacy extends only as far as the various settings on various websites. Any dedicated hacker would find it quite simple to discover his identity.

Taking to the Airwaves: For eight seasons, the reality-competition show Lion's Den has broken network television ratings records. Centered around various entrepreneurs and inventors pitching their products to a panel of investors with the goal of receiving corporate backing. Rumor has it that Jim has been bankrolling production on this show in order to sift out the truly inspiring inventors from the talent pool before any of the panelists have a chance to partner with them.

Anarch Sympathies: Jim looks to the future and the advancement of both human and vampire society. While his Victorian sentimentality is comfortable with a rigid social hierarchy, he also understands that he doesn't have to be a weatherman to know which way the wind is blowing. It may take relatively little prodding in order to scoot Jim over the party-line.

MORE ➤
THE COURT OF
PRINCE SAMANTHA (PART III)

VAMPIRE
THE MASQUERADE
WINTER'S TEETH

MASK AND MIEN:

Ever since his mortal life, Jim has always dressed himself with the latest fashion, constantly keeping up with the most relevant trends for young, attractive men. While always ensuring to dress within his age demographic, Jim also keeps his style in accordance with his own personality and temperament. Blending contemporary street-fashion with timeless aesthetics, Jim takes credit for bringing back vintage menswear. (**Looks: Beautiful**)

When operating among mortal circles, Jim tends to prefer using proxies as opposed to dealing with individuals directly. As a young man who appears to be in his late twenties, he recognizes that, many times, the appearance of an aged, established man is more soothing to investors than upstart young entrepreneurs. Still, he does maintain several fake names and shell companies for the purposes of navigating mortal business affairs. (**Mask 2**)

———————— ● ————————

ATTRIBUTES:
Strength 2
Dexterity 2
Stamina 2
Charisma 3
Manipulation 3
Composure 3
Intelligence 4
Wits 3
Resolve 3

SECONDARY ATTRIBUTES:
Health 5
Willpower 6

SKILLS:

Athletics 2	Subterfuge 3
Brawl 1	Academics 3 (Research)
Craft 2 (Automotive Repair)	Awareness 2
Drive 3	Finances 3
Firearms 2	Investigation 2
Animal Ken 1	Medicine 1
Etiquette 3	Occult 1
Insight 2	Science 2 (Engineering)
Persuasion 3 (Pitching)	Politics 3 (Camarilla)
Streetwise 2	Technology 4

DISCIPLINES:
Auspex 4
Celerity 2
Presence 3

JIM GERSHWIN

SIRE: HENRIETTA L'ABADIE

EMBRACED: 1833

AMBITION: TO SPONSOR AN ADVANCEMENT THAT WILL CHANGE THE WORLD.

CONVICTIONS: "PROGRESS MUST NEVER BE STYMIED."

TOUCHSTONES: GERSHWIN HAS GROWN FIXATED WITH BRITISH TECH MOGUL AND PHILANTHROPIST RICH LANCER, WHO MADE HIS FORTUNE OVERSEEING THE MUSIC LABEL COQUETTE RECORDS. JIM VIEWS LANCER'S PLAYBOY ATTITUDE AND "TECH-BRO" DEMEANOR AS SOMETHING WORTH ASPIRING TO AND FURTHER RESPECTS HIS SHREWD BUSINESS INSTINCTS.

HUMANITY: 6

GENERATION: 10

BLOOD POTENCY: 2

WINTER'S TEETH
VAMPIRE
THE MASQUERADE

Name	Concept	Predator
Chronicle	Ambition	Clan
Sire	Desire	Generation

ATTRIBUTES

Physical		*Social*		*Mental*	
Strength	ooooo	Charisma	ooooo	Intelligence	ooooo
Dexterity	ooooo	Manipulation	ooooo	Wits	ooooo
Stamina	ooooo	Composure	ooooo	Resolve	ooooo

Health □□□□□ □□□□□   Willpower □□□□□ □□□□□

SKILLS

Athletics	ooooo	Animal Ken	ooooo	Academics	ooooo
Brawl	ooooo	Etiquette	ooooo	Awareness	ooooo
Craft	ooooo	Insight	ooooo	Finance	ooooo
Drive	ooooo	Intimidation	ooooo	Investigation	ooooo
Firearms	ooooo	Leadership	ooooo	Medicine	ooooo
Larceny	ooooo	Performance	ooooo	Occult	ooooo
Melee	ooooo	Persuasion	ooooo	Politics	ooooo
Stealth	ooooo	Streetwise	ooooo	Science	ooooo
Survival	ooooo	Subterfuge	ooooo	Technology	ooooo

DISCIPLINES

ooooo	ooooo	ooooo
ooooo	ooooo	ooooo

Resonance ....   Hunger □□□□□   Humanity □□□□□ □□□□□

WINTER'S TEETH
VAMPIRE
THE MASQUERADE

Chronicle Tenets	Touchstones & Convictions	Clan Bane

Advantages & Flaws

	OOOOO
	OOOOO
	OOOOO
	OOOOO
	OOOOO
	OOOOO
	OOOOO
	OOOOO
	OOOOO
	OOOOO
	OOOOO

Notes

Blood Potency OOOOO OOOOO

Blood Surge	Mend Amount
Power Bonus	Rouse Re-Roll
Feeding Penalty	Bane Severity

Total Experience ....

Spent Experience ....

True age
Apparent age
Date of birth
Date of death
Appearance
Distinguishing features
History

VAMPIRE

THE MASQUERADE

CHARACTER NOTES

VAMPIRE

THE MASQUERADE

CHARACTER NOTES

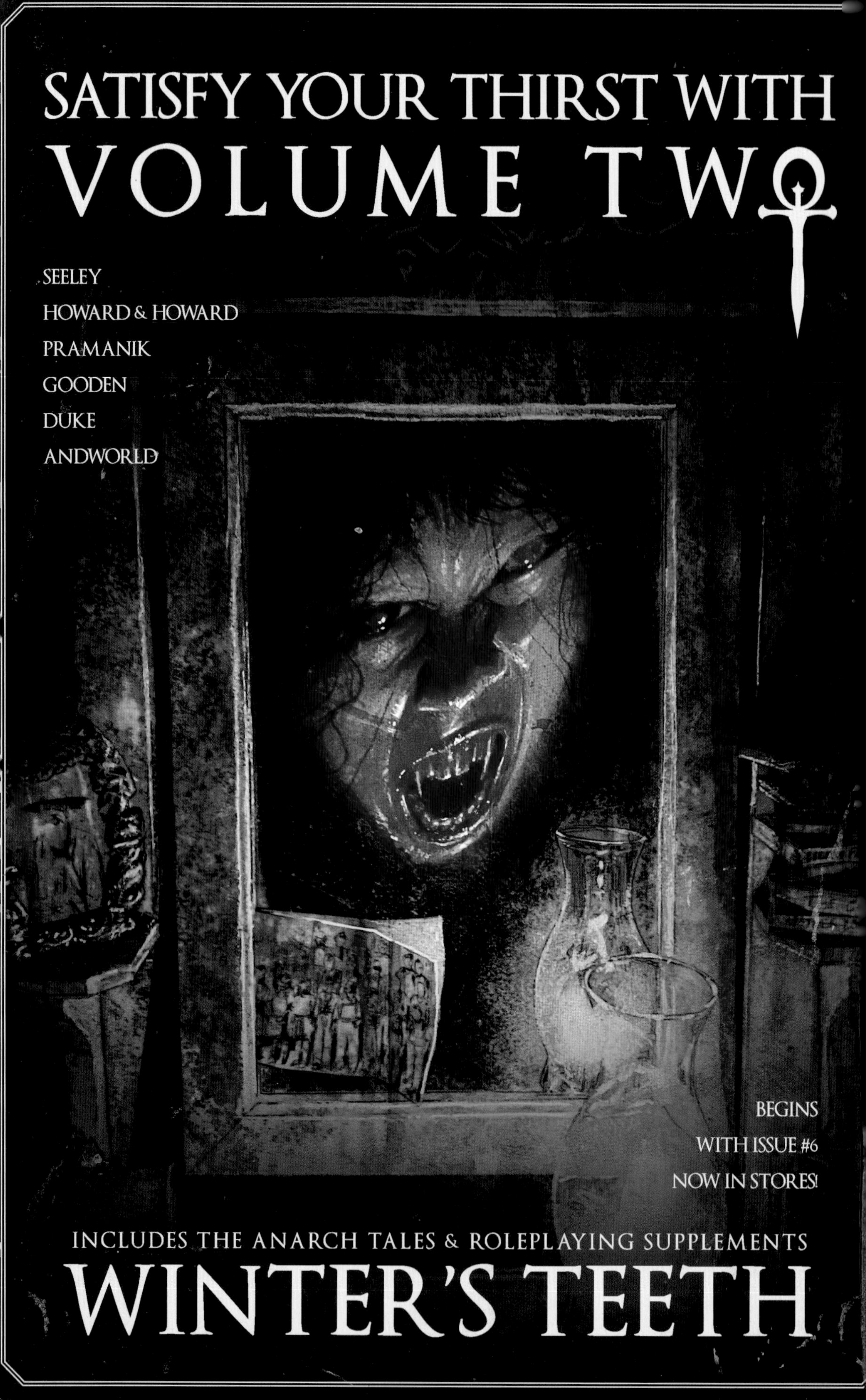

SATISFY YOUR THIRST WITH
VOLUME TWO
SEELEY
HOWARD & HOWARD
PRAMANIK
GOODEN
DUKE
ANDWORLD
BEGINS
WITH ISSUE #6
NOW IN STORES!
INCLUDES THE ANARCH TALES & ROLEPLAYING SUPPLEMENTS
WINTER'S TEETH